MW00678363

THE
BIRKMAN
METHOD®
MANUAL

First Edition

Copyright © 2008
by Roger W. Birkman, Fabian Elizondo,
Larry G. Lee, Patrick L. Wadlington, and
Matthew W. Zamzow
Houston, Texas (USA)

Design and Layout
by Four Solutions Graphic Design - Julián M. Mondragón
julian@foursolutions.net
Houston, Texas (USA)

ISBN-13
978-0-9817099-0-1

Print Executors:
Print Printers Inc / Citicap Channels Ltd
connect@printprinters.com   www.printprinters.com

All rights reserved
Reproduction in whole or in part is strictly forbidden without
the prior written consent of the publisher.

Birkman International, Inc.
3040 Post Oak Blvd., Suite 1425
Houston, Texas 77056 USA
Office: 713.623.2760
Fax: 713.963.9142
Email: info@birkman.com
Web site: www.birkman.com

The Birkman Promise

"The three generation Birkman family is dedicated to enhancing

the effectiveness and quality of life for individuals, teams, organizations,

and cultures who experience The Birkman Method®.

Our promise is to keep this central in everything we do."

Roger W. Birkman

Acknowledgements

The authors would like to acknowledge our gratitude to previous

Birkman senior psychometricians Roy Mefferd, Tim Sadler, and

Frank Larkey for building a solid foundation for

The Birkman Method® and what it has become today.

In addition, we thank Scott Davies, Elizabeth Wadlington,

and Barbara Walker for reviewing this manuscript and providing

suggestions to improve its technical content and style.

EXECUTIVE SUMMARY

The Birkman Method® is an assessment that uses "self" and "most people" perceptions to gather important motivational and behavioral insights. The prototype of The Birkman Method® began in 1951 and it has clear lineage and professional oversight up to the present time. Over the years, The Birkman Method® has been constantly reviewed, updated, and improved by qualified psychometricians and organizational psychologists. Today, Birkman International, Inc. continues to maintain and improve The Birkman Method® using both classical test theory (CTT) and item response theory (IRT). As a result, The Birkman Method® demonstrates strong psychometric properties and significant value.

The first few chapters of the manual provide an overview of The Birkman Method®, the history of the founder, and the subsequent development of the instrument. Initially, Roger Birkman developed a theory and a psychometric instrument for understanding the structure and dynamics of personality based on self and other perspectives. One of the most important Birkman discoveries was how to identify need (expectation) requirements and how need fulfillment or frustration precipitated either productive or less-than-productive behaviors. His work eventually led to developing ways to understand, manage, and improve need fulfillment, which ultimately increases behavioral effectiveness.

The Birkman Method® Component scales are based on, and supported by, many different theories of social perception and personality. Strong relationships have been demonstrated between a person's view of self and of others. The perceptions a person has, however normal or abnormal, are real to that person and influence behavior in the context of the social environment. The Birkman Method® is unique within the self-other assessment arena in that it compares a person's own perspectives with their perspectives of most people. In effect, it defines a person's social worldview. Reports are comprised of the motivations and behaviors of individuals who have similar self and other scores.

Another unique contribution of The Birkman Method® is that it corrects for socially desirable answers. It is well known that individuals also have the tendency to present themselves in a socially desirable light when answering personality questionnaires. The Birkman Method® integrates social desirability into its process and effectively corrects this problem along with the problem of "faking" that is overlooked or ignored in many personality assessments available today.

Interests in The Birkman Method® measure ten general interest themes indicating one's preference for activities or tasks. The scale scores are derived from responses to items containing occupations relevant to a particular interest area. Convergent validity was demonstrated with Holland's types, and factor analyses revealed the Birkman Interests scales load consistently with Holland's six types. Internal consistency and test-retest reliabilities of the Birkman Interests are adequate. Taken together, the Interests scales provide clear indications of high or low interest preferences.

The main body of this technical manual is dedicated to the psychometric properties of the instrument, especially the Component scales. This section describes the following: the validity and reliability attributes of The Birkman Method®, the application of CTT and IRT to the development and characteristics of the original and revised instrument, the alignment with the Five Factor Model (FFM) of personality, and how The Birkman Method® aligns with other psychological and sociological instruments. These characteristics demonstrate strong support for The Birkman Method® when used in the intended applications.

The last chapters specifically define each scale of The Birkman Method® and describe both low and high scale attributes. This section also provides many report examples and provides insight into the "look and feel" of The Birkman Method® reports, the various report applications, and the face value they provide to a client working with a certified Birkman consultant. These examples also demonstrate the positive language and intent of every Birkman report. At this time, The Birkman Method® has been translated into 13 languages with each conveying this same positive tone.

The administration and scoring of The Birkman Method® is similar to and consistent with other instruments and best practices for assessments with similar applications. Specifically, in terms of administration and audience, The Birkman Method® is administered by trained Birkman certified consultants familiar with the application and interpretation of the instrument. Birkman International, Inc., computes scores and all data are kept strictly confidential. In terms of audience, The Birkman Method® is meant for normally functioning individuals, preferably in the workforce, 18 years of age and above, although it can also be used in educational settings. As should be anticipated, The Birkman Method® does not cause adverse impact to protected groups.

In conclusion, The Birkman Method® is a valid and reliable assessment that aligns with personality but also goes beyond personality to assess key social interactions based on self and other perceptions, as well as general interests. By doing so, The Birkman Method® provides important self-other insights that define the social context and expectations of individuals as they work together. Fifty years of experience and millions of respondents demonstrate that clients using these insights consistently and intentionally create new approaches to increase effectiveness and efficiency within organizations.

TABLE OF CONTENTS

CONTENTS

CONTENTS

CONTENTS

LIST OF TABLES

TABLES

TABLES

LIST OF FIGURES

FIGURES

SECTION I

INTRODUCTION/HISTORY

CHAPTER 1
Guide to Using The Birkman Method® Manual

INTRODUCTION

This manual is a complete revision and update of the Birkman Reliability and Validity Manual (Birkman & Sadler, 2001). Three factors have prompted this update of the Manual.

First, Birkman has linked The Birkman Method® to the Five Factor Model (FFM) of personality. Originally, The Birkman Method® was not developed to define or measure personality; it was developed in light of the personal characteristics most impacting personal and interpersonal functioning. At one level, it is not surprising that The Birkman Method® incorporates the FFM or that it is much more than the FFM. This manual explains how The Birkman Method® is connected to personality and other constructs.

Second, many new research-based comparative studies have been conducted, applications have been developed, and reporting capabilities have recently been added to The Birkman Method®. This manual keeps clients and customers up to date on the latest research and reports currently available.

Third, Birkman International, Inc. (BI) has moved to improve and maintain the psychometric properties of The Birkman Method® with the addition of item response theory (IRT) as a complementary diagnostic tool to classical test theory (CTT). IRT has become the measurement model of choice for test development because it adds several benefits to item level data analysis. This manual describes the IRT model used for analysis of The Birkman Method® so that psychometricians and sophisticated users of The Birkman Method® can benefit from this information.

Reasons for Current Revision

The current version of The Birkman Method® is the result of recent updates to the psychometric properties of the assessment. The revision

In This Section

- Introduction
- Using the Manual
- Historical Synopsis
- Integrated System
- Scale Type Dynamics
- Dynamic Utility

"This manual is the culmination of our most thorough, in depth, and detailed analysis of the properties of The Birkman Method®. It contains something for everyone. It has been written so that practitioners and PhDs can understand the instrument and apply it with confidence. I believe you will find it useful."

-Roger W. Birkman

further examines the reliability and validity of the instrument. The reason for the revisions involved re-evaluating the Components (scales) and presenting further construct validity with additional measures not previously reported. Refinement of the instrument was examined using CTT, factor analysis, and IRT methodologies. Additionally, analyses revealed The Birkman Method® aligns to the FFM (Digman, 1990; Goldberg, 1992) of personality. The current version continues to present 125 items for "self" and "most"; however, only 88 items are used for scale and subscale scoring. The remaining items are used for field testing, to continually revise and update items and the psychometric properties of the instrument. Validity studies were conducted to demonstrate criterion-related validity evidence, linking the assessment to work-related outcomes. IRT enabled detailed item analyses, allowing creation of a pre-equated item pool.

Maximizing the Usefulness of this Manual

This manual is designed to be useful to many types of readers and at various levels of depth. For example, the individual who wants an overview of the manual should read Chapter 1 and the chapter summaries. For readers who appreciate the journey of discovery, read Chapter 1 and the historical chapters (2-3). Professionals who want to critically evaluate this instrument with deeper understanding should review the entire manual.

Description of The Birkman Method®

The Birkman Method® is a complex set of psychological instruments and interpretive reports that use score profiles to predict significant behavioral and motivational patterns by asking respondents about their perception of how "most people" view the world and comparing those responses with "self" perception responses. What Roger Birkman discovered was that certain answer patterns consistently predicted unique motivations and behaviors in the respondents.

The Birkman Method® is unique in that it integrates a full set of measures and reports into a comprehensive whole. Therefore, understanding The Birkman Method® as an integrated system is the foundation for discussing everything in this manual. The history, theoretical background, development, reliability, validity, instrument comparisons, derived scales, administration, interpretation, and applications all hinge on the utility of this system.

What will be demonstrated in subsequent chapters is that The Birkman Method®:

- *Assesses self perception, social perception, and occupational interests for typical adults in many different cultures*
- *Is non-clinical, online, valid, reliable, and without "adverse impact"*
- *Identifies personal, interpersonal, and situational motivators*
- *Identifies "effective" and "less than effective" behaviors*
- *Identifies practical interventions to improve effectiveness*
- *Identifies the career choices most likely to appeal to the respondent*

- *Provides respondents with a unique problem-solving approach that can be applied to many situations beyond those situations identified in the reports*

The Birkman Method® is a multifaceted self-report tool that provides practical insights into everyday issues confronting adults as they live and work. It provides a unique way of discovering how their perceptions about themselves and others affect how they accomplish goals or miss opportunities.

Historical Synopsis

Ultimately, The Birkman Method® evolved in business and industrial settings in which validation rests on measurable changes in motivation, performance, and stability that are reflected directly in dollars and cents. Today, BI supports for-profit and non-profit organizations.

Roger Birkman, the developer of The Birkman Method®, began his exploration of individual differences while a pilot and pilot instructor for the U.S. Air Force in the 1940s. His experience with the impact of misperceptions (both visual and interpersonal) on pilot performance and student learning led him to the study of psychology. Based on his observations, Birkman developed his instrument, The Birkman Method®, to measure the human characteristics that influence perceptions, behaviors, and motivations in normally functioning adults.

The instrument was developed as a self-report questionnaire eliciting responses about perception of self, perception of social context, and perception of occupational opportunities. In the 1950s, Birkman developed the scales empirically by comparing self-report item results with descriptions of likes, dislikes, and behaviors provided by third parties. The scale development efforts took part primarily with supervisor/direct report pairs in business environments. These individuals completed the questionnaire and then took part in one-on-one interviews. During the private interviews, each member of the pair was asked to describe the behaviors as well as the perceived likes and perceived dislikes of the other member of the pair. Birkman then matched self-report results, item by item, with these third party behavioral descriptions. Eventually, these scales and the relationships between these scales became the working model of perceptual and interest interactions. Rigorous sets of factor analysis studies were ongoing throughout the development of The Birkman Method®, but no effort was made to hypothesize direct causal relationships.

There were two reasons for this non-traditional approach. First, Birkman was interested in application rather than academic study. While other researchers studied why respondents behaved the way they did, Birkman identified which behaviors resulted from the respondents' self and other responses making certain that all the core human dynamics were included in his instrument. Second, Birkman knew he was working on fundamental human factors because much of his work was based on that of leading psychologists of his time, factor analysis, and current studies relating to psychiatric psychoses (schizophrenia, bipolar disorder, depression, etc.). Unique to Birkman, was his self-other perceptual orientation and his focus on normal functioning adults. Specifically, Birkman wanted to understand, integrate, and apply what could be known about the preconditions to psychotic disorders and not the clinical psychoses themselves.

Birkman simply assumed he captured the essential human factors, an assumption which has been validated decades later. Even today, the comparing of self and other perspectives is overlooked. Specifically, in the last twenty years, researchers have studied many aspects of self and other perceptions (Biernat, Manis, & Kobrynowicz, 1997; Sande, Goethals, & Radloff, 1988; Sala, 2003; Karniol, 2003) without fully exploring the implications of the self and other perceptions on the individual having these perceptions.

THE BIRKMAN METHOD® AS AN INTEGRATED SYSTEM

The Birkman Method® consists of ten scales describing "occupational preferences" (Interests), 11 scales describing "effective behaviors" (Usual behavior) and 11 scales describing interpersonal and environmental expectations (Needs). A corresponding set of 11 scale values was derived to describe "less than effective" behaviors (Stress behavior). Together, these sets of 11 scales are titled Components. Each of the Components' (Usual, Needs, and Stress) descriptors have been derived from interviews aimed at identifying the most frequent behaviors and motivations that described positive and negative aspects of interpersonal relationships.

> Note:
> Needs are often referred to as "Expectations." The Component scales were primarily developed for application and use by the respondents based on several theories of personality structure available at that time. At this time, BI can empirically establish that the FFM is a subset of the Components contained within The Birkman Method®.

In terms of reporting, two sets of scales describe motivations (Interests and Needs) and two describe behaviors (Usual and Stress). The integrative engine of The Birkman Method® is illustrated in Figure 1.1.

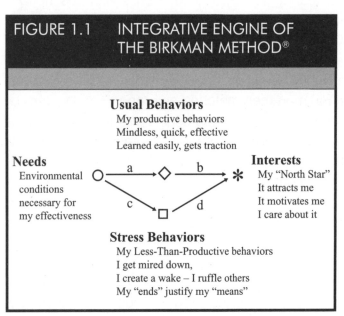

FIGURE 1.1   INTEGRATIVE ENGINE OF THE BIRKMAN METHOD®

Usual Behaviors
My productive behaviors
Mindless, quick, effective
Learned easily, gets traction

Needs
Environmental conditions necessary for my effectiveness

Interests
My "North Star"
It attracts me
It motivates me
I care about it

Stress Behaviors
My Less-Than-Productive behaviors
I get mired down,
I create a wake – I ruffle others
My "ends" justify my "means"

Notes: Specific scale titles and definitions are presented in Chapters 7 and 11.

Typically, the Interests scales are presented in one distinct section of a report and the Component (Usual, Needs, and Stress) scales are presented together. This format is used because the Component scales are intrinsically related to one another and should be interpreted together.

Interest Scales

Interest scales describe an expressed motivational construct. Individuals with high scale values tend to prefer to be engaged in activities consistent with the commonly expected responsibilities of the interest scale meaning. The scales interact to form measures of general interest beyond measures of specific interest. The scale values measure intensity of desire to be involved with these activities; they do not measure level of expected skill or proficiency with these responsibilities. Birkman had many authorities to draw from as he developed his Interest scales. Roy Mefferd, Birkman's first psychometrician, created distinct and efficient statistical methods to identify respondent Interests.

The reporting of the Interest scales is based on the Pareto Chart format. It ranks Interests in order of highest to lowest values. Figure 1.2 depicts a typical Interest profile for a respondent.

Long bars indicate a strong preference or attraction while short bars indicate minimal interest and possibly disinterest or avoidance.

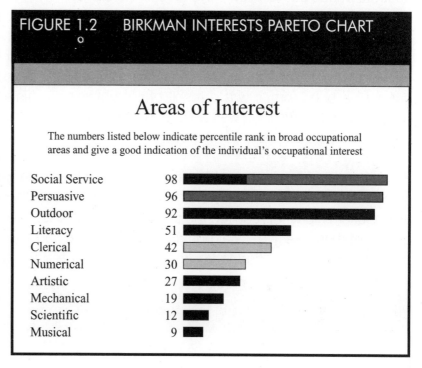

FIGURE 1.2   BIRKMAN INTERESTS PARETO CHART

Areas of Interest

The numbers listed below indicate percentile rank in broad occupational areas and give a good indication of the individual's occupational interest

Social Service	98
Persuasive	96
Outdoor	92
Literacy	51
Clerical	42
Numerical	30
Artistic	27
Mechanical	19
Scientific	12
Musical	9

Needs/Expectations Scales

The Needs scales were derived to identify which set of conditions predicted Needs fulfillment or Needs frustration for the respondent. Birkman could not directly observe another's Needs, but he was able to identify the positive or negative behaviors associated with Needs fulfillment or Needs frustration. Baumeister, Heatherton, and Tice (1994) and others have a long standing interest in studying the related topic of Self-Regulation and the attending behavioral implications. Through interviews with paired associates, spouses, and friends, Birkman found that when an individual was in a situation or relationship that proceeded in a manner that was consistent with their underlying Needs or expectations (Needs fulfillment) that individual felt good about self, was adaptable, and exhibited positive, productive behavior (Usual). Birkman reasoned that Needs were fulfilled when the relationship or situation treated the individual in a manner consistent with the individual's Needs and required the individual to frequently behave in a manner that was consistent with the individual's underlying expectations. By understanding the productive behaviors, Birkman was able to explore the conditions (Needs) necessary to create them. Conversely, Birkman also found that individuals tended to exhibit less-than-effective behaviors (Stress) when these individuals were in important relationships or situations that proceeded in a manner that was inconsistent with their own Needs (Needs frustration). When this occurred, the paired associate, spouse, or friend often described the individuals as "stressed," "frustrated," or "upset" in their behaviors. It is important to note that Birkman recognized the affect state but focused on the behaviors associated with that condition because he wanted to help individuals understand and manage their behaviors with better results.

Ultimately, Birkman found that the conditions that created less-than-effective behaviors varied greatly. The only precise way for Birkman to define the "frustrating" conditions was by noting that they were not the "fulfillment" conditions. In other words, there were an infinite number of ways to frustrate needs but very few ways to fulfill the same.

Through knowledge of psychological processes and the Needs behavior dynamics, Birkman established the logical relationships of his system as depicted in Figure 1.1. Productive behaviors resulted from an individual receiving sufficient fulfillment conditions. If an individual did not exhibit productive behaviors, it was a result of not obtaining sufficient fulfillment conditions. Equally important was that Birkman was able to identify these Needs fulfilling conditions through the "most people" responses in the questionnaire.

Birkman crafted the scales so that individuals with low scale values needed situations and relationships that demanded one style of response and those with high scale values needed situations and relationships that required the opposite style of response. No value judgment was attached to direction; therefore, Needs at both ends of the scale had equal value. The scale values described how an individual needed to be treated or what type situation an individual prefers, not intensity or frequency of need alone. For example, Figures 1.3 to 1.5 describe the low and high scale descriptions of the Advantage scale.

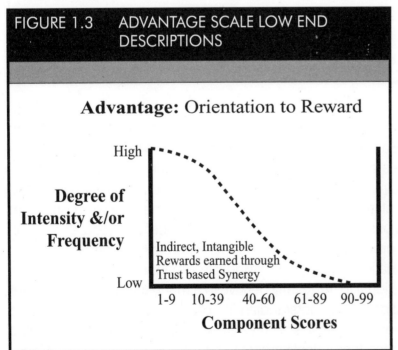

FIGURE 1.3   ADVANTAGE SCALE LOW END DESCRIPTIONS

Advantage: Orientation to Reward

Degree of Intensity &/or Frequency

High

Low

Indirect, Intangible Rewards earned through Trust based Synergy

1-9   10-39   40-60   61-89   90-99

Component Scores

If written from the Needs viewpoint, Figure 1.3 describes the intense need for an environment that provides indirect, intangible rewards for respondents scoring on the low end of the scale. As the scores move to the high end, the intensity and/or frequency for indirect motivators is extinguished.

Figure 1.4 describes the intense need for an environment that provides direct and tangible rewards for respondents scoring on the high end of the scale. As the scores move to the low end, the intensity and/or frequency for direct motivators is extinguished.

Figure 1.5 demonstrates both low and high descriptive anchors for the entire Advantage scale.

The last major point that must be discussed about the Needs scales is that they are the statistical anchors for the behavioral Component scales (Usual and Stress). They are the anchors because they represent scales unaffected by social desirability. This is reasonable, given the following points. First, because the Needs scales are derived from "most people" responses, they cannot be measuring the inclination to present "oneself" in a manner that will be viewed favorably by others. Second, after aggregating data from thousands of respondents, it is found that Needs scores are distributed evenly across all possible responses. The lack of skewness across each factor scale suggests that the scales for Needs are less likely influenced by social bias.

Each specific Needs scale has a specific number of items associated with it. Percentile values are assigned to each item and aggregated to create a scale score. These same Needs item percentiles are used to score the corresponding Usual scales. By using the non-biased Needs percentiles as the base, the Usual score profiles demonstrate the degree to which they are sensitive to social bias.

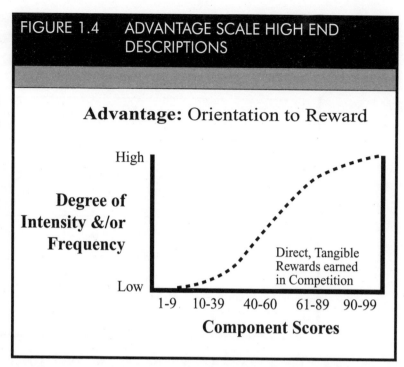

FIGURE 1.4   ADVANTAGE SCALE HIGH END DESCRIPTIONS

Advantage: Orientation to Reward

Degree of Intensity &/or Frequency — High / Low

Direct, Tangible Rewards earned in Competition

1-9   10-39   40-60   61-89   90-99
Component Scores

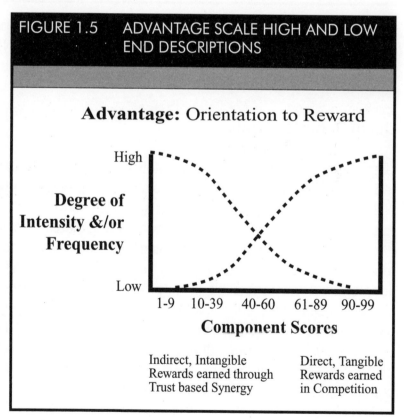

FIGURE 1.5   ADVANTAGE SCALE HIGH AND LOW END DESCRIPTIONS

Advantage: Orientation to Reward

Degree of Intensity &/or Frequency — High / Low

1-9   10-39   40-60   61-89   90-99
Component Scores

Indirect, Intangible Rewards earned through Trust based Synergy

Direct, Tangible Rewards earned in Competition

FIGURE 1.6 . INTERACTION PREFERENCE SCALE USUAL VERSUS NEEDS

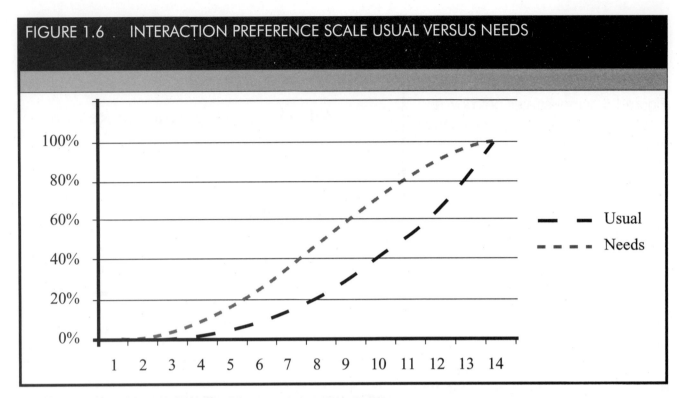

Figure 1.6 depicts a representative Component (Interaction Preference) across the 13 item scale for Needs and Usual scores. The relative flatness of the Needs score values, except at the very low and high ends, illustrates the lack of bias, especially as compared to the Usual scores which consistently display a high bias.

Usual Behavior Scales

Usual behavior is expressed in a variety of situations and is readily observable by others. It is seen most often in the early stages of a relationship or when the individual is in unfamiliar or formal social and work circumstances. These scales describe an individual's effective style of dealing with relationships and tasks. These behaviors are typically described as positive or effective in manner (though not necessarily in result). Birkman hypothesized that reward effectiveness was impacted more by the target of the motivation than by the skills of the one motivating. Using the full descriptions of the Advantage scale (Figure 1.5), it is easy to envision two equally skilled individuals, one excellent at initiating indirect, intangible rewards and the other excellent at initiating direct and tangible rewards. Regardless of personal skills, the target of the reward motivation is to seek and be persuaded by motivators that align with their Needs. Theoretically, this is similar to the FIRO-B Elements® assessment (Schutz, 1994), which assumes that an individual's behavior is independent of their desired environmental conditions.

Again, each scale is constructed as a bidirectional descriptor of style so that individuals with a low scale value are described as approaching relationships or tasks in one manner and those with a high scale value are described as approaching them in an opposite but equally effective manner.

Again, the scale values describe style of behavior, not level of effectiveness. However, the expectations of the observer (Needs) may affect the judgment of effectiveness in some situations.

Usual behavior occurs when the situation appears to require "good" behavior or when others are expected to judge or evaluate the behavior or results of the behavior – as long as the individual feels good about self and the situation. Thus, it is "socially correct" behavior, as the individual understands socially correct. Most observers will judge this type of behavior as positive and effective behavior in many situations. This judged effectiveness will occur for Usual behavior from both ends of the scale.

The scales in this group are derived from self-description responses and are known to be influenced by perceptions of social desirability. The scaling technique compares "self perception" responses against the evenly distributed "most people" percentiles. Thus, the instrument draws both a distinction and a comparison between the "socially correct" behaviors an individual exhibits in formal or early contact situations (Usual) and how the individual wants to be treated by others on an ongoing basis (Needs). This distinction recognizes that significant numbers of people "know how to act" in a relationship or task but would rather have a life that didn't require that particular style of action for extended periods of time.

Stress Behavior Scales

Scale values presented in this grouping are bidirectional and describe an individual's ineffective style of dealing with relationships or tasks. The "stress" behaviors are typically described as "how he acts when he is under stress, "how she behaves when she is frustrated," or in similar terms. Within The Birkman Method®, stress is described as ineffective, negative and non-productive behavior (or practically productive, but costly in terms of relationships). A quick review of Chapter 9 demonstrates the correlations between The Birkman Method® scales and the popular MBTI® types. One of the most striking differences between these two instruments is that in the MBTI® types, one has to refer to other works (Quenk, 1993) to reveal insights into less-than-productive behaviors and the 16 possible intervention sets to correct them. By way of contrast, The Birkman Method® integrates less-than-productive behavioral interventions into the reports.

When exhibiting Stress behavior, people are less productive and often report that they are not pleased with themselves. Individuals with low scale values tend to act out their frustrations with one style of ineffective behavior and individuals with high scale values act out in the opposite but equally ineffective manner. The scale values describe style of behavior, not level of ineffectiveness. Further insights into the causes of Stress behavior and descriptions of various less-than-productive behaviors have been studied by many researchers (e.g., Baumann & Kuhl, 2005; Baumeister & Vohs, 2004; Higgins, 1997; Muraven & Baumeister, 2000; Vohs & Heatherton, 2000) within the self-regulation literature.

Stress behavior describes the style of behavior that an individual expresses when the individual does not feel good about self or the situation. This type of behavior occurs more often when the individual is with close friends or family members (socially safer situations) and less often in formal situations, especially work situations where an individual higher in the power hierarchy is present. It is readily observable and indeed may be known to be characteristic of the individual. These scales are derived from the relationship between the Usual behavior value and the underlying Needs value for a given construct. The scaling method used is very closely related to the method for measuring the underlying Needs but differs somewhat based on internal indicators that predict typical or atypical Stress behaviors.

SCALE TYPE DYNAMICS

Building on the independently functioning single scales, it is the interactions of the scales that make The Birkman Method® a dynamic, integrated system. Birkman knew that occupational interests motivated individuals, but interest alone did not move individuals closer to occupations of their choice. Behaviors move individuals closer to, or farther away from, their Interests. In Figure 1.7, it is line "b" that describes the condition when an individual uses productive behaviors (Usual) to move towards what motivates him or her (Interests).

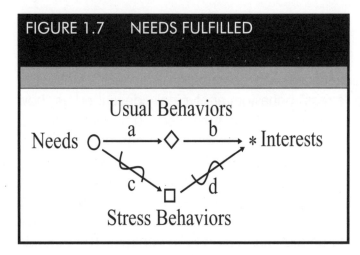

FIGURE 1.7   NEEDS FULFILLED

FIGURE 1.8   NEEDS FRUSTRATION

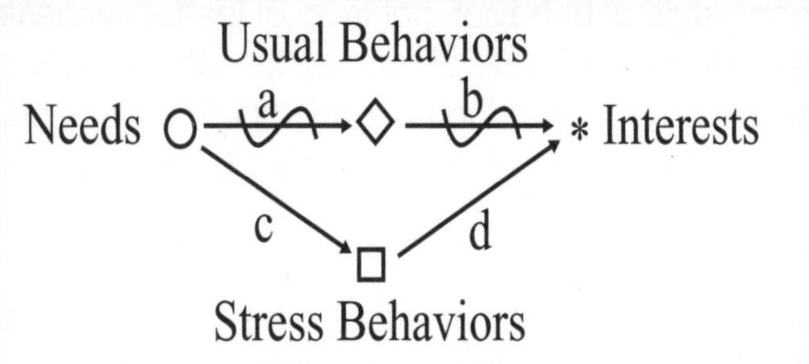

What Birkman also found was that individuals were productive if, and only if, they had a sufficient level of Needs fulfillment (line "a"). Figure 1.7 demonstrates what Birkman found when an individual's Needs were fulfilled. The idea is that, "If I get my needs met, I use my most productive behaviors to accomplish that which is most important to me."

What is unsaid in the storyline is as important as what was left said. Unsaid in the original storyline is that Needs fulfillment virtually precluded Stress behaviors in the normal adult population. Of course, not all situations provided Needs fulfillment. Figure 1.8 illustrates Needs frustration dynamics.

The wavy line over line "a" represents Needs frustration, and the wavy line over line "b" indicates that productive behaviors are not available or at least not used by the individual. Line "c" represents the individual's choice, either consciously or unconsciously, to use less-than-effective Stress behaviors. Line "d" represents a dual dynamic. First, Stress behaviors were activated. Second, the individual tends to rationalize this behavior using "ends justify the means" language, which is more evidence of less-than-productive behavior.

Basically, there are many ineffective behaviors that are not for the purpose of some important goal or interest. Figure 1.9 depicts individuals using their Stress behaviors to get their Needs met (line "c") rather than meet a goal or commitment.

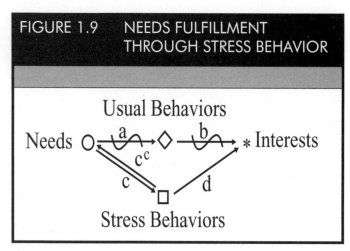

FIGURE 1.9 NEEDS FULFILLMENT THROUGH STRESS BEHAVIOR

Summary of Scale Dynamics

The four types of scales are linked into a dynamic system that primarily respond to Needs fulfillment or Needs frustration. Once activated by fulfillment or frustration, individuals tend to react in predictable, effective or less-than-effective behaviors.

DYNAMIC UTILITY

Understanding the scales and their interconnections are the basis for over 40 report sets in The Birkman Method®. They range from overview reports and high level career guidance to specific, "one-on-one" reports that compare the Usual behaviors and underlying Needs/Expectations of one individual to another individual. There is also a mix of personal, interpersonal, and organizational reports that range from Coaching to Team Building. Together, the reports provide dynamic utility to the data gathered and integrated through The Birkman Method®. In terms of reports, the primary relationships among the Components are illustrated Figure 1.10 (*see page 14*).

Construction of the Component Scales

The purpose of this section is to provide one example of how scores are utilized within The Birkman Method®, so we can correctly interpret specific scales and low and high scores in light of their original meanings. For the purpose of explaining this approach, let's create a fictitious Component named "Handedness." Low scores indicate a left-handed approach to solving dexterity problems and high scores indicate right-handed preferences. One way to differentiate the pure lefties from other lefties (those who merely prefer left or like to keep up their left hand skills or prefer not to use their left hands very much) is to create a scale. The following scale (Table 1.1, *see page 15*) uses numbers to indicate the degree to which the left hand is preferred.

Conversely, we could explain Handedness from the right-handers perspective using the same scale (Table 1.2, *see page 15*). The logic of the bidirectional scoring is illustrated well here.

FIGURE 1.10   BIRKMAN UTILITY MOLECULE

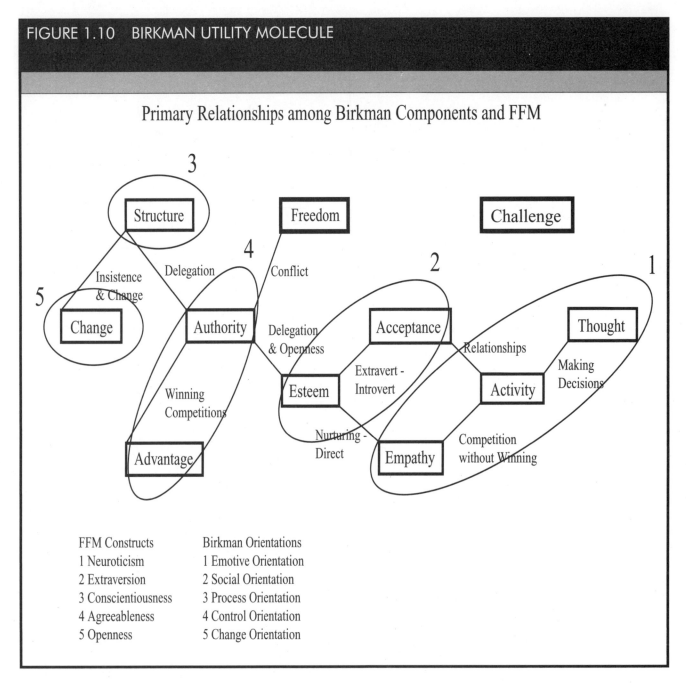

Primary Relationships among Birkman Components and FFM

FFM Constructs
1 Neuroticism
2 Extraversion
3 Conscientiousness
4 Agreeableness
5 Openness

Birkman Orientations
1 Emotive Orientation
2 Social Orientation
3 Process Orientation
4 Control Orientation
5 Change Orientation

If the Handedness score (or bandwidth) is between 1 and 9, the right hand is never used and, by default, the left hand is always used (unless hurt).

The two outer bandwidths (scores of 1-9 and 90-99) are the pure forms of opposing preferences; they are differences of kind. For some individuals, the pure forms are more than "preferences." They are viewed as the "right" way. This is either caused by or can lead to being judgmental or a potential inability to see things from another's perspective. As you might suspect, the three middle bands (scores of 10-39, 40-60, and 61-89) are differences of degree, that is, they are blends of the two pure preferences.

TABLE 1.1 HANDEDNESS: FROM A LEFT-HANDER'S PERSPECTIVE

COMPONENT: HANDEDNESS					
LEFT-HANDER'S PERSPECTIVE					
Score	1-9	10-39	40-60	61-89	90-99
Always Left	■				
Mostly Left		■			
Alternates Left			■		
Some Left				■	
Never Left					■

Notes: 1-9: Only use Left-Hand, if left hand is usable; 10-39: Predominantly Left-Handed; 40-60: Left-handed 50%, but must use left hand regularly; 61-89: Left-Handed occasionally, sometimes rarely; 90-99: Never use Left-Hand—unless right hand unusable.

TABLE 1.2 HANDEDNESS: FROM A RIGHT-HANDER'S PERSPECTIVE

COMPONENT: HANDEDNESS					
RIGHT-HANDER'S PERSPECTIVE					
Score	1-9	10-39	40-60	61-89	90-99
Always Right					■
Mostly Right				■	
Alternates Right			■		
Some Right		■			
Never Right	■				

Notes: 1-9: Never use Right-Hand - unless left hand unusable; 10-39: Right-Handed occasionally, sometimes rarely; 40-60: Right-handed 50%, but must use right hand regularly; 61-89: Predominantly Right-Handed; 90-99: Only use Right-Hand, if right hand is usable.

The Birkman Method® utilizes this approach for all Components. The Component reports, regardless of the numerical values, actually portray five "bandwidths" of behavioral/motivational descriptions. The meaning and interpretation of finer distinctions is reserved for advanced applications. Figure 1.11 (*see page 16*) depicts only the low side of a Component scale to illustrate the scale to behavior connections.

Figure 1.12 (*see page 17*) shows the perceived accuracy of the reports when reviewed with respondents. The low and high ends of the scale are much more accurate than the center section. This is consistent with expectations, in that middle scores indicate a mixture of styles.

FIGURE 1.11   BIRKMAN SCALE BANDWIDTHS

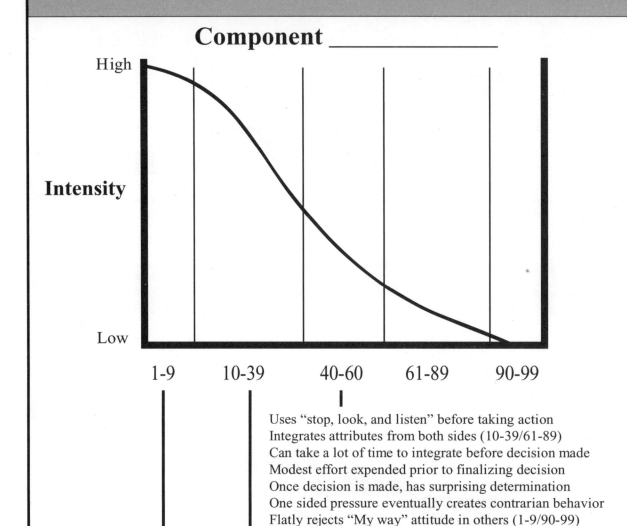

Component _____

Intensity — High to Low

| 1-9 | 10-39 | 40-60 | 61-89 | 90-99 |

Uses "stop, look, and listen" before taking action
Integrates attributes from both sides (10-39/61-89)
Can take a lot of time to integrate before decision made
Modest effort expended prior to finalizing decision
Once decision is made, has surprising determination
One sided pressure eventually creates contrarian behavior
Flatly rejects "My way" attitude in others (1-9/90-99)
(and, unless pushed, this opinion is usually left unsaid)

Consistent, predictable preference in attitudes / behaviors
Moderately high energy level and decisiveness
Occasionally, integrates other perspective
Copes with (1-9) and (40-60) effectively
(1-9) sees them as not quite pure/consistent/energetic enough
(40-60) sees them as not integrated/considerate enough

Intense, constant, high energy levels, capable of "instant" decisions
Honed skills to a high degree, often efficient, "unconsciously competent"
Rarely in doubt, except in understanding why others are so slow to "understand"
Rarely sees the value in "slowing down" to explore "other" options / approaches
Can be seen as "too much" of a good thing, especially by (40-99)

FIGURE 1.12   LEVEL OF BEHAVIORAL ACCURACY

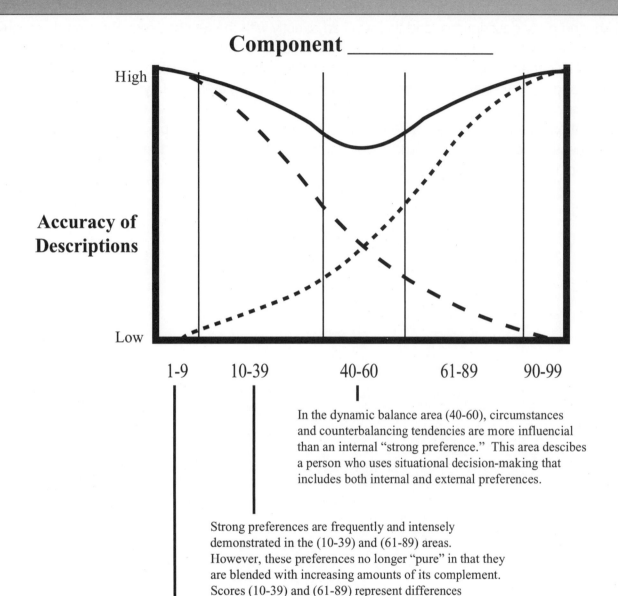

In the dynamic balance area (40-60), circumstances and counterbalancing tendencies are more influencial than an internal "strong preference." This area descibes a person who uses situational decision-making that includes both internal and external preferences.

Strong preferences are frequently and intensely demonstrated in the (10-39) and (61-89) areas. However, these preferences no longer "pure" in that they are blended with increasing amounts of its complement. Scores (10-39) and (61-89) represent differences of degree for the Component.

The accuracy of the Birkman descriptions varies across the Component scores. The desciptions for (1-9) are virtually "pure," that is, unmixed with the attributes of the other end of the scale (90-99). The inverse is also true. Scores (1-9) and (90-99) represent differences of kind for the Component.

CHAPTER 1 SUMMARY

The Birkman Method® is an assessment that uses "self" and "most people" perceptions to gather important motivational and behavioral insights. It was developed through direct respondent interviews and second party descriptions, and then verified directly with the respondents. Birkman discovered how to identify Needs requirements and how Needs fulfillment or frustration precipitated either productive or less-than-productive behaviors. His work eventually led to developing ways to understand, manage, and improve Needs fulfillment within a complex, integrated, and dynamic system.

In application, The Birkman Method® provides a method of improving personal and interpersonal effectiveness, articulating issues and resolving them, and revealing hidden assumptions that directly affect interpersonal effectiveness.

CHAPTER 2
History of Birkman International

HISTORY OVERVIEW

Roger W. Birkman began his exploration of individual differences while a pilot and pilot instructor for the U.S. Air Force. His experience with the impact that misperceptions (both visual and interpersonal) had on pilot performance and student learning led him to the study of psychology. From these beginnings, Birkman developed his instrument, the Test of Social Comprehension, to measure the human characteristics that he saw influence perceptions, behaviors, and motivations in normally functioning adults.

The history of The Birkman Method® and Birkman International dates back to 1951. The Birkman journey already spans more than five decades and continues to grow stronger than ever. Since 1951, his discoveries have affected millions of individuals and thousands of organizations.

1930s AND 1940s

In 1939, Roger Birkman was one of the first inductees in the military draft. During the war, he was stationed in the European theatre as a B-17 bomber pilot. His role provided a rich point of observation for viewing the results of stress and its effects on human actions. Birkman began to notice the environment's impact on human perception. "The power of perception became very evident to me during World War II. As a B-17 bomber pilot, I witnessed times when my fellow pilots, under great stress, wasted valuable ammunition on targets they perceived to be there (but actually were not). Since then, I have tried to identify, analyze, and learn how to eliminate many other types of perception problems" (Birkman, 1997, p. xvii).

After the war was over, Birkman took advantage of the new G.I. Bill and obtained his B.A. and M.A. in psychology from the University of Houston. He then began working for the Veteran's Administration conducting aptitude tests in order to determine the best career fit for returning

"In many ways, the history of Birkman International is a personal history. In fact, it is the history of my whole family. What you will read in this chapter is just a taste of the lifelong adventure of building a life and a company that contributes to building up individuals, teams, and organizations to be their very best."

-Roger W. Birkman

GIs. After completing his tenure with the U.S. Air Force, he returned, this time as a psychology assistant and liaison for a project being jointly conducted by the Air Force and the University of Texas. During this period, Birkman enrolled as a Ph.D. student at the university.

1950s

Up to this point, most of Birkman's work had been with aptitude testing, but he was more interested in the effect of personality and interests on the work that people do. During this time, Birkman read two journal papers that influenced him. One dealt with the effects of placing subjects in engineered environments, in which scale and perspective of everyday items like walls and windows were deliberately distorted to disorient the observer (Ames, 1951). A psychologist named George Lehner wrote the other article. He demonstrated that when individuals complete personality questionnaires asking about themselves and other people, they tend to generate two very different sets of answers (Lehner, 1949). Two questions were not addressed in the paper – "Why does this occur?" and "What insights can be gleaned from these differences?"

Together, these ideas raised an interesting possibility – the self-description method chosen for personality-oriented questionnaires might yield undesirable results because people can't "see" themselves objectively. In fact, this had been suspected for some time. Personality inventories did (and still do) compensate for the tendency of respondents to see themselves in a "socially desirable" light, and scores are typically manipulated to take account for this tendency. However, Birkman saw a way to utilize social desirability, rather than discount it, and began to explore new territory. His original investigation was to determine if asking the respondent about other people, rather than himself, would generate more accurate information about the respondent. He found that when respondents answered questions about "other people," the report was a more accurate depiction of themselves than self-description questions. Ultimately, the answer to this original research question led Birkman to the development of his first personality questionnaire, the "Test of Social Comprehension."

In 1951, Birkman & Associates was founded. Roger and his wife Sue, whom he'd met just after the war and married in 1945, would commit themselves full-time to what would become The Birkman Method®. It was during this time that the instrument would expand to include self-description items as well as an interest survey.

The remainder of the decade saw Birkman working with large organizations within the city of Houston as he continued to refine the instrument. Eventually, the items of the questionnaire would be standardized, with the patterns that resulted serving as the basis for various report formats.

1960s

In 1961, Roger W. Birkman earned his Ph.D. at the University of Texas under the direction of Benjamin Fruchter. Fruchter was himself a student of J. P. Guilford, whose expertise was both personality and multivariate analysis. Birkman continued with his research and led the company he had started. In the mid-'60s, Birkman's company became more well known to companies in Southeast Texas, but he was limited by the time it took to hand score each questionnaire. At that time, five reports could consume an entire day. Jim Thomas, a banker working with one of Roger's clients, was the first to suggest to Birkman that the process of scoring questionnaires could be programmed into a computer. This was a delicate issue, since most psychologists at the time did not believe that personality or other important human attributes could be identified by means of computerized assessments or calculation processes. Computer scoring, however, proved to be more efficient than hand scoring.

Eventually, Birkman met Roy B. Mefferd, Jr., on the campus of the University of Texas. Mefferd was a statistician/psychometrician and would later prove instrumental in the analysis of Birkman's assessments. Mefferd had a formal education in agricultural biology, genetics, and plant physiology, bacteriology, and biochemistry, and held professorships in psychiatry and the behavioral sciences. Mefferd also wrote a multitude of papers for many academic journals and was a leading expert on schizophrenia. In addition, Mefferd was a colleague of H.J. Eysenck with whom he sat on the board of the journal *Psychological Reports*. Mefferd also worked closely with Raymond Cattell, creator of the 16PF. Cattell spoke of Mefferd's "provocative and intensive thinking...at the turning points of scientific history only a few pioneers realize the direction in which things are heading. Dr. Mefferd has been such a pioneer in the No Man's Land between psychology and physiology" (Cattell, 1966, p. 686).

Mefferd's credentials became well established. He went on to publish over 200 scientific publications over a wide range of topics with a particular emphasis in complex multivariate statistical techniques. He held the positions of adjunct Professor of Psychology, Graduate School, and Clinical Professor of Psychology, Department of Psychology, University of Houston; Director of Psychiatric and Psychosomatic Research Laboratory, Veterans Administration Hospital in Houston; Professor of Physiology, Departments of Psychiatry and Physiology, Baylor College of Medicine, Houston.

Against the advice of many in the psychological community, Mefferd decided to use Birkman's assessments as the primary tools in his own research. Ultimately, Mefferd became Birkman's research partner.

In speaking about the unique blend of interdisciplinary scientists then associated with the University of Texas/Air Force Project, Mefferd singled Roger Birkman out. "The whole group of psychologists there, and especially Birkman, were very interested in both perception and personality. That was an exciting time at the University of Texas. The psychologists were eagerly absorbing the emerging reports on perception by Adelbert Ames, William H. Ittelson, James J. Gibson, Herman A. Witkin, and others. Blake and Ramsey (1951) were completing their book relating perception and personality, and Blake and Mouton (1964) were already formulating what became the Management Grid. Chairman Karl M. Dallenbach was publishing and editor of the *American Journal of Psychology* there. Wayne Holtzman shortly would be working on the Holtzman Ink Blot Test (Holtzman, 1958). In this heady atmosphere, Birkman was excited by the report by Lehner (1949) about the results he had obtained...Birkman recognized the potential power of such an approach" (Mefferd, 1992).

1970s

The '70s were marked by continual growth of The Birkman Method® and Birkman's company. Mefferd had contacts within the government that allowed the organization to win governmental contracts while the organizational clients continued to grow. During this time, Birkman received a grant from the National Science Foundation to conduct research.

In the late '70s, Mefferd introduced his protégé Tim Sadler, Ph.D., to Birkman, a relationship that would continue for decades. Sadler helped Mefferd use the data collected with the instrument to develop occupational scores. These scores helped with the creation of profiles that could predict potential success of individuals within different jobs.

1980s

The computer continued to be a key instrument in the development of The Birkman Method®. Early in the decade, a mainframe computer scored the questionnaire. Personal PCs provided the vision that would eventually drive the organization in the years that followed.

The '80s also brought a shift in the Birkman organization. The new model began using internal consultants to provide solutions to individuals and organizations. The organization saw the growth potential in the independent consultant market, a market that needed a powerful tool to reach organizations around the globe.

Sadler's role at Birkman continued to be two-fold. He continued to be instrumental in the research conducted by the organization. In addition, he acted as a trainer.

1990s

In an effort to bring the network of growing consultants together, the first of many Birkman® Conventions was held in 1991. By the mid '90s, the international market was expanding and there was a growing demand for The Birkman Method® to be translated. Efforts began on several translations as additional countries continued to discover the value The Birkman Method® could provide. As a result, "Birkman and Associates" changed its name to "Birkman International, Inc."

As the company grew in client base and revenues, technology was increasingly used to score assessments. Birkman2000® was developed as "a client-based" software that allowed consultants to dial into the Birkman computers and download their entire database of respondents. This approach provided each Birkman consultant with instant access to the multitude of available Birkman report formats. It was during this time that Internet access became popular.

2000 & BEYOND

In 2001, BI introduced BirkmanDirect®, an online delivery system that precipitated many changes. Consultants sent out questionnaires via the Internet, central computers scored the questionnaires, and consultants selected and printed reports within minutes.

During this same period, Birkman researchers continued to develop the instrument, add innovative reports, and link the original concepts to current personality and social constructs. Now, as throughout its history, BI is committed to ongoing research and the development of new products. Birkman psychologists continually query the database for additional research insights, perform instrument comparisons, and develop new hypotheses to test. For research purposes, the database maintains approximately one million assessments at any given time.

Roger Birkman comes into his office every day to develop new insights and applications. However, his daughter Sharon Birkman Fink now serves as President and CEO of Birkman International. She is dedicated to preserving her father's legacy and enhancing the lives of individuals and organizations through The Birkman Method®.

CHAPTER 2 SUMMARY

This chapter highlights the key events in the history of Birkman International, Inc., and sets the stage for future developments. New applications, expanded reports, and web-based interactive report capabilities are currently being developed. In every dimension, the historical trend of growth anticipates even more growth as staff and capabilities expand.

CHAPTER 3
Development of the Instrument

CHAPTER 3
OVERVIEW

In This Section

- History of Development
- Six Phases of Development
- Dynamic Testing
- Current Version
- Normative Data Set

PURPOSE

This chapter focuses on the development of The Birkman Method®, including how the original assessment was developed, changes that have been made, recent revisions to the instrument, and the current structure of The Birkman Method®. Detailed information will be found in Chapters 7-9.

HISTORY OF DEVELOPMENT

The Birkman Method® was developed in the 1950s as a self-report questionnaire eliciting responses about perception of self and perception of social context. Later, a third section (Interests) was added to include perception concerning occupational opportunities. The original item pool for this instrument was similar to items other authors were using in psychological scale development at the time, and they were purposefully written in simple language so that people with a broad range of verbal skills would understand them.

The creation of an operational form was a multi-step process, which included extensive literature reviews, item content analyses, factor analyses, and several form revisions. The first forms were constructed with the intent of presenting the same 100 items twice. First, the "True/False" items were presented in the "Test of Social Comprehension" which measured respondent beliefs about "most people." Then the same items were presented as a "Self-Inventory." The first set of items was related to the behavior and attitudes of "most people," and the second set of items was presented in the typical self-report format used by most personality assessments.

Initial process experiments confirmed that when the Test of Social Comprehension was taken before the Self-Inventory, results were much more accurate and reliable. It was assumed that this order of presentation increased respondent objectivity and reduced defensiveness. See Table 3.1 and 3.2 for sample items.

"From the very beginning, talented professionals were attracted to the methodology. This chapter defines the lineage of the instrument and those who made it what it is today."

-Roger W. Birkman

TABLE 3.1	EXAMPLE FACTOR ITEMS FROM THE OTHER PERSPECTIVE		
ITEM TEXT		**RESPONSE OPTION**	
Expect too much of themselves		True	False
Do not like changes		True	False
Sometimes say the first thing that they think of		True	False

TABLE 3.2	EXAMPLE FACTOR ITEMS FROM THE SELF PERSPECTIVE		
ITEM TEXT		**RESPONSE OPTION**	
Expect too much of myself		True	False
Do not like changes		True	False
Sometimes say the first thing that I think of		True	False

Initial Item Development

Before the first form of The Birkman Method® was developed, an extensive literature review was conducted on personality assessments with an emphasis placed on widely used questionnaires that were considered effective in discriminating between personality groups. All items were studied carefully with an emphasis placed on those relating to deeper attitudes and experiences not easily identifiable as true or false by casual observation. The less that items reflected factual, definite, or easily observable attitudes and motives, the more the subject would be required to fall back upon their own experiences and inferences in order to arrive at a definite true or false response. It was determined that items constructed along this line would make possible a deeper probing of the basic organization and structure of the individual's personality.

Thousands of possible items were considered suitable for the forms. Factor analyses were conducted and preference was given to items with high loadings on well-defined factors. Consideration was given to Cattell's (1946) 16 primary personality source factors. Items with high factor loadings were analyzed for general content, rather than exact wording, to gain insight into the feelings and attitudes expressed. Factor analysis was only an initial guide as items were further developed from the content of items and general themes identified through factor analysis results. Selection or exclusion of items for the forms relied on brevity, simplicity in wording, ease of interpretation, ease of classification, and general suitability.

Administration of Initial Provisional Forms and Successive Revisions

After many items were developed and analyzed, 100 of the most promising items were selected for field testing, in the first of a series of forms. Two provisional forms were first administered to 160 participants: 24 graduate and 136 undergraduate students at universities located in central Texas.

The results from the initial field testing demonstrated that students generally described "most people" much more negatively than they did themselves. For example, a shift from "True" on the Test of Social Comprehension to "False" on the Self-Inventory, on the same item, was usually in the more socially desirable direction. Items having a stronger social stigma caused the change in response style more consistently than other items. The more an item appeared to have an apparent social stigma, the more respondents consistently changed the response from the socially undesirable on the Test of Social Comprehension to a more socially desirable response on the Self-Inventory. Collectively, responses for "most people" were generally less socially desirable than for self-descriptive items. This supported the assumption that defensiveness (faking) could be minimized, to some extent, by administering the Test of Social Comprehension first. Due to these findings, all further administrations of the forms presented "most people" items before self-report items.

Interesting to note that during the administrations, items were less ambiguous to respondents when items were first asked about "most people" than for self. More questions were raised by respondents as to the full meaning or intent behind particular items in the self-descriptive form, even though the exact wording remained the same from one form to the other (with the exception of substituting "you" for "most people").

Data gathered from field testing allowed further item analyses, which allowed for item revisions and further provisional form development. Comparing total group responses of the same item, from self to most, revealed information regarding the sensitivity of items. More discriminant items elicited a greater response shift. Response trends were observed with items causing a greater shift in response from "most" to "self," whether it was a change from "True" to "False" or vice versa. Items not causing significant changes in response patterns were considered neutral and were eliminated from further forms. Items characterizing a marked response shift were kept because it was believed that the shift indicated the respondents made a conscious understanding of the intent of the item and an effort to try to obscure any negative implications of endorsing such an item. Items were also analyzed to ensure they were not skewed, either positively or negatively. The inclusion of items which involved a strong social stigma, along with those which most persons would consider complimentary, was intended to add to the scope of the questionnaire and increase the sensitivity of the instruments.

Following the original field testing of the forms, seven successive revisions of the instrument were performed to improve the accuracy, reliability, and validity. Each version was administered to more than 1,000 individuals selected from a business or industrial setting. After each testing, responses were recorded and analyzed for compatibility. Each new form represented an improvement and variation of the previous form. After seven revisions administered to several thousand participants from professional sales to non-professional employees, the initial operational form was introduced in 1957. The items in this operational form were determined to be sensitive to personality differences. In the 1960s, the name of the assessment changed to "The Birkman Method®," a name that has not changed since, although The Birkman Method® has continuously evolved since its inception in business, industrial, educational, and community settings.

Original Scale Development

Scales on the original assessment were derived empirically from the item level responses. The theory and literature behind assessing normal personality characteristics from a standpoint of self versus others perspectives is described in the next chapter. Birkman, observing how individuals vary in perception of self versus others, used this idea as a unique way of measuring personality and social perception. The actual scales within the assessment were developed empirically using behavioral interviewing.

The process for scale construction began by comparing self-report item results with the descriptions of the likes, dislikes, and behaviors of these individuals, as provided by third parties. The scale development efforts were conducted primarily with supervisor/direct report pairs from a business setting. These individuals completed the questionnaire and then took part in one-on-one interviews. Spousal pairs took part as well, but most information came from established work teams. During the private interviews, each member of the pair was asked to describe the behaviors, as well as the perceived likes and dislikes of the other member of the pair. Birkman then matched self-report results, item by item, with these third party behavioral descriptions. When developing scales from this effort, Birkman focused on describing behaviors that were important for understanding work relationships, important for understanding differences in approach for common work functions or important for understanding career preferences. Items were phrased to sample a well-recognized psychological attribute such as Self-Consciousness or Sociability. The scales were not intended to be all-inclusive or to describe a person's behavior completely. Consideration was given to how respondents' patterns of answers matched or failed to match those of group patterns of a variety of types and occupations. It has been stated that one of the most important attributes of The Birkman Method® is that it describes aspects of behaviors that are related to life situations (Justice & Birkman, 1972).

The scale development process resulted in 11 scales describing effective behaviors (Usual behavior) and 11 scales describing interpersonal and environmental preferences or expectations (Needs). A corresponding set of 11 scale values was derived to describe "less than effective" behaviors (Stress behaviors). These scales represent a set of descriptors chosen to be useful in understanding behaviors and motivations that frequently were discussed when describing positive and negative aspects of relationships, team work, career success, etc. For Interests, the scale development process resulted in ten scales describing occupational preferences. Refer to Chapter 6 for more information on Interests.

2000 REVISION

The number of scales and construct structures of the scales were established in the early development of the instrument and did not change significantly over the years. Re-standardization efforts occurred periodically and criterion-referenced scales were added as criterion data accumulated. However, in 2000, a systematic reevaluation of the basic scales was undertaken and the item structure of each scale was reexamined. The item content of the instrument remained essentially constant over the years except for minor and subtle rewordings of a few items from time to time to account for shifts in language usage. Throughout the years, however, a set of non-scored items was distributed throughout the instrument. By this time, the length of the instrument had increased from 100 to 125 items about "self" and "most." These items were changed periodically as data accumulated so that new items, which would contribute to measurement of the original constructs, would be available for later use. The 2000 revisions utilized these items as well as original items to revise the scales throughout. Revisions included adding items, shifting items, and deleting items. One scale, the Challenge scale, was originally derived through a ratio of more basic scales. In the 2000 scaling, this scale was converted to a direct item-based scale.

Revisions undertaken in 2000 were intended to increase internal consistency of the existing constructs, not replace them or add new constructs. The revised scales were in most instances extremely close to the original scales in construct meaning (*See Table 3.3 page 30*). For a few scales, the original scale had either a small number of items or an overly large number of items; but even in these cases, the revised scale was still close in meaning to the original scale. The correlations between original and revised scales were quite high. Most revised scales were essentially identical with their original scales (correlations in the range of .90). Others were merely extremely close in meaning (correlations in the .80 range). Only one revised scale had a correlation with its original scale at level less than .75 (Freedom Usual). Thus, the revisions increased internal consistency (see Chapter 8, Reliability) and in many instances increased the number of items in the scale but, by design, did not alter the basic construct meaning of the scales.

The 2000 revisions were, of necessity, accompanied by re-norming of the scales. For these purposes, a sample of 10,033 persons who had completed The Birkman Method® during the years 1993 to 1999 and who were between the ages of 25 and 65 were utilized. These persons completed the instrument in the United States and are presumed to be primarily representative of the U.S. culture. They completed the questionnaire in paper form or desktop computer-based administration. Instructions and items were the same for all administrations. The normative sample was selected from the larger database utilizing reported education level to build a sample roughly representative of the educational accomplishments reported from the 1990 census in the U.S. This balancing effort was deemed necessary because the general database was heavily loaded with persons reporting advanced educational attainment, and earlier research with the instrument has indicated that level of education and level of organizational responsibility may be associated with different scale results. Table 3.4 (*see page 31*) provides demographic information for the sample used for re-norming purposes.

TABLE 3.3	CORRELATIONS BETWEEN ORIGINAL SCALES AND 2000 SCALING FOR INDIVIDUALS WHO COMPLETED THE QUESTIONNAIRE BETWEEN 1993 AND 1999			
COMPONENT	USUAL	NEEDS	INTEREST SCALE	
Esteem	.93	.93	Persuasive	.89
Acceptance	.94	.96	Social Service	.94
Structure	.90	.92	Scientific	.80
Authority	.93	.89	Mechanical	.98
Advantage	.82	.94	Outdoor	.96
Activity	.95	.95	Numerical	.93
Empathy	.93	.92	Clerical	.93
Change	.94	.93	Artistic	.89
Freedom	.67	.81	Literary	.91
Thought	.75	.79	Musical	.97
Challenge	.80			

Notes: N = 91,672.

Norms were updated in the current version using a stratified sample representative of the U.S. workforce, including 15 of the 22 U.S. Department of Labor categories (N = 4,300). Several name changes were made to the Components (scales), which had remained the same for decades until this revision. They are intended to be aligned with the FFM of personality; and along with the sub-scales, they describe both high scores and low scores for each dimension. Refer to Chapter 7 of this manual for a detailed discussion of the current structure of the instrument and the statistical analyses involved in the revision.

TABLE 3.4		DEMOGRAPHICS OF NORMATIVE SAMPLE FOR 2000 SCALING					
AGE		GENDER		RACE		EDUCATION	
Range	25-65	Male	51.6%	White	80.9%	Less than HS	4.1%
Mean	39.98	Female	48.4%	Black	9.7%	HS	23.6%
25-30	16.3%			Hispanic	5.6%	Some College	36.9%
31-40	37.5%			Other	4.8%	4 Year Degree	27.2%
41-50	33.4%					Post Grad Degree	8.2%
51-60	12.2%						
61-65	0.6%						

Notes: N = 10,033. All demographic information based on self-report data. Instructions make entry of this information voluntary at the time the person completes the questionnaire. Race breakdown based on a sample of 4,790 who reported race.

HISTORY OF BIRKMAN INSTRUMENT DEVELOPMENT

Initial (Phase 1) Development (late 1940s to early 1960s)

Roger Birkman. Birkman created the instrument from insight he gained by interviewing hundreds of employees. Major contributions included:

- *Creation of the theoretical framework for Usual, Needs, and Stress behaviors*
- *Creation of the Component scales in the form of a social comprehension instrument (1st version of The Birkman Method®)*
- *Creation of patterns for personality profiles*

Phase 2 Development (mid-1960s to 1994)

Roger Birkman, Roy B. Mefferd, Jr., and Tim Sadler. Mefferd and Sadler worked as researchers examining and revising the instrument as far as psychometric properties. Major contributions included:

- *Development of new items*
- *Established construct validity*
- *Clarification of the factor structure*
- *Development of career-focused scales*

Phase 3 Development (1995 to 2002)

Roger Birkman and Tim Sadler. Sadler worked as the lead researcher examining and revising the instrument as far as psychometric properties. Major contributions included:

- *Revision of Component and Interest scales*
- *Creation of the career report based on profiling methodology*
- *Creation of managerial styles*
- *Cross validation of career profiling*

Phase 4 Development (2003 to 2005)

Roger Birkman, Frank Larkey, Jennifer L. Knight, and Paul Cruz. Larkey worked as the lead researcher examining and revising the instrument. The Research and Development department continued the validation and documentation of the utility of the Birkman instrument. Major contributions included:

- *Revision of the reliability and validity summary report*
- *Conducted additional criterion-related and construct validity studies in support of the instrument*
- *Creation of Research and Development archives*

Phase 5 Development (2006 to 2007)

Roger Birkman, Larry G. Lee, Patrick L. Wadlington, and Fabian Elizondo. This team has made several improvements to the psychometric and theoretical properties of the Birkman instrument. Major contributions include:

- *Reconstruction of Component scales via CTT, factor analytic, and IRT methodologies*
- *Establishment of construct validity aligning the Components with the FFM personality constructs*
- *Establishment of criterion-related validity to job performance, job satisfaction, retention, and management/leadership development*
- *Validation of Usual/Needs/Stress behavior patterns*
- *Development of subfactor scales*
- *Creation of a pre-equated item pool via IRT*
- *Development of 2007 national norms*
- *Development of selection profiling methodology*

Present (Phase 6) Development

The Birkman Research and Development Department will continue to focus its efforts in five areas:
- *Improvements to the item quality, reliability, and validity of the Birkman instruments through internal and external resources*
- *Development of new instrument reports and applications*

- *Publication of empirical findings demonstrating the validity and utility of Birkman instruments in organizational and educational settings*
- *Differential reliability and validity and differential item and test functioning (DIF, DTF)*
- *Dynamic testing platform creation and implementation*

DYNAMIC TESTING

The last item, dynamic testing, is so important to enhancing The Birkman Method® that it deserves further explanation. BI is working towards a dynamic testing platform to enhance The Birkman Method®. This task will take several years; yet, the payoff will be immense.

For the most part, personnel testing today uses static (versus dynamic) assessment platforms, especially in regards to personality tests. Static platforms use one or two forms of items over an extended period of time; thus, all applicants see the same one or two sets of items. On the other hand, dynamic platforms use an infinite number of items replenished on a regular basis. This bank of items is presented in alternate forms spiraled across test takers or in computer adaptive algorithms.

In large scale and/or high-risk personnel testing, several problems can arise by staying with a static platform (Davies & Wadlington, 2007; Wadlington & Davies, 2006).

- *Using the same set of items over time never lets the user discover the full potential of the predictor space (unless it is an incredibly long test or a very narrow predictor construct).*
- *Whatever part of the predictor is covered by the static set of items is the only part ever used for prediction of performance.*
- *Item exposure from a static platform can create test security issues. Items and keys can be stolen and then the form is compromised. Fortunately, it does not have to be blatant to have an impact. For instance, there have been many books and websites written specifically to coach test takers on how to respond to certain item types. When this approach has a positive outcome for test takers, the test is compromised to some degree.*
- *With item exposure comes score mean shift, thus, test takers start getting better scores, on average; and then it becomes very difficult to make comparisons across time and examinees. Additionally, score shift leads to skewness with the scale distributions and the resulting skewness means less variance. Less variance results in less covariance, thus less validity for the instrument.*

A dynamic testing platform can address all of these issues. Best practices in test development and maintenance call for some form of dynamic testing in large scale, high stakes testing systems - particularly if there is reason to question item security and associated score mean shift (Segal, Moreno, Bloxom, & Hetter, 1997). Many similar efforts have already been made in educational testing (e.g., MCAT, GRE, PRAXIS, GMAT, SAT, ASVAB, GATB). Additionally, according to professional and legal guidelines (AERA, APA, NCME; 1999, 2004; EEOC, 1978), dynamic testing is best practices in testing and leads to score equivalence and test fairness, if done in a rigorous manner.

To be done in a rigorous manner means that dynamic testing must have a detailed testing development and maintenance process in place (Wadlington, Little, & Turner, 2007). To stay on track with dynamic testing, BI will have a test maintenance cycle/operations similar to that used in large sale educational testing houses. These operations are necessary for dynamic test system development and maintenance. Note that substantial item writing resources are required for these operations to function smoothly. These item writing resources include: 1) computerized item banking and tracking software, 2) large data collection opportunities for field testing and validation studies, 3) internal psychometricians devoted to item analysis and forms creation, and 4) an Internet platform capable of supporting operational administration of dynamic tests. In Figure 3.1, the detailed process/cycle of BI's future dynamic testing operations is illustrated.

Additionally, a major concern in dynamic testing is equivalent validity across alternate forms. BI plans to keep equivalent validity as a foremost priority in its dynamic testing efforts. Equivalent validity of The Birkman Method® alternate forms will be established with the necessary research studies on the equivalence of test length, test content, test reliability, and internal structure as well as studies establishing construct validation. Construct validation with the dynamic testing platform will be shown via the validation of the item bank and ongoing studies of convergent and discriminant validity with alternate forms.

SEGUE TO CURRENT VERSION

With a new normative sample and IRT capabilities available, the form was transformed into its current version. The goal was to align The Birkman Method® scales with the FFM constructs as well as

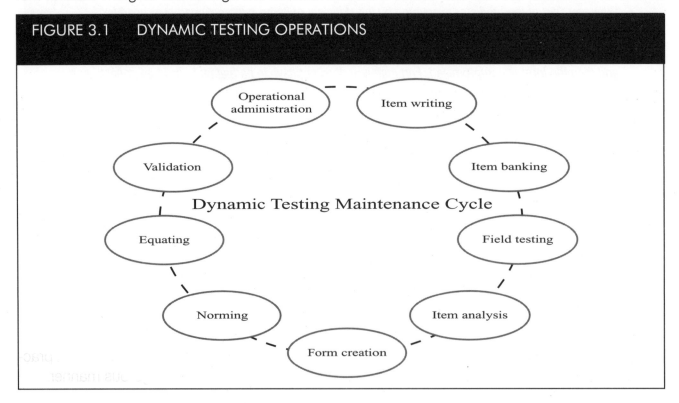

FIGURE 3.1   DYNAMIC TESTING OPERATIONS

Dynamic Testing Maintenance Cycle

Operational administration — Item writing — Item banking — Field testing — Item analysis — Form creation — Norming — Equating — Validation

improve the reliability and validity of the instrument from factor analytic, CTT, and IRT psychometric approaches. The following sections describe these approaches and how they lead to the current version of The Birkman Method®. Below the construct agreement is demonstrated between the previous versions and the current version of the Birkman instrument. To remain anchored to this vast amount of validity data from previous versions, the current version of the instrument was carefully and methodically developed following widely used and accepted procedures. Tables 3.5 through 3.8 demonstrate the strong relationship between previous version scales and current version scales. Note that all uncorrected Birkman Usual correlations, excluding Personal Autonomy, between prior and current same constructs are 0.87 or above. Personal Autonomy was changed to a greater extent due to increased psychometric understanding via modern test theory analyses.

TABLE 3.5	CURRENT-TO-PRIOR UNCORRECTED CORRELATION MATRIX (OBSERVABLE) – USUAL										
	Current (Prior) Name	PRIOR VERSION									
		1	2	3	4	5	6	7	8	9	10
1	Activity	**.87**	-.60	-.65	-.44	.27	.21	-.22	-.06	-.24	-.42
2	Empathy	-.54	**a**	.59	.46	-.27	-.18	.31	.18	.32	.37
3	Thought	-.48	.59	**.79**	.47	-.22	-.15	.24	.03	.31	.24
4	Communication (Esteem)	-.46	.45	.52	**.98**	-.51	-.07	.16	-.12	.18	.11
5	Interaction (Acceptance)	.34	-.27	-.27	-.49	**a**	.04	-.11	.09	.02	-.25
6	Process (Structure)	.45	-.31	-.54	-.19	.10	**.91**	-.32	-.03	-.22	-.42
7	Incentive (Advantage)	-.08	.24	.16	.15	-.02	-.14	**.79**	.36	.23	.35
8	Authority	-.03	.23	.08	.04	.03	-.06	.32	**.89**	.31	.31
9	Change	-.12	.29	.23	.20	.02	-.13	.16	.26	**.96**	.09
10	Personal Autonomy (Freedom)	-.50	.69	.58	.56	-.46	-.21	.46	.30	.45	**.53**

Notes: a = perfect correlation; **bold** indicates scales measuring the same construct.
Source: 2007 normative database.

TABLE 3.6		CURRENT-TO-PRIOR CORRECTED CORRELATION MATRIX (LATENT) – USUAL										
		Current (Prior) Name	PRIOR VERSION									
			1	2	3	4	5	6	7	8	9	10
Current Version	1	Activity	a	-.73	-.87	-.55	.34	.27	-.32	-.08	-.33	-.73
	2	Empathy	-.70	a	.78	.58	-.34	-.24	.44	.24	.44	.64
	3	Thought	-.76	.89	a	.71	-.34	-.24	.42	.05	.52	.51
	4	Communication (Esteem)	-.59	.56	.70	a	-.64	-.09	.24	.16	.25	.19
	5	Interaction (Acceptance)	.44	-.34	-.36	-.61	a	.05	-.17	.12	.03	-.44
	6	Process (Structure)	.62	-.40	-.76	-.26	.13	a	-.49	-.04	-.32	-.76
	7	Incentive (Advantage)	-.13	.36	.27	.22	-.03	-.23	a	.59	.39	.73
	8	Authority	-.05	.33	.12	.06	.04	-.09	.54	a	.49	.62
	9	Change	-.16	.39	.34	.28	.02	-.18	.26	.39	a	.16
	10	Personal Autonomy (Freedom)	-.70	.92	.84	.76	-.63	-.30	.73	.44	.67	a

Notes: a = perfect correlation; **bold** indicates scales measuring the same construct.
Source: 2007 normative database.

Note that all corrected Birkman Usual correlations between prior and current same constructs align with a coefficient of 1.00.

Note that all uncorrected Birkman Needs correlations, excluding Personal Autonomy, between prior and current same constructs are 0.82 or above. Personal Autonomy was changed to a greater extent due to increased psychometric understanding via modern test theory analyses.

TABLE 3.7	CURRENT-TO-PRIOR UNCORRECTED CORRELATION MATRIX (OBSERVABLE) – NEEDS AND CHALLENGE											

	Current (Prior) Name	1	2	3	4	5	6	7	8	9	10	11
							PRIOR VERSION					
1	Activity	**.82**	-.65	-.69	-.52	.46	.43	-.53	-.30	-.41	-.60	.54
2	Empathy	-.57	**a**	.68	.52	-.43	-.40	.61	.47	.48	.63	-.53
3	Thought	-.48	.64	**.83**	.48	-.36	-.33	.52	.36	.48	.48	-.51
4	Communication (Esteem)	-.52	.52	.59	**.97**	-.49	-.38	.48	.21	.38	.34	-.58
5	Interaction (Acceptance)	.60	-.43	-.47	-.49	**a**	.50	-.47	-.10	-.15	-.49	.56
6	Process (Structure)	.70	-.49	-.64	-.50	.55	**.93**	-.62	-.22	-.28	-.61	.61
7	Incentive (Advantage)	-.42	.57	.55	.50	-.35	-.40	**.88**	.53	.48	.67	-.52
8	Authority	-.27	.53	.46	.37	-.19	-.24	.61	**.89**	.48	.53	-.42
9	Change	-.21	.43	.45	.39	-.16	-.18	.41	.38	**.93**	.33	-.32
10	Personal Autonomy (Freedom)	-.58	.77	.70	.57	-.53	-.46	.74	.54	.59	**.79**	-.60
11	Perspective Alignment (Challenge)	.51	-.55	-.58	-.54	.50	.43	-.54	-.35	-.35	-.53	**.92**

Notes: a = perfect correlation; **bold** indicates scales measuring the same construct.
Source: 2007 normative database.

Note that all corrected Birkman Needs correlations between prior and current same constructs align with a coefficient of 1.00.

TABLE 3.8   CURRENT-TO-PRIOR CORRECTED CORRELATION MATRIX (LATENT) – NEEDS AND CHALLENGE

Current (Prior) Name	PRIOR VERSION										
	1	2	3	4	5	6	7	8	9	10	11
1 Activity	a	-.84	-.96	-.69	.63	.58	-.67	-.44	-.60	-.81	.68
2 Empathy	-.73	a	.88	.66	-.55	-.51	.74	.66	.67	.80	-.64
3 Thought	-.74	.94	a	.73	-.56	-.51	.76	.61	.81	.74	-.74
4 Communication (Esteem)	-.70	.66	.81	a	-.66	-.51	.61	.31	.56	.46	-.73
5 Interaction (Acceptance)	.80	-.55	-.64	-.64	a	.66	-.60	-.15	-.22	-.66	.70
6 Process (Structure)	.92	-.61	-.86	-.65	.72	a	-.77	-.31	-.40	-.80	.75
7 Incentive (Advantage)	-.58	.75	.78	.68	-.49	-.56	a	.80	.72	.92	-.67
8 Authority	-.39	.73	.67	.53	-.27	-.34	.82	a	.76	.77	-.57
9 Change	-.32	.63	.70	.59	-.25	-.28	.59	.63	a	.50	-.45
10 Personal Autonomy (Freedom)	-.74	.95	.93	.73	-.69	-.59	.90	.76	.82	a	-.73
11 Perspective Alignment (Challenge)	.74	-.76	-.86	-.77	.73	.62	-.74	-.56	-.55	-.77	a

Current Version (row axis label)

Notes: a = perfect correlation; **bold** indicates scales measuring the same construct.
Source: 2007 normative database.

Development of National Normative Data Set

The first step in the psychometric procedure for distributional projection is to collect a large (i.e., $n > 1,500$) sample on an operational anchor form of an instrument for which there are known parameter estimates for the population of interest. The number of individuals needed for a representative sample depends on three factors:

1. *Heterogeneity of the population*
2. *Variance in the instrument*
3. *Latent trait of interest (dictates which IRT model is chosen and the number of parameters to be estimated)*

A norming sample representative of the U.S. workforce was drawn from 17,537 working adults who had been administered The Birkman Method® from 2002-2006. The final sample contained 4,300 working adults from a variety of industries including management, healthcare, engineering, transportation, protective services, retail, financial services, and education. This sample was representative of 15 of the 22 U.S. Department of Labor categories. The data set was comprised of 47.4% female. By race, the data set was made up of 9.6% Blacks, 8.0% Hispanics, 6.9% Asian/Pacific Islanders, 1.5% Native Americans/Alaskan Natives, 74.0% Whites, and 3.0% not indicated. The average age of the individuals was 43.17 years.

CHAPTER 3 SUMMARY

The prototype of The Birkman Method® began in 1951 and it has clear lineage and professional oversight up to the present time. Over the years, The Birkman Method® has been constantly reviewed, updated, and improved by qualified psychometricians and organizational psychologists. Today, Birkman International continues to maintain and improve this assessment using both CTT and IRT. As a result, The Birkman Method® demonstrates strong psychometric properties and significant value.

SECTION I SUMMARY

This section answers: "What is The Birkman Method® and how did it evolve to its present state?"

In order to answer that question, this section described the Birkman history and system. Chapter 1 explained The Birkman Method® in non-technical language. Chapter 2 described the history of the company, including the singular contributions of various researchers and psychometricians who contributed to the instrument. Chapter 3 briefly described the development of the instrument from the beginning to the present time. The goal of this section was to provide a brief history of the founder and the instrument.

SECTION II

THEORETICAL BACKGROUND

CHAPTER 4
Theoretical Background of The Birkman Method®

This chapter briefly describes Roger Birkman's initial conceptual work and an overview of the research available at that time.

It begins with an excerpt from Birkman's dissertation. "When I was first introduced to existing knowledge in the field of psychological tests and measurement while doing undergraduate work at the University of Houston, the potential contribution which could be made to education, business, and industry captured my imagination and has absorbed much of my thought and effort since" (Birkman, 1961).

Initially, Birkman hoped to contribute a unique approach to the measurement of personality. The central problem appeared to be one of developing a theory for understanding the structure and dynamics of personality, which would lend itself to the construction of a more sensitive psychometric instrument and to a more meaningful analysis and interpretation of data obtained from the instrument.

Prior to 1961, questionnaires were most widely used for the study of individual differences in personality. Few studies had been conducted to identify the usefulness of personality measures in the workplace. In fact, in 1965, Guion and Gottier (1965) published an article criticizing the validity of personality measures in personnel selection, which led to a decline in their use for several decades. According to Birkman, most of the existing personality instruments at that time were based on an inadequate theoretical framework. Clearly, there was a need for understanding the structure and dynamics of personality. At the time, there was no general consensus on five factors of personality as there is now (Digman, 1990; Goldberg, 1992); and there was no discrimination between groups based on differences in personality, unless they represented clinical extremes.

Birkman also noted that most personality assessments at that time had significant limitations. For example, assessments were prone to defensiveness and falsification of responses (i.e., faking). Individuals tended to respond to items in a particularly defensive way, so as to present

"In the beginning, we didn't have the technical resources we have today. So, I looked at the best social, personality, and organizational psychologists and began to use their diverse insights to develop The Birkman Method®. This chapter explains the early theories that originally impacted me, and those which followed after."

-Roger W. Birkman

themselves in a positive light. Another notable problem was that most instruments did not account for social desirability, or they used methods to "detect" faking or falsification of responses.

Birkman also noted that many assessments used discrete categories to measure behavior, which failed to fully convey the dynamics of personality. Further, Birkman found that the use of discrete data lost valuable information that was necessary to make assessments more accurate. This was an important issue because the personality traits still needed to be determined and defined.

DISCUSSION OF THE THEORY OF PERSONALITY STRUCTURE

After a thorough consideration of the then current literature and his own observations, Birkman believed that a more sensitive analysis of individual personality differences could be obtained by creating an instrument that measured both social and self-perceptions.

Birkman suggested a new approach to the assessment of personality differences. He proposed that behavior is a function of the meaning the individual assigns to stimuli. During his research, he found that the attitudes, motives, and behavior of the majority of people in an individual's surroundings were more critical than any series of statements they made concerning their own attitudes and beliefs. The hypothesis implicit in this theoretical position is that a close relationship exists between the way individuals judge the motives, attitudes, and behavior of others on the one hand and their characteristic mode of thinking and performing on the other. Each person attributes to others their own thoughts, attitudes, and motives for action. Essentially, individuals are as they see others.

Birkman made two further observations. The first is that behavior is not determined so much by objective facts as by the particular meanings the individual attaches to these facts. The individual's reaction to meanings of events, rather than the events themselves, comprises the most significant data concerning their behavior. The second was that the perceptions of some individuals may actually be illusory, irrational, and unreal. Nevertheless, these perceptions are real and reasonable to the individual, and greatly influence their behavior. They are constantly reacting to an environment distinctly and uniquely their own in a manner which, at the instant of behavior, appears to them most logical, effective, and desirable.

Birkman's theoretical framework and methodology was similar to projective methods used at the time for measuring personality. The difference was that the stimuli presented consisted of word descriptors of the attitudes, feelings, and actions of "most people" presented as true or false statements in the questionnaire. Individuals' judgments made concerning the feelings, attitudes, and behaviors of the "average" person, "people in general," the "majority of people," "almost everyone," etc., were found to be more crucial and relevant for insights into the way an individual performed than any statement(s) made by them concerning their own attitudes, sentiments, behaviors, or needs, regardless of how skillfully statements were phrased or presented. After many questionnaire iterations, the phrase "most people" was considered particularly effective in this technique of personality measurement. Judgments made about the behavior of "most people" were found to be the best means of obtaining the examinee's perception of the social environment to which they were constantly seeking to orient their behavior. Furthermore, by thinking in terms of "most people" rather than "everyone" or some similar all-inclusive term, individuals could make allowances for those whom they knew would be exceptions in the general population. Thus, the individual's responses were not distorted because of some sweeping statements. At the same time the "most people" phrase was sufficiently broad to obtain the subject's general, consistent, and compelling attitudinal and behavioral orientation in the form of their social expectancy. It was also found that judgments made concerning "most people" were likely to elicit the most discriminating responses since this phrase was frequently used in everyday conversation.

Measuring differences in perception of "most people" was thought to have the following advantages:

1. *The individual was challenged to answer to the best of their ability, since questions concerning "most people" take the form of an objective task, in which there was conceivably a right answer.*
2. *Intentional and unintentional defensiveness in responding to questionnaire items about "most people" was likely to be minimized. The meaning of an item would be less subject to the distortion of defensive reasoning.*
3. *Errors resulting from the examinee's inability to assess themselves and their own behavior accurately in self-inventory type questionnaires would in all probability be reduced.*
4. *The questionnaire itself could be made more discriminating and meaningful in analyzing performance differences among the normal population. Items could be phrased simply and briefly. They needed not be phrased in the manner intended to conceal their real purpose and meaning. It was therefore probable that their discriminative and diagnostic value would be proportionately increased.*
5. *The questionnaire itself could be made brief yet permit a wide latitude of responses. There would be no necessity to stress length and add to the number of questions in order to encourage more accurate reporting by the individual.*
6. *The questionnaire would have the merit of more rational construction throughout because of the intelligibility and comparative simplicity of the theoretical assumptions on which it was based. This approach was in contrast to items constructed and validated according to clinical phraseology and norms that appeared to lose their discriminative power because of frequent obscurity and complexity.*

Personality differences were likely to emerge more clearly in a social perception type of questionnaire. One of the problems of self-description questionnaires was that every individual was successful to some extent in controlling their behavior in order to adapt more effectively to environmental influences. As a result, both their observable behavior and their responses to questionnaires could be misleading, since their true nature was often concealed, even to themselves, on a conscious level. As a result, underlying personality dynamics tended to be at least partially concealed.

A study of personality differences in terms of social perception made it possible to clarify and verify theoretical concepts, which found widespread acceptance among leading theoreticians and a way to develop items taken from common speech. The goal was to develop a social perception questionnaire that would shed new light upon those motivational aspects of personality by which people could be compared. As a result, major personality differences, initially identified through logic and observation and only partially verified by psychometric devices, could become more susceptible to measurement.

One of the basic findings of the study was that there were two pivotal points around which personality and perception seemed to organize – a need to see "most people" in a socially acceptable light on the one hand and the counter-need to see "most people" in a socially unacceptable manner on the other.

Social acceptability, operationally defined, was determined by noting the direction of change after groups respond first to items describing "most people" and then respond to the same items in terms of self-description. The greater frequency of endorsement by the group of either the true or false answer to each of the "most people" items over the same answer to the corresponding self-descriptive item was assumed to reflect both the socially desirable response and the response indicating positive perception. For example, if the majority in a norm group tended to assume a trait true for others, false for self, the false for self was assumed the most socially desirable. If an item was answered false for others and true for self by the majority in a group, the true for self answer was then considered the socially desirable response indicating a positive perception, and the false for self answer the socially undesirable response indicating a negative perception.

The assumptions that 1) social perception can be used to discriminate differences among "normal" personalities and that 2) the perception variables of social acceptability or unacceptability are in fact a basic and valid categorization of opposing forces within personality, were believed to introduce special requirements in the area of scoring. Any study conducted along this line was best directed toward examining the functional interdependence of traits. It was believed that the comparison of one personality with another could be facilitated by an exhaustive analysis of relationships between combinations of variables rather than between single variables. The theoretical construct combining (1) social and self-perception as a basis for building a questionnaire and (2) the analysis of social and self-perception in terms of two basic points of view suggested the possibility of developing a pattern analysis by the application of statistical techniques.

Research findings subsequent to these original assumptions, concepts, and theses affirm the value and contribution of the resulting self-other assessment approach, and in particular, The Birkman Method® as it has evolved. For an in-depth review of the instrument as it evolved, refer to Chapter 3 of this manual.

OVERVIEW OF GENERAL THEORETICAL PERSPECTIVES AND RESEARCH AVAILABLE AT THE TIME FROM BIRKMAN'S DISSERTATION

Attributing one's own thoughts, attitudes, and actions to others is a social mechanism that has been a subject of considerable theoretical speculation. George Mead (1934) considered this mechanism essential and basic to personality development. He introduced the concept of role taking, in which the individual takes on roles and attitudes of others in the community. With this view, personality is influenced by attitudes of those around us. As individuals develop, they take on different roles according to what is observed through social roles. An individual then acquires a "generalized other" concept, which represents the general norm within the social environment. The "generalized other" represents what kind of behavior is expected within a social setting. Personality, in turn, arises through social interactions. For Mead, behavior arises through social experiences.

Alfred Adler (1917) recognized that there is a relationship between the feelings one has towards oneself and the feelings one has towards others. Feelings of inferiority that arise in individuals become impelling forces for the development of their psyches. Feelings of inferiority, according to Adler, cause a derogatory tendency to disparage others. Fromm (1939) observed that the failure to love the self is accompanied by a basic hostility toward others, that self-love and love of others go hand in hand.

Harry Stack Sullivan (1940) gave this phenomenon clear and explicit expression in Conceptions of Modern Psychiatry:

"...as one respects oneself, so one can respect others. That is one of the peculiarities of personality that can always be depended on. If there is a valid and real attitude toward the self, that attitude will manifest as valid and real toward others. It is not that as ye judge so shall ye be judged, but as you judge yourself so shall you judge others; strange but true so far as I know, and with no exception." (Sullivan, 1940, p. 244).

Sears (1937) and Healy, Bronner, and Bowers (1930) defined this phenomenon in terms of "ideas of reference" which are essentially projections of feelings of self-criticism or guilt or the false idea that others are noticing or speaking of them. McDougall (1926) advanced a sensitization theory. According to this theory, sensitization of the sentiments of self-regard occurs when the individual seeks to repress some weakness or guilt of which he is aware. Murray and Morgan (1945) theorized that so-called projection is in fact a closure in perception of social relations in the direction of adequacy of stimulus.

Groups and Conformity

Regarding estimates of group opinion and social norms, there is considerable research on the ability to judge others. As early as 1929, Sweet (1929) found that boys' estimates of group opinions were valuable in diagnostic adjustment problems.

Asch (1940), Moore (1921), Marple (1933), and Sherif (1936) have each observed that individuals tend to modify their opinions to make them conform to those of the group with whom they identify themselves. The roles of personal values and needs are organizing factors in perception (Bruner & Postman, 1948; Bruner & Goodman, 1947; Bruner & Postman, 1947; Goodman, 1953; Hanfmann, Stein, & Bruner, 1947; Postman, Bruner, & McGinnies, 1948).

Asch (1940) noted that the views individuals have of groups (positive or negative) have effects on their judgment and behavior and are often used as standards for arriving at conclusions. Studies on group opinions go as far back as Moore (1921) Marple (1933), Sherif (1935), and Sherif (1936) who found that group majority opinion was more effective in changing individuals' judgments than expert opinions.

Previous Questionnaires on Self versus Others Views

Carl Rogers (1949) mentioned two studies his students were conducting (Sheerer, 1949; Stock, 1949) in which attitudes towards oneself were compared with attitudes towards others, in a search to increase understanding about "the self" in therapy and personality. Sheerer (1949) and Stock (1949) gathered data using behavioral observations during patient therapy sessions in a clinical setting. Phillips (1951) noted their findings and took it a step further by devising a brief questionnaire in which patients in a clinical setting were asked to answer questions about the attitudes towards themselves, as compared to attitudes towards others. In this analysis, attitudes towards self and others were very highly correlated, and the author noted further research was needed to investigate the implications for personality measurement (Phillips, 1951). Similar findings using this questionnaire were found by Berger (1952) and McIntyre (1952). Omwake (1954) compared these relationships using three personality inventories. Although the inventories did not delve deeply into personality dynamics, "there is evidence that in a normal population, as well as in those undergoing therapy, attitudes toward the self appear to be reflected in attitudes toward other people: the lower the opinion of the self, the lower the opinion of others. The results support the hypothesis in that there is a marked relation between the way an individual sees himself and the way he sees others; those who accept themselves tend to be acceptant of others and to perceive others as accepting themselves; those who reject themselves hold a correspondingly low opinion of others, and perceive others as being self-rejectant" (Omwake, 1954, p. 445-446). Suinn (1961) found that there is a relationship between self-acceptance and acceptance of others using a learning theory analysis. Though these studies were conducted on adults, similar results have been found in children (Epstein & Feist, 1988).

Travers (1941), Wallen (1943), and Goodman (1953) noted a persistent and surprisingly strong correlation between a person's own attitude and their estimate of group opinion. Gage and Suci (1951), Tobolski and Kerr (1952), Van Zelst (1952), Kelly and Fiske (1951), Chowdhry and Newcomb (1952), and Newcomb (1943) all confirmed that a general relationship exists between the individual's estimate of group opinion and their own performance in various settings.

The foregoing studies have a bearing on social perception, but the specific hypotheses involving "the generalized other concept" advanced by Mead were not tested. Most of the foregoing studies employed as the frame of reference a particular, specific group.

The small amount of research which had been carried out to investigate the "generalized other" concept as an approach to measuring differences in personality was surprising in view of the plausibility of the concept. One possible explanation was that the full significance of the relationship existing between individuals and their social environment had been to some degree overlooked. Attention apparently had been centered largely on the individual, without due regard to the dynamics operating in the external world as they see it. Most experimental examinations involving "other concepts" placed primary emphasis on mass empathy and self-regarding attitudes, perhaps largely as a result of the established research trend.

A study investigating the relationships between scores for self and projected "average" scores on the Test of Personality by George Lehner was reported in the September 1949 issue of the *American Psychologist*. Lehner (1949) found that women tended to devalue the personality of others more than men. Furthermore, he noted that these differences in social perceptions were paralleled by differences in scores reported for self.

As part of Section A in their "Sentiments" examination, Murray and Morgan (1945) asked subjects to guess what the majority of people believe or prefer, e.g. "what are the three most popular things to do?" Norman and Ainsworth (1954) investigated hypotheses concerning the measurement of empathic abilities by requiring the individual to judge "most people." But again, attention was directed away from perceptual differences between groups. Instead, factors of empathy and other correlates were given primary consideration in their investigation.

Hillson and Worchel (1957) used the Self-Activity Inventory developed by Worchel in connection with U. S. Air Force research. The Self-Activity Inventory is designed to give measures of the individual's "other concepts" in addition to their "self-concepts" and "ideal concepts." Here again the discrepancies between self and ideal concepts were noted primarily, and only incidental attention was given to "others concepts" scores.

CHAPTER 4 SUMMARY

The Birkman Method® is based on, and supported by, many different theories of social perception and personality. The "Test of Social Comprehension" takes into consideration a person's own perspectives and the same person's perspectives of most people. Birkman hoped to develop a theory for understanding the structure and dynamics of personality by way of a psychometric instrument. The perceptions a person has, however normal or abnormal, are real to that person and influence behavior in the context of the social environment. Research has shown a strong relationship between a person's view of self and view of others. Individuals have the tendency to present themselves in a socially desirable light when answering personality questionnaires.

An assumption made in measuring personality via self and social perceptions is that individuals who tend to perceive others in a negative way, yet themselves in a positive way, demonstrate the impact of social desirability. Since The Birkman Method® integrates social desirability into its process, it effectively corrects this problem and the problem of "faking" that is overlooked in many personality assessments available today.

The Birkman Method® was, and is, solidly based on theories of social perception and personality. Its unique contribution is that it takes into consideration a person's own perspectives and the same person's perspectives of most people. Carefully and systematically comparing these two perspectives provides insight into the behaviors and motivations of typical, everyday people.

"In essence, an individual is how he or she sees others" (Birkman, 1961).

CHAPTER 5
Five Factor Model of Personality

THE FIVE FACTOR MODEL AND THE BIRKMAN METHOD®

Roger Birkman conducted a series of factor analyses as part of the original development of The Birkman Method® and the instrument has remained relatively unchanged since its original creation. Birkman relied heavily on factor analysis methodologies and was inspired by the work of Cattell (1946). Although the item review in the initial development of The Birkman Method® focused on some of Cattell's work, Birkman also studied other instruments and conducted behavioral interviewing to devise items for scales. Birkman and Mefferd continued to update the original Test of Social Comprehension with the original 11 Components as the FFM was being developed. At the time, the FFM had not been fully researched and described, and Cattell's work inspired others (e.g., Tupes & Christal, 1961; Norman, 1963, Ashton & Lee, 2002) to attempt to replicate his findings, only to arrive at five, six, seven, or as many as 30 factors (SHL, 1984a, 1993a). The differences in numbers of factors identified across authors are driven in large part by the need for specificity in interpretation of test results. In other words, in an academic setting, a five factor solution may provide adequate specificity for research; but in an applied leadership development setting, more factors (i.e., scales) are needed to provide the level of feedback required. With this in mind, it is not surprising that five broad factors can be identified within each of these more complex factor solutions. Based on current studies with data from The Birkman Method®, a stable structure of five factors is identifiable. The original 11 scales in the Test of Social Comprehension provide the specificity necessary for feedback in applied settings, yet continue to uphold the five factor structure. As is true of other applied personality measures, several scales in the Test of Social Comprehension are considered FFM subscales.

The current revision of The Birkman Method® was undertaken to review items and reconstruct the scales via CTT, factor analysis, and IRT, to see how it would align to the FFM of personality. The current revision

> "The original work predates the Five Factor Model. However, we assumed that we had identified the major behavior denominators of personality by paying attention to the best things that psychology had to offer. It is very gratifying to me now that the linkages are so clear."
>
> -Roger W. Birkman

included exploratory and confirmatory factor analyses, and revealed the existence of five factors within the items of The Birkman Method®. IRT analyses allowed efficient revision of items and created a basis for developing the revised operational form. The five factor structure was identified for both Usual behaviors and Needs. Within the five, some of the original scales aligned as primary factors, and some fit as subfactors within the overall five factors. Two of the previous scales (Freedom and Challenge) are not measures of personality traits and were excluded from the revised factor structure. These additional scales will be explained in Chapter 11. Chapter 7 explains the development of the instrument as it was revised. Chapter 11 explains definitions, interpretations, and application of the factors and subfactors. As research continues to support the five general factors, The Birkman Method® now includes assessment of personality via a five factor model. The development efforts supporting this design will be described in the Chapter 7.

FIVE FACTOR MODEL OF PERSONALITY

The Five Factor Model of personality (also referred to as the "Big Five") has become widely accepted as a means of measuring normal functioning personality. Allport and Odbert (1936) sought to identify personality traits using words from English dictionaries. Out of 17,953 terms, they identified approximately 4,500 terms describing relatively stable personality traits. Cattell (1943) used factor analysis with these terms and attempted to develop a taxonomy of personality factors. Eventually, he identified 16 factors to be used in his 16PF measure. Many attempted to replicate Cattell's findings but failed to uphold a 16 factor structure. The work of Fiske (1949), Tupes (1957), Tupes and Christal (1961), and Norman (1963) demonstrated that there were five main factors of personality, as opposed to the 16 proposed by Cattell. There are many names for the five factors, but Norman (1963) gave them labels that have since upheld, for the most part. These were (a) Extroversion or Surgency, (b) Agreeableness, (c) Conscientiousness, (d) Emotional Stability, and (e) Culture. Culture is usually referred to as "Openness to Experience" or "Intellect," and Emotional Stability is often labeled "Neuroticism."

Extensive work has been conducted on the FFM. Goldberg (1981) conducted a lexical analysis of English trait terms and described the "Big Five" factors as being robust. Additionally, he suggested "standard markers of the Big-Five" (Goldberg, 1990; Goldberg, 1992). Costa and McCrae (1985) devised the NEO Personality Inventory (NEO-PI), which focused on Neuroticism, Extraversion, and Openness. Additional studies would align the NEO-PI to the Big Five (Costa & McCrae, 1988; McCrae & Costa, 1987). Based on decades of research and the consistent findings of five factors of personality traits, the use and acceptance of the FFM is widespread.

Cross-cultural studies have also consistently revealed five factors among a multitude of languages and cultures. The work of Goldberg (1990) demonstrated that five factors uphold to various groups of English terms. Angleitner, Ostendorf, and John (1990) found five factors to uphold using German adjectives (Wiggins & Pincus, 1992). Yang and Bond (1990) found five factors among an indigenous Chinese population, administering a translation of American adjectives used in FFM measures. Trull and Geary (1997) used Goldberg's (1992) items and administered them to Chinese and American students, confirming a hypothesized five factor model for both samples, as well as high intercorrelations among the items found in each factor, suggesting the utility of using FFM measures in the Chinese culture. McCrae and Costa (1997) found similarities with the NEO-PI and translations in German, Portuguese, Hebrew, Chinese, Korean, and Japanese. A robust five factor structure upheld in Canada, Finland, Poland, and Germany in a study by Paunonen, Jackson, Trzebinski, and Forsterling (1992). Hendriks et al. (2003) found "clear five-factor structures" in ten data sets of European and non-European countries, including Belgium, England, Germany, the Netherlands, USA, Italy, Spain, Croatia, Czech Republic, Slovakia, Israel, Hungary, and Japan.

The precedence of the FFM allows a direct method of quantifying personality traits among normal functioning individuals. This has allowed the application of the model into the workplace and beyond. In the workplace, organizations tend to rely on personality measures for job selection, teamwork, coaching, and conflict resolution, as well as employee and leader development.

THE ROLE OF PERSONALITY IN ORGANIZATIONS

In the 1960s, the role of personality as a predictor of performance was criticized by Guion and Gottier (1965). This led to a decline in the use of personality in the workforce until the 1990s, when a series of meta-analyses were conducted to demonstrate the relationship between personality and job selection. Barrick and Mount (1991) investigated the relationship between FFM dimensions and job performance across several occupational groups, where Conscientiousness was shown to be related to performance criteria across all groups. Tett, Jackson, and Rothstein (1991) used confirmatory research strategies to provide FFM scale validities and found higher validities than previously reported using exploratory methods. Meta-analyses have also revealed that FFM constructs are valid predictors of job performance in European samples (Salgado, 1998; Salgado, 2003).

The relationship between personality and leadership was examined by Judge, Bono, Ilies, and Gerhardt (2002). Judge et al. found support for the leader trait perspective when using the FFM, and relatively high correlations were found for the five factors where Extraversion was the strongest indicator of leadership. The FFM has also been linked to several dimensions of transformational leadership (Judge & Bono, 2000; Bono & Judge, 2004). Goffin, Rothstein, and Johnston (1996) found incremental validity using personality measures over assessment centers in managerial selection. Overall, there seems to be a direct relationship between personality, leadership, and managerial performance.

The study of personality and team performance has recently gained substantial interest (Rothstein & Goffin, 2006). Extraversion seems to be a consistent predictor of team performance. This was examined by Barrick, Stewart, Neubert, and Mount (1998) and Barry and Stewart (1997). Leadership emergence in teams has also been predicted by Extraversion (Kickul & Neuman, 2000). Extraversion and Conscientiousness are also related to contextual performance in a team setting (Morgeson, Reider, & Campion, 2005).

The use of personality testing in the workplace is increasing greatly, for various workplace related issues. As many as 20% of employers are using personality tests in their organizations in one form or another (Piotrowski & Armstrong, 2006). Heller (2005) noted that 30% of American companies use personality testing for job selection purposes, with a yearly growth of 20%. Given the wide-spread use of personality testing in organizations, it is important that they be used accurately and effectively. The Uniform Guidelines on Employee Selection Procedures (Equal Employment Opportunity Commission, 1978) specifies selection procedures (which can include the use of personality assessments) be valid and fair. Unfortunately, even if valid personality measures are being used for the purposes of job selection, they are not always used properly. Whether the purpose is job selection or employee development (e.g., executive coaching, performance appraisal, teambuilding, culture), those using the measures need to be knowledgeable on how to use them correctly.

CHAPTER 5 SUMMARY

The Birkman Method® was originally developed using factor analysis. Inspired by the work of Raymond B. Cattell, Birkman and Mefferd continued to revise and update The Birkman Method® using factor analysis, as the FFM was emerging through the work of other researchers. The current version of The Birkman Method® aligns to the FFM of personality, and is useful in determining important workplace outcomes such as job performance, job satisfaction, teamwork, etc. The use of personality assessments in the workforce is increasing, as the significance of successful work-related outcomes becomes more crucial to organizations across the world. Consistent with findings of other FFM measures, The Birkman Method® is useful in applications such as job performance, leadership development, team performance, among other organizational functions.

CHAPTER 6
Interests Overview

INTERESTS MEASURED VIA THE BIRKMAN METHOD®

The Interests section of The Birkman Method® measures broad interest themes that are characteristic of many occupations. This section stands apart from behavior in that it directly indicates preference of activities but does not indicate how an individual will go about engaging in these activities. Scores are meant to measure one's preference for activities or tasks; they are not meant to measure skill. When Interest scale scores are particularly high or low, they strongly influence an individual's choice of recreation and occupation.

Interest tests generally involve asking respondents to indicate whether they would like or dislike a particular activity or occupation. Responses tend to be indicators of occupations the individual will likely enter, given adequate opportunity. Edward K. Strong was one of the earliest to investigate interest measurement. The original development of the Strong Vocational Interest Blank (Strong, 1927) included contrasting items administered to people in certain occupational groups to those of a general population group. Frederick Kuder (1946) constructed scales based on general interest areas he identified. Kuder investigated differences among people within the actual occupational groups, as opposed to a general population group. Kuder's methodology also differed from Strong's in that he used a forced-choice format for items, asking respondents to choose the most and least preferred from a set of three items. The Birkman Method® applies a similar methodology used for the Interests section of the report. See Table 6.1 for a sample Interest item.

General interest patterns can be inferred from a pattern of occupational choices, as with the Birkman Interests; and occupations can be inferred from a pattern of interests in general activities, as with the Kuder or Strong surveys. Reliable measurements of occupational interests can be obtained from either type of instrument. The occupational approach, however, yields a direct non-inferential statement about occupational interests, one that is based not only on mere positive selection of specific occupations but also on the rejection of other specific occupations. For example,

"In my day, among the best at determining interests were Strong and Kuder. One of my first tasks was to create an improved interest assessment based on their work. Dr. Roy Mefferd, a leading research psychologist of the time, also provided innovative psychometric insights that improved the interpretive data in the interest survey. His approach is still in use today."

-Roger W. Birkman

TABLE 6.1	EXAMPLE INTEREST ITEM	
JOB TITLE	**1ST CHOICE**	**2ND CHOICE**
Purchasing agent		
Psychiatrist		
Store clerk		
Office manager		

one need not infer an interest in the health professions on the basis of a generalized vocational interest such as reading books. Many people of many occupations other than the health professions may also choose to read a book instead of taking part in other activities. On the other hand, even before high school, children know in general what physicians, nurses, dentists, veterinarians and other vocational practitioners do, and whether or not this kind of vocational activity interests them.

People spend a great deal of their youth considering a range of occupational choices. Even in the face of these differing levels of vocational integration, a high degree of familiarity with specific activities does not appear to be required for the determination of interest patterns. Someone need not know what a forest ranger does in detail to know that he is interested in general in outdoors occupations.

The original development of Birkman Interests resulted in the identification of ten areas of interest, commonly found in other interest measures (e.g., Kuder Preference Record). Table 6.2 lists the ten Birkman Interests scales and their definitions. These scales describe an individual's expressed preference for job titles based on instructions to assume equal economic reward. The scaling methods utilize first and second choices of job titles only and do not include avocational activities or relationship preferences. The Interests survey consists of 48 items consisting of groups of four occupations each. From each of the four options, the respondent makes a first and second choice of preference. The scales comprising the Interests allow description of individual differences in occupational preferences.

Individuals have interests that result in their selection of occupations in characteristic clusters. The specific occupations often may appear to be unrelated. Each occupational interest cluster is composed of several different occupations (e.g., there are a possible two dozen or so occupations involving persuasion and public contact which are individually contrasted with six dozen or so non-persuasive and non-public contact occupations, and so on). Failure to choose a few critical occupations in a cluster for whatever reason, as well as the selection of a few contraindicated occupations, may be compensated for by the selection of other pertinent occupations. Uncertainty or unfamiliarity about the parameters of one, or even of several occupational titles, is compensated for by the selection of other related common occupations. Uneven familiarity with the occupations in a quartet is further compensated for by the fact that two occupations are not selected, permitting dislikes to enter directly into these selections.

TABLE 6.2	THE BIRKMAN METHOD® INTERESTS SCALES AND DEFINITIONS
SCALE	**DEFINITION**
Artistic	The Artistic Interest scale measures a preference for career and/or opportunities involving photography, architecture, design, and representational art endeavors.
Clerical	The Clerical Interest scale measures a preference for career and/or opportunities involving internal administrative support, secretarial, and public contact administrative or service activities.
Literary	The Literary Interest scale measures a preference for career and/or opportunities involving writing, editing, reporting, and general involvement with books and the literary arts.
Mechanical	The Mechanical Interest scale measures a preference for career and/or opportunities involving skilled and semi-skilled mechanical crafts, repair and trouble-shooting responsibilities, hands-on electronics work, and engineering.
Musical	The Musical Interest scale measures a preference for career and/or opportunities involving performing music, working with musical instruments, or general involvement with music and the musical arts.
Numerical	The Numerical Interest scale measures a preference for career and/or opportunities involving bookkeeping and accounting, auditing, financial and statistical analysis, and mathematics.
Outdoor	The Outdoor Interest scale measures a preference for career and/or opportunities involving agricultural and building activities, adventure-oriented activities (performed outside), and working with animals.
Persuasive	The Persuasive Interest scale measures a preference for career and/or opportunities involving persuading, selling, communicating, and various influencing responsibilities such as management.
Scientific	The Scientific Interest scale measures a preference for career and/or opportunities involving medicine (and allied professions), research, and applied sciences.
Social Service	The Social Service Interest scale measures a preference for career and/or opportunities involving counseling, supporting, guiding, educating, and ministering to others as clergy.

DESCRIPTIVE STATISTICS AND RELIABILITY OF BIRKMAN INTERESTS

Internal Consistency

Table 6.3 presents the descriptive statistics and reliabilities for the Birkman Interests. Note that some means appear to be skewed (e.g., Literary) or higher than the number of items possible (e.g., Artistic). This is due to the fact that for each item corresponding to a scale, there is a possible associated raw value of 0, 1, or 2. This means that it is possible for someone to get a value of 28 on Artistic, for example. Also note that the total number of all items in Table 6.3 is 158. There would be an expected total of 192 (48 item quartets equals 192), however, not all items are used to score the scales, and some items are duplicates within the 48 quartets. The internal consistency of the Birkman Interests was analyzed using Cronbach's alpha. As seen in Table 6.3, the internal consistency of the various scales is adequate. Reliability coefficients range from .74 (Scientific) to .91 (Mechanical). For the most part reliability coefficients are moderately high. The few exceptions can be accounted for by the low number of items on these scales (Fried & Ferris, 1987).

TABLE 6.3	BIRKMAN INTERESTS DESCRIPTIVE STATISTICS AND INTERNAL CONSISTENCY RELIABILITIES				
SCALE	N OF ITEMS	M	SD	ALPHA	TEST-RETEST
Artistic	14	14.75	6.56	.84	.86
Clerical	22	9.69	8.36	.90	.89
Literary	11	10.23	5.84	.85	.85
Mechanical	18	10.45	8.49	.91	.93
Musical	10	8.22	5.75	.87	.86
Numerical	19	10.59	8.53	.90	.92
Outdoor	16	12.94	7.77	.88	.90
Persuasive	15	10.92	6.04	.79	.92
Scientific	14	11.57	5.42	.74	.90
Social Service	19	17.35	8.13	.86	.92

Notes: N = 4,300 from 2007 normative sample; N = 115 for test-retest statistics, employees at a financial services organization.

Test-Retest Reliability

A recent test-retest study was conducted on the Birkman Interests and is summarized in Table 6.3. This study was conducted by Birkman researchers in March 2008. The results for short-term test-retest are comparable to those found for similar instruments. The study consisted of a sample of 115 employees at a financial services organization. Results indicate reasonably high reliability coefficients for the scales. The two-week sample test-retest reliabilities range from .85 (Literary) to .93 (Mechanical).

Intercorrelations

Table 6.4 presents the Birkman Interests scales intercorrelations. The results indicate that the Artistic scale is positively correlated with the Literary and Musical scales, and negatively correlated with the Clerical, Numerical, and Persuasive scales. Clerical correlates positively with Numerical and negatively with Musical and Outdoor. Literary is positively correlated with Musical and negatively correlated with Mechanical and Numerical. Mechanical correlates positively with Outdoor and Sci-

TABLE 6.4	BIRKMAN INTERESTS SCALES INTERCORRELATIONS								
	BIRKMAN SCALES								
	ART	CLE	LIT	ME	MUS	NUM	OUT	PER	SCI	SOC
Artistic										
Clerical	-.28									
Literary	.46	-.25								
Mechanical	-.19	-.27	-.38							
Musical	.46	-.41	.50	-.26						
Numerical	-.37	.48	-.33	.01	-.27					
Outdoor	-.02	-.43	-.19	.57	-.18	-.35				
Persuasive	-.30	-.09	.02	-.33	.00	-.17	-.25			
Scientific	.02	-.29	-.09	.32	.10	-.09	.15	-.31		
Social Service	-.24	-.03	-.05	-.48	-.08	-.15	-.27	.33	-.29	

Notes: N = 4,300 from 2007 normative sample. Art = Artistic, Cle = Clerical, Lit = Literary, Me = Mechanical, Mus = Musical, Num = Numerical, Out = Outdoor, Per = Persuasive, Sci = Scientific, Soc = Social Service.

entific, and negatively with Social Service and Persuasive. Musical correlates negatively with Numerical, and Outdoor correlates negatively with Persuasive. Lastly, Persuasive correlates negatively with Scientific, and Scientific correlates negatively with Social Service. These findings indicate that aesthetically-oriented Interests (e.g., Literary, Musical, Artistic) contrast with more factually-oriented Interests (e.g., Mechanical, Numerical), as expected.

VALIDITY OF THE BIRKMAN INTERESTS

John Holland (1976) identified "types," representing six general interest areas that are widely used by many in the field of interest measurement. These areas represent Realistic, Investigative, Artistic, Social, Enterprising, and Conventional types. A principal components analysis of Birkman Interests was conducted to determine how closely they might reflect the Holland types. Using the 2000 scale revisions, this analysis was conducted on a sample of individuals who completed the Birkman Interests between 1993 and 1999 ($N = 91,672$). Principal components factors were rotated using a direct oblimin rotation. Factoring was taken to 6 factors for comparison purposes (factoring to this level factors to eigen values of .54 and above, and extracts 88.3% of the variance). The results are presented in Table 6.5.

TABLE 6.5	ROTATED FACTOR STRUCTURE (OBLIMIN) OF INTERESTS SCALES					
	SIX FACTOR					
SCALE	FACTOR I	FACTOR II	FACTOR III	FACTOR IV	FACTOR V	FACTOR VI
Artistic	.53	-.15	.34	-.12	-.53	-.68
Clerical	-.77	-.46	.05	-.26	-.09	.43
Literary	.65	-.35	.31	-.28	-.07	-.57
Mechanical	-.14	.78	.36	.47	-.16	.28
Musical	.89	.28	.16	-.03	-.13	-.38
Numerical	-.41	-.21	.14	-.05	-.13	.91
Outdoor	.00	.88	.11	.18	-.18	-.25
Persuasive	.05	-.22	-.28	-.29	.94	-.12
Scientific	.14	.20	.20	.97	-.23	-.02
Social Service	-.04	-.22	-.96	-.24	.31	-.09

Notes: N = 91,672.

Factor I for the Birkman Interests scales appears to be a direct contrast of the Numerical and Clerical scales with the Artistic, Literary, and Musical scales. Items that make up the Numerical and Clerical scales relate to accounting, bookkeeping, administering, and secretarial duties. Items that make up the Artistic, Literary, and Musical scales relate to representational art, writing, and musical occupations. The item content of these opposing scales suggests that this factor represents a bidirectional pairing of two of the Holland types (Conventional and Artistic).

Factor II consists of the Birkman Mechanical and Outdoor scales. Items that make up these scales relate to basic and skilled crafts, repair and inspection, and agricultural and other outdoor occupations. The item content of these scales suggests that this factor relates to Holland's Realistic type.

Factor III consists of the Birkman Social Service scale. Items from this scale relate to educational, counseling and therapeutic, social agency, and church-related careers. The item content of this scale suggests that this factor, and the single scale involved, relates to Holland's Social type.

Factor IV consists of the Birkman Scientific scale. Items of this scale relate to medicine, meteorology, science, and research occupations. This item content suggests that this factor, and the single scale involved, relates to Holland's Investigative type.

Factor V consists of the Birkman Persuasive scale. Items of this scale relate to sales, sales management, public speaking, and political occupations. The item content suggests that this factor, and the single scale involved, relates to Holland's Enterprising type.

Factor VI appears to be another direct contrast of the Birkman Numerical and Clerical scales with the Artistic, Literary, and Musical scales. It is possible that we could interpret Factor I as representing the Holland Artistic type and Factor VI as representing the Holland Conventional type. However, because the two factors represent vastly different contributions to the overall variance, this probably isn't warranted.

It appears from the results that the Birkman Interests scales measure constructs similar in some degree to the Holland types. Correlations and joint factor analytic results based on the original scaling (presented in Tables 6.6 and 6.7, see page 62) support this conclusion. Correlations with the Holland types are generally consistent with the findings discussed above. The joint factor analysis resulted in five factors that combined the Realistic and Investigative types and found Birkman's Scientific Interest loading with the Artistic type. Since the 2000 revisions doubled the length of almost all of the Interest scales, and oblique rotation was chosen for the current analyses, these minor differences are understandable.

TABLE 6.6 — BIRKMAN INTERESTS AND HOLLAND GENERAL OCCUPATIONAL THEMES CORRELATIONS FOR TWO SAMPLES

HOLLAND SCALES	BIRKMAN SCALES									
	PER	SOC	SCI	ME	OUT	NUM	CLE	ART	LIT	MUS
Enterprising		.56/ .47								
Social			.78/ .62							
Realistic				.76/ .68	.64/ .45	.58/ .48				
Investigative				.42/ .29	.38/ .26					
Artistic								.81/ .55	.72/ .58	.80/ .59
Conventional							.51/ .38			

Notes: The first coefficient represents 318 entering college freshmen ages 17-18. The second coefficient represents 271 adults receiving career counseling.

TABLE 6.7 — FACTOR STRUCTURE OF THE COMBINED BIRKMAN AND HOLLAND SCALES

I.		II.		III.		IV.		V.	
Realistic	.91	Conventional	.76	Social	.79	Enterprising	.84	Artistic	.87
Investigative	.54	Num	.86	Soc	.74	Per	.78	Art	.71
Me	.79	Cle	.69	Sci	-.60			Lit	.74
Out	.60	Out	-.56					Mus	.78
Soc	-.46							Sci	.40

Notes: N = 271 adults during career counseling. The Holland scales were based on the Strong-Campbell Interest Survey; both the Birkman and Holland scales were derived from occupational choices. Varimax rotation of the principal components with associated eigen values of 1.0 or greater.

CHAPTER 6 SUMMARY

Interests in The Birkman Method® measure ten general interest themes indicating one's preference for activities or tasks. Interest measurements usually consist of items asking about preference for either activities or occupations. The Birkman Interests use a forced-choice format for items by asking respondents to choose two out of a group of four occupations. The scale scores are derived from responses to items containing occupations relevant to a particular interest area.

Internal consistency and test-retest reliabilities of the Birkman Interests are adequate. Convergent validity was demonstrated with Holland's types, and factor analyses revealed Birkman Interests scales load consistently with Holland's six types. Taken together, the Interests scales provide clear indications of high or low interest preferences.

SECTION II SUMMARY

This section answers: "Does The Birkman Method® have historical and current theoretical support?"

In order to answer that question, this section described the theoretical development for the assessment. Chapter 4 explained the initial and continuing theoretical support for the "self" and "most people" questionnaire design. Chapter 5 demonstrated how The Birkman Method® aligns with the Five Factor Model of personality used by the majority of personality researchers and practitioners today. Chapter 6 substantiated the approach to assessing Interests based on direct comparisons to similar instruments. The following section provides the specific information by which a technical evaluation can be made of The Birkman Method®.

SECTION III

PSYCHOMETRIC PROPERTIES OF THE BIRKMAN METHOD®

CHAPTER 7
Classical and IRT Based Item and Scale Analysis

BIRKMAN SCALE DESCRIPTION

The current scales in The Birkman Method® are briefly described below. For more detailed definitions, refer to Chapter 11.

Orientations/Personality Factors

The five construct scales for the instrument are:

Emotive Orientation - measures the degree to which an individual expresses emotions, makes decisions, and their preferred pace of action. This construct aligns to Emotional Stability or Neuroticism of the FFM.

Social Orientation - measures the degree to which an individual seeks social interaction. This construct aligns to Extraversion of the FFM.

Process Orientation - (formerly known as Structure) measures the degree to which an individual wants to give or receive clear direction, to follow instructions carefully, to finish tasks, to deal with detailed tasks, to work for accuracy, and to use systematic approaches. This construct aligns to Conscientiousness of the FFM.

Control Orientation - measures the degree to which an individual approaches others. This construct aligns to Agreeableness of the FFM.

Change Orientation - measures the degree to which an individual is restless. It involves focused or wandering attention, the ease or trouble in sitting still, the frequency of needing to change focus, and working fast enough to optimize the inflow of new stimuli. This construct aligns to Openness to Experience of the FFM.

Preferences/Personality Subfactors

The seven primary subscales for the instrument are:

"The construction of The Birkman Method® was an intense, iterative process. It's a blessing to be able to assemble the right talent to get the whole thing done. I could not have done it alone, the job was too big and the skills needed exceeded my own."

-Roger W. Birkman

Empathy - measures the degree to which an individual is comfortable with emotional expression and involvement of feelings.

Activity - measures the degree to which an individual prefers action, quick thinking, and physical expression of energy.

Thought - measures the degree to which an individual approaches forming conclusions and making decisions; concerns for making the right decision the first time; and concerns over consequences of decisions.

Communication (formerly known as Esteem) - measures a sensitivity-based construct that includes shyness, saying no, praising and being praised, sensitivity about correcting others or being corrected by others, getting one's feelings hurt, and concerns about embarrassing or being embarrassed.

Interaction (formerly known as Acceptance) - measures the degree to which an individual wants to be talkative, enjoy people in groups, social laughter (even at one's own expense), comfort in talking to strangers, enjoying parties and group activities, and approachability.

Incentive (formerly known as Advantage) - measures the degree to which an individual prefers to drive for personal rewards or to share in team rewards.

Authority - measures the degree to which an individual wants to persuade, speak up, express opinions openly and forcefully, and/or argue.

Social Environment Anchored Scales

The two macro-level scales for the instrument are:

Personal Autonomy (formerly known as Freedom) - measures the degree to which an individual provides conventional or unconventional answering patterns across the instrument.

Perspective Alignment (formerly known as Challenge) - measures the degree to which an individual approaches and understands the issues of socially correct behavior and especially social image.

Item Content

Items for all scales in The Birkman Method® have been screened extensively for content that might seem offensive or invade an examinee's privacy. There are no items concerning religious beliefs, sexual preference, criminal offenses, drug incidents, or racial/ethnic attitudes. Lastly, no items exist that reference physical or mental disabilities.

The Flesch-Kincaid reading level analysis shows that the instrument is written at the third grade level. Readability statistics conducted on the 88 items indicated an average of 1.28 syllables per word, an average word length of 3.9 letters, and an average sentence length of 9.5 words.

CLASSICAL TEST THEORY (CTT) DESCRIPTIVE STATISTICS

CTT is the most established and widely used methodology for instrument development and validation. CTT was used to examine the psychometric properties of The Birkman Method® factor scales. CTT statistics for the Birkman Orientation, Preference, and Social Environment Anchored scales are shown in Tables 7.1, 7.2, and 7.3.

TABLE 7.1		CLASSICAL TEST THEORY SCALE STATISTICS FOR ORIENTATION SCALES					
	SCALE	N OF ITEMS	M	SD	ALPHA	AVE. ITEM-TOTAL r	SEM
USUAL	Emotive	22	5.27	4.80	.88	.481	1.66
	Social	25	17.07	5.16	.86	.397	1.93
	Process	15	9.67	2.93	.71	.312	1.58
	Control	19	5.26	3.07	.70	.277	1.68
	Change	7	3.29	1.94	.67	.387	1.11
NEEDS	Emotive	22	8.35	5.41	.88	.479	1.87
	Social	25	11.68	4.86	.82	.354	2.06
	Process	15	6.38	3.46	.78	.386	1.62
	Control	19	8.51	3.98	.80	.369	1.78
	Change	7	3.62	1.70	.58	.307	1.10

Source: 2007 normative database

These tables explain the central tendency, dispersion, reliability, and precision level of the Birkman scales from the CTT standpoint. The difference in distributions on the same Birkman scale across the two perspectives illustrates the influence of the target of the stimuli. The magnitudes of these scale differences may be accounted for by many variables (e.g., perception differences, social desirability). While most of the coefficient alphas are relatively high, a few scales have more modest reliabilities. The low number of items can account for the lower reliabilities on these scales (Fried & Ferris, 1987). The average item total correlations are all moderately high. The standard errors of measurements provide sufficient precision evidence for the five bandwidth interpretation used in the Birkman reporting structure.

TABLE 7.2		CLASSICAL TEST THEORY SCALE STATISTICS FOR PREFERENCE SCALES					
	SCALE	N OF ITEMS	M	SD	ALPHA	AVE. ITEM-TOTAL r	SEM
USUAL	Activity	6	3.96	1.95	.81	.570	0.85
	Empathy	13	2.48	2.69	.81	.461	1.17
	Thought	3	0.75	0.93	.54	.354	0.63
	Communication	12	4.70	3.10	.80	.439	1.39
	Interaction	13	9.77	2.84	.80	.413	1.27
	Incentive	9	1.68	1.51	.54	.251	1.02
	Authority	10	3.58	2.09	.60	.282	1.32
NEEDS	Activity	6	3.05	1.92	.74	.488	0.98
	Empathy	13	4.00	3.15	.82	.456	1.34
	Thought	3	1.40	1.08	.56	.371	0.72
	Communication	12	7.86	2.67	.74	.377	1.36
	Interaction	13	7.55	2.97	.75	.364	1.49
	Incentive	9	3.73	2.22	.70	.375	1.22
	Authority	10	4.77	2.19	.65	.316	1.30

Source: 2007 normative database.

Note that the mean for the Perspective Alignment scale is negative. This is possible because the scale is constructed from delta differences. Perspective Alignment scale scores range from -70 to 32 in the 2007 Birkman normative database.

TABLE 7.3	CLASSICAL TEST THEORY SCALE STATISTICS FOR SOCIAL ENVIRONMENT ANCHORED SCALES					
SCALE	N OF ITEMS	M	SD	ALPHA	AVE. ITEM-TOTAL r	SEM
Personal Autonomy: Usual	18	3.40	2.51	.68	.265	1.42
Personal Autonomy: Needs	18	5.12	3.55	.80	.376	1.59
Perspective Alignment	4*	-15.00	12.79	.64	.425	7.67

Notes: * not dichotomous items, scale deltas; SEM = Standard Error of Measurement.
Source: 2007 normative database.

IRT BASED ITEM ANALYSIS

IRT was used to examine the Birkman scales at the item and scale level. IRT greatly increases the information that can be gathered about an instrument more than by CTT methods alone (Embretson & Reise, 2000; Hambleton & Swaminathan, 1985).

IRT relates characteristics of items (item parameters) and characteristics of individuals (latent traits) to the probability of a positive response on a common scale. A variety of IRT models has been developed for dichotomous and polytomous data. In each case, the probability of answering correctly or endorsing a particular response category can be represented graphically by an item (option) response function (IRF/ORF). These functions represent the nonlinear regression of a response probability on a latent trait such as conscientiousness or verbal ability (Hulin, Drasgow, & Parsons, 1983).

Numerous IRT models are available for examining dichotomous and polytomous data. Ultimately, the choice of a model should be based on both theoretical and empirical considerations, i.e., model-data fit. One of the most commonly used models among applied psychologists is the Three-Parameter Logistic Model (3PL). The 3PL has been used primarily for modeling cognitive ability data, but recently 3PL has been applied to personality data as well (Embretson & Reise, 2000). The 3PL model is a more general form of the one parameter (1PL or Rasch Model) and two parameter logistic model (2PL; Birnbaum, 1968). It contains three parameters representing item discrimination "a", item location "b", and the lower asymptote parameter "c". Note that the 2PL model can be obtained from 3PL by setting "c" = 0; the 1PL model may be obtained by setting "c" = 0 and "a" = 1. For the 3PL model, the probability (P) that an examinee with latent trait (θ) will endorse item j is

$$P_j(\theta) \equiv P(x_j = 1 | \theta; a_j, b_j, c_j) = \frac{c_j + (1 - c_j)}{\left\{ 1 + \exp\left[-Da_j\left(\theta - b_j\right)\right]\right\}}$$

where x_j is the response to the item, D is a scaling constant equal to 1.702, and a, b, and c are the parameters characterizing an item. The parameters for the operational items must be estimated using an IRT program (e.g., BILOG, MULTILOG, TESTFACT).

IRT ANALYSIS RESULTS

Tables 7.4 through 7.8 provide estimated discrimination "a", difficulty "b", and guessing "c" parameters for the Birkman items from the self perspective. These estimates provide invariant (i.e., population) information on the individual items that can be used to determine the quality of each.

Table 7.4 presents the results from the IRT analysis of the Emotive Orientation Usual scale items and overall scale. The "a" or discrimination parameters range from 0.672 to 3.005 and have a mean of 1.473. An "a" parameter above 0.500 is considered a conservative criterion for adequately discriminating between examinees on the latent trait (e.g., Emotive Orientation). All of the items on the Emotive Orientation Usual scale meet these criteria. The "a" parameter is analogous to the item-total correlation or factor loading. The high "a" parameters reported here provide support for the unidimensionality of the Emotive Orientation Usual scale at the item level.

The "b" or difficulty parameters for the Emotive Orientation Usual scale range from 0.038 to 2.088 and have a mean of 1.138. A value of 0.000 on the underlying theta scale (i.e., Emotional Stability Usual) was established as the population mean for the latent trait continuum. This indicates that the mean of the set of Emotive Orientation Usual items included in this analysis (i.e., the operational Birkman items) is somewhat higher than the mean level of Emotive Orientation in the population from the self perspective.

The "c" parameters range for the Emotive Orientation Usual scale from 0.010 to 0.133 and have a mean of 0.047. Recent advances in research suggest that the c-parameter is a measure of how dynamic the components (guessing, self-presentation, identity) are that make up the item level responses across the theta continuum; however, more research is necessary before any conclusions can be made.

Overall, the IRT parameters demonstrate that the Emotive Orientation Usual scale is well constructed for use in differentiating between examinees throughout the moderate-to-high range of the Emotive Orientation latent trait from the self perspective. The best discrimination and highest information points are within one standard deviation above the scale mean.

Table 7.5 (*see page 74*) presents the results from the IRT analysis of the Social Orientation Usual scale items and the overall scale. The "a" or discrimination parameters range from 0.511 to 1.905 and have a mean of 0.991. All of the items on the Social Orientation Usual scale meet the criteria of "a" > .500. The "a" parameter is analogous to the item-total correlation or factor loading. The high "a" parameters reported here provide support for the unidimensionality of the Social Orientation Usual scale at the item level.

The "b" or difficulty parameters range from -2.870 to 1.376 and have a mean of -0.456. This indicates that the mean of the set of Social Orientation Usual items included in this analysis (i.e., the operational Birkman items) is approximately the same as the mean level of Social Orientation in the population from the self perspective.

TABLE 7.4	IRT PARAMETERS FOR THE EMOTIVE ORIENTATION USUAL SCALE		
	ESTIMATED PARAMETERS		
Item	a_i	b_i	c_i
1	1.423	0.699	.051
2	1.099	1.208	.048
3	1.706	1.079	.022
4	1.500	0.136	.054
5	1.718	0.819	.016
6	1.085	0.038	.077
7	0.672	0.856	.133
8	1.313	0.477	.092
9	1.680	1.276	.026
10	0.792	1.809	.044
11	1.231	2.088	.048
12	1.440	1.618	.021
13	0.995	2.013	.056
14	1.814	1.108	.027
15	1.118	0.491	.074
16	1.716	1.837	.031
17	3.005	1.446	.010
18	1.989	1.314	.019
19	2.784	1.278	.017
20	1.081	0.803	.085
21	1.363	1.213	.034
22	0.879	1.425	.053
Average	1.473	1.138	.047

	ESTIMATED PARAMETERS		
Item	a_i	b_i	c_i
1	0.620	-0.373	.389
2	0.853	-0.774	.374
3	0.766	-0.672	.238
4	0.846	1.376	.081
5	1.905	-0.128	.135
6	0.511	-2.870	.500
7	0.829	0.776	.135
8	1.371	-0.331	.227
9	1.797	-0.125	.158
10	1.243	-0.005	.071
11	1.771	-0.654	.146
12	0.512	0.407	.337
13	1.165	-0.489	.213
14	0.518	-1.760	.430
15	0.672	0.253	.176
16	1.511	-0.286	.109
17	0.738	-1.577	.500
18	0.539	-0.905	.329
19	1.556	-0.323	.107
20	0.601	-0.434	.376
21	1.300	-0.500	.105
22	0.928	0.368	.079
23	1.100	-0.792	.229
24	0.544	-2.038	.497
25	0.587	0.454	.442
Average	0.991	-0.456	.255

TABLE 7.5   IRT PARAMETERS FOR THE SOCIAL ORIENTATION USUAL SCALE

The "c" or difficulty parameters range from 0.071 to 0.500 and have a mean of 0.255. Similar to the other Birkman scales, the "c" parameters vary across items within Social Orientation Usual scale. Overall, the IRT parameters demonstrate that the Social Orientation Usual scale is a soundly-constructed scale for use in differentiating between examinees throughout the range of the Social Orientation latent trait from the self perspective. The best discrimination and highest information points are within one standard deviation of the scale mean, meaning that the scale measures best where the majority of the population scores.

Table 7.6 presents the results from the IRT analysis of the Process Orientation Usual items and the overall scale. The "a" or discrimination parameters range from 0.427 to 1.923 and have a mean of 0.930. Fourteen of the 15 items on the Process Orientation Usual scale meet the criteria of "a">.500. The "a" parameter is analogous to the item-total correlation or factor loading. The high "a" parameters support the unidimensionality of the Process Orientation Usual scale at the item level.

TABLE 7.6	IRT PARAMETERS FOR THE PROCESS ORIENTATION USUAL SCALE		
	ESTIMATED PARAMETERS		
Item	a_i	b_i	c_i
1	1.123	-0.135	.181
2	0.532	1.947	.355
3	1.240	0.371	.120
4	0.509	0.794	.282
5	1.027	-0.966	.367
6	1.923	-0.396	.211
7	0.427	1.069	.405
8	1.145	-0.570	.397
9	0.825	1.055	.186
10	0.754	-1.124	.457
11	0.775	0.856	.112
12	0.967	-0.226	.160
13	0.681	-2.463	.500
14	1.037	0.343	.189
15	0.982	-1.095	.500
Average	0.930	-0.036	.295

The "b" or difficulty parameters range from -2.463 to 1.947 and have a mean of -0.036. This indicates that the mean of the set of Process Orientation Usual items included in this analysis (i.e., the operational Birkman items) is approximately the same as the mean level of Process Orientation in the population from the self perspective.

The "c" or difficulty parameters of the Process Orientation Usual scale range from 0.112 to 0.500 and have a mean of 0.295. Given the wide range of "c" parameters, interpretations at the scale level may be misleading, hence the real need for item level IRT analyses.

Overall, the IRT parameters demonstrate that the Process Orientation Usual scale is a soundly-constructed scale for use in differentiating between examinees throughout the range of the Process Orientation latent trait from the self perspective. The best discrimination and highest information points are within one standard deviation of the scale mean, meaning that the scale measures best where the majority of the population scores.

Table 7.7 presents the results from the IRT analysis of the Control Orientation Usual items and the overall scale. The "a" or discrimination parameters range from 0.712 to 1.052 and have a mean of 0.995. An "a" parameter above 0.500 is considered a conservative criterion for adequately discriminating between examinees on the latent trait. All of the items on the Control Orientation Usual scale meet this criterion. The "a" parameter is analogous to the item-total correlation or factor loading. The high "a" parameters reported here provide support for the unidimensionality of the Control Orientation Usual scale at the item level.

The "b" or difficulty parameters for the Control Orientation Usual scale range from 0.171 to 2.745 and have a mean of 1.631. This indicates that the mean of the set of Control Orientation Usual items included in this analysis (i.e., the operational Birkman items) is somewhat higher than the mean level of Control Orientation in the population from the self perspective.

The "c" parameters for the Control Orientation Usual scale range from 0.034 to 0.500 and have a mean of 0.147. Given the wide range of "c" parameters, interpretations at the scale level may be misleading, hence the real need for item level IRT analyses.

Overall, the IRT parameters demonstrate that the Control Orientation Usual scale is well constructed for use in differentiating between examinees throughout the range of the Control Orientation latent trait from the self perspective. The best discrimination and highest information points are one standard deviations above the scale mean, meaning that the scale measures best where the majority of the workforce population scores.

Table 7.8 presents the results from the IRT analysis of the Change Orientation Usual items and overall scale. The "a" or discrimination parameters range from 0.558 to 2.196 and have a mean of 1.340. An "a" parameter above 0.500 is considered a conservative criterion for adequately discriminating between examinees on the latent trait. All of the items on the Change Orientation Usual scale meet this criterion. The "a" parameter is analogous to the item-total correlation or factor loading. The fairly high "a" parameters reported here provide support for the unidimensionality of the Change Orientation Usual scale at the item level.

The "b" or difficulty parameters for the Change Orientation Usual scale range from -0.599 to 1.226 and have a mean of 0.484. This indicates that the mean of the set of Change Orientation Usual items included in this analysis (i.e., the operational Birkman items) is approximately the same as the mean level of Change Orientation in the population from the self perspective. Another set of Change Orientation Usual items calibrated to the current operational items could have a higher or lower mean in relation to the population mean, but the population mean will remain fairly static or fixed.

TABLE 7.7	IRT PARAMETERS FOR THE CONTROL ORIENTATION USUAL SCALE		
	ESTIMATED PARAMETERS		
Item	a_i	b_i	c_i
1	1.024	2.745	.035
2	1.010	1.766	.133
3	1.018	2.409	.083
4	1.052	1.924	.034
5	0.963	0.492	.281
6	1.041	1.818	.042
7	1.024	2.489	.055
8	1.013	2.666	.049
9	1.003	2.096	.162
10	1.020	1.810	.207
11	1.031	2.307	.076
12	0.989	2.078	.391
13	0.985	1.541	.247
14	1.042	1.569	.034
15	0.977	0.448	.168
16	0.712	0.287	.500
17	0.987	1.367	.102
18	0.988	1.014	.060
19	1.030	0.171	.132
Average	0.995	1.631	.147

The "c" parameters range for the Change Orientation Usual scale from 0.042 to 0.352 and have a mean of 0.174. Given the wide range of "c" parameters, interpretations at the scale level may be misleading, hence the real need for item level IRT analyses.

Overall, the IRT parameters demonstrate that the Change Orientation Usual scale is well constructed for use in differentiating between examinees throughout the range of the Change Orientation latent trait from the self perspective. The best discrimination and highest information points are within one standard deviation above the scale mean.

TABLE 7.8	IRT PARAMETERS FOR THE CHANGE ORIENTATION USUAL SCALE		
	ESTIMATED PARAMETERS		
Item	a_i	b_i	c_i
1	0.789	1.226	.352
2	2.161	0.771	.042
3	0.558	0.005	.219
4	1.336	-0.599	.200
5	1.208	0.809	.192
6	1.136	0.990	.122
7	2.196	0.188	.091
Average	1.340	0.484	.174

Tables 7.9 through 7.13 provide estimated discrimination "a", difficulty "b", and guessing "c" parameters for the Birkman items from the other perspective. These estimates provide invariant (i.e., population) information on the individual items that can be used to determine the quality of each.

Table 7.9 presents the results from the IRT analysis of the Emotive Orientation Needs scale items and overall scale. The "a" or discrimination parameters range from 0.702 to 2.374 and have a mean of 1.219. An "a" parameter above 0.500 is considered a conservative criterion for adequately discriminating between examinees on the latent trait (e.g., Emotive Orientation). All of the items on the Emotive Orientation Needs scale meet these criteria. The "a" parameter is analogous to the item-total correlation or factor loading. The high "a" parameters reported here provide support for the unidimensionality of the Emotive Orientation Needs scale at the item level.

The "b" or difficulty parameters for the Emotive Orientation Needs scale range from -0.640 to 1.491 and have a mean of 0.617. A value of 0.000 on the underlying theta scale (i.e., Emotive Orientation) was established as the population mean for the latent trait continuum. This indicates that the mean of the set of Emotive Orientation Needs items included in this analysis (i.e., the operational Birkman items) is a little higher than the mean level of Emotive Orientation in the population from the other perspective. Another set of Emotive Orientation Needs items calibrated to the current operational items could have a higher or lower mean in relation to the population mean, but the population mean will remain fairly static or fixed.

TABLE 7.9	IRT PARAMETERS FOR THE EMOTIVE ORIENTATION NEEDS SCALE		
	ESTIMATED PARAMETERS		
Item	a_i	b_i	c_i
1	0.702	0.567	.150
2	1.276	0.468	.093
3	1.561	0.726	.040
4	1.075	-0.159	.093
5	1.708	0.374	.046
6	0.984	-0.640	.202
7	0.891	1.491	.065
8	0.807	0.255	.099
9	0.803	0.878	.065
10	0.909	-0.043	.113
11	1.475	1.055	.052
12	1.441	1.302	.033
13	1.352	0.457	.045
14	1.095	-0.175	.110
15	0.932	1.440	.059
16	1.340	0.936	.042
17	2.374	1.165	.017
18	1.465	1.004	.044
19	1.341	1.456	.019
20	0.854	-0.009	.136
21	1.025	0.642	.090
22	1.417	0.391	.085
Average	1.219	0.617	.077

The "c" parameters for the Emotive Orientation Needs scale range from 0.017 to 0.202 and have a mean of 0.077. Recent advances in research suggest that the c-parameter is a measure of how dynamic the components (guessing, self-presentation, identity) are that make up the item level responses across the theta continuum; however, more research is necessary before any conclusions can be made.

Overall, the IRT parameters demonstrate that the Emotive Orientation Needs scale is well constructed for use in differentiating between examinees throughout the range of the Emotive Orientation latent trait from the other perspective. The best discrimination and highest information points are within one standard deviation of the scale mean, meaning that the scale measures best where the majority of the population scores.

Table 7.10 presents the results from the IRT analysis of the Social Orientation Needs scale items and the overall scale. The "a" or discrimination parameters range from 0.559 to 2.095 and have a mean of 1.045. All of the items on the Social Orientation Needs scale meet the criteria of "a" > .500. The "a" parameter is analogous to the item-total correlation or factor loading. The high "a" parameters reported here provide support for the unidimensionality of the Social Orientation Needs scale at the item level.

The "b" or difficulty parameters range from -1.328 to 2.032 and have a mean of 0.541. This indicates that the mean of the set of Social Orientation Needs items included in this analysis (i.e., the operational Birkman items) is approximately the same as the mean level of Social Orientation in the population from the other perspective.

The "c" or difficulty parameters range from 0.048 to 0.463 and have a mean of 0.194. Similar to the other Birkman scales, the "c" parameters vary across items within Social Orientation Needs scale.

Overall, the IRT parameters demonstrate that the Social Orientation Needs scale is a soundly-constructed scale for use in differentiating between examinees throughout the range of the Social Orientation latent trait from the other perspective. The best discrimination and highest information points are within one standard deviation of the scale mean, meaning that the scale measures best where the majority of the population scores.

Table 7.11 (*see page 82*) presents the results from the IRT analysis of the Process Orientation Needs items and the overall scale. The "a" or discrimination parameters range from 0.596 to 1.659 and have a mean of 1.079. All of the items on the Process Orientation Needs scale meet the criteria of "a" > .500. The "a" parameter is analogous to the item-total correlation or factor loading. The high "a" parameters support the unidimensionality of the Process Orientation Needs scale at the item level.

The "b" or difficulty parameters range from -.866 to 2.126 and have a mean of 0.724. This indicates that the mean of the set of Process Orientation Needs items included in this analysis (i.e., the operational Birkman items) is approximately the same as the mean level of Process Orientation in the population from the other perspective.

TABLE 7.10	IRT PARAMETERS FOR THE SOCIAL ORIENTATION NEEDS SCALE		
	ESTIMATED PARAMETERS		
Item	a_i	b_i	c_i
1	0.619	0.881	.218
2	1.120	0.047	.426
3	0.836	0.177	.158
4	1.540	1.636	.068
5	2.066	1.202	.060
6	0.769	-1.159	.302
7	0.940	1.637	.084
8	1.055	1.344	.082
9	2.095	1.076	.048
10	1.032	0.461	.072
11	1.646	0.540	.102
12	1.116	1.300	.171
13	1.384	0.530	.193
14	0.664	-0.425	.215
15	1.252	1.158	.122
16	1.059	0.466	.401
17	0.732	-1.328	.463
18	0.591	-0.565	.242
19	0.881	0.122	.134
20	0.559	1.216	.429
21	0.898	-0.474	.380
22	0.763	2.032	.119
23	0.854	0.013	.123
24	0.752	-0.042	.133
25	0.890	1.674	.094
Average	1.045	0.541	.194

The "c" or difficulty parameters of the Process Orientation Needs scale range from 0.049 to 0.419 and have a mean of 0.166. Given the wide range of "c" parameters, interpretations at the scale level may be misleading, hence the real need for item level IRT analyses.

Overall, the IRT parameters demonstrate that the Process Orientation Needs scale is a soundly-constructed scale for use in differentiating between examinees throughout the range of the Process Orientation latent trait from the other perspective. The best discrimination and highest information points are within one standard deviation of the scale mean, meaning that the scale measures best where the majority of the population scores.

TABLE 7.11   IRT PARAMETERS FOR THE PROCESS ORIENTATION NEEDS SCALE

Item	ESTIMATED PARAMETERS		
	a_i	b_i	c_i
1	1.451	0.357	.078
2	0.596	2.126	.280
3	1.420	0.713	.055
4	0.838	1.864	.092
5	0.996	-0.314	.247
6	1.659	0.322	.071
7	0.669	1.345	.321
8	1.483	0.257	.136
9	0.881	1.210	.182
10	1.110	0.877	.072
11	1.012	1.202	.069
12	1.129	0.724	.115
13	0.644	-0.866	.419
14	1.473	1.011	.049
15	0.825	0.037	.303
Average	1.079	0.724	.166

Table 7.12 presents the results from the IRT analysis of the Control Orientation Needs items and the overall scale. The "a" or discrimination parameters range from 0.476 to 1.758 and have a mean of 1.081. An "a" parameter above 0.500 is considered a conservative criterion for adequately dis-

TABLE 7.12   IRT PARAMETERS FOR THE CONTROL ORIENTATION NEEDS SCALE

Item	ESTIMATED PARAMETERS		
	a_i	b_i	c_i
1	0.820	0.901	.107
2	1.210	2.186	.042
3	1.135	1.045	.108
4	1.758	-0.407	.157
5	0.703	0.032	.289
6	0.958	1.023	.036
7	1.216	1.553	.197
8	1.502	-0.113	.062
9	1.496	0.095	.049
10	1.029	1.839	.193
11	1.345	1.347	.050
12	0.995	0.285	.190
13	1.161	0.328	.082
14	0.940	1.561	.425
15	1.021	-0.395	.154
16	0.784	1.372	.261
17	1.348	1.610	.053
18	0.476	-1.547	.500
19	0.646	-0.413	.263
Average	1.081	0.647	.169

criminating between examinees on the latent trait. Eighteen of the 19 items on the Control Orientation Needs scale meet this criterion. The "a" parameter is analogous to the item-total correlation or factor loading. The high "a" parameters reported here provide support for the unidimensionality of the Control Orientation Needs scale at the item level.

The "b" or difficulty parameters for the Control Orientation Needs scale range from -1.547 to 2.186 and have a mean of 0.647. This indicates that the mean of the set of Control Orientation Needs items included in this analysis (i.e., the operational Birkman items) is a little higher than the mean level of Control Orientation in the population from the other perspective. Another set of Control Orientation Needs items calibrated to the current operational items could have a higher or lower mean in relation to the population mean, but the population mean will remain fairly static or fixed.

The "c" parameters range for the Control Orientation Needs scale from 0.036 to 0.500 and have a mean of 0.169. Given the wide range of "c" parameters, interpretations at the scale level may be misleading, hence the real need for item level IRT analyses.

Overall, the IRT parameters demonstrate that the Control Orientation Needs scale is well constructed for use in differentiating between examinees throughout the range of the Control Orientation latent trait from the other perspective. The best discrimination and highest information points are within one standard deviation of the scale mean, meaning that the scale measures best where the majority of the population scores.

Table 7.13 presents the results from the IRT analysis of the Change Orientation Needs items and overall scale. The "a" or discrimination parameters range from 0.704 to 1.570 and have a mean of 1.097. An "a" parameter above 0.500 is considered a conservative criterion for adequately discriminating between examinees on the latent trait. All of the items on the Change Orientation Needs scale meet this criterion. The "a" parameter is analogous to the item-total correlation or factor loading. The fairly high "a" parameters reported here provide support for the unidimensionality of the Change Orientation Needs scale at the item level.

The "b" or difficulty parameters for the Change Orientation Needs scale range from -1.352 to 1.237 and have a mean of 0.423. This indicates that the mean of the set of Change Orientation Needs items included in this analysis (i.e., the operational Birkman items) is approximately the same as the mean level of Change Orientation in the population from the other perspective. Another set of Change Orientation Needs items calibrated to the current operational items could have a higher or lower mean in relation to the population mean, but the population mean will remain fairly static or fixed.

The "c" parameters range for the Change Orientation Needs scale from 0.034 to 0.410 and have a mean of 0.242. Given the wide range of "c" parameters, interpretations at the scale level may be misleading, hence the real need for item level IRT analyses.

Overall, the IRT parameters demonstrate that the Change Orientation Needs scale is well constructed for use in differentiating between examinees throughout the range of the Change Orientation latent trait from the other perspective. The best discrimination and highest information points are within one standard deviation of the scale mean, meaning that the scale measures best where the majority of the population scores.

TABLE 7.13   IRT PARAMETERS FOR THE CHANGE ORIENTATION NEEDS SCALE

Item	ESTIMATED PARAMETERS		
	a_i	b_i	c_i
1	0.902	1.132	.410
2	1.570	0.978	.034
3	0.704	-0.027	.405
4	1.145	-1.352	.346
5	1.013	1.237	.241
6	0.916	0.474	.172
7	1.432	0.516	.084
Average	1.097	0.423	.242

Test Characteristic Curves

Using these parameters, test characteristic curves (TCCs) provide a detailed map of a scale functioning across the entire θ continuum. TCCs denote a link between the observable examinee scale performance (correct and incorrect responses) and the unobservable traits underlying the performance on the test.

For any individual item, a TCC provides a graphical representation of functioning. The "a" parameter affects the steepness of the curve; as "a" increases the slope of the TCC increases. Larger "a" parameters provide better discrimination among examinees and are analogous to item-total correlation in CTT. The "a" parameter is also an indicator of the amount of information regarding θ that an item is measuring, similar to an item's factor loading. Figures 7.1 and 7.2 demonstrate how the item characteristic curve changes as "a" increases.

The "b" parameter represents the location of the TCC along the horizontal axis, theta. It is commonly called the item difficulty, or threshold, parameter. The "b" is related to the proportion-correct score, "p", in CTT, but the two are inversely related. Large values of "p" indicate relatively "easy" items, whereas, large values of "b" indicate "difficult" items. Note that when "c" = 0 and "b" equals the value of theta, then the probability of a positive response is 0.5. Figures 7.3 and 7.4 demonstrate how the item characteristic curve changes as "b" increases.

FIGURE 7.1   SMALL "A" PARAMETER

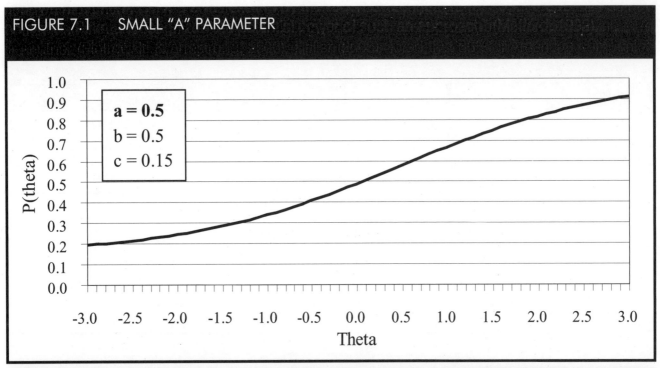

FIGURE 7.2   LARGE "A" PARAMETER

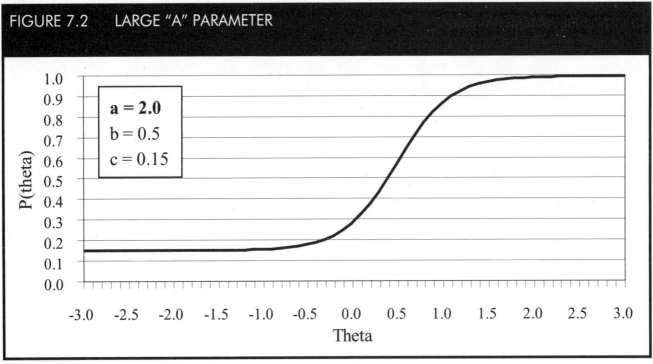

The "c" parameter indicates the probability of responding positively for examinees having very low theta (Chuah, Lee, & Wadlington, 2001). Multiple lines of thought exist as to how to interpret the "c" parameter. The conventional idea is that "c" is a pseudo guessing parameter such that it is the likelihood that an examinee could answer the item correctly by guessing. Other researchers believe that the larger "c" parameters are more transparent in regards to what the correct answer is (Zickar,

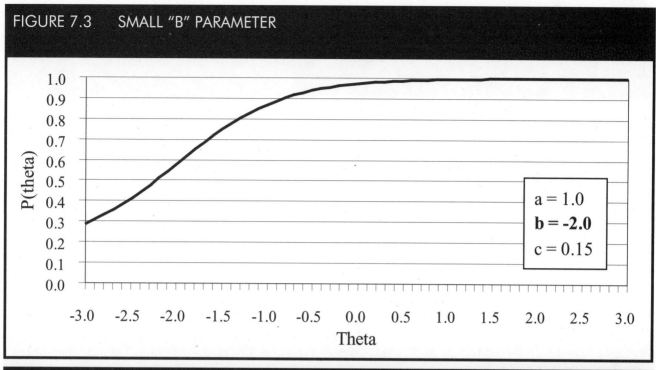

FIGURE 7.3   SMALL "B" PARAMETER

a = 1.0
b = -2.0
c = 0.15

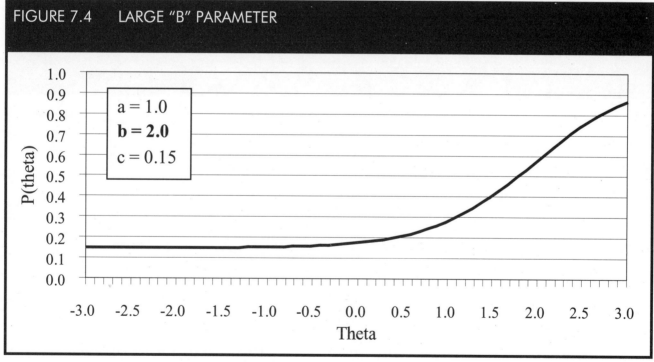

FIGURE 7.4   LARGE "B" PARAMETER

a = 1.0
b = 2.0
c = 0.15

2001). These ideas, while having merit, have not been able to fully explain the "c" parameter. They are necessary but not sufficient because they are only static components of the missing dynamic model. A recent idea is that the "c" parameter explains the relationship of the dynamic components (guessing, self-presentation, identity) that make up the item level responses across the theta distribution (Davies, Norris, Turner, & Wadlington, 2005).

Figures 7.5 and 7.6 demonstrate how the item characteristic curve changes as "c" increases.

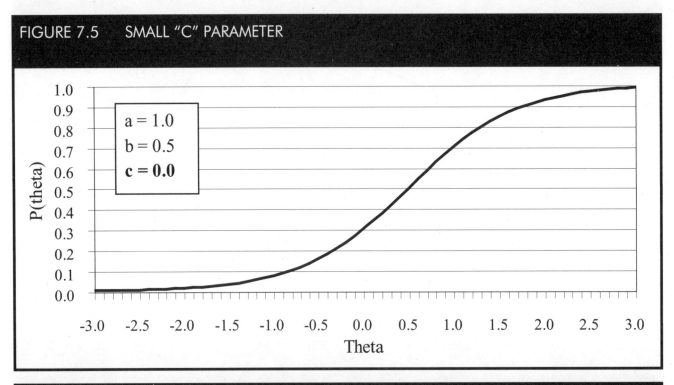

FIGURE 7.5   SMALL "C" PARAMETER

a = 1.0
b = 0.5
c = 0.0

P(theta)

Theta

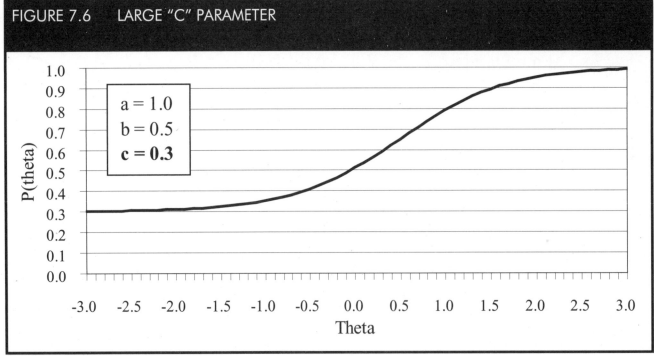

FIGURE 7.6   LARGE "C" PARAMETER

a = 1.0
b = 0.5
c = 0.3

P(theta)

Theta

This will make the Birkman instrument the first large scale, high stakes personality/social perception assessment to use IRT for operational development (see Embretson & Reise, 2000). This situation exists due to a lack of: a) technical expertise, b) existing item data in sufficient numbers, and c) less than adequate data collection facilities for most other personality test developers. However, BI has more than adequate resources in these areas to be the IRT pioneer of operational personality and social perception test development and maintenance.

In Figure 7.7, the TCC for the Emotive Orientation Usual scale illustrates three main points: 1) The slope of the curve shows the scale measures best between 0.50 standard deviations below and 2.25 standard deviations above the population mean, indicating that 67.9% of the population are measured with high precision under a standard normal distribution; 2) The point of inflection shows that on average the items are somewhat less likely to be endorsed than not; and 3) The lower asymptote shows that those with extremely low Emotive Orientation from the self perspective have a 5 percent chance, on average, to endorse an item.

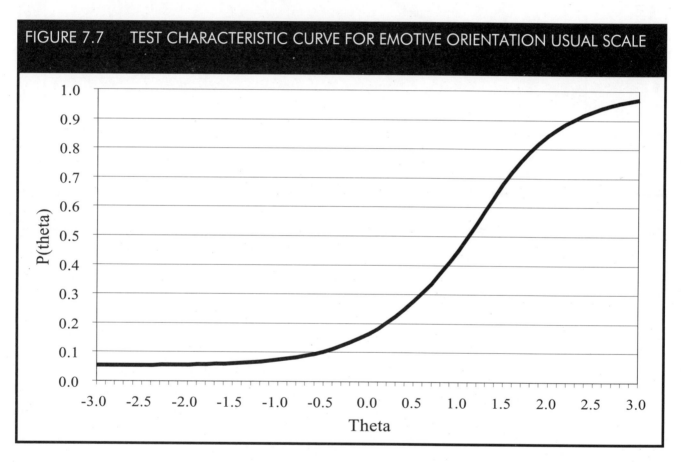

FIGURE 7.7   TEST CHARACTERISTIC CURVE FOR EMOTIVE ORIENTATION USUAL SCALE

In Figure 7.8, the TCC for the Social Orientation Usual scale illustrates three main points: 1) The slope of the curve shows that the scale measures best between 1.75 standard deviations below and 1.25 standard deviations above the population mean, indicating that 85.4% of the population are measured with high precision under a standard normal distribution; 2) The point of inflection shows that on average the items are somewhat more likely to be endorsed than not; and 3) The lower asymptote shows that those with extremely low Social Orientation from the self perspective have a 29 percent chance, on average, to endorse an item.

FIGURE 7.8   TEST CHARACTERISTIC CURVE FOR SOCIAL ORIENTATION USUAL SCALE

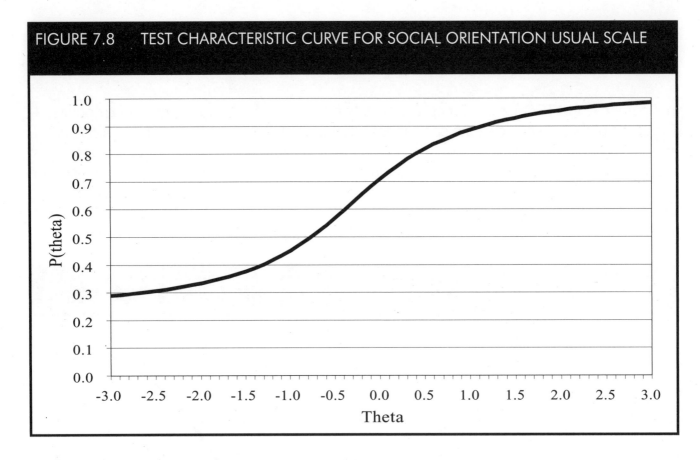

In Figure 7.9, the TCC for the Process Orientation Usual scale illustrates three main points: 1) The slope of the curve shows that the scale measures best +/- two standard deviations around the population mean, indicating that 95.4% of the population are measured with high precision under a standard normal distribution; 2) The point of inflection shows that on average the items are equally likely to be endorsed or not endorsed; and 3) The lower asymptote shows that those with extremely low Process Orientation from the self perspective have a 31 percent chance, on average, to endorse an item.

In Figure 7.10, the TCC for the Control Orientation Usual scale illustrates three main points: 1) The slope of the curve shows that the scale measures best between 0.50 standard deviations below and 2.50 standard deviations above the population mean, indicating that 68.5% of the population are measured with high precision under a standard normal distribution; 2) The point of inflection shows that on average the items are somewhat less likely to be endorsed than not; and 3) The lower asymptote shows that those with extremely low Control Orientation from the self perspective have a 15 percent chance, on average, to endorse an item.

FIGURE 7.9   TEST CHARACTERISTIC CURVE FOR PROCESS ORIENTATION USUAL SCALE

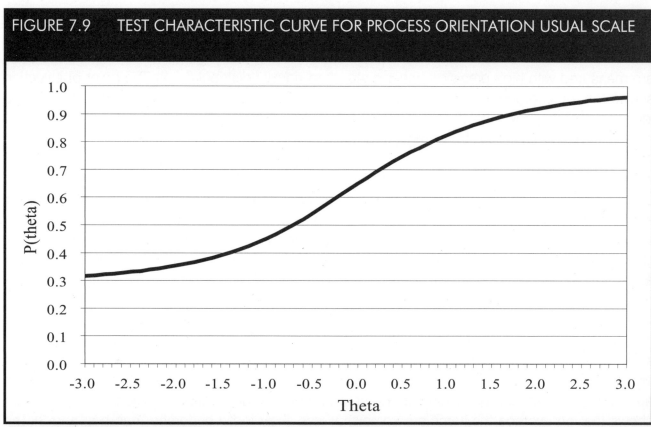

FIGURE 7.10   TEST CHARACTERISTIC CURVE FOR CONTROL ORIENTATION USUAL SCALE

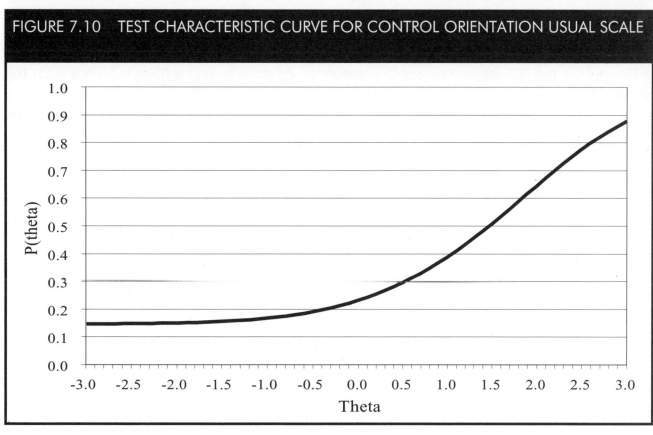

In Figure 7.11, the TCC for the Change Orientation Usual scale illustrates three main points: 1) The slope of the curve shows that the scale measures best between 1.50 standard deviations below and 2.25 standard deviations above the population mean, indicating that 92.1% of the population are measured with high precision under a standard normal distribution; 2) The point of inflection shows that on average the items are somewhat less likely to be endorsed than not; and 3) The lower asymptote shows that those with extremely low Change Orientation from the self perspective have a 19 percent chance, on average, to endorse an item.

In Figure 7.12, the TCC for the Emotive Orientation Needs scale illustrates three main points: 1) The slope of the curve shows that the scale measures best between 1.00 standard deviations below and 2.00 standard deviations above the population mean, indicating that 81.9% of the population are measured with high precision under a standard normal distribution; 2) The point of inflection shows that on average the items are slightly less likely to be endorsed than not; and 3) The lower asymptote shows that those with extremely low Emotive Orientation from the other perspective have a nine percent chance, on average, to endorse an item.

In Figure 7.13, the TCC for the Social Orientation Needs scale illustrates three main points: 1) The slope of the curve shows that the scale measures best between 1.50 standard deviations below and 2.50 standard deviations above the population mean, indicating that 92.6% of the population are measured with high precision under a standard normal distribution; 2) The point of inflection shows that on average the items are somewhat less likely to be endorsed than not; and 3) The lower asymptote shows that those with extremely low Social Orientation from the other perspective have a 20 percent chance, on average, to endorse an item.

In Figure 7.14, the TCC for the Process Orientation Needs scale illustrates three main points: 1) The slope of the curve shows that the scale measures best between 1.25 standard deviations below and 2.25 standard deviations above the population mean, indicating that 88.2% of the population are measured with high precision under a standard normal distribution; 2) The point of inflection shows that on average the items are somewhat less likely to be endorsed than not; and 3) The lower asymptote shows that those with extremely low Process Orientation from the other perspective have a 18 percent chance, on average, to endorse an item.

FIGURE 7.11   TEST CHARACTERISTIC CURVE FOR CHANGE ORIENTATION USUAL SCALE

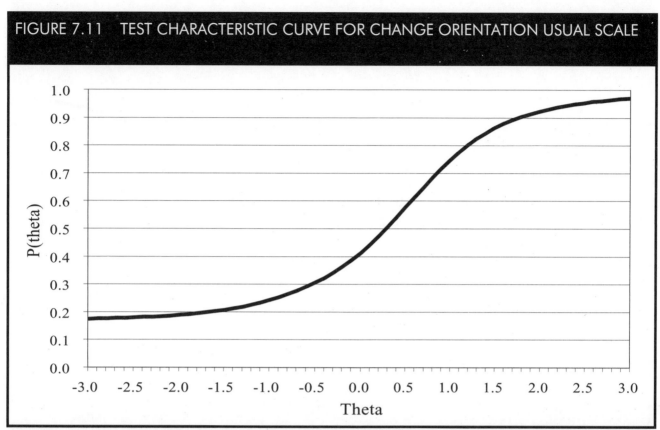

FIGURE 7.12   TEST CHARACTERISTIC CURVE FOR EMOTIVE ORIENTATION NEEDS SCALE

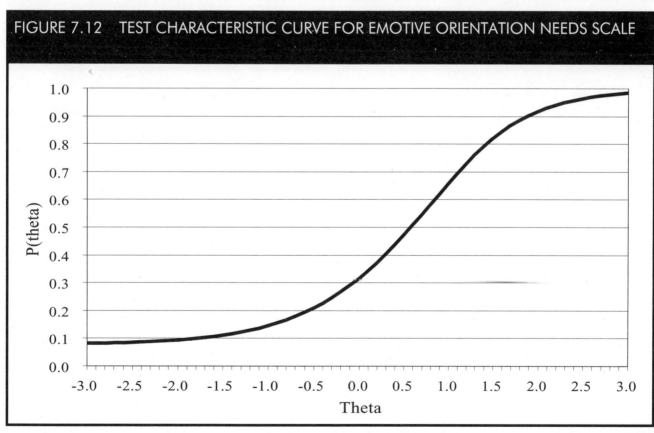

FIGURE 7.13   TEST CHARACTERISTIC CURVE FOR SOCIAL ORIENTATION NEEDS SCALE

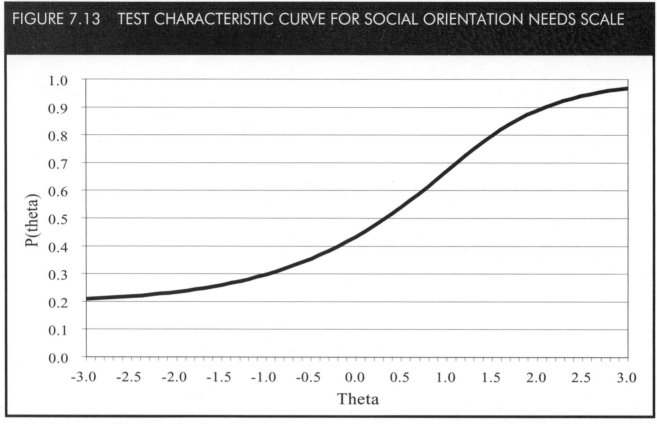

FIGURE 7.14   TEST CHARACTERISTIC CURVE FOR PROCESS ORIENTATION NEEDS SCALE

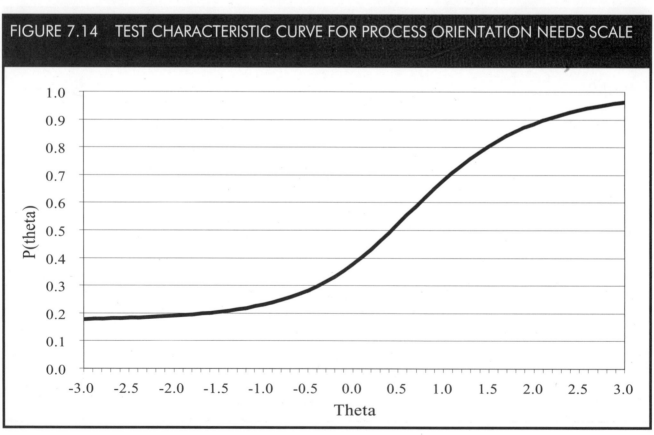

In Figure 7.15, the TCC for the Control Orientation Needs scale illustrates three main points: 1) The slope of the curve shows that the scale measures best between 1.25 standard deviations below and 2.50 standard deviations above the population mean, indicating that 88.8% of the population are measured with high precision under a standard normal distribution; 2) The point of inflection shows that on average the items are somewhat less likely to be endorsed than not; and 3) The lower asymptote shows that those with extremely low Control Orientation from the other perspective have a 18 percent chance, on average, to endorse an item.

FIGURE 7.15   TEST CHARACTERISTIC CURVE FOR CONTROL ORIENTATION NEEDS SCALE

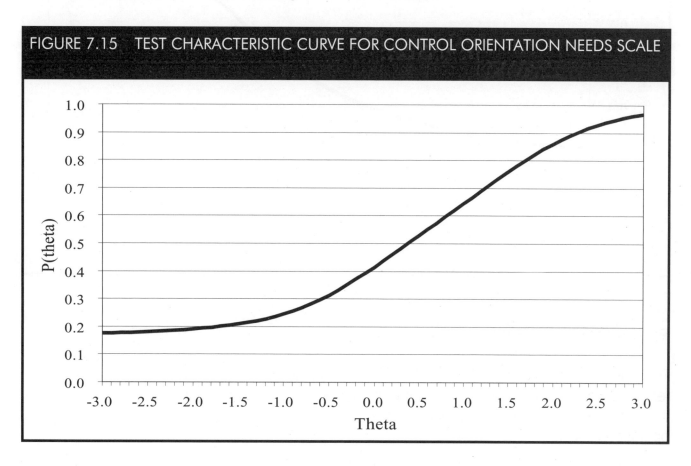

In Figure 7.16, the TCC for the Change Orientation Needs scale illustrates three main points: 1) The slope of the curve shows that the scale measures best between 1.50 standard deviations below and 1.75 standard deviations above population mean, indicating that 89.3% of the population are measured with high precision under a standard normal distribution; 2) The point of inflection shows that on average the items are less likely to be endorsed than not; and 3) The lower asymptote shows that those with extremely low Change Orientation from the other perspective have a 25 percent chance, on average, to endorse an item.

FIGURE 7.16   TEST CHARACTERISTIC CURVE FOR CHANGE ORIENTATION NEEDS SCALE

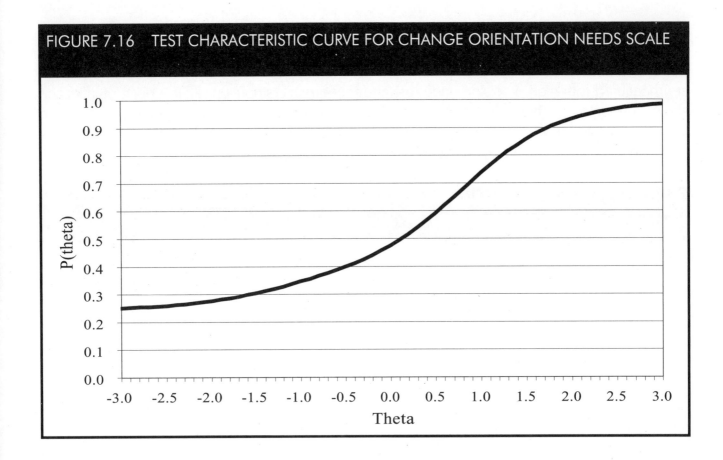

Pre-Equated Item Pool

To create the pre-equated item pools for The Birkman Method® scales, new items were administered with the operational items in an appropriate field test design. It is important to note that the new items do not have to be administered together; rather one can field test new items across operational forms.

While holding the parameters of the operational items constant, the parameters of the new items were estimated. This step places the parameters of the new items on the same metric as the operational items.

Having the theta distribution set to a (0,1) distribution for the population, one may use the theta distribution of any set of new items from the pre-equated item pool to scale the theta scores for the population into raw scores for the population. Thereby, the expected distribution of raw scores on a new form for the population is a derived distribution. This scaling procedure can be done with an IRT scaling program (e.g., ST). Computationally, the last two steps of this distributional projection procedure, formally known as a *two-stage model-based projection of an observed score distribution*, can be represented by the following two formulas:

Population Mean

$$\overline{\overline{x^+}} = N^{-1} \sum_{i=1}^{N} \int S(x) \int p(x|\theta) p(\theta|u_i) \, d\theta \, dx$$

Population Variance

$$\overline{\overline{\sigma_X^2}} = N^{-1} \sum_{i=1}^{N} \int \int \left(S(x) - \overline{\overline{x^+}} \right)^2 p(x|\theta) p(\theta|u_i) \, d\theta \, dx$$

As described above, distributional projection can create a synthetic population distribution for any item combination selected from the pre-equated item pool. In other words, distributional projection creates a population normative data set without administering the selected set of items together as a form to any examinees (Wadlington, Davies, & Phillips, 2006).

The Birkman Method® Needs IRT parameters were used as the IRT parameters for their Usual item counterparts for scoring purposes. This technique, while unconventional in previous IRT academic research, was critical to understanding the difference in socially accepted versus personally held beliefs. See the chapters on applications for further explanation. However, for psychometric standard rigor and to examine deltas on the "b" parameters for the same items with different stimuli, the Usual items' IRT parameters were estimated and subject to scrutiny in the creation of this version. No items were included that did not meet the psychometric standards set from either the Usual or Needs perspective.

FACTOR STRUCTURE

Factor analysis is a rigorous method for assessing the psychometric quality of a test. This method is based on the idea that every psychological measure has an underlying latent structure that describes and gives rise to correlations of the items on the measure as well as external measures. This is true whether or not the measure was developed with a latent structure in mind. If the items on a measure empirically covary with one another or with any external measure, this is due to the variance these items share on a latent psychological dimension. Because of this, it is: (a) useful to understand underlying structure for measures that provide decision-making support and (b) necessary to use the latent structure for test validation and maintenance activities. Understanding the structure allows theoretical statements to be derived and research hypotheses to be formulated and tested. In applied measurement situations (e.g., personnel testing), knowledge of the structure provides the basis for assessing unidimensionality that is essential for scaling, scoring, calibrating field test items using IRT, and test validation work.

The family of statistical analyses used to identify the latent structure in complex data sets is called covariance structure modeling. Structural equation modeling, factor analysis, multiple linear regression, and analysis of variance methods are all special cases of this family of statistical methods. It is common practice in psychological test development to first apply principal components analysis (a procedure similar to factor analysis) to test data for a number of factors; then use exploratory factor analyses to look for the factor loading; and finally, to use confirmatory factor analyses models with large, representative data sets to cross-validate. Each method represents an increase in statistical rigor and provides incremental support for the underlying latent structure of the test data.

Self Perspective Scales (Usual, Self)

First, BI conducted a principal components analysis of The Birkman Method® scales using an intercorrelation matrix of 125 items from model testing random half of the Birkman 2007 normative sample (see Appendix A). Based on the scree plot, a five-component solution via an orthogonal varimax rotation was determined based on the "elbow" or differences in eigenvalues across components. These data provided initial support for the primary scale and subscale structure for The Birkman Method® items. However, a few items loaded on more than one scale. This is one drawback of the principal components approach to assessing underlying factor structure-i.e., difficulties in interpreting the results.

Second, researchers at BI followed a covariance structure modeling approach. Factor analysis is a specific case of covariance structure modeling and differs from the more common approach of principal component analysis in a very important way. Factor analysis separates unique variance for each observed variable (i.e., indicator) from the shared (i.e., common) latent dimension variance across observed variables. Principal components analysis models error and unique variance with the common variance into component scores. This approach, unlike factor analysis, allows the error terms to be correlated due to sampling error and does not provide a true estimation of the degree to which the variables are measuring the same latent dimension in the population. Using maximum Wishart likelihood extractions with direct oblimin rotation, exploratory factor analyses at the item level supported the proposed five-factor solution. The largest factor loadings for items were found for their targeted scales. The results support unidimensional scale structures sufficient for testing confirmatory factor models and IRT models on the cross-validation sample.

Third, BI researchers tested a second-order confirmatory factor model using the cross-validation random split half from the Birkman 2007 normative sample with an $N = 2,154$ (see Appendix A). Using the LISREL program, a maximum Wishart likelihood extraction was conducted with the five primary and seven secondary scales specified as oblique latent factors and the 88 chosen items as indicators. An a priori model was posited for significance testing against fit to the Birkman data. To assess overall fit, there are several metrics available; but the root mean squared error of approximation (RMSEA) is one of the most conservative. The RMSEA is a function of the estimated discrepancy between the population covariance matrix and the model-implied covariance matrix, with a value of less than or equal to .05 indicating close fit and a value between .05 and .08 indicating a "reasonable error of approximation" (Browne & Cudeck, 1993, p. 144). The hypothesized factor analytic model for the Birkman latent structure is presented graphically in Figure 7.17.

FIGURE 7.17   BIRKMAN FACTORIAL MODEL FOR SELF PERSPECTIVE (USUAL)

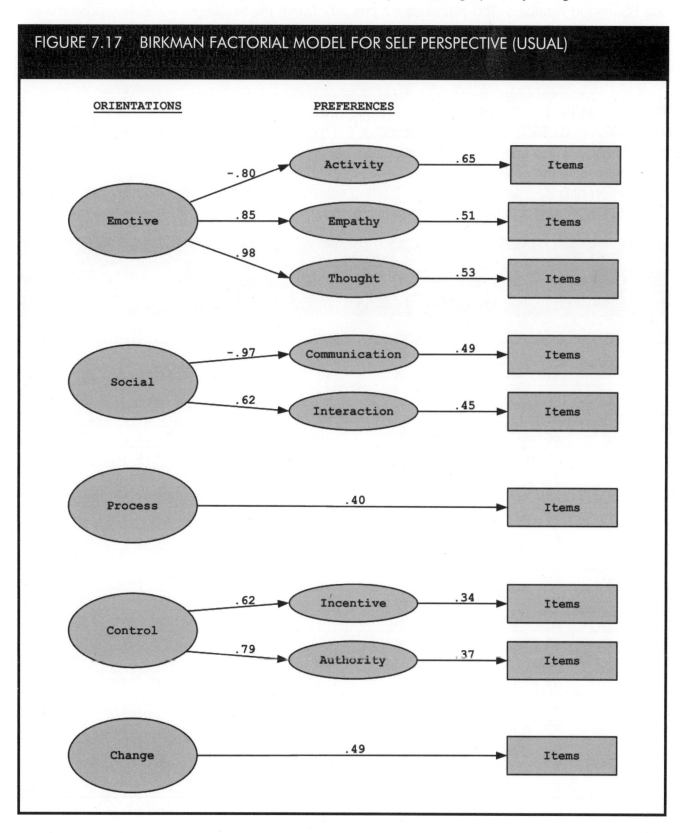

The model presented in Figure 7.17 describes the variance in items' scores in terms of shared variance on five primary latent correlated variables, seven secondary latent correlated variables, and 88 unique variables. The estimates for paths between the five latent variables and items are interpretable as standardized beta weights because the variance in the latent variables is set to unit values. Also, because the paths between the unique and manifest variables (items) are set to a unit value, the variance term for each of them is estimated and is used as an error term.

The model in Figure 7.17 provides good "close" overall fit to the Birkman data, as evidenced by the RMSEA of 0.053. Thus, cross-validation of the model showed equivalent fit. Evidence for the model's utility is also seen in the fact that most parameter estimates of item factor loadings on their respective scales were significant. Only seven of the 88 factor loading were lower than the practical criterion of 0.20. The average factor loading estimate was 0.45. Table 7.14 provides the point estimates of the factor loadings from the self perspective.

TABLE 7.14   MAXIMUM WISHART LIKELIHOOD ESTIMATES OF FREE PARAMETERS IN DEPENDENCE RELATIONSHIPS FOR BIRKMAN FACTOR MODEL FROM SELF PERSPECTIVE

ITEM	FACTOR LOADING	ITEM	FACTOR LOADING	ITEM	FACTOR LOADING	ITEM	FACTOR LOADING
1	.35	23	.33	45	.52	67	.25
2	.31	24	.46	46	.21	68	.31
3	.33	25	.48	47	.25	69	.45
4	.35	26	.41	48	.54	70	.51
5	.66	27	.76	49	.19	71	.10
6	.74	28	.13	50	.52	72	.26
7	.63	29	.39	51	.28	73	.13
8	.48	30	.60	52	.41	74	.50
9	.74	31	.76	53	.63	75	.40
10	.67	32	.68	54	.03	76	.22
11	.63	33	.61	55	.48	77	.46
12	.57	34	.31	56	.35	78	.47
13	.50	35	.56	57	.31	79	.66
14	.57	36	.26	58	.39	80	.42
15	.42	37	.44	59	.49	81	.19
16	.72	38	.61	60	.19	82	.27
17	.71	39	.26	61	.46	83	.67
18	.50	40	.34	62	.31	84	.34
19	.66	41	.76	63	.20	85	.47
20	.60	42	.30	64	.28	86	.47
21	.52	43	.68	65	.72	87	.50
22	.51	44	.56	66	.23	88	.73

Source: 2007 normative database.

Other Perspective Scales (Needs, Most, Expectations)

First, BI researchers conducted a principal components analysis of Birkman items using an intercorrelation matrix of 125 items from model testing random half of the 2007 normative sample with an $N = 2,154$ (see Appendix A). Based on the scree plot, a five-component solution via an orthogonal varimax rotation was determined based on the "elbow" or differences in eigenvalues across components. These data provided initial support for the primary scale and subscale structure for Birkman items. However, a few items loaded on more than one scale. This is one drawback of the principal components approach to assessing underlying factor structure-i.e., difficulties in interpreting the results.

Second, BI researchers followed a covariance structure modeling approach. Factor analysis is a specific case of covariance structure modeling and differs from the more common approach of principal component analysis in a very important way. Factor analysis separates unique variance for each observed variable (i.e., indicator) from the shared (i.e., common) latent dimension variance across observed variables. Principal components analysis models error and unique variance with the common variance into component scores. This approach, unlike factor analysis, allows the error terms to be correlated due to sampling error and does not provide a true estimation of the degree to which the variables are measuring the same latent dimension in the population. Using maximum Wishart likelihood extractions with direct oblimin rotation, exploratory factor analyses at the item level supported the proposed five-factor solution. The largest factor loadings for items were found for their targeted scales. The results support unidimensional scale structures sufficient for testing confirmatory factor models and IRT models on the cross-validation sample.

Third, BI researchers tested a second-order confirmatory factor model using the cross-validation random split half from Birkman 2007 normative sample. Using the LISREL program, a maximum Wishart likelihood extraction was conducted with the five primary scales specified as oblique latent factors and the 88 items as indicators. An a priori model was posited for significance testing against fit to Birkman data. To assess overall fit, there are several metrics available; but the root mean squared error of approximation (RMSEA) is one of the most conservative. The RMSEA is a function of the estimated discrepancy between the population covariance matrix and the model-implied covariance matrix, with a value of less than or equal to .05 indicating close fit and a value between .05 and .08 indicating a "reasonable error of approximation" (Browne & Cudeck, 1993, p. 144). The hypothesized factor analytic model for Birkman latent structure is presented graphically in Figure 7.18 (see page 102).

The model presented in Figure 7.18 describes the variance in items scores in terms of shared variance on five primary latent, correlated variables, the seven secondary latent correlated variables, and 88 unique variables. The estimates for paths between the five latent variables and items are interpretable as standardized beta weights because the variance in the latent variables is set to unit values. Also, because the paths between the unique and manifest variables (items) are set to a unit value, the variance term for each of them is estimated and is used as an error term.

FIGURE 7.18   BIRKMAN FACTORIAL MODEL FOR OTHER PERSPECTIVE (NEEDS)

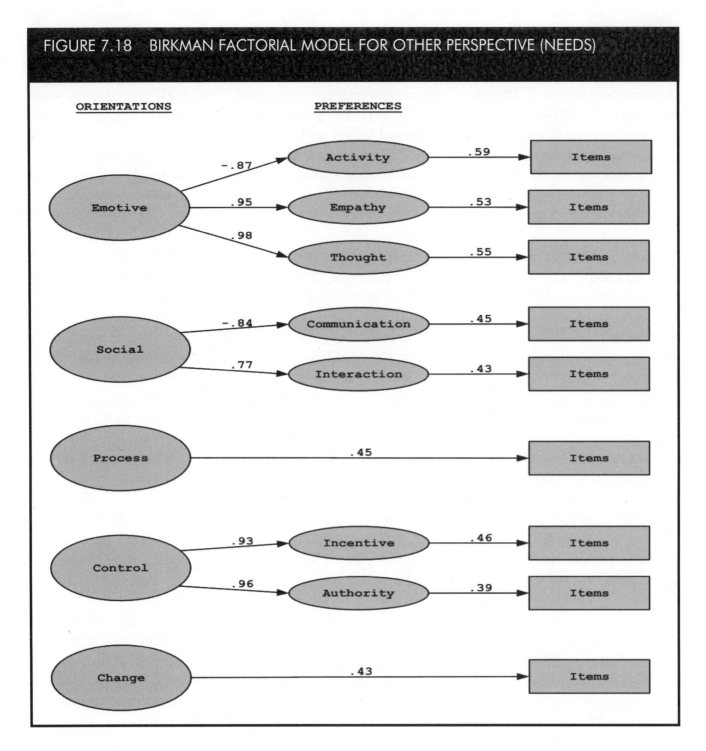

The model in Figure 7.18 provides good "close" overall fit to the Birkman data, as evidenced by the RMSEA of 0.048. Thus, cross-validation of the model showed equivalent fit. Evidence for the model's utility is also seen in the fact that all parameter estimates of item factor loadings on their respective scales were significant. Only three of the 88 factor loading was lower than the practical criterion of 0.20. The average factor loading estimate was 0.46. Table 7.15 provides the point estimates of the factor loadings from the other perspective.

TABLE 7.15	MAXIMUM WISHART LIKELIHOOD ESTIMATES OF FREE PARAMETERS IN DEPENDENCE RELATIONSHIPS FOR BIRKMAN FACTOR MODEL FROM OTHER PERSPECTIVE						

ITEM	FACTOR LOADING	ITEM	FACTOR LOADING	ITEM	FACTOR LOADING	ITEM	FACTOR LOADING
1	.58	23	.38	45	.53	67	.50
2	.45	24	.45	46	.51	68	.50
3	.42	25	.47	47	.43	69	.61
4	.50	26	.46	48	.62	70	.47
5	.64	27	.59	49	.17	71	.24
6	.72	28	.40	50	.60	72	.43
7	.58	29	.33	51	.31	73	.24
8	.58	30	.42	52	.51	74	.54
9	.59	31	.67	53	.67	75	.67
10	.53	32	.57	54	.25	76	.23
11	.37	33	.55	55	.61	77	.36
12	.48	34	.38	56	.35	78	.56
13	.49	35	.51	57	.52	79	.61
14	.41	36	.44	58	.42	80	.27
15	.58	37	.51	59	.52	81	.36
16	.65	38	.39	60	.29	82	.27
17	.68	39	.33	61	.55	83	.65
18	.57	40	.35	62	.39	84	.30
19	.63	41	.45	63	.16	85	.33
20	.62	42	.20	64	.40	86	.32
21	.46	43	.37	65	.68	87	.48
22	.49	44	.18	66	.24	88	.64

Source: 2007 normative database.

Relationship among Personality Orientation Factors

Few, if any, psychological constructs are not related in some way. Orthogonal (i.e., uncorrelated factors) models may be inappropriate in view of previous research findings. Therefore, it is rational and prudent to use oblique models in factor analytic work. The intercorrelations of the Orientation scales are provided in Table 7.16 and the intercorrelations of the latent factors are provided in Table 7.17. These two sets of results provide: (a) the degree to which the scales overlap in real world data and (b) the degree to which the overlap is due to measurement error. Overlap in observable scales may be best understood as shared variance (i.e., r^2), which averaged 0.11, with a minimum of 0.03 and a maximum value of 0.40. Magnitude of the true score correlations between factors was higher than the correlations between observable scale scores in every case, providing support for the view that the overlap is due to the actual underlying structure of the Birkman scales and not unexplained shared error.

TABLE 7.16   INTERCORRELATIONS BETWEEN ORIENTATION OBSERVABLE SCORES

		SCALE	1	2	3	4	5	6	7	8	9
USUAL	1	Emotive	---								
	2	Social	-.48								
	3	Process	-.37	.17							
	4	Control	.25	-.01	-.14						
	5	Change	.30	-.10	-.16	.30					
NEEDS	6	Emotive	.52	-.24	-.19	.27	.25				
	7	Social	-.31	.30	.22	-.20	-.19	-.62			
	8	Process	-.31	.21	.42	-.23	-.20	-.55	.60		
	9	Control	.35	-.20	-.10	.45	.20	.63	-.43	-.45	
	10	Change	.27	-.14	-.07	.21	.34	.47	-.31	-.25	.49

Source: 2007 normative database.

Relationship among Personality Preference Subactors

The intercorrelations of the Preference scales are provided in Table 7.18 and the intercorrelations of the latent factors are provided in Table 7.19. These two sets of results provide: (a) the degree to which the scales overlap in real world data and (b) the degree to which the overlap is due to measurement error. Overlap in observable scales may be best understood as shared variance (i.e., r^2), which averaged 0.30, with a minimum of 0.008 and a maximum value of 0.65. Magnitude of the true score correlations between factors was higher than the correlations between observable scale scores in every case, providing support for the view that the overlap is due to the actual underlying structure of the Birkman scales and not unexplained shared error.

TABLE 7.17 INTERCORRELATIONS BETWEEN ORIENTATION TRUE SCALE SCORES

		SCALE	1	2	3	4	5	6	7	8	9
USUAL	1	Emotive	---								
	2	Social	-.55								
	3	Process	-.46	.22							
	4	Control	.31	-.01	-.20						
	5	Change	.39	-.13	-.23	.44					
NEEDS	6	Emotive	.59	-.27	-.25	.34	.32				
	7	Social	-.36	.35	.29	-.27	-.26	-.73			
	8	Process	-.38	.26	.56	-.31	-.27	-.67	.75		
	9	Control	.42	-.24	-.14	.61	.27	.75	-.53	-.57	
	10	Change	.38	-.20	-.10	.33	.54	.66	-.45	-.38	.72

Source: 2007 normative database.

TABLE 7.18 INTERCORRELATIONS BETWEEN PREFERENCE OBSERVABLE SCORES

		SCALE	1	2	3	4	5	6	7	8	9	10	11	12	13
USUAL	1	Activity	---												
	2	Empathy	-.60												
	3	Thought	-.52	.59											
	4	Communication	-.44	.45	.47										
	5	Interaction	.27	-.27	-.22	-.51									
	6	Incentive	-.14	.24	.16	.07	-.02								
	7	Authority	-.12	.23	.09	-.01	.03	.44							
NEEDS	8	Activity	.47	-.36	-.29	-.23	.12	-.17	-.17						
	9	Empathy	-.40	.49	.33	.25	-.13	.23	.23	-.65					
	10	Thought	-.32	.32	.32	.20	-.10	.17	.18	-.57	.64				
	11	Communication	-.25	.25	.18	.31	-.13	.19	.19	-.52	.52	.48			
	12	Interaction	.22	-.23	-.15	-.17	.29	-.10	-.12	.46	-.43	-.36	-.49		
	13	Incentive	-.30	.32	.25	.24	-.13	.41	.31	-.47	.57	.48	.44	-.35	
	14	Authority	-.23	.26	.20	.19	-.07	.28	.39	-.38	.53	.44	.35	-.19	.62

Source: 2007 normative database.

		SCALE	1	2	3	4	5	6	7	8	9	10	11	12	13
USUAL	1	Activity	---												
	2	Empathy	-.74												
	3	Thought	-.78	.89											
	4	Communication	-.55	.56	.72										
	5	Interaction	.33	-.34	-.33	-.63									
	6	Incentive	-.22	.36	.29	.10	-.03								
	7	Authority	-.18	.34	.16	-.01	.04	.77							
NEEDS	8	Activity	.60	-.46	-.47	-.30	.16	-.28	-.26						
	9	Empathy	-.49	.60	.49	.30	-.16	.35	.33	-.84					
	10	Thought	-.47	.47	.58	.30	-.15	.30	.31	-.88	.94				
	11	Communication	-.33	.33	.29	.40	-.16	.30	.29	-.70	.66	.75			
	12	Interaction	.28	-.30	-.24	.21	.37	-.15	-.18	.62	-.55	-.55	-.65		
	13	Incentive	-.40	.42	.41	.32	-.18	.67	.47	-.66	.75	.77	.61	-.49	
	14	Authority	-.32	.36	.33	.26	-.09	.48	.63	-.55	.73	.73	.51	-.27	.92

TABLE 7.19   INTERCORRELATIONS BETWEEN PREFERENCE TRUE SCALE SCORES

Source: 2007 normative database.

Relationship among Social Environment Anchored (SEA) Factors

The intercorrelations of the SEA scales are provided in Table 7.20, and the intercorrelations of the latent factors are provided in Table 7.21. These two sets of results provide: (a) the degree to which the scales overlap in real world data and (b) the degree to which the overlap is due to measurement error. Overlap in observable scales may be best understood as shared variance (i.e., r^2), which averaged 0.40, with a minimum of 0.21 and a maximum value of 0.62. Magnitude of the true score correlations between factors was higher than the correlations between observable scale scores in every case, providing support for the view that the overlap is due to the actual underlying structure of the Birkman scales and not unexplained shared error.

Current Version Construction

Having IRT and CTT (descriptive and factor analytic) statistics on all the Birkman items, the current version of The Birkman Method® was constructed with four goals in mind:

1) Retain construct validity of original and past versions

TABLE 7.20	INTERCORRELATIONS BETWEEN SEA OBSERVABLE SCORES		
	SCALE	1	2
1	Personal Autonomy: Usual	---	
2	Personal Autonomy: Needs	.42	
3	Perspective Alignment	.19	-.62

Source: 2007 normative database.

TABLE 7.21	INTERCORRELATIONS BETWEEN SEA TRUE SCALE SCORES		
	SCALE	1	2
1	Personal Autonomy: Usual	---	
2	Personal Autonomy: Needs	.57	
3	Perspective Alignment	.29	-.87

Source: 2007 normative database.

2) *Improve reliability of instrument across each of the five continuums*
3) *Decrease number of operational items - thereby creating spots for field test items for future development and research*
4) *Increase amount of construct relevant information gathered for each respondent*

CHAPTER 7 SUMMARY

In Chapter 7, the development and characteristics of the original and revised Birkman Method® was explained using factor analysis, CTT, and IRT. The alignment with the FFM factors was also demonstrated empirically for The Birkman Method® scales. The capacity for field testing new items was also demonstrated via a pre-equated item pool. Together, these characteristics demonstrate strong support for the intended applications.

CHAPTER 8
Reliability

RELIABILITY ESTIMATES

Several methods exist for estimating test reliability using a variety of study and analysis designs. Here, we report reliability estimates from the most common approaches: a) temporal stability through a test-retest study design, b) internal consistency as estimated through Cronbach's alpha, and c) IRT based item analyses.

Reliability refers to the consistency or stability of an instrument. There are various ways of measuring reliability. When a test is administered, it should provide consistent results. One form of reliability is called test-retest, and it measures stability over time. To measure test-retest, individuals are administered the same test at two different intervals, and the results are compared. The test is considered stable over time if similar scores are found for the two administrations. Individuals should receive the same scores upon multiple administrations of the same instrument. Another type of reliability is internal consistency reliability. This is a way of making sure the test correlates with itself. Items from scales are compared with each other and should highly relate to each other. For The Birkman Method® scales, Coefficient Alpha was used to compute internal consistency. This chapter provides a detailed description of the IRT methodology used to compute reliability for The Birkman Method®.

Test-Retest Reliability

The test-retest statistics provide evidence that the Birkman scales and constructs measured are stable across time and other variables.

As shown in Table 8.1 via product-moment Pearson correlations, the stability/reliability of the Birkman scales has been empirically determined with a two-week period between repeated measures of the instrument.

"Even in the beginning, we tested and retested to make sure we were on the right path. Now, sophisticated software takes a lot of the work out of it. This gives us great confidence in the market place applications."

-Roger W. Birkman

TABLE 8.1   TEST-RETEST RELIABILITIES ACROSS A TWO-WEEK PERIOD

SCALE	USUAL	NEEDS
Emotive Orientation	.91	.84
Social Orientation	.91	.77
Process Orientation	.88	.79
Control Orientation	.86	.72
Change Orientation	.80	.62
Activity Preference	.84	.74
Empathy Preference	.88	.83
Thought Preference	.80	.57
Communication Preference	.87	.70
Interaction Preference	.89	.75
Incentive Preference	.75	.70
Authority Preference	.82	.64
Personal Autonomy	.85	.80
Perspective Alignment	.74	

Notes: N = 115 professional employees in the financial industry.

Coefficient Alpha

See Table 7.1 through 7.3 for CTT reliability statistics.

ITEM RESPONSE THEORY RELIABILITY STATISTICS

In complementary fashion to CTT, IRT was utilized to gain additional optimal psychometric insight into the reliability of the Birkman scales.

Test Information Functions

One of the major contributions of IRT is the extension of the reliability concept. Reliability refers to the precision of measurement (i.e., the degree to which measurement is free of error). In the realm of CTT, it is measured using a single index defined in various ways such as the ratio of true and observed score variance. This index is helpful in characterizing a test's average reliability, yet reliability is not uniform across the entire range of test scores. For example, scores at the edges of the test's range are known to have more error than scores closer to the middle.

IRT uses the broader and more versatile idea of information as opposed to reliability. Information (I) is a function model determined by item parameters. Item level information with the simplest of models, the Rasch model, is defined as the probability of a correct response multiplied by the probably of an incorrect response, or:

$$I(\theta) = p_i(\theta) * q_i(\theta)$$

The more information at a point along the θ continuum, the more reliable the scale is at that point. The Birkman scales have been developed to gather the most information where the majority of the population scores. Ninety-five percent of the population scores between -2 and +2 on the θ continuum.

Test information functions (TIFs) give scale level visual representation of the amount of information measured across the theta continuum. The more information, the more accurate the measurement is. Information is the inverse of the standard error. The amount of information at a point on the theta continuum is determined by a combination of the "a", "b", and "c" parameters. The "a" parameter establishes the amount of potential information that can be gathered across the theta continuum by the scale. The "b" parameter determines at what point on the theta continuum most of the information will be gathered. The "c" parameter has a negative influence on the amount of information that can be gathered. The "c" function directly reduces the information function and shifts the theta point of maximum information to the right. Because TIFs are not standardized, comparison of theta points within a scale is the best practice for the statistic. Comparing TIFs between scales can cause misinterpretation, especially when one gets two larger information values (e.g., > 10). If one is to view TIFs in absolute terms, it is recommended to: 1) choose a value of conditional standard error (CSE) that is acceptable for the given scale and situation, 2) find the conditional information (CI) magnitude that corresponds to the CSE value, and 3) set all information values which are above this value to be equal to this value. By proceeding in this manner, large values of information will not be interpreted incorrectly.

An additional note of caution is that the definition of 'information' within this context concerns precision and not necessarily interpretability. For example, an individual may obtain a very low score on a scale. With such a low score, the behavioral and motivational implications for the individual may be very interpretable; yet, due to the majority of "b" parameters being more toward the middle of the theta distribution, this individual would be difficult to distinguish from another individual with a very low score as well.

For interpretation purposes, the following benchmarks in Table 8.2 are utilized and a standard normal distribution is assumed.

TABLE 8.2	CORRESPONDING CI AND CSE BENCHMARKS		
AMOUNT OF INFORMATION	CI RANGE	AMOUNT OF STANDARD ERROR	CSE RANGE
large	> 10	little-to-none	< .30
moderate	5 to 9.9	modest	0.30 to 0.44
modest	1.0 to 4.9	moderate	0.45 to 0.99
little-to-none	< 1.0	large	> 0.99

The TIFs across the θ continuum for each Birkman scale are shown in Figure 8.1 through Figure 8.10.

In Figure 8.1, the TIF for the Emotive Orientation Usual scale is illustrated across the θ continuum. Reading from left to right across the θ continuum, from -3.00 to -1.00, "little-to-no" discriminant information is known. In effect, this instrument does not provide discriminant information about 16 percent of respondents within the lowest portion of the θ continuum. A modest amount of discriminant information is provided across -1.00 to -0.25, a moderate amount from -0.25 to 0.50, a large amount from 0.50 to 2.25, a moderate amount (again) from 2.25 to 2.50, and a modest amount (again) from 2.50 to 3.00. This scale provides the most amount of discriminant information for respondents in the moderate-to-high side of the θ continuum. In respect to Birkman interpretative reports, the Emotive Orientation Usual scale has sufficient precision to discriminate between 84 percent of examinees across the entire θ continuum.

FIGURE 8.1   TEST INFORMATION FUNCTION FOR EMOTIVE ORIENTATION USUAL SCALE

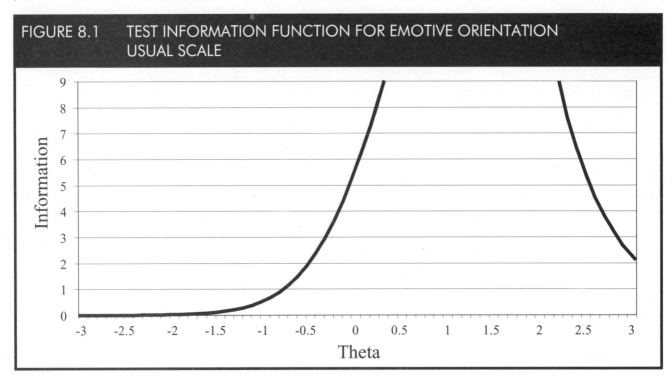

In Figure 8.2, the TIF for the Social Orientation Usual scale is illustrated across the θ continuum. Reading from left to right across the θ continuum, from -3.00 to -1.75 and from 2.25 to 3.00, "little-to-no" discriminant information is known. In effect, this instrument does not provide discriminant information about five percent of respondents within the lowest and highest portions of the θ continuum. A modest amount of discriminant information is provided across -1.75 to -1.25, a moderate amount from -1.25 to -0.75, a large amount from -0.75 to 0.25, a moderate amount (again) from 0.25 to 0.75, and a modest amount (again) from 0.75 to 2.25. This scale provides the most amount of discriminant information for respondents in the middle range of the θ continuum. In respect to Birkman interpretative reports, the Social Orientation Usual scale has sufficient precision to discriminate between 95 percent of examinees across the entire θ continuum.

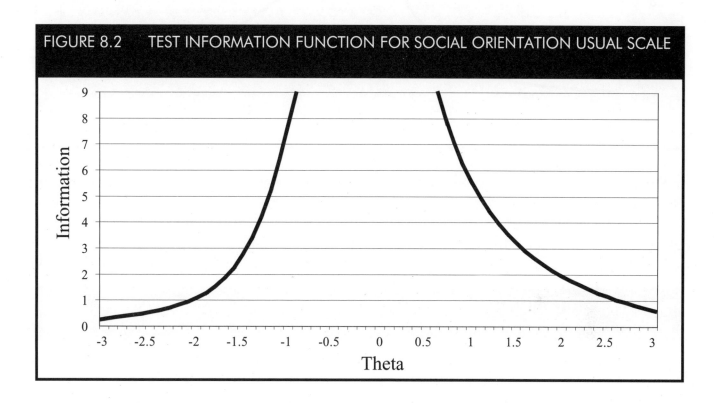

FIGURE 8.2   TEST INFORMATION FUNCTION FOR SOCIAL ORIENTATION USUAL SCALE

In Figure 8.3, the TIF for the Process Orientation Usual scale is illustrated across the θ continuum. Reading from left to right across the θ continuum, from -3.00 to -1.50 and from 2.25 to 3.00, "little-to-no" discriminant information is known. In effect, this instrument does not provide discriminant information about eight percent of respondents within the lowest and highest portions of the θ continuum. A modest amount of discriminant information is provided across -1.50 to -0.50, a moderate amount from -0.50 to 0.00, and a modest amount (again) from 0.00 to 2.25. This scale provides the most amount of discriminant information for respondents in the moderate range of the θ continuum. In respect to Birkman interpretative reports, the Process Orientation Usual scale has sufficient precision to discriminate between 92 percent of examinees across the entire θ continuum.

FIGURE 8.3   TEST INFORMATION FUNCTION FOR PROCESS ORIENTATION
              USUAL SCALE

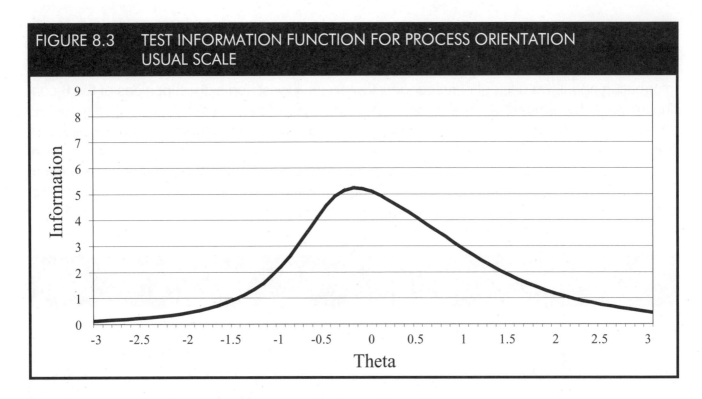

In Figure 8.4, the TIF for the Control Orientation Usual scale is illustrated across the **θ** continuum. Reading from left to right across the **θ** continuum, from -3.00 to -0.50, "little-to-no" discriminant information is known. In effect, this instrument does not provide discriminant information about 31 percent of respondents within the lowest portion of the **θ** continuum. A modest amount of discriminant information is provided across -0.50 to -0.75, and a moderate amount from -0.75 to 3.00. This

FIGURE 8.4   TEST INFORMATION FUNCTION FOR CONTROL ORIENTATION
              USUAL SCALE

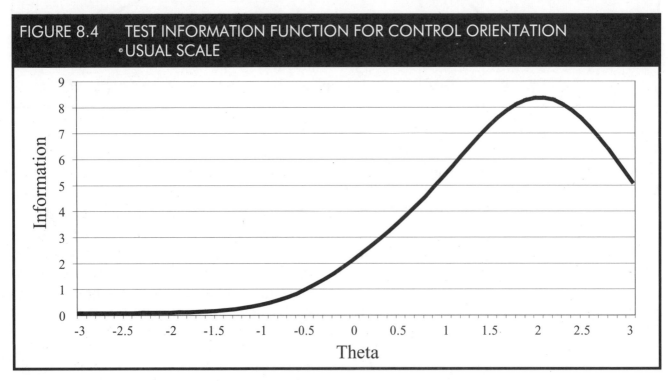

scale provides the most amount of discriminant information for respondents in the moderate-to-high side of the θ continuum. In respect to Birkman interpretative reports, the Control Orientation Usual scale has sufficient precision to discriminate between 69 percent of examinees across the entire θ continuum.

In Figure 8.5, the TIF for the Change Orientation Usual scale is illustrated across the θ continuum. Reading from left to right across the θ continuum, from -3.00 to -0.75 and from 2.00 to 3.00, "little-to-no" discriminant information is known. In effect, this instrument does not provide discriminant information about 25 percent of respondents within the moderate-to-low and highest portions of the θ continuum. A modest amount of discriminant information is provided across -0.75 to -0.25, a moderate amount from -0.25 to 1.00, and a modest amount (again) from 1.00 to 2.00. This scale provides the most amount of discriminant information for respondents in the moderate-to-high range of the θ continuum. In respect to Birkman interpretative reports, the Change Orientation Usual scale has sufficient precision to discriminate between 75 percent of examinees across the entire θ continuum.

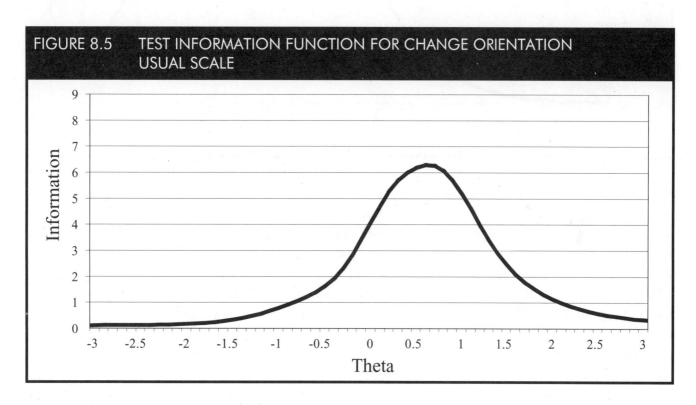

FIGURE 8.5   TEST INFORMATION FUNCTION FOR CHANGE ORIENTATION USUAL SCALE

In Figure 8.6, the TIF for the Emotive Orientation Needs scale is illustrated across the θ continuum. Reading from left to right across the θ continuum, from -3.00 to -1.25, "little-to-no" discriminant information is known. In effect, this instrument does not provide discriminant information about 11 percent of respondents within the lowest portion of the θ continuum. A modest amount of discriminant information is provided across -1.25 to -0.50, a moderate amount from -0.50 to 0.00, a large amount from 0.00 to 1.75, a moderate amount (again) from 1.75 to 2.25, and a modest

amount (again) from 2.25 to 3.00. This scale provides the most amount of discriminant information for respondents in the moderate-to-high range of the θ continuum. In respect to Birkman interpretative reports, the Emotive Orientation Needs scale has sufficient precision to discriminate
between 89 percent of examinees across the entire θ continuum.

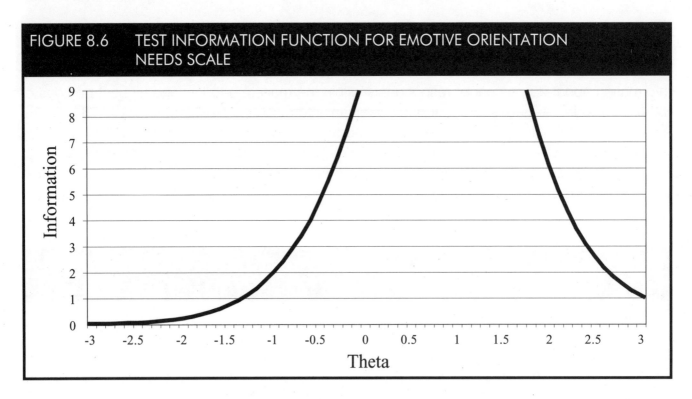

FIGURE 8.6   TEST INFORMATION FUNCTION FOR EMOTIVE ORIENTATION
              NEEDS SCALE

In Figure 8.7, the TIF for the Social Orientation Needs scale is illustrated across the θ continuum.
Reading from left to right across the θ continuum, from -3.00 to -1.50, "little-to-no" discriminant
information is known. In effect, this instrument does not provide discriminant information about
seven percent of respondents within the lowest portion of the θ continuum. A modest amount of
discriminant information is provided across -1.50 to -0.25, a moderate amount from -0.25 to 0.50,
a large amount from 0.50 to 1.50, a moderate amount (again) from 1.50 to 2.25, and a modest
amount (again) from 2.25 to 3.00. This scale provides the most amount of discriminant information
for respondents in the moderate-to-high range of the θ continuum. In respect to Birkman interpretative reports, the Social Orientation Needs scale has sufficient precision to discriminate between 93
percent of examinees across the entire θ continuum.

In Figure 8.8, the TIF for the Process Orientation Needs scale is illustrated across the θ continuum.
Reading from left to right across the θ continuum, from -3.00 to -0.75, "little-to-no" discriminant
information is known. In effect, this instrument does not provide discriminant information about 23
percent of respondents within the lowest portion of the θ continuum. A modest amount of discriminant information is provided across -0.75 to -0.25, a moderate amount from -0.25 to 0.50, a large
amount from 0.50 to 0.75, a moderate amount (again) from 0.75 to 1.50, and a modest amount
(again) from 1.50 to 3.00. This scale provides the most amount of discriminant information for re-

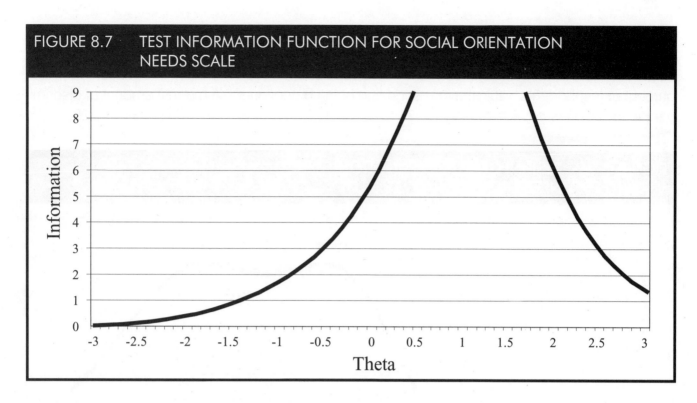

FIGURE 8.7   TEST INFORMATION FUNCTION FOR SOCIAL ORIENTATION
NEEDS SCALE

spondents in the moderate-to-high range of the θ continuum. In respect to Birkman interpretative reports, the Process Orientation Needs scale has sufficient precision to discriminate between 77 percent of examinees across the entire θ continuum.

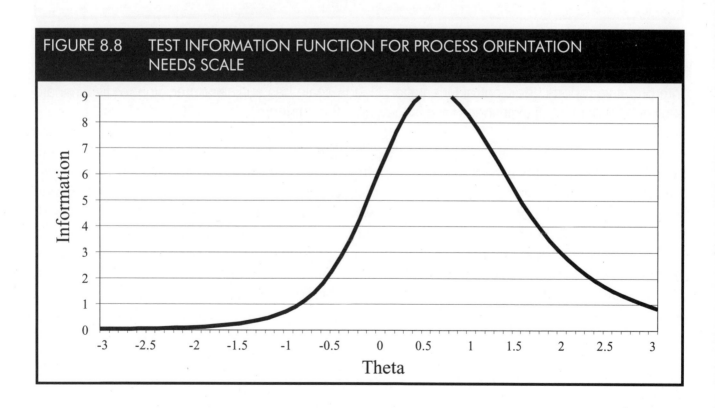

FIGURE 8.8   TEST INFORMATION FUNCTION FOR PROCESS ORIENTATION
NEEDS SCALE

In Figure 8.9, the TIF for the Control Orientation Needs scale is illustrated across the θ continuum. Reading from left to right across the θ continuum, from -3.00 to -1.25, "little-to-no" discriminant information is known. In effect, this instrument does not provide discriminant information about ten percent of respondents within the lowest portion of the θ continuum. A modest amount of discriminant information is provided across -1.25 to -0.50, a moderate amount from -0.50 to 2.25, and a

FIGURE 8.9   TEST INFORMATION FUNCTION FOR CONTROL ORIENTATION NEEDS SCALE

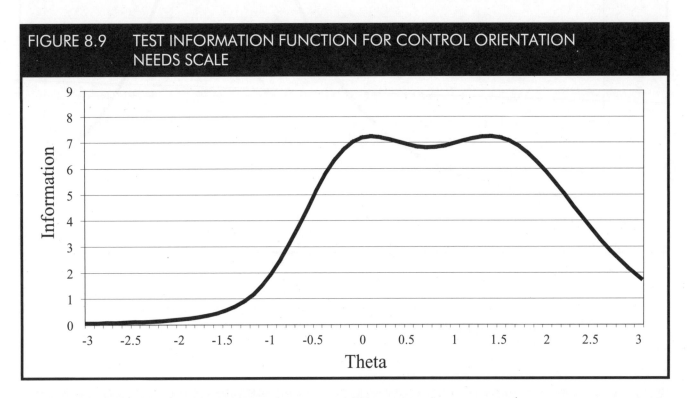

modest amount (again) from 2.25 to 3.00. This scale provides the most amount of discriminant information for respondents in the moderate-to-high range of the θ continuum. In respect to Birkman interpretative reports, the Control Orientation Needs scale has sufficient precision to discriminate between 90 percent of examinees across the entire θ continuum.

In Figure 8.10, the TIF for the Change Orientation Needs scale is illustrated across the θ continuum. Reading from left to right across the θ continuum, from -3.00 to -0.50 and from 2.25 to 3.00, "little-to-no" discriminant information is known. In effect, this instrument does not provide discriminant information about 42 percent of respondents within the moderate-to-low and highest portions of the θ continuum. A modest amount of discriminant information is provided from -0.50 to 2.25. This scale provides the most amount of discriminant information for respondents in the moderate-to-high range of the θ continuum. In respect to Birkman interpretative reports, the Change Orientation Needs scale has sufficient precision to discriminate between 58 percent of examinees across the entire θ continuum.

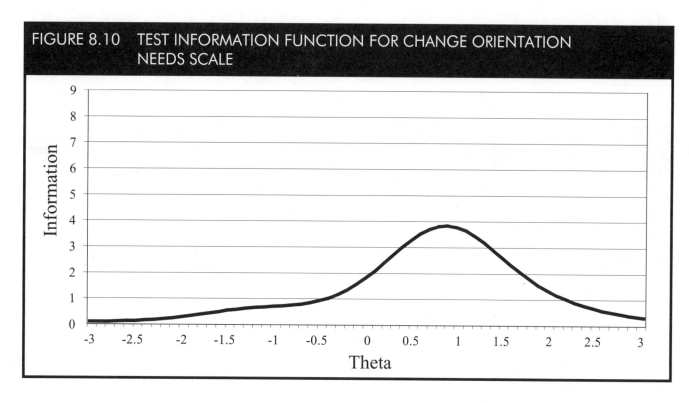

FIGURE 8.10   TEST INFORMATION FUNCTION FOR CHANGE ORIENTATION NEEDS SCALE

Test Standard Error Functions

The Conditional Standard Error of estimation (CSE) is the reciprocal of the test information at any particular point on the θ continuum. Hence, more information implies less error of measurement (Baker, 2001). The smaller the standard error at a point along the θ continuum, the more reliable the scale is at that point.

Test Standard Error Functions (TSEFs) give the scale level visual representation of the amount of measurement error that exists across the theta continuum. The more measurement error there is, the less reliable and valid the measure. The amount of information at a point on the theta continuum is determined by a combination of the "a", "b", and "c" parameters. The "a" parameter has a negative relationship with measurement error. The "b" parameter determines at what point on the theta continuum the least amount of measurement error will exist. The "c" parameter creates measurement error in a dynamic manner. TSEFs are standardized and can be compared across scales readily. The TSEFs across the θ continuum for each Birkman scale are shown in Figure 8.11 through Figure 8.20. The TSEFs interpretations are guided by Table 8.2.

In Figure 8.11, the TSEF for the Emotive Orientation Usual scale is illustrated across the θ continuum. Reading from left to right across the θ continuum, from -3.00 to -1.00, a large amount of standard error exists. In effect, this instrument has too much standard error to be discriminant between the 16 percent of respondents within the lowest portion of the θ continuum. A moderate amount of standard error exists across -1.00 to -0.25, a modest amount from -0.25 to 0.50, little-to-none from 0.50 to 2.25, a modest amount (again) from 2.25 to 2.50, and a moderate amount (again) from 2.50 to 3.00. This scale has the least amount of standard error for respondents in the moderate-to-high side of the θ continuum. In respect to Birkman interpretative reports, the Emotive Orientation Usual scale has sufficient precision to discriminate between 84 percent of examinees across the entire θ continuum.

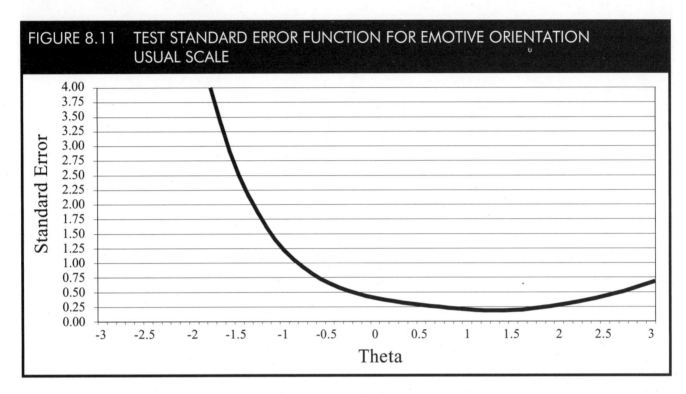

FIGURE 8.11   TEST STANDARD ERROR FUNCTION FOR EMOTIVE ORIENTATION USUAL SCALE

In Figure 8.12, the TSEF for the Social Orientation Usual scale is illustrated across the θ continuum. Reading from left to right across the θ continuum, from -3.00 to -1.75 and from 2.25 to 3.00, a large amount of standard error exists. In effect, this instrument has too much standard error to discriminate between the five percent of respondents coming from the lowest and highest portions of the θ continuum. A moderate amount of standard error exists across -1.75 to -1.25, a modest amount from -1.25 to -0.75, little-to-none from -0.75 to 0.25, a modest amount (again) from 0.25 to 0.75, and a moderate amount (again) from 0.75 to 2.25. This scale has the least amount of standard error for respondents in the middle range of the θ continuum. In respect to Birkman interpretative reports, the Social Orientation Usual scale has sufficient precision to discriminate between 95 percent of examinees across the entire θ continuum.

In Figure 8.13, the TSEF for the Process Orientation Usual scale is illustrated across the θ continuum. Reading from left to right across the θ continuum, from -3.00 to -1.50 and from 2.25 to 3.00, a large amount of standard error exists. In effect, this instrument has too much standard error to discriminate between the eight percent of respondents coming from the lowest and highest portions of the θ continuum. A moderate amount of standard error exists across -1.50 to -0.50, a modest amount from -0.50 to 0.00, and a moderate amount (again) from 0.00 to 2.25. This scale provides the least amount of standard error for respondents in the moderate range of the θ continuum. In

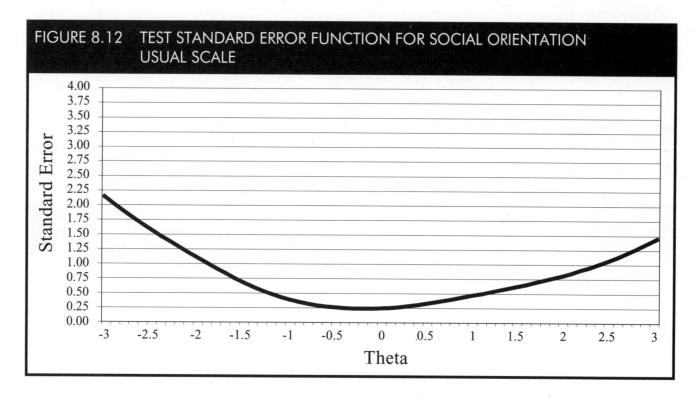

FIGURE 8.12   TEST STANDARD ERROR FUNCTION FOR SOCIAL ORIENTATION USUAL SCALE

respect to Birkman interpretative reports, the Process Orientation Usual scale has sufficient precision to discriminate between 92 percent of examinees across the entire θ continuum.

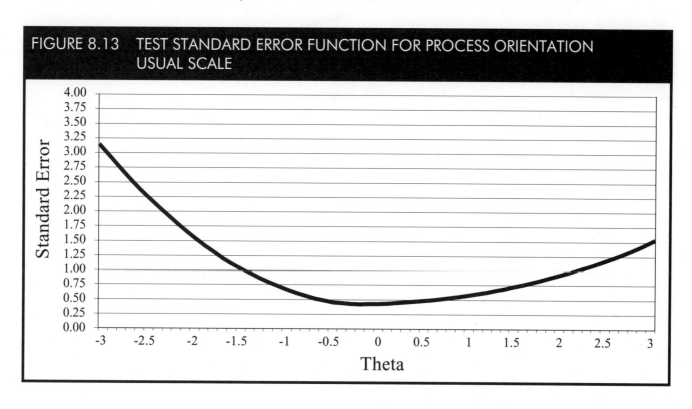

FIGURE 8.13   TEST STANDARD ERROR FUNCTION FOR PROCESS ORIENTATION USUAL SCALE

In Figure 8.14, the TSEF for the Control Orientation Usual scale is illustrated across the θ continuum. Reading from left to right across the θ continuum, from -3.00 to -0.50, a large amount of standard error exists. In effect, this instrument has too much standard error to discriminate between the 31 percent of respondents coming from the lowest portion of the θ continuum. A moderate amount of standard error exists across -0.50 to -0.75 and a modest amount from -0.75 to 3.00. This scale provides the least amount of standard error for respondents in the moderate-to-high side of the θ continuum. In respect to Birkman interpretative reports, the Control Orientation Usual scale has sufficient precision to discriminate between 69 percent of examinees across the entire θ continuum.

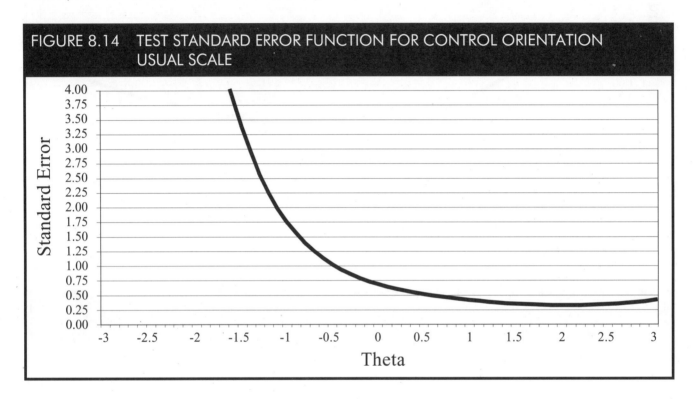

FIGURE 8.14   TEST STANDARD ERROR FUNCTION FOR CONTROL ORIENTATION USUAL SCALE

In Figure 8.15, the TSEF for the Change Orientation Usual scale is illustrated across the θ continuum. Reading from left to right across the θ continuum, from -3.00 to -0.75 and from 2.00 to 3.00, a large amount of standard error exists. In effect, this instrument has too much standard error to discriminate between the 25 percent of respondents coming from the moderate-to-low and highest portions of the θ continuum. A moderate amount of standard error exists across -0.75 to -0.25, a modest amount from -0.25 to 1.00, and a moderate amount (again) from 1.00 to 2.00. This scale provides the least amount of standard error for respondents in the moderate-to-high range of the θ continuum. In respect to Birkman interpretative reports, the Change Orientation Usual scale has sufficient precision to discriminate between 75 percent of examinees across the entire θ continuum.

In Figure 8.16, the TSEF for the Emotive Orientation Needs scale is illustrated across the θ continuum. Reading from left to right across the θ continuum, from -3.00 to -1.25, a large amount of stan-

FIGURE 8.15   TEST STANDARD ERROR FUNCTION FOR CHANGE ORIENTATION USUAL SCALE

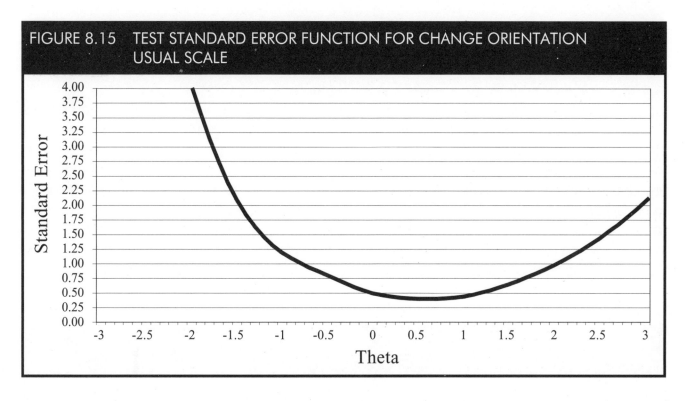

dard error exists. In effect, this instrument has too much standard error to discriminate between the 11 percent of respondents coming from the lowest portion of the θ continuum. A moderate amount of standard error exists across -1.25 to -0.50, a modest amount from -0.50 to 0.00, little-none from 0.00 to 1.75, a modest amount (again) from 1.75 to 2.25, and a moderate amount (again) from 2.25 to 3.00. This scale provides the least amount of standard error for respondents in the moderate-to-

FIGURE 8.16   TEST STANDARD ERROR FUNCTION FOR EMOTIVE ORIENTATION NEEDS SCALE

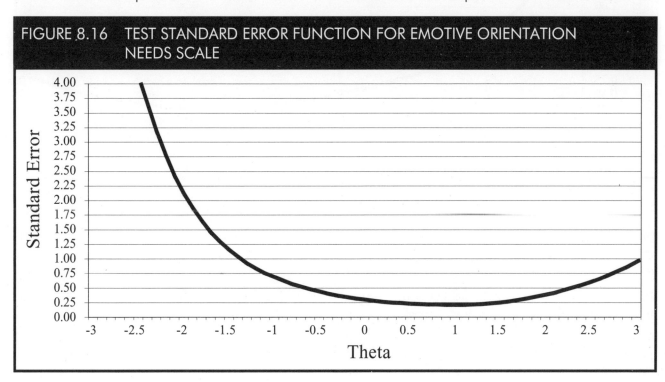

high range of the θ continuum. In respect to Birkman interpretative reports, the Emotive Orientation Needs scale has sufficient precision to discriminate between 89 percent of examinees across the entire θ continuum.

In Figure 8.17, the TSEF for the Social Orientation Needs scale is illustrated across the θ continuum. Reading from left to right across the θ continuum, from -3.00 to -1.50, a large amount of standard error exists. In effect, this instrument has too much standard error to discriminate between the seven percent of respondents coming from the lowest portion of the θ continuum. A moderate amount of standard error exists across -1.50 to -0.25, a modest amount from -0.25 to 0.50, little-to-none from 0.50 to 1.50, a modest amount (again) from 1.50 to 2.25, and a moderate amount (again) from 2.25 to 3.00. This scale provides the least amount of standard error for respondents in the moderate-to-high range of the θ continuum. In respect to Birkman interpretative reports, the Social Orientation Needs scale has sufficient precision to discriminate between 93 percent of examinees across the entire θ continuum.

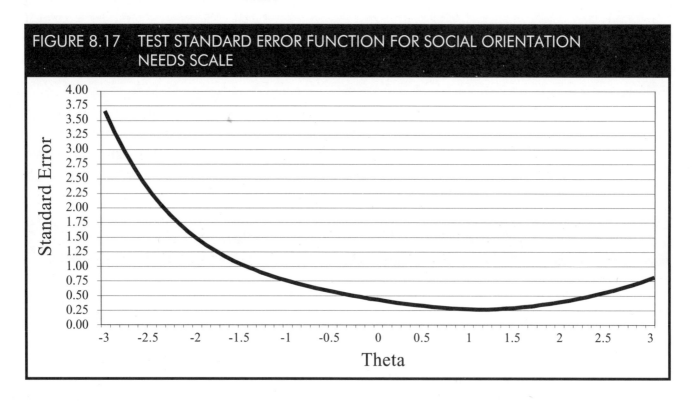

FIGURE 8.17   TEST STANDARD ERROR FUNCTION FOR SOCIAL ORIENTATION NEEDS SCALE

In Figure 8.18, the TSEF for the Process Orientation Needs scale is illustrated across the θ continuum. Reading from left to right across the θ continuum, from -3.00 to -0.75, a large amount of standard error exists. In effect, this instrument has too much standard error to discriminate between the 23 percent of respondents coming from the lowest portion of the θ continuum. A moderate amount of standard error exists across -0.75 to -0.25, a modest amount from -0.25 to 0.50, little-to-none from 0.50 to 0.75, a modest amount (again) from 0.75 to 1.50, and a moderate amount (again) from 1.50 to 3.00. This scale provides the least amount of standard error for respondents in the moderate-to-high range of the θ continuum. In respect to Birkman interpretative reports, the Process Orientation Needs scale has sufficient precision to discriminate between 77 percent of examinees across the entire θ continuum.

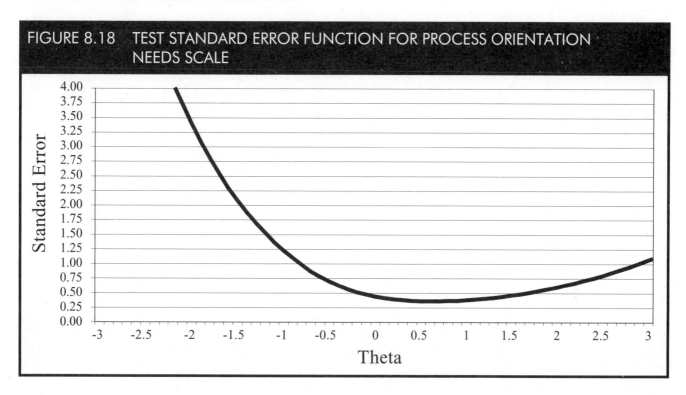

FIGURE 8.18   TEST STANDARD ERROR FUNCTION FOR PROCESS ORIENTATION NEEDS SCALE

In Figure 8.19, the TSEF for the Control Orientation Needs scale is illustrated across the θ continuum. Reading from left to right across the θ continuum, from -3.00 to -1.25, a large amount of standard error exists. In effect, this instrument has too much standard error to discriminate between the ten percent of respondents coming from the lowest portion of the θ continuum. A moderate amount of standard error exists across -1.25 to -0.50, a modest amount from -0.50 to 2.25, and a moderate amount (again) from 2.25 to 3.00. This scale provides the least amount of standard error for respondents in the moderate-to-high range of the θ continuum. In respect to Birkman interpretative reports, the Control Orientation Needs scale has sufficient precision to discriminate between 90 percent of examinees across the entire θ continuum.

In Figure 8.20, the TSEF for the Change Orientation Needs scale is illustrated across the θ continuum. Reading from left to right across the θ continuum, from -3.00 to -0.50 and from 2.25 to 3.00, a large amount of standard error exists. In effect, this instrument has too much standard error to discriminate between the 42 percent of respondents coming from the moderate-to-low and highest portions of the θ continuum. A moderate amount of standard error exists from -0.50 to 2.25. This scale provides the least amount of standard error for respondents in the moderate-to-high range of the θ continuum. In respect to Birkman interpretative reports, the Change Orientation Needs scale has sufficient precision to discriminate between 58 percent of examinees across the entire θ continuum.

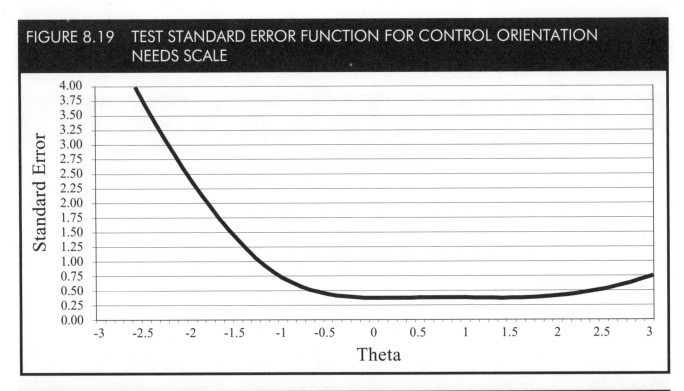

FIGURE 8.19 TEST STANDARD ERROR FUNCTION FOR CONTROL ORIENTATION NEEDS SCALE

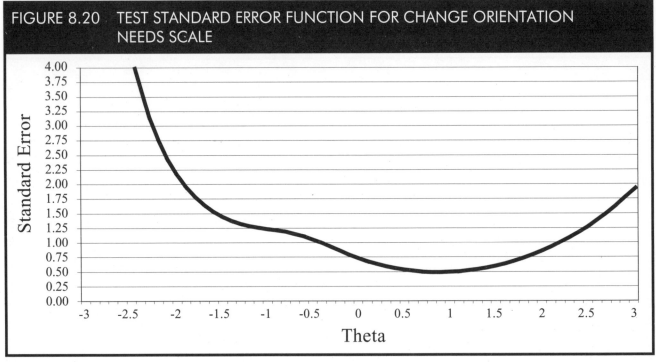

FIGURE 8.20 TEST STANDARD ERROR FUNCTION FOR CHANGE ORIENTATION NEEDS SCALE

IRT Cutoff Score Analysis

The existing scale scores for each Birkman scale are determined according to the number right (*NR*) metric. If cutoff scores are to be utilized for particular applications of The Birkman Method® (e.g., selection), it is beneficial to translate cutoff scores on the *NR* metric to their respective values on the IRT theta (θ) metric in order to assess the item's quality.

To discover the expected θ of the examinees with the specified *NR* score x, denoted by $u_{\theta|x}$. The joint distribution of θ and x is given by

$$f(\theta, x) = f(x|\theta) f(\theta).$$

Then based on Bayes' theorem, the conditional distribution of θ given x is given by

$$f(\theta|x) = \frac{f(x|\theta) f(x)}{f(x)}.$$

The expected θ given *NR* score x then can be determined by

$$u_{\theta|x} = f(x)^{-1} \int \theta f(x|\theta) f(\theta) d\theta.$$

No numerically exact expression exists; however, the value can be approximated by

$$u_{\theta|x} \approx \left[K f(x) \right]^{-1} \sum_{q=1}^{n_q} \theta_q f(x|\theta_q) f(\theta_q),$$

where $\theta_1, ..., \theta_{n_q}$ are $n_q = 601$ ordinal points equally spaced on the -3 to +3 continuum, $f(\theta)$ is a standard normal density, and *K* is a constant used for normalization provided by

$$K = \sum_{q=1}^{n_q} f(\theta_q).$$

Using item response functions, Lord's (1980) recursive observed score generation algorithm generates the unconditional and conditional *NR* distributions. These θ values are the most important points on the metric for focusing on the precision of measurement for these scales. In addition, the deltas for each Orientation across perspectives can be analyzed with much greater precision and thus greater understanding. Table 8.3 (*see page 128*) and Table 8.4 (*see page 129*) show the conversion from *NR* to IRT θ metric for each Birkman Orientation scale.

An illustration of the utility of these conversions follows. If the *NR* cutoff score for Emotive Orientation Usual is set to 5, then the *NR* score corresponds to a θ of 0.32, meaning $\mu_{\theta|x=5} = \mathbf{0.32}$. Additionally, if the *NR* cutoff score for Emotive Orientation Needs is 5 which corresponds to a θ of -0.38, meaning $\mu_{\theta|x=5} = \mathbf{-0.38}$. The resulting $\mu_{\theta|D}$ for Emotion Orientation is 0.70.

TABLE 8.3   NR TO IRT θ CONVERSION FOR ORIENTATION USUAL SCALES

EMOTIVE		SOCIAL		PROCESS		CONTROL		CHANGE	
NR	$\mu_{\theta\mid x}$	NR	$\mu_{\theta\mid x}$	NR	$\mu_{\theta\mid x}$	NR	$\mu_{\theta\mid x}$	NR	$\mu_{\theta\mid x}$
0	-1.38	0	-3.76	0	-4.00	0	-2.64	0	-1.75
1	-1.25	1	-3.52	1	-3.33	1	-2.32	1	-1.43
2	-0.86	2	-3.43	2	-2.87	2	-1.30	2	-0.64
3	-0.30	3	-3.30	3	-2.81	3	-1.21	3	-0.06
4	0.11	4	-3.25	4	-2.45	4	-0.47	4	0.42
5	0.32	5	-3.23	5	-1.95	5	-0.05	5	0.81
6	0.50	6	-3.18	6	-1.35	6	0.42	6	1.30
7	0.64	7	-2.47	7	-0.93	7	0.77	7	2.27
8	0.77	8	-1.98	8	-0.53	8	1.10		
9	0.89	9	-1.67	9	-0.24	9	1.31		
10	1.02	10	-1.33	10	0.05	10	1.55		
11	1.12	11	-1.04	11	0.33	11	1.74		
12	1.19	12	-0.87	12	0.70	12	1.96		
13	1.32	13	-0.70	13	1.10	13	2.16		
14	1.41	14	-0.55	14	1.91	14	2.35		
15	1.49	15	-0.37	15	3.49	15	2.57		
16	1.62	16	-0.26			16	2.86		
17	1.76	17	-0.12			17	3.14		
18	1.90	18	0.02			18	3.61		
19	2.16	19	0.21			19	3.89		
20	2.42	20	0.40						
21	2.81	21	0.61						
22	3.24	22	0.88						
		23	1.23						
		24	1.91						
		25	2.74						

TABLE 8.4 NR TO IRT θ CONVERSION FOR ORIENTATION NEEDS SCALES

EMOTIVE		SOCIAL		PROCESS		CONTROL		CHANGE	
NR	$\mu_{\theta|x}$	NR	$\mu_{\theta|x}$	NR	$\mu_{\theta|x}$	NR	$\mu_{\theta|x}$	NR	$\mu_{\theta|x}$
0	-2.41	0	-3.49	0	-2.20	0	-2.46	0	-2.23
1	-2.31	1	-3.36	1	-1.94	1	-2.29	1	-2.10
2	-1.90	2	-3.15	2	-1.45	2	-2.12	2	-1.82
3	-1.19	3	-2.81	3	-1.18	3	-1.76	3	-0.46
4	-0.70	4	-2.54	4	-0.61	4	-1.31	4	0.39
5	-0.38	5	-2.02	5	-0.20	5	-0.90	5	0.97
6	-0.18	6	-1.64	6	0.08	6	-0.52	6	1.49
7	0.02	7	-1.23	7	0.30	7	-0.28	7	2.18
8	0.15	8	-0.85	8	0.52	8	-0.04		
9	0.31	9	-0.51	9	0.72	9	0.20		
10	0.45	10	-0.22	10	0.96	10	0.38		
11	0.58	11	0.04	11	1.20	11	0.67		
12	0.72	12	0.27	12	1.44	12	0.87		
13	0.83	13	0.40	13	1.80	13	1.09		
14	0.95	14	0.61	14	2.33	14	1.37		
15	1.06	15	0.71	15	3.65	15	1.62		
16	1.20	16	0.89			16	1.88		
17	1.33	17	1.03			17	2.25		
18	1.52	18	1.19			18	2.65		
19	1.71	19	1.35			19	3.19		
20	1.98	20	1.48						
21	2.40	21	1.70						
22	3.01	22	1.92						
		23	2.20						
		24	2.81						
		25	3.58						

Test Precision Analysis

The conditional information function of a **NR** score is given by:

$$I(\theta, x) = \frac{\left[\sum_{i=1}^{n} P_i'(\theta)\right]^2}{\sum_{i=1}^{n} P_i(\theta) Q_i(\theta)},$$

where $P_i(\theta)$ is 3PL model for item *i* given item parameters a_i, b_i, c_i; $P_i'(\theta)$ is the derivative of $P_i(\theta)$ with respect to θ; and **n** is the total number of scale items (Lord, 1980).

An illustration of the exemplar **NR** cutoff scores for the Emotive Orientation scales being evaluated using information functions is shown in Figure 8.21 and Figure 8.22. High information exists at the cutoff scores for both scales. In fact, information peaks near the cutoff score for both scales.

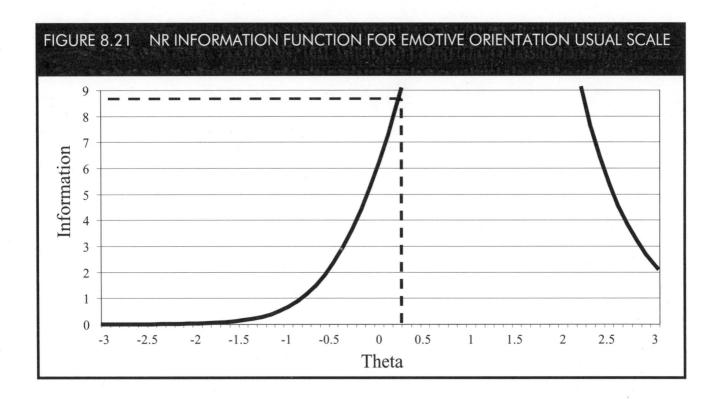

FIGURE 8.21   NR INFORMATION FUNCTION FOR EMOTIVE ORIENTATION USUAL SCALE

PRE-EQUATING

With certain assumptions having been met (e.g., unidimensionality and item parameters being known), the recursive observed-score algorithm (Lord, 1980) can be utilized to derive/estimate cumulative distributions of **NR** scores for each Birkman Orientation scale. With the IRT item parameters in conjunction with a specified theta distribution, these estimated expected distributions are derived. Via pretesting, having known item parameters makes it possible for form(s) to be devel-

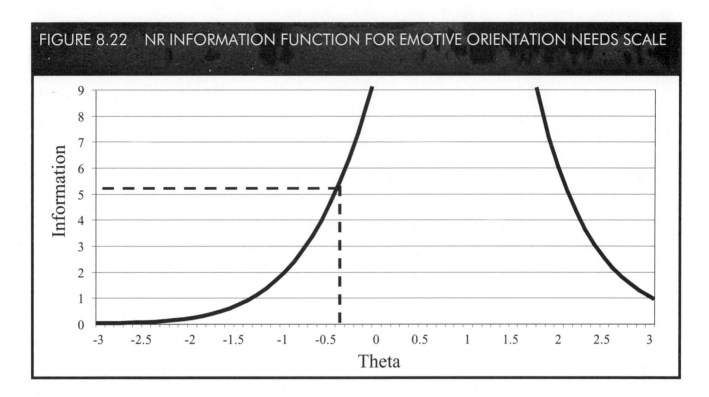

FIGURE 8.22   NR INFORMATION FUNCTION FOR EMOTIVE ORIENTATION NEEDS SCALE

oped and equated prior to using the forms operationally. Having determined which items to include in a new scale, the observed score algorithm can be used to determine the new form's *NR* cumulative distribution and the *NR* cumulative distribution of associated alternative forms. The procedure of equating can be done through the use of mean, linear, equipercentile, and/or IRT methods. Of these methods, IRT and equipercentile are considered optimal.

The exactness of the observed score algorithms for each Birkman Orientation scale was scrutinized using the 2007 normative operational data set. Assuming a standard normal distribution [i.e., $\theta \sim N(0,1)$] for each Birkman Orientation scale of interest, the estimated item parameters for their respective scale were used to estimate the observed score distributions. The empirical cumulative distribution functions of *NR* scale scores based on actual data for the scales were then compared to the estimated/expected cumulative distribution functions (CDF). The CDFs were estimated using mean, linear, and equipercentile, and IRT methods. After making decisions as to the accuracy of the methods, the IRT CDFs were used in the empirical comparisons. The two CDFs for each scale of interest are shown in Figure 8.23 through Figure 8.32. The differences between the two CDFs for each respective scale are illustrated in Figure 8.33 through Figure 8.42. The CDFs for each scale differ by varying percentage points throughout the θ continuum. The differences being small, averaging 2.58 percentile points across all ten scales for the majority of the θ continuum, indicate that the empirical *NR* distributions are closely and adequately estimated by the IRT method of score distributions. In addition, these results indicate that an equating using this pre-equating method to estimate *NR* distributions will closely and adequately match the equating obtained from empirical *NR* scores collected after future field-tested items are incorporated into alternative forms and become operational.

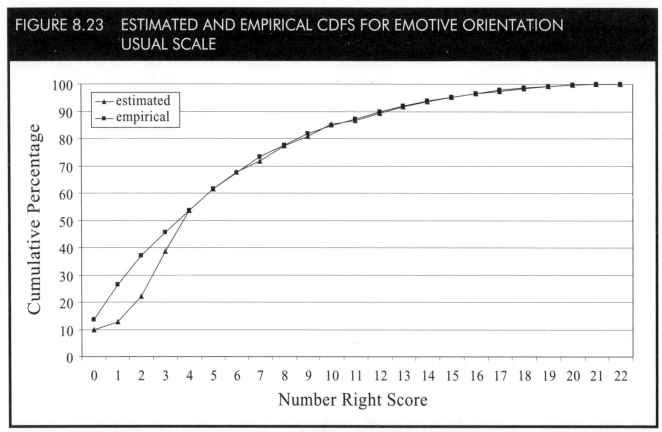

FIGURE 8.23   ESTIMATED AND EMPIRICAL CDFS FOR EMOTIVE ORIENTATION
USUAL SCALE

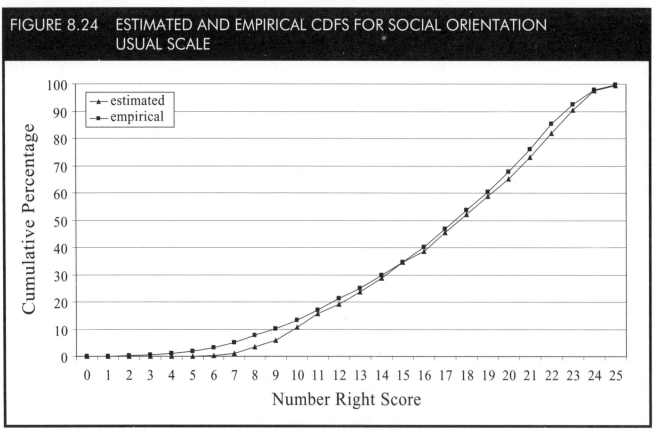

FIGURE 8.24   ESTIMATED AND EMPIRICAL CDFS FOR SOCIAL ORIENTATION
USUAL SCALE

FIGURE 8.25   ESTIMATED AND EMPIRICAL CDFS FOR PROCESS ORIENTATION
USUAL SCALE

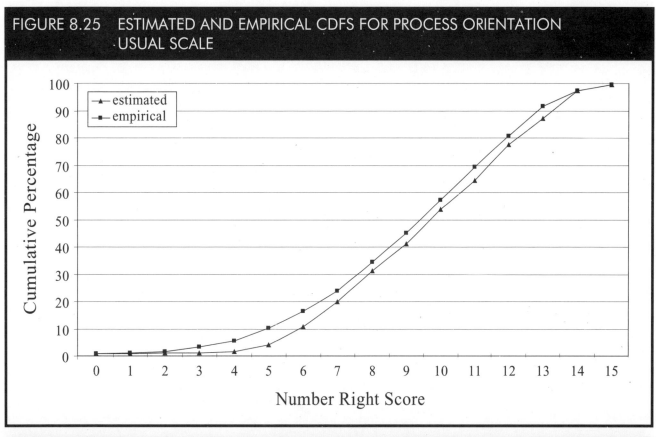

FIGURE 8.26   ESTIMATED AND EMPIRICAL CDFS FOR CONTROL ORIENTATION
USUAL SCALE

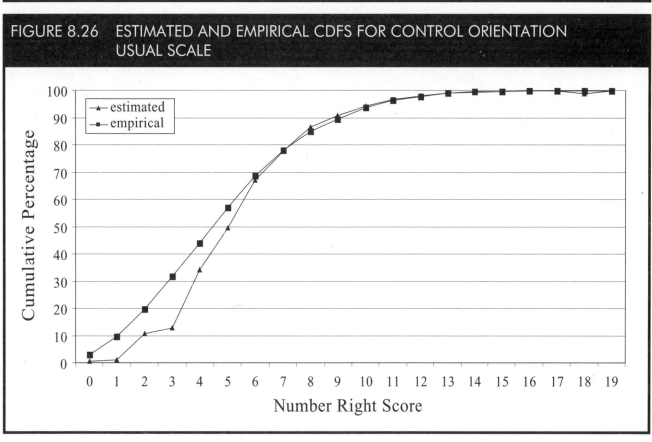

FIGURE 8.27   ESTIMATED AND EMPIRICAL CDFS FOR CHANGE ORIENTATION
USUAL SCALE

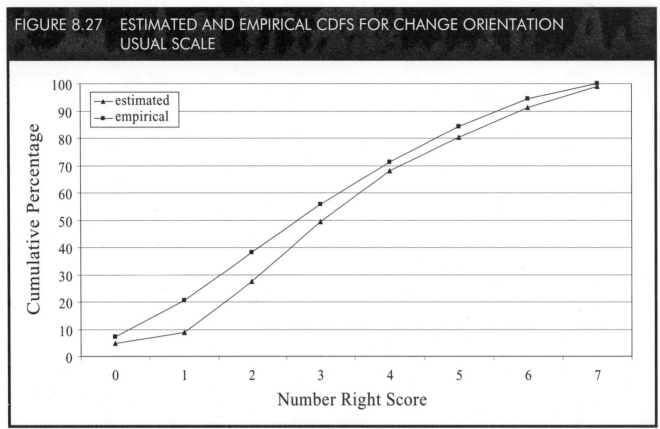

FIGURE 8.28   ESTIMATED AND EMPIRICAL CDFS FOR EMOTIVE ORIENTATION
NEEDS SCALE

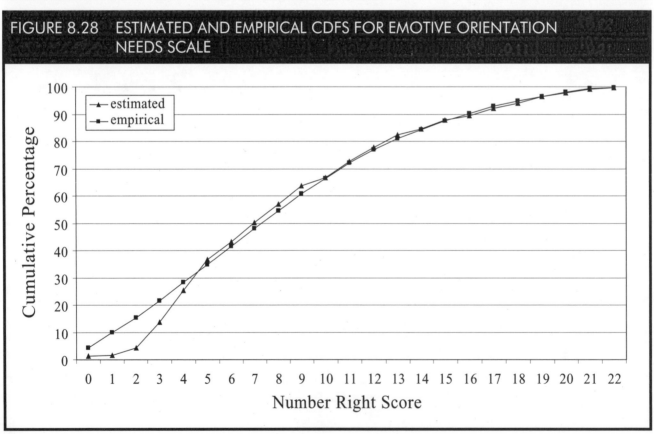

FIGURE 8.29   ESTIMATED AND EMPIRICAL CDFS FOR SOCIAL ORIENTATION
NEEDS SCALE

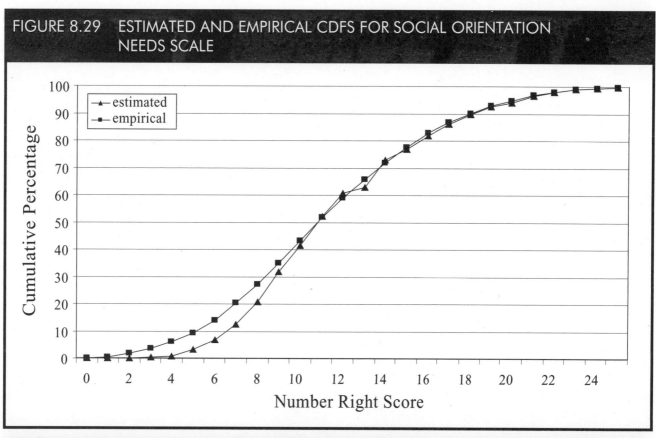

FIGURE 8.30   ESTIMATED AND EMPIRICAL CDFS FOR PROCESS ORIENTATION
NEEDS SCALE

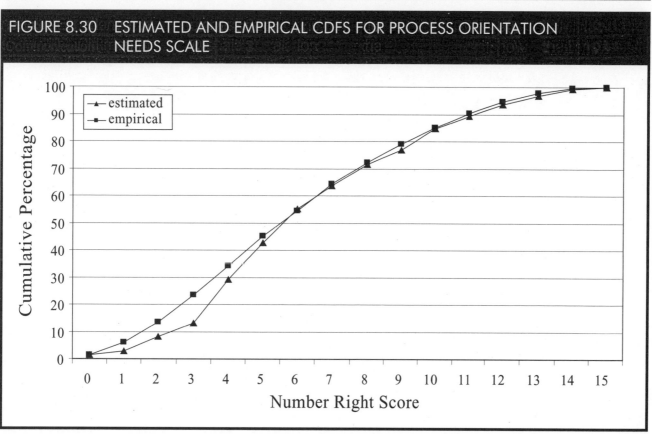

FIGURE 8.31   ESTIMATED AND EMPIRICAL CDFS FOR CONTROL ORIENTATION
NEEDS SCALE

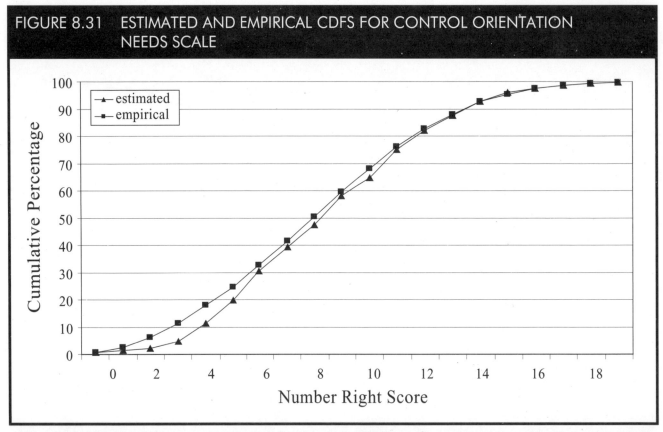

FIGURE 8.32   ESTIMATED AND EMPIRICAL CDFS FOR CHANGE ORIENTATION
NEEDS SCALE

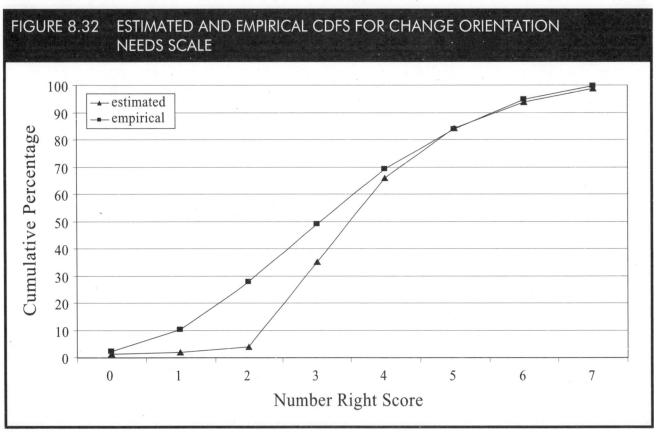

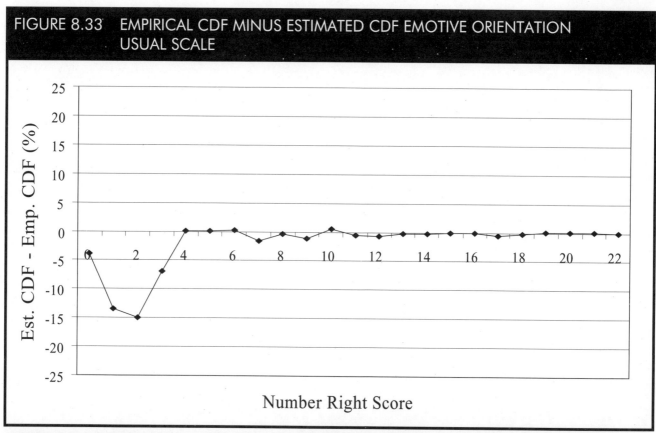

FIGURE 8.33 EMPIRICAL CDF MINUS ESTIMATED CDF EMOTIVE ORIENTATION USUAL SCALE

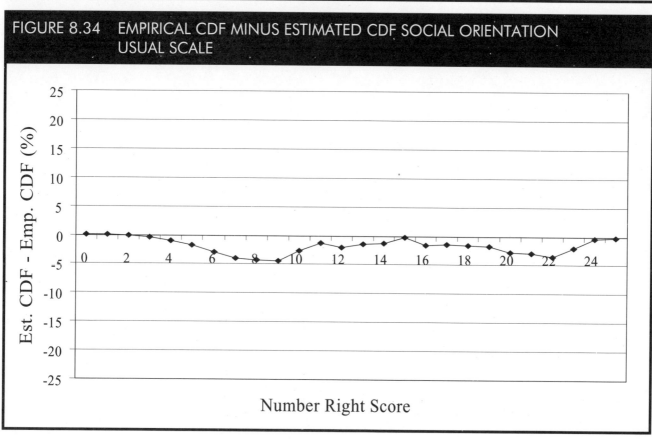

FIGURE 8.34 EMPIRICAL CDF MINUS ESTIMATED CDF SOCIAL ORIENTATION USUAL SCALE

FIGURE 8.35   EMPIRICAL CDF MINUS ESTIMATED CDF PROCESS ORIENTATION
               USUAL SCALE

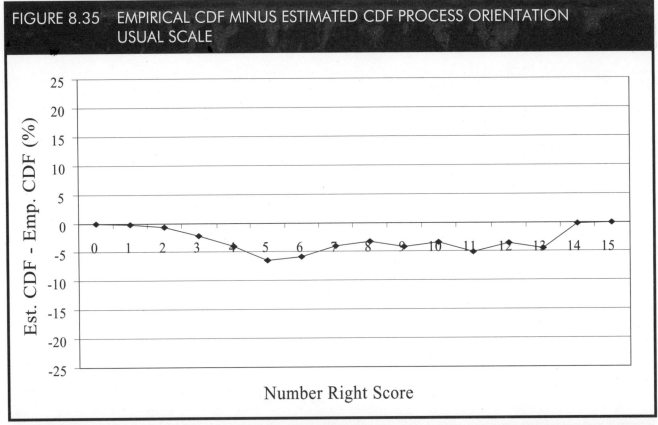

Number Right Score

FIGURE 8.36   EMPIRICAL CDF MINUS ESTIMATED CDF CONTROL ORIENTATION
               USUAL SCALE

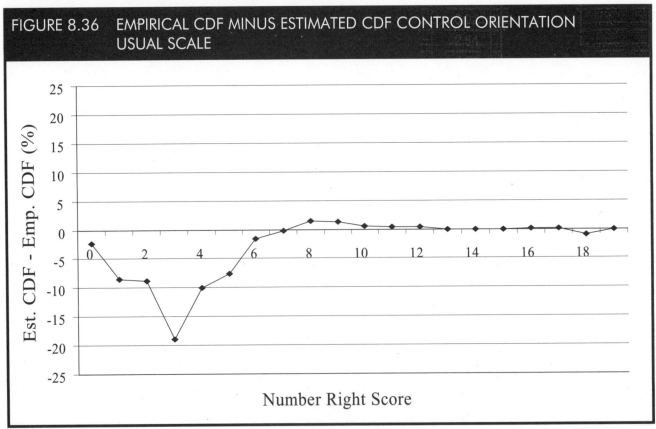

Number Right Score

FIGURE 8.37   EMPIRICAL CDF MINUS ESTIMATED CDF CHANGE ORIENTATION
USUAL SCALE

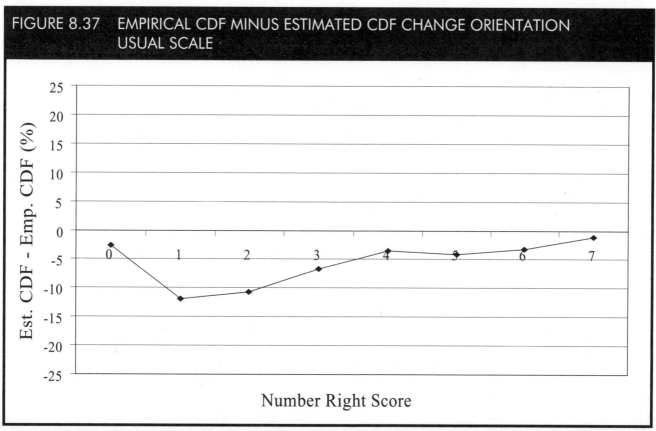

FIGURE 8.38   EMPIRICAL CDF MINUS ESTIMATED CDF EMOTIVE ORIENTATION
NEEDS SCALE

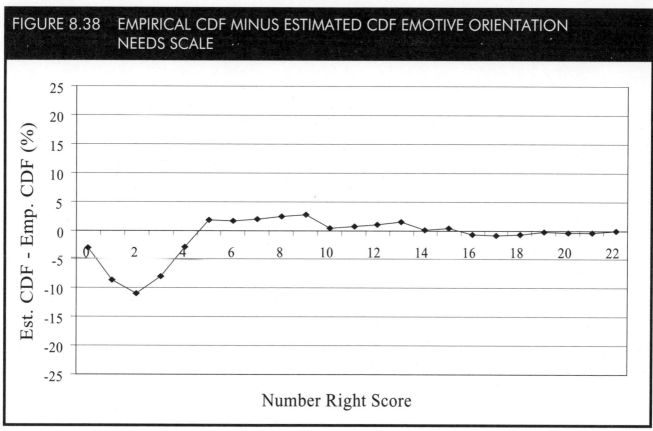

FIGURE 8.39   EMPIRICAL CDF MINUS ESTIMATED CDF SOCIAL ORIENTATION NEEDS SCALE

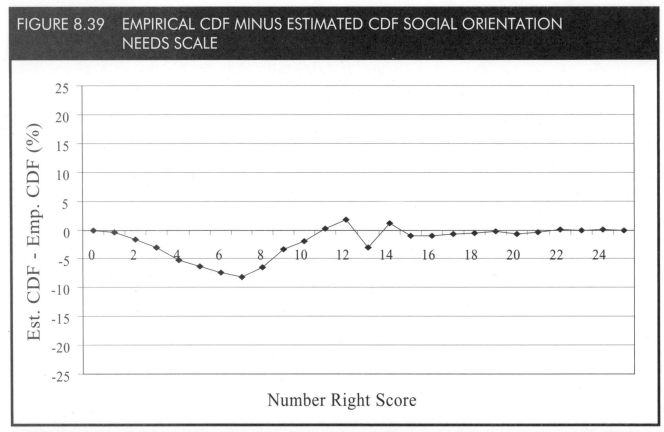

Number Right Score

FIGURE 8.40   EMPIRICAL CDF MINUS ESTIMATED CDF PROCESS ORIENTATION NEEDS SCALE

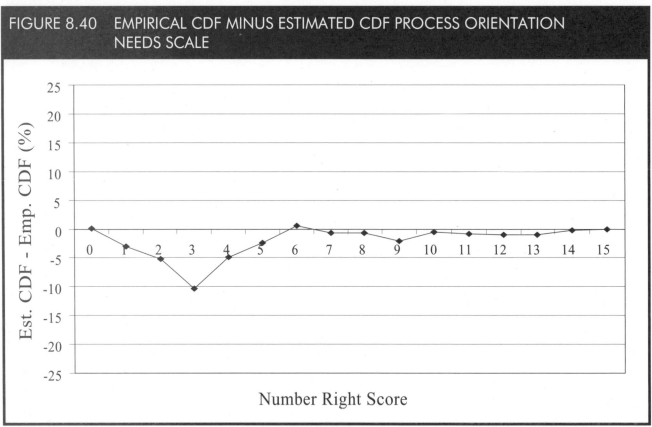

Number Right Score

FIGURE 8.41   EMPIRICAL CDF MINUS ESTIMATED CDF CONTROL ORIENTATION NEEDS SCALE

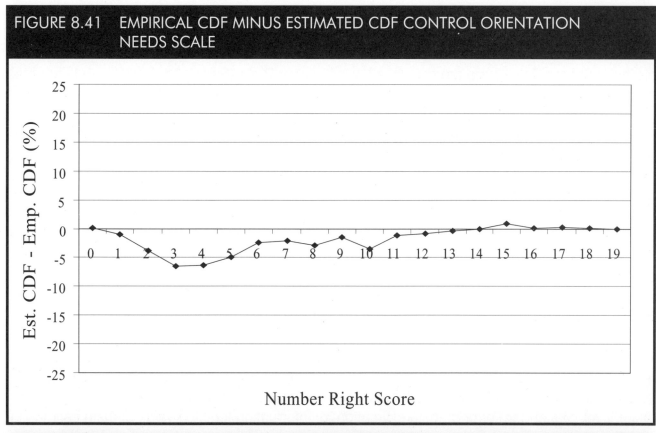

Number Right Score

FIGURE 8.42   EMPIRICAL CDF MINUS ESTIMATED CDF CHANGE ORIENTATION NEEDS SCALE

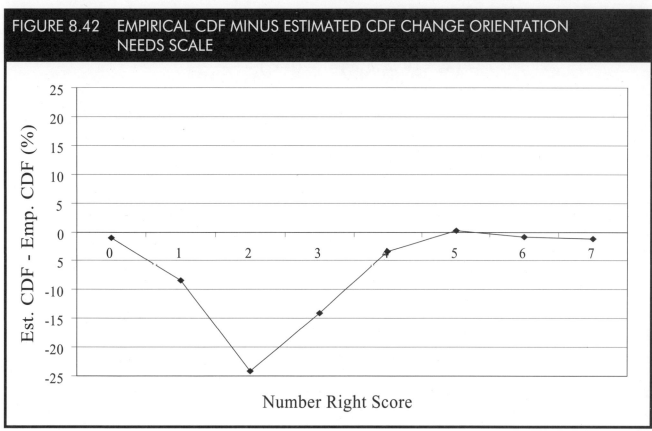

Number Right Score

SCORING METHODOLOGY

For quality control and psychometric insight, the Birkman Orientation scales are scored in two distinct manners. The scales are calculated with Number Right (Endorsed) Scoring and Expected A Posteriori Scoring (EAPS).

Number Right Scoring (NRS) is simply based on the number of items endorsed per scale. Once the number is calculated, the raw score is transformed into a percentile score using the 2007 normative data set. CTT is used to calculate standard error statistics (constant across construct continuum) and then 95 percent confidence intervals.

EAPS is based on theta score estimations ($\hat{\theta}$s) of IRT item parameters and examinees' item level responses. IRT is utilized to calculate CSEs by which 95 percentile confidence intervals can be computed around an examinee's $\hat{\theta}$ scores.

EAPS Calculations

The equations that follow are utilized in the EAPS calculations. In respective order, these equations represent: 1) three parameter logistic model, 2) joint probability for response set for locally independent items, 3) density or weights for standard normal distribution [prior], 4) theta estimation of factor level, 5) standard error of theta estimation, 6) information function value of theta estimation, and 7) theta-to-raw score transformation.

$$P\left(X_{ir}=1\middle|\hat{\theta}_r,a_i,b_i,c_i\right)=c_i+\left(1-c_i\right)\frac{e^{(a_i(\theta_s-b_i))}}{1+e^{(a_i(\theta_s-b_i))}}$$

a	= discriminant item parameter [known]
b	= difficulty item parameter [known]
c	= pseudo-guessing parameter [known]
$\hat{\theta}$	= estimate of an examinee's latent trait score (theta) on a factor [unknown]
i	= item
r	= quadrature point
e	= 2.71828

$$L\left(\underline{X}\right)=P_1Q_2P_3P_i,\ldots,P_n$$

$\underline{X}$	= response set
P	= probability of endorsing item (X=1)
Q	= probability of not endorsing item (X=0); $1 - P$
i	= item
n	= total number of items within factor

$$F(\theta) = \left[\frac{1}{\sqrt{(2)(3.14)}} \right] e^{-\theta^2/2}$$

e = 2.71828

$$\hat{\theta} = \frac{\sum_{r=1}^{241} Q_r \times L(Q_r) \times W(Q_r)}{\sum_{r=1}^{241} L(Q_r) \times W(Q_r)}$$

$\hat{\theta}$ = estimate of an examinee's theta score on a factor
r = quadrature point
Q_r = θ on latent trait/theta continuum at r
$L(Q_r)$ = likelihood of response set at r
$W(Q_r)$ = density value of the standard normal distribution (prior) at r

$$SE(\hat{\theta}) = \sqrt{\frac{\sum_{r=1}^{241} (Q_r - \hat{\theta}) \times L(Q_r) \times W(Q_r)}{\sum_{r=1}^{241} L(Q_r) \times W(Q_r)}}$$

$\hat{\theta}$ = estimate of an examinee's theta score on a factor
r = quadrature point
Q_r = θ on latent trait/theta continuum at r
$L(Q_r)$ = likelihood of response set at r
$W(Q_r)$ = density value of the standard normal distribution (prior) at r

$$I(\hat{\theta}) = \frac{1}{SE^2}$$

$$\hat{\theta}^* = SD(\hat{\theta}) + \bar{X}$$

$\hat{\theta}^*$ = raw score estimate of an examinee's number of items endorsed
SD = standard deviation of the raw score distribution of a factor
$\hat{\theta}$ = estimate of an examinee's theta score on a factor
$\bar{X}$ = mean of the raw score distribution of a factor

Using the prior equations, the EAPS methodology can be carried out in 20 steps for each factor per examinee.

CHAPTER 8 SUMMARY

In Chapter 8, reliability evidence via CTT and IRT was presented in support of The Birkman Method® scales. In addition, Birkman scoring methodology was explained demonstrating quality control and increased understanding using multiple scoring methods. The Birkman Method® scales are reliable when used in the intended applications.

CHAPTER 9
Validity

A general definition of validity is the degree to which a questionnaire, test, or psychological instrument measures what it claims to measure. This chapter will discuss the different types of validity of The Birkman Method®.

FACE VALIDITY

Face validity is the most basic type of validity, and it is defined as the mere appearance that the results are relevant, important, or make sense to the test taker. This validity is important since it is a measure of the perceived accuracy of the test. The Birkman Method® has always received positive feedback on its face validity by both individuals and groups. A large measure of the success consultants experience during feedback sessions using The Birkman Method® is attributed to face validity. Perhaps the strongest case for face validity is the large number of organizations that have perceived that the instrument is relevant, important, or makes sense. For over 50 years, The Birkman Method® has been perceived as a major tool in organizational analysis, promotion, team building, selection, manager development, coaching, merger and acquisitions, and decision-making. The Birkman items and scales were developed and validated using employees from a multitude of organizations. The item content uses everyday non-clinical language. The instrument has been used within thousands of organizations across most industries throughout five decades within the U. S. and abroad. These include but are not limited to: telecommunications, utilities, insurance, education, petrochemical, engineering, financial, healthcare, government, retail, manufacturing, aerospace, service, and energy. Various Birkman clients in these industries have used The Birkman Method® and endorsed it as face valid, meaning they consider it relevant.

CONSTRUCT VALIDITY

Construct validity is defined as the extent to which a test measures the "construct" (e.g., attribute, characteristic, trait, etc.) that it is designed

"As you know, if it's not valid, then nothing else matters. Throughout our history, we have been engaged in validation studies and cultural comparisons. It is very clear now that The Birkman Method® is consistent with other measures, and it brings something unique to the domain. Ultimately, "self" and "other" perspectives help individuals see themselves, their teams and organizations in their own distinctive perceptual context."

-Roger W. Birkman

to measure. When comparing psychological/sociological instruments, construct validity deals with the strength of the relationship between similar and non-similar constructs. Several comparisons were made with The Birkman Method® and personality inventories available from the International Personality Item Pool (IPIP; Goldberg, 1999; Goldberg, Johnson, Eber, Hogan, Ashton, Cloninger, & Gough, 2006). Birkman researchers have established construct validity with directly comparable instruments such as the NEO Personality Inventory-IPIP, MBTI® Step II, 16PF Questionnaire-IPIP, HPI-IPIP, the Job Descriptive Index, Emotional Intelligence-IPIP, Personal Attribute Survey-IPIP, Positive and Negative Affect Schedule, 6PF-IPIP, Risk-Avoidance facet, HEXACO-IPIP, Abridged Big Five-Dimensional Circumplex-IPIP, Ability scales, and Adjective Checklists. The sections that follow will describe the different types of validity, including convergent and divergent, and comparisons of The Birkman Method® with other instruments.

CONVERGENT CONSTRUCT VALIDITY

Convergent construct validity is conducted when instruments measuring similar constructs are compared. Examples include comparing an intelligence test with another intelligence test or a personality test with another personality test. When comparing different instruments that measure similar constructs, the correlations between each respective construct should be relatively high. In order to establish convergent construct validity, the same group of individuals must complete each instrument; and results must be compared using Pearson product moment correlations.

To align The Birkman Method® constructs with other personality factors, Birkman scales have been correlated with other instruments that assess personality-related constructs. These associations are shown in Table 9.3 through Table 9.29.

In addition, to demonstrate other construct associations and disassociations, The Birkman Method® constructs have been correlated with non-FFM personality, affect, and other constructs. These non-FFM associations are shown in Table 9.30 through Table 9.38.

It is important to review these validity coefficients, with the relevant reliability coefficients in mind, since reliability determines the upper bound of validity.

The Birkman Method® Factor and Interests Comparison

The correlations between The Birkman Method® factors and Interests are shown in Table 9.1. Many of The Birkman Method® Interest scales display significant and severable profiles across The Birkman Method® factor scales. This is consistent with expectations. The Persuasion Interest scale has particularly strong indicators that combine high social interaction, influence, and incentive with low emotive tendencies. Interestingly, Social Service has a similar profile with the notable exception of low incentive scores rather than high scores.

	BIRKMAN INTEREST SCALES				
BIRKMAN FACTOR SCALES	ART	CLE	LIT	MEC	MUS
Orientation Usual Scales					
Emotive	**.16**	.09	**.11**	-.02	**.10**
Social	**-.10**	**-.18**	.01	**-.13**	.04
Process	**-.18**	**.11**	**-.22**	.08	**-.18**
Control	-.03	**-.14**	-.02	**.11**	.03
Change	.04	-.04	-.01	-.03	.01
Orientation Needs Scales					
Emotive	.04	.02	.06	-.01	.07
Social	-.04	.07	**-.10**	-.03	-.08
Process	-.09	.09	**-.18**	.03	**-.12**
Control	-.04	.04	-.06	.07	-.01
Change	.02	.05	-.02	-.03	.00
Preference Usual Scales					
Activity	**-.16**	**-.11**	**-.10**	.04	-.08
Empathy	**.13**	.03	**.11**	.01	**.11**
Thought	**.12**	**.11**	.05	-.04	.04
Communication	**.13**	**.20**	-.01	.04	-.01
Interaction	-.04	**-.11**	.01	**-.19**	.06
Incentive	.02	-.06	.02	.03	.05
Authority	-.06	**-.15**	-.04	**.13**	.00
Preference Needs Scales					
Activity	-.07	-.03	-.06	.04	-.06
Empathy	.03	.00	.06	.01	.06
Thought	.02	.03	.03	.01	.04
Communication	.05	-.05	.07	.00	.07
Interaction	-.02	.07	**-.10**	-.04	-.07
Incentive	.01	.04	-.02	.03	.02
Authority	-.07	.03	-.09	**.10**	-.03
Other Scales					
Personal Autonomy: Usual	.08	.05	.03	.08	.04
Personal Autonomy: Needs	-.02	.02	.00	.04	.03
Perspective Alignment	.09	.08	-.01	.03	-.02

Notes: ART = Artistic, CLE = Clerical, LIT = Literary, MEC = Mechanical, MUS = Musical; **Bold** indicates a correlation coefficient equal to or greater than .10.
Source: 2007 normative database.

TABLE 9.2	CORRELATION OF THE BIRKMAN METHOD® FACTOR SCALES AND THE BIRKMAN METHOD® INTEREST SCALES (CONTINUED)				

	BIRKMAN INTEREST SCALES				
BIRKMAN FACTOR SCALES	NUM	OUT	PER	SCI	SOC
Orientation Usual Scales					
Emotive	-.05	.01	**-.21**	.02	**-.12**
Social	**-.11**	-.07	**.44**	**-.12**	**.20**
Process	**.18**	-.02	.01	.03	.01
Control	-.03	.07	**.16**	.05	**-.14**
Change	-.06	.05	.09	-.04	-.01
Orientation Needs Scales					
Emotive	-.06	.03	-.06	-.01	-.03
Social	.07	-.06	.04	.00	.02
Process	.07	-.02	.02	.01	.03
Control	.02	.01	-.01	.03	-.08
Change	-.04	.02	-.02	-.03	.01
Preference Usual Scales					
Activity	.04	.01	**.22**	-.01	**.10**
Empathy	-.06	.03	**-.17**	.02	**-.12**
Thought	-.03	-.03	**-.16**	.00	-.05
Communication	.06	.02	**-.39**	.07	**-.13**
Interaction	**-.14**	**-.10**	**.37**	**-.14**	**.22**
Incentive	-.01	-.01	**.14**	.02	**-.14**
Authority	-.03	**.11**	**.13**	.06	**-.11**
Preference Needs Scales					
Activity	.05	.00	.06	.00	.02
Empathy	-.05	.04	-.05	-.01	-.03
Thought	-.03	.01	-.04	-.01	-.03
Communication	-.07	.04	-.03	.00	.00
Interaction	.06	-.06	.04	.00	.04
Incentive	.01	-.02	-.02	.02	-.07
Authority	.03	.04	.00	.04	-.08
Other Scales					
Personal Autonomy: Usual	-.01	.06	**-.17**	.06	**-.17**
Personal Autonomy: Needs	-.02	.02	-.01	-.01	-.04
Perspective Alignment	.04	.01	-.17	.06	**-.11**

Notes: NUM = Numerical, OUT = Outdoor, PER = Persuasive, SCI = Scientific, SOC = Social Service; **Bold** indicates a correlation coefficient equal to or greater than .10.
Source: 2007 normative database.

The Birkman Method® and MBTI® Primary Scales Comparison

In Table 9.3, The Birkman Method® scales were correlated with the Myers-Briggs Type Indicator® (MBTI®; Briggs-Myers, McCaulley, Quenk, & Hammer, 2003).

Table 9.3 correlates The Birkman Method® scales and the primary MBTI® scales. The MBTI® attitudes (E/I and J/P) have the highest correlations, .66 and -.46 for the corresponding Social and Process Birkman Method® Orientations.

The Birkman Method® Interaction Preference scale is a subscale of the Social Orientation scale and has the highest correlation, -.74 with the MBTI® EI scale.

The MBTI® measures internal mental functions in the SN and TF scales. The Birkman Method® measures perception rather than mental functioning. High correlations are not expected among these scales.

In general, The Birkman Method® Needs scales have fewer and lower correlations with MBTI® scales. This is consistent with expectations in that the MBTI® does not measure "other" perceptions or expectations.

Table 9.4 compares The Birkman Method® scales and MBTI® EI scales. Consistent with expectations, MBTI® EI scales have strongly noticeable mean differences in the aligned The Birkman Method® Social, Communication, and Interaction scales. Also consistent is the fact that no other scales register strongly noticeable differences. This demonstrates that The Birkman Method® scales are not only correlated (see Table 9.3) but also measure across the entire EI scale.

Table 9.5 compares The Birkman Method® scales and MBTI® SN scales. Consistent with expectations, MBTI® SN scales do not have noticeable mean differences in the aligned Birkman Method® scales. This is consistent with earlier correlations and expectations because The Birkman Method® measures perceptions rather than mental functions.

Table 9.6 compares The Birkman Method® scales and MBTI® TF scales. Consistent with expectations, MBTI® TF scales have few noticeable mean differences in the aligned Birkman Method® scales. This is consistent with earlier correlations and expectations because The Birkman Method® measures perceptions rather than mental functions.

Table 9.7 compares The Birkman Method® scales and MBTI® JP scales. Consistent with expectations, MBTI® JP scales have strongly noticeable mean differences in the corresponding Birkman Method® Process scale. Also consistent is the fact that no other scales register strongly noticeable differences. This demonstrates that The Birkman Method® scale is not only correlated (see Table 9.3) but it also measures across the entire JP scale.

TABLE 9.3	CORRELATIONS BETWEEN THE BIRKMAN METHOD® FACTOR SCALES AND THE PRIMARY MBTI® SCALES			
	MBTI® PRIMARY SCALES			
BIRKMAN SCALE	EI	SN	TF	JP
Orientation Usual Scales				
Emotive	**.21**	**.24**	**.20**	**.24**
Social	**-.66**	.09	-.08	-.08
Process	-.07	**-.16**	-.11	**-.46**
Control	-.09	.09	**-.14**	.13
Change	**-.19**	**.19**	**.18**	.11
Orientation Needs Scales				
Emotive	.12	**.17**	**.24**	.12
Social	-.10	-.03	-.13	.04
Process	-.11	-.09	**-.16**	**-.17**
Control	.05	.12	.12	**.26**
Change	.03	.08	**.21**	.15
Preference Usual Scales				
Activity	**-.22**	-.10	**-.14**	**-.19**
Empathy	**.15**	**.28**	**.19**	**.20**
Thought	.14	**.17**	**.15**	**.20**
Communication	**.40**	-.04	**.20**	.10
Interaction	**-.74**	.12	.08	-.04
Incentive	-.04	.11	-.03	.13
Authority	-.10	.04	**-.19**	.08
Preference Needs Scales				
Activity	-.13	-.05	**-.22**	-.05
Empathy	.10	**.20**	**.22**	**.16**
Thought	.05	**.18**	**.14**	.04
Communication	.03	.06	**.17**	.02
Interaction	**-.14**	.00	-.07	.07
Incentive	.13	.11	.12	**.24**
Authority	-.05	.10	.07	**.19**
Other Scales				
Personal Autonomy: Usual	**.17**	**.14**	.13	**.28**
Personal Autonomy: Needs	.04	**.22**	**.25**	**.21**
Perspective Alignment	**.20**	-.02	-.13	.12

Notes: N = 216; EI = Extraversion-Introversion, SN = Sensing-Intuitive, TF = Thinking-Feeling, JP = Judging-Perceiving; **Bold** indicates a correlation coefficient significant at *p* < .05.
Source: 2008 MBTI®/The Birkman Method® study.

TABLE 9.4   THE BIRKMAN METHOD® SCALE STATISTICS ACROSS MBTI® EXTRAVERSION-INTROVERSION TYPES

BIRKMAN SCALE	MBTI® - E		MBTI® - I		OVERALL	
	M	SD	M	SD	M Diff	d
Orientation Usual Scales						
Emotive	4.73	4.10	6.34	4.52	**-1.61**	0.38
Social	20.34	2.69	14.78	4.58	**5.55**	**1.61**
Process	8.10	3.05	7.41	2.51	0.69	
Control	5.92	2.96	5.39	2.45	0.52	
Change	3.77	1.84	3.22	1.83	**0.55**	0.30
Orientation Needs Scales						
Emotive	8.25	4.98	9.24	4.41	-0.99	
Social	11.20	4.72	10.03	3.96	1.17	
Process	5.80	2.75	4.89	2.45	**0.91**	0.34
Control	8.19	3.17	8.50	3.02	-0.31	
Change	3.52	1.77	3.78	1.60	-0.26	
Preference Usual Scales						
Activity	4.21	1.70	3.49	2.01	**0.72**	0.40
Empathy	2.41	2.41	3.04	2.63	-0.63	
Thought	0.53	0.77	0.78	0.95	**-0.26**	-0.31
Communication	3.25	2.18	5.36	2.78	**-2.12**	**0.88**
Interaction	11.58	1.41	8.15	2.48	**3.44**	**1.87**
Incentive	2.06	1.70	2.03	1.44	0.03	
Authority	3.86	1.94	3.36	1.69	0.49	
Preference Needs Scales						
Activity	3.17	1.73	2.69	1.77	0.48	
Empathy	4.12	2.91	4.57	2.77	-0.45	
Thought	1.30	1.08	1.36	1.08	-0.06	
Communication	8.12	2.51	8.45	2.13	-0.33	
Interaction	7.32	2.92	6.47	2.46	**0.84**	0.30
Incentive	3.46	1.96	4.05	1.65	**-0.60**	0.32
Authority	4.73	1.81	4.45	1.98	0.29	
Other Scales						
Personal Autonomy: Usual	3.13	2.29	3.92	2.21	**-0.79**	0.35
Personal Autonomy: Needs	4.88	3.30	5.15	2.87	-0.27	
Perspective Alignment	-17.24	10.64	-13.28	11.45	**-3.96**	0.36

Notes: N = 142 for E, N = 74 for I; **Bold** indicates significant mean difference (*M* Diff) at *p* < .05; Underline indicates moderate effect size (*d*), **Bold** indicates large effect size (*d*).
Source: 2008 MBTI®/The Birkman Method® study.

TABLE 9.5 THE BIRKMAN METHOD® SCALE STATISTICS ACROSS MBTI® SENSING-INTUITIVE TYPES

BIRKMAN SCALE	MBTI® - S		MBTI® - N		OVERALL	
	M	SD	M	SD	M Diff	d
Orientation Usual Scales						
Emotive	4.56	3.69	5.52	4.48	-0.96	
Social	17.54	4.99	18.73	4.08	-1.20	
Process	8.48	2.85	7.65	2.88	0.83	
Control	5.65	2.64	5.77	2.86	-0.12	
Change	3.22	1.62	3.70	1.91	-0.48	
Orientation Needs Scales						
Emotive	7.43	4.38	8.98	4.89	**-1.56**	0.33
Social	11.11	4.70	10.69	4.44	0.42	
Process	5.89	2.85	5.36	2.62	0.53	
Control	8.00	2.94	8.40	3.17	-0.40	
Change	3.44	1.57	3.67	1.76	-0.22	
Preference Usual Scales						
Activity	4.06	1.72	3.93	1.88	0.12	
Empathy	2.17	2.34	2.78	2.54	-0.61	
Thought	0.44	0.63	0.67	0.90	**-0.23**	0.27
Communication	4.37	2.84	3.84	2.51	0.53	
Interaction	9.91	2.61	10.57	2.39	-0.67	
Incentive	1.85	1.48	2.11	1.65	-0.26	
Authority	3.80	1.88	3.65	1.88	0.14	
Preference Needs Scales						
Activity	3.11	1.83	2.97	1.73	0.14	
Empathy	3.54	2.46	4.52	2.95	**-0.98**	0.35
Thought	1.00	0.97	1.43	1.10	**-0.43**	0.40
Communication	7.80	2.27	8.38	2.42	-0.58	
Interaction	6.91	2.88	7.07	2.78	-0.16	
Incentive	3.41	1.89	3.75	1.87	-0.34	
Authority	4.59	1.72	4.65	1.92	-0.06	
Other Scales						
Personal Autonomy: Usual	3.13	1.89	3.49	2.41	-0.36	
Personal Autonomy: Needs	4.13	2.66	5.25	3.26	**-1.12**	0.36
Perspective Alignment	-14.24	11.30	-16.43	10.96	2.19	

Notes: N = 54 for S, *N* = 162 for N; **Bold** indicates significant mean difference (*M* Diff) at *p* < .05; Underline indicates moderate effect size (*d*), **Bold** indicates large effect size (*d*).
Source: 2008 MBTI®/The Birkman Method® study.

TABLE 9.6	THE BIRKMAN METHOD® SCALE STATISTICS ACROSS MBTI® THINKING-FEELING TYPES					

	MBTI® - T		MBTI® - F		OVERALL	
BIRKMAN SCALE	M	SD	M	SD	M Diff	d
Orientation Usual Scales						
Emotive	4.81	4.23	5.84	4.36	-1.02	
Social	18.58	4.43	18.26	4.24	0.33	
Process	8.03	2.78	7.66	3.02	0.36	
Control	6.06	2.76	5.35	2.81	0.71	
Change	3.34	1.87	3.87	1.80	**-0.53**	0.29
Orientation Needs Scales						
Emotive	7.68	4.46	9.69	4.99	**-2.02**	0.43
Social	11.33	4.45	10.15	4.49	1.18	
Process	5.80	2.73	5.12	2.59	0.67	
Control	8.02	3.05	8.63	3.18	-0.62	
Change	3.23	1.57	4.07	1.78	**-0.84**	0.51
Preference Usual Scales						
Activity	4.10	1.76	3.80	1.92	0.31	
Empathy	2.41	2.55	2.89	2.42	-0.48	
Thought	0.51	0.78	0.74	0.90	**-0.24**	0.28
Communication	3.63	2.57	4.39	2.59	**-0.76**	0.29
Interaction	10.21	2.43	10.64	2.48	-0.43	
Incentive	2.11	1.69	1.97	1.52	0.14	
Authority	3.95	1.86	3.38	1.85	**0.57**	0.31
Preference Needs Scales						
Activity	3.21	1.65	2.76	1.84	0.46	
Empathy	3.70	2.63	4.96	2.99	**-1.26**	0.45
Thought	1.19	1.05	1.49	1.10	**-0.30**	0.28
Communication	7.88	2.33	8.65	2.40	**-0.77**	0.33
Interaction	7.21	2.80	6.81	2.79	0.41	
Incentive	3.55	1.83	3.80	1.93	-0.25	
Authority	4.47	1.86	4.84	1.88	-0.37	
Other Scales						
Personal Autonomy: Usual	3.28	2.42	3.54	2.13	-0.26	
Personal Autonomy: Needs	4.42	2.85	5.63	3.38	**-1.21**	0.39
Perspective Alignment	-14.31	10.48	-17.79	11.49	**3.48**	0.32

Notes: N = 118 for T, N = 98 for F; **Bold** indicates significant mean difference (M Diff) at p < .05; Underline indicates moderate effect size (d), **Bold** indicates large effect size (d).
Source: 2008 MBTI®/The Birkman Method® study.

TABLE 9.7   THE BIRKMAN METHOD® SCALE STATISTICS ACROSS MBTI® JUDGING-PERCEIVING TYPES

BIRKMAN SCALE	MBTI® - J		MBTI® - P		OVERALL	
	M	SD	M	SD	M Diff	d
Orientation Usual Scales						
Emotive	4.40	3.79	6.01	4.58	**-1.61**	0.38
Social	18.67	4.40	18.24	4.29	0.44	
Process	9.06	2.59	6.86	2.75	**2.20**	**0.82**
Control	5.50	2.61	5.93	2.95	-0.43	
Change	3.36	1.80	3.76	1.88	-0.41	
Orientation Needs Scales						
Emotive	7.98	4.46	9.10	5.03	-1.12	
Social	10.83	4.44	10.77	4.56	0.06	
Process	5.96	2.80	5.10	2.53	**0.86**	0.32
Control	7.50	3.06	8.96	3.02	**-1.46**	0.48
Change	3.35	1.73	3.83	1.68	**-0.48**	0.28
Preference Usual Scales						
Activity	4.22	1.72	3.75	1.91	0.48	
Empathy	2.10	2.15	3.06	2.69	**-0.96**	0.39
Thought	0.52	0.74	0.69	0.92	-0.17	
Communication	3.87	2.68	4.06	2.54	-0.19	
Interaction	10.54	2.32	10.30	2.57	0.24	
Incentive	1.90	1.45	2.17	1.74	-0.27	
Authority	3.60	1.76	3.76	1.97	-0.16	
Preference Needs Scales						
Activity	3.05	1.71	2.97	1.80	0.08	
Empathy	3.74	2.60	4.71	3.00	**-0.97**	0.34
Thought	1.29	1.05	1.36	1.11	-0.07	
Communication	8.10	2.42	8.34	2.37	-0.24	
Interaction	6.93	2.71	7.11	2.88	-0.18	
Incentive	3.21	1.85	4.03	1.83	**-0.82**	0.45
Authority	4.29	1.88	4.92	1.82	**-0.64**	0.35
Other Scales						
Personal Autonomy: Usual	2.92	2.11	3.80	2.36	**-0.88**	0.39
Personal Autonomy: Needs	4.24	2.68	5.58	3.40	**-1.33**	0.43
Perspective Alignment	-16.53	11.48	-15.35	10.73	-1.18	

Notes: N = 98 for J, N = 118 for P; **Bold** indicates significant mean difference (*M* Diff) at *p* < .05; Underline indicates moderate effect size (*d*), **Bold** indicates large effect size (*d*).
Source: 2008 MBTI®/The Birkman Method® study.

The Birkman Method® and MBTI® Step II Comparison

In Table 9.8 through Table 9.12, The Birkman Method® scales were correlated with the MBTI® Step II (Quenk, Hammer, & Majors, 2001).

The most pronounced correlations in Table 9.8 are The Birkman Method® Social Orientation Usual scale and the MBTI® Extraversion facet scales. Correlations range from -.40 to -.68 indicating that the high Birkman Method® Social Orientation Usual scale is very similar to each of the Initiating, Expressive, Gregarious, Active, and Enthusiastic MBTI® facets. This is consistent with expectations.

The second most pronounced correlation is The Birkman Method® Process Orientation Usual scale and the MBTI® Judging facet scales. Correlations range from -.34 to -.43 indicating that the high Birkman Method® Process Orientation Usual scale is very similar to each of the Systematic, Planful, Early Starting, Scheduled, and Methodical MBTI® facets. This is consistent with expectations.

Also consistent with expectations is the fact that The Birkman Method® correlates most highly with the MBTI® attitudes, or orientations, which are not internal functions within individuals. To put it another way, The Birkman Method® was not designed to describe internal human functioning, such as the MBTI® S/N and T/F facets; and it does not describe internal facets as well as the behavioral aspects of the MBTI®.

Interestingly, The Birkman Method® Emotive Orientation Usual scale correlates across almost all of the MBTI® facets, possibly indicating the universal applicability of emotion to most aspects of humanness.

Table 9.9 portrays The Birkman Method® Needs scales and MBTI® facet scales. There are relatively few significant correlations, suggesting that the MBTI® facet scales and The Birkman Method® Needs scales measure different attributes. This is consistent with expectations in that the MBTI® measures only self descriptors.

The noteworthy exception is that The Birkman Method® Emotive Needs are correlated across all MBTI® SN facet scales.

Table 9.10 correlates The Birkman Method® Preference Usual scales and MBTI® facet scales. Consistent with expectations, The Birkman Method® Communication Preference Usual and Interaction Preference Usual (which comprise Social Orientation) are the highest correlates to the MBTI® facet scale Extraversion. Interestingly, the direction of the correlations suggests that MBTI® Extraversion combines high social interaction combined with significant amounts of Contained, Intimate, Reflective, and Quiet interactions. This suggests that the stereotype extravert may have more complexity than what is commonly attributed to them.

The second most notable correlates combine the MBTI® Thinking scale to The Birkman Method® Authority Preference Usual scale. Correlations range from -.17 to -.33, indicating that The Birkman Method® Authority Preference Usual scale is associated with the MBTI® Logical, Reasonable, Questioning, Critical, and Tough facets. This is consistent with expectations in that Authority Usual is negatively correlated to Agreeableness within the FFM of personality.

Also to be noted, The Birkman Method® Activity Preference Usual correlations are virtually all negative indicating that initiating physical activity may increase MBTI® ESTJ preferences.

Table 9.11 correlates The Birkman Method® Needs scales and MBTI® facet scales. Two MBTI® facet scales (Gregarious-Intimate and Reasonable-Compassionate) correlate with five of the seven Birkman Method® Needs scales. This may add complexity and completeness to the understanding of how these facets are deployed in everyday interactions.

The most notable correlates center on The Birkman Method® Needs scales for Empathy and Thought and the MBTI® Intuitive facet which includes the Abstract, Imaginative, Conceptual, Theoretical, and Original scales. Together, these point towards the classical definition of Intuition and the environment it requires as well as adds to it the complexities of requiring an empathetic environment.

The single highest correlation is .25 for the MBTI® Spontaneous and The Birkman Method® Incentive Preference. This may infer that an environment that provides incentive may also promote spontaneous behavior.

Also to be noted, The Birkman Method® Activity Preference Needs correlations are virtually all negative indicating that an environment that requires physical activity on an individual may increase MBTI® ESTJ preferences in that individual.

Table 9.12 correlates two non-personality Birkman Method® scales and MBTI® facet scales. The Birkman Method® scale Personal Autonomy has no direct theoretical tie to any MBTI® construct. However, from a practical perspective, Personal Autonomy Usual, a contrarian construct, does correlate with all MBTI® Perceiving facets. Correlation values range from .18 to .24. Environments that provide Intuitive and Perceiving opportunities also correlate with Personal Autonomy. This suggests that certain environments, combined with certain personal attributes, may increase or decrease, contrarian behavior.

The most notable characteristic of The Birkman Method® scale Perspective Alignment to the MBTI® scales is the interspersed correlations. Perspective Alignment correlates with facets of Introversion, Sensing, Thinking, and Perceiving. Aligned perspectives are correlated with Open-Ended, Pressure-Prompted, Receiving, Contained, Reflective, Practical, Reasonable, and Critical facets. This is consistent with aligning, at a personal level, with the diverse attributes of an individual. Perspective Alignment has no direct MBTI® facet scale equivalent.

| TABLE 9.8 | CORRELATION OF THE BIRKMAN METHOD® ORIENTATION USUAL SCALES AND MBTI® STEP II FACET SCALES |

MBTI® STEP II FACET SCALE	BIRKMAN ORIENTATION USUAL SCALE				
	EMO	SOC	PRO	CON	CHA
E-I Facet Scales					
Initiating-Receiving	**.19**	**-.68**	-.11	**-.13**	-.12
Expressive-Contained	.08	**-.43**	-.03	-.06	-.12
Gregarious-Intimate	**.20**	**-.40**	-.02	-.02	**-.25**
Active-Reflective	**.18**	**-.52**	-.07	-.08	**-.16**
Enthusiastic-Quiet	**.18**	**-.52**	-.03	-.06	**-.24**
S-N Facet Scales					
Concrete-Abstract	**.16**	.11	-.11	.07	**.15**
Realistic-Imaginative	**.19**	.14	-.12	.08	**.16**
Practical-Conceptual	**.20**	.07	-.07	.04	.06
Experimental-Theoretical	**.16**	.06	**-.16**	.08	**.13**
Traditional-Original	**.22**	.13	**-.19**	.07	**.17**
T-F Facet Scales					
Logical-Empathetic	**.15**	-.01	-.06	**-.14**	**.15**
Reasonable-Compassionate	**.18**	-.10	-.12	**-.17**	**.14**
Questioning-Accommodating	.01	**-.18**	.13	**-.29**	.00
Critical-Accepting	-.07	-.04	-.03	**-.31**	.06
Tough-Tender	**.15**	-.13	-.11	**-.15**	**.14**
J-P Facet Scales					
Systematic-Casual	**.20**	-.08	**-.38**	.09	.06
Planful-Open-Ended	**.20**	**-.14**	**-.43**	.07	.08
Early Starting-Pressure-Prompted	**.20**	-.03	**-.40**	.10	**.18**
Scheduled-Spontaneous	**.20**	-.07	**-.39**	.13	.09
Methodical-Emergent	**.13**	-.01	**-.34**	.13	.08

Notes: EMO = Emotive, SOC = Social, PRO = Process, CON = Control, CHA = Change; $N = 216$; **Bold** indicates a correlation coefficient significant at $p < .05$.
Source: 2008 MBTI®/The Birkman Method® study.

TABLE 9.9   CORRELATION OF THE BIRKMAN METHOD® ORIENTATION NEEDS SCALES AND MBTI® STEP II FACET SCALES

MBTI® STEP II FACET SCALE	BIRKMAN NEEDS ORIENTATION SCALE				
	EMO	SOC	PRO	CON	CHA
E-I Facet Scales					
Initiating-Receiving	.11	-.09	-.09	-.02	.00
Expressive-Contained	-.02	-.02	-.03	.05	-.02
Gregarious-Intimate	**.22**	**-.21**	-.10	**.17**	.10
Active-Reflective	.10	-.07	-.08	.02	.06
Enthusiastic-Quiet	.12	-.12	**-.13**	.06	.01
S-N Facet Scales					
Concrete-Abstract	**.15**	-.02	-.02	**.13**	.04
Realistic-Imaginative	**.14**	.03	-.07	.07	**.13**
Practical-Conceptual	**.20**	**-.14**	**-.13**	.15	.07
Experimental-Theoretical	**.15**	-.08	-.10	.07	.02
Traditional-Original	**.18**	-.04	-.10	.11	**.15**
T-F Facet Scales					
Logical-Empathetic	**.19**	-.08	-.11	.07	**.23**
Reasonable-Compassionate	**.25**	**-.15**	**-.20**	.13	**.23**
Questioning-Accommodating	.04	.04	.03	**-.13**	.04
Critical-Accepting	.07	-.09	.04	-.01	**.18**
Tough-Tender	**.19**	-.13	**-.16**	.09	**.17**
J-P Facet Scales					
Systematic-Casual	.12	-.01	-.11	**.21**	**.18**
Planful-Open-Ended	.08	.03	**-.16**	.17	.11
Early Starting-Pressure-Prompted	.04	.06	-.08	.08	.05
Scheduled-Spontaneous	.10	.04	**-.16**	**.25**	.09
Methodical-Emergent	.07	-.01	-.06	**.15**	.10

Notes: EMO = Emotive, SOC = Social, PRO = Process, CON = Control, CHA = Change; N = 216; **Bold** indicates a correlation coefficient significant at $p < .05$.
Source: 2008 MBTI®/The Birkman Method® study.

TABLE 9.10   CORRELATION OF THE BIRKMAN METHOD® PREFERENCE USUAL SCALES AND MBTI® STEP II FACET SCALES

MBTI® STEP II FACET SCALE	BIRKMAN PREFERENCE USUAL SCALE						
	ACT	EMP	THO	COM	INT	INC	AUT
E-I Facet Scales							
Initiating-Receiving	**-.22**	**.14**	.12	**.45**	**-.72**	-.08	-.12
Expressive-Contained	**-.13**	.00	**.15**	**.17**	**-.58**	-.01	-.08
Gregarious-Intimate	**-.15**	**.19**	.13	**.24**	**-.46**	.02	-.04
Active-Reflective	**-.22**	.11	.09	**.30**	**-.60**	-.01	-.11
Enthusiastic-Quiet	**-.22**	**.14**	.06	**.30**	**-.60**	.01	-.11
S-N Facet Scales							
Concrete-Abstract	-.07	**.20**	.08	-.06	.12	.05	.05
Realistic-Imaginative	-.11	**.19**	**.16**	-.06	**.19**	**.13**	.01
Practical-Conceptual	**-.14**	**.18**	**.20**	-.07	.06	.09	-.01
Experimental-Theoretical	.01	**.23**	**.15**	-.03	.08	.08	.06
Traditional-Original	**-.14**	**.22**	**.16**	-.09	**.13**	.10	.02
T-F Facet Scales							
Logical-Empathetic	-.09	**.15**	**.14**	.12	.11	-.05	**-.17**
Reasonable-Compassionate	**-.15**	**.15**	**.17**	**.17**	.01	-.06	**-.21**
Questioning-Accommodating	-.02	.00	.01	**.21**	-.10	-.12	**-.32**
Critical-Accepting	.01	-.08	-.09	**.14**	.08	**-.17**	**-.33**
Tough-Tender	**-.14**	.12	.09	**.25**	.03	-.02	**-.20**
J-P Facet Scales							
Systematic-Casual	**-.18**	**.16**	**.16**	.12	-.01	**.13**	.02
Planful-Open-Ended	**-.20**	**.13**	**.21**	.11	**-.13**	.10	.02
Early Starting-Pressure-Prompted	**-.13**	**.20**	**.15**	.04	-.01	.09	.07
Scheduled-Spontaneous	**-.15**	**.19**	**.13**	.05	-.08	.12	.10
Methodical-Emergent	-.06	**.14**	.09	.05	.04	.08	.12

Notes: ACT = Activity, EMP = Empathy, THO = Thought, COM = Communication, INT = Interaction, INC = Incentive, AUT = Authority; $N = 216$; **Bold** indicates a correlation coefficient significant at $p < .05$.
Source: 2008 MBTI®/The Birkman Method® study.

	BIRKMAN PREFERENCE NEEDS SCALE						
MBTI® STEP II FACET SCALE	ACT	EMP	THO	COM	INT	INC	AUT
E-I Facet Scales							
Initiating-Receiving	-.11	.09	.07	.04	-.12	.08	-.11
Expressive-Contained	-.03	-.06	.00	-.02	-.05	.11	-.04
Gregarious-Intimate	**-.18**	**.21**	.11	**.13**	**-.23**	**.22**	.06
Active-Reflective	-.07	.12	.01	.01	-.11	.09	-.05
Enthusiastic-Quiet	**-.13**	.12	.02	.05	**-.15**	**.13**	-.04
S-N Facet Scales							
Concrete-Abstract	-.01	**.18**	**.16**	.04	.00	.09	.12
Realistic-Imaginative	-.06	**.15**	**.14**	.05	.08	.05	.07
Practical-Conceptual	-.12	**.17**	**.22**	**.16**	-.09	.17	.09
Experimental-Theoretical	-.03	**.17**	**.15**	.11	-.03	.06	.05
Traditional-Original	-.06	**.20**	**.17**	.08	.00	.11	.07
T-F Facet Scales							
Logical-Empathetic	**-.16**	.18	**.13**	.12	-.03	.08	.04
Reasonable-Compassionate	**-.24**	**.22**	**.15**	**.19**	-.08	**.14**	.07
Questioning-Accommodating	-.07	.02	.01	-.01	.06	-.08	**-.13**
Critical-Accepting	-.10	.04	.04	.08	-.08	-.01	-.01
Tough-Tender	**-.18**	**.18**	.09	**.17**	-.06	.06	.10
J-P Facet Scales							
Systematic-Casual	-.10	**.13**	.05	.07	.04	.19	**.16**
Planful-Open-Ended	-.07	.08	.04	.01	.06	.16	.12
Early Starting-Pressure-Prompted	.08	.12	.01	.01	.10	.05	.09
Scheduled-Spontaneous	-.03	**.16**	-.03	.00	.07	**.25**	**.17**
Methodical-Emergent	-.01	.11	.01	.04	.01	**.14**	.11

TABLE 9.11 CORRELATION OF THE BIRKMAN METHOD® PREFERENCE NEEDS SCALES AND MBTI® STEP II FACET SCALES

Notes: ACT = Activity, EMP = Empathy, THO = Thought, COM = Communication, INT = Interaction, INC = Incentive, AUT = Authority; N = 216; **Bold** indicates a correlation coefficient significant at $p < .05$.
Source: 2008 MBTI®/The Birkman Method® study.

	BIRKMAN OTHER SCALE		
MBTI® STEP II FACET SCALE	PA: USUAL	PA: NEEDS	PEA
E-I Facet Scales			
Initiating-Receiving	**.20**	.01	**.24**
Expressive-Contained	.05	-.05	**.17**
Gregarious-Intimate	**.13**	**.21**	-.01
Active-Reflective	**.15**	.04	**.17**
Enthusiastic-Quiet	.12	.06	.12
S-N Facet Scales			
Concrete-Abstract	.10	**.21**	-.05
Realistic-Imaginative	.12	**.14**	-.02
Practical-Conceptual	.09	**.19**	**-.14**
Experimental-Theoretical	.10	**.18**	-.04
Traditional-Original	**.15**	**.23**	-.05
T-F Facet Scales			
Logical-Empathetic	.08	**.21**	-.12
Reasonable-Compassionate	.08	**.25**	**-.16**
Questioning-Accommodating	-.04	-.01	.01
Critical-Accepting	-.06	.06	**-.14**
Tough-Tender	.09	**.20**	-.10
J-P Facet Scales			
Systematic-Casual	**.22**	**.19**	.09
Planful-Open-Ended	**.24**	**.14**	**.15**
Early Starting-Pressure-Prompted	**.24**	.06	**.18**
Scheduled-Spontaneous	**.23**	**.19**	.11
Methodical-Emergent	**.18**	**.19**	.08

TABLE 9.12 CORRELATION OF THE BIRKMAN METHOD® OTHER SCALES AND MBTI® STEP II FACET SCALES

Notes: PA = Personal Autonomy, PEA = Perspective Alignment; N = 216; **Bold** indicates a correlation coefficient significant at $p < .05$.
Source: 2008 MBTI®/The Birkman Method® study.

161

The Birkman Method® Interests and MBTI® Primary Scales Comparison

Since the factor scales within The Birkman Method® are social perception, it is anticipated that they would correlate highly with the MBTI® attitudes (i.e., EI, JP) and not the MBTI® functions (i.e., SN, TF). Since both The Birkman Method® Interest scales and the MBTI® primary scales measure internal preferences, it should be expected that they would correlate. The results in Table 9.13 are consistent with expectations.

TABLE 9.13	CORRELATIONS BETWEEN THE BIRKMAN METHOD® INTEREST SCALES AND THE PRIMARY MBTI® SCALES			
	MBTI® PRIMARY SCALES			
BIRKMAN INTEREST SCALE	EI	SN	TF	JP
Artistic	-0.02	**0.34**	0.11	0.13
Clerical	0.08	**-0.34**	0.01	**-0.26**
Literary	0.07	**0.34**	0.13	0.05
Mechanical	**0.19**	**-0.16**	**-0.15**	0.09
Musical	-0.08	**0.32**	**0.17**	0.13
Numerical	0.13	**-0.29**	**-0.20**	**-0.30**
Outdoor	0.01	-0.03	-0.08	**0.20**
Persuasive	**-0.38**	0.08	-0.04	-0.01
Scientific	**0.18**	-0.03	-0.13	0.08
Social Service	-0.06	-0.02	**0.24**	0.00

Notes: N = 216; EI = Extraversion-Introversion, SN = Sensing-Intuitive, TF = Thinking-Feeling, JP = Judging-Perceiving; **Bold** indicates a correlation coefficient significant at $p < .05$.
Source: 2008 MBTI®/The Birkman Method® study.

As seen in Table 9.14, The Birkman Method® Persuasive and Scientific Interest scales have significant mean differences when compared to the MBTI® Extraversion-Introversion types.

As seen in Table 9.15, The Birkman Method® Artistic, Clerical, Literary, Mechanical, Musical, Numerical, and Outdoor Interest Scales have significant mean differences when compared to the MBTI® Sensing-Intuitive types.

As seen in Table 9.16, The Birkman Method® Mechanical, Musical, and Social Service Interest scales have significant mean differences when compared to the MBTI® Thinking-Feeling types.

As seen in Table 9.17, The Birkman Method® Clerical and Numerical Interest scales have significant mean differences when compared to the MBTI® Judging-Perceiving types.

TABLE 9.14   THE BIRKMAN METHOD® INTEREST SCALE STATISTICS ACROSS MBTI® EXTRAVERSION-INTROVERSION TYPES

	MBTI – E		MBTI – I		OVERALL	
BIRKMAN SCALE	M	SD	M	SD	M Diff	d
Artistic	15.92	6.05	15.99	6.38	-0.07	
Clerical	6.11	5.92	6.69	7.18	-0.58	
Literary	13.31	4.84	13.62	5.03	-0.31	
Mechanical	6.06	5.91	8.01	7.58	-1.95	
Musical	11.54	4.87	11.12	5.94	0.41	
Numerical	6.24	6.49	6.66	6.49	-0.42	
Outdoor	11.42	6.98	11.19	7.16	0.23	
Persuasive	14.60	6.12	10.50	5.87	**4.10**	0.68
Scientific	8.75	5.20	10.64	5.22	**-1.88**	0.36
Social Service	22.20	7.80	22.42	6.82	-0.21	

Notes: N = 142 for E, N = 74 for I; **Bold** indicates significant mean difference (M Diff) at p < .05; Underline indicates moderate effect size (d), **Bold** indicates large effect size (d).
Source: 2008 MBTI®/The Birkman Method® study.

TABLE 9.15   THE BIRKMAN METHOD® INTEREST SCALE STATISTICS ACROSS MBTI® SENSING-INTUITIVE TYPES

	MBTI – S		MBTI – N		OVERALL	
BIRKMAN SCALE	M	SD	M	SD	M Diff	d
Artistic	12.69	6.57	17.02	5.62	**-4.34**	**0.74**
Clerical	9.02	9.10	5.40	4.85	**3.62**	0.58
Literary	10.70	5.48	14.32	4.34	**-3.62**	**0.78**
Mechanical	8.94	7.80	5.99	5.96	**2.95**	0.46
Musical	8.56	5.61	12.34	4.78	**-3.78**	**0.76**
Numerical	9.65	8.84	5.30	5.05	**4.35**	0.70
Outdoor	13.11	7.94	10.75	6.61	**2.36**	0.34
Persuasive	12.17	6.91	13.54	6.11	-1.37	
Scientific	9.96	5.21	9.21	5.29	0.75	
Social Service	21.52	7.75	22.53	7.37	-1.01	

Notes: N = 54 for S, N = 162 for N; **Bold** indicates significant mean difference (M Diff) at p < .05; Underline indicates moderate effect size (d), **Bold** indicates large effect size (d).
Source: 2008 MBTI®/The Birkman Method® study.

TABLE 9.16	THE BIRKMAN METHOD® INTEREST SCALE STATISTICS ACROSS MBTI® THINKING-FEELING TYPES					
	MBTI – T		MBTI – F		OVERALL	
BIRKMAN SCALE	M	SD	M	SD	M Diff	d
Artistic	15.24	6.29	16.79	5.90	-1.55	
Clerical	6.10	6.16	6.55	6.63	-0.45	
Literary	13.03	4.94	13.89	4.82	-0.86	
Mechanical	7.55	6.92	5.74	6.02	**1.81**	0.28
Musical	10.60	5.41	12.35	4.91	**-1.75**	0.34
Numerical	7.16	6.88	5.45	5.85	1.71	
Outdoor	12.07	7.06	10.47	6.91	1.60	
Persuasive	13.61	6.54	12.69	6.06	0.92	
Scientific	9.88	5.32	8.82	5.18	1.07	
Social Service	21.00	7.32	23.82	7.37	**-2.82**	<u>0.38</u>

Notes: N = 118 for T, *N* = 98 for F; **Bold** indicates significant mean difference *(M* Diff) at *p* < .05; <u>Underline</u> indicates moderate effect size *(d)*, **Bold** indicates large effect size *(d)*.
Source: 2008 MBTI®/The Birkman Method® study.

TABLE 9.17	THE BIRKMAN METHOD® INTEREST SCALE STATISTICS ACROSS MBTI® JUDGING-PERCEIVING TYPES					
	MBTI – J		MBTI – P		OVERALL	
BIRKMAN SCALE	M	SD	M	SD	M Diff	d
Artistic	15.44	6.46	16.36	5.88	-0.92	
Clerical	7.51	7.73	5.31	4.77	**2.21**	<u>0.35</u>
Literary	13.15	5.13	13.64	4.70	-0.48	
Mechanical	6.05	6.51	7.30	6.60	-1.25	
Musical	10.86	5.65	11.84	4.88	-0.98	
Numerical	8.05	7.67	5.00	4.91	**3.05**	<u>0.48</u>
Outdoor	10.46	7.31	12.08	6.72	-1.62	
Persuasive	13.24	6.40	13.15	6.29	0.09	
Scientific	8.84	5.34	9.86	5.19	-1.03	
Social Service	22.56	7.21	22.04	7.68	0.52	

Notes: N = 98 for J, *N* = 118 for P; **Bold** indicates significant mean difference *(M* Diff) at *p* < .05; <u>Underline</u> indicates moderate effect size *(d)*, **Bold** indicates large effect size *(d)*.
Source: 2008 MBTI®/The Birkman Method® study.

Correlations between The Birkman Method® Interest scales and MBTI® Step II facet scales are consistent with the prior The Birkman Method® Interest scale statistics across MBTI® types, as seen in Table 9.18 and Table 9.19. Overall congruence at the MBTI® primary and facet level is consistent with expectations. Without exception, The Birkman Method® Interest scales identify both the low and high ends of the bidirectional MBTI® Step II facet scales.

TABLE 9.18 · CORRELATIONS BETWEEN THE BIRKMAN METHOD® INTEREST SCALES AND MBTI® STEP II FACET SCALES

MBTI® STEP II FACET SCALE	BIRKMAN PREFERENCE USUAL SCALE				
	ART	CLE	LIT	MEC	MUS
E-I Facet Scales					
Initiating-Receiving	-.04	.06	.01	**.17**	-.04
Expressive-Contained	.02	.01	.10	.10	-.03
Gregarious-Intimate	.06	-.03	.12	**.19**	-.07
Active-Reflective	.03	.01	**.14**	**.15**	.02
Enthusiastic-Quiet	-.06	.08	.00	**.20**	-.11
S-N Facet Scales					
Concrete-Abstract	**.29**	**-.24**	**.33**	**-.20**	**.26**
Realistic-Imaginative	**.34**	**-.34**	**.27**	-.12	**.36**
Practical-Conceptual	**.29**	**-.21**	**.49**	**-.23**	**.26**
Experimental-Theoretical	**.23**	**-.25**	**.29**	**-.16**	**.24**
Traditional-Original	**.32**	**-.36**	**.24**	.03	**.29**
T-F Facet Scales					
Logical-Empathetic	**.15**	.02	.05	**-.17**	.13
Reasonable-Compassionate	-.01	.07	.12	**-.18**	**.16**
Questioning-Accommodating	-.11	**.25**	**-.17**	.05	-.10
Critical-Accepting	.01	**.20**	.05	**-.15**	.04
Tough-Tender	.09	.03	**.17**	-.05	**.14**
J-P Facet Scales					
Systematic-Casual	.13	**-.15**	.07	.04	**.14**
Planful-Open-ended	.10	**-.19**	.02	**.15**	.04
Early Starting-Pressure Prompted	.07	**-.16**	.06	.01	.05
Scheduled-Spontaneous	**.16**	**-.23**	.11	.04	**.14**
Methodical-Emergent	-.04	-.13	-.10	.12	-.05

Notes: ART = Artistic, CLE = Clerical, LIT = Literary, MEC = Mechanical, MUS = Musical; *N* = 216; **Bold** indicates a correlation coefficient significant at *p* < .05.
Source: 2008 MBTI®/The Birkman Method® study.

TABLE 9.19   CORRELATIONS BETWEEN THE BIRKMAN METHOD® INTEREST SCALES AND MBTI® STEP II FACET SCALES (CONTINUED)

MBTI® STEP II FACET SCALE	BIRKMAN INTEREST SCALE				
	NUM	OUT	PER	SCI	SOC
E-I Facet Scales					
Initiating-Receiving	0.06	0.01	**-0.34**	**0.21**	0.01
Expressive-Contained	0.06	-0.01	**-0.23**	**0.14**	-0.05
Gregarious-Intimate	0.03	0.06	**-0.28**	**0.16**	-0.12
Active-Reflective	0.06	0.02	**-0.33**	**0.15**	-0.09
Enthusiastic-Quiet	**0.14**	0.09	**-0.35**	**0.15**	-0.07
S-N Facet Scales					
Concrete-Abstract	**-0.20**	-0.11	0.06	0.01	0.01
Realistic-Imaginative	**-0.22**	-0.01	0.06	-0.04	-0.06
Practical-Conceptual	**-0.25**	-0.12	0.04	-0.05	0.03
Experimental-Theoretical	**-0.30**	-0.07	**0.16**	-0.06	0.03
Traditional-Original	**-0.26**	0.13	-0.02	0.05	-0.12
T-F Facet Scales					
Logical-Empathetic	**-0.18**	-0.10	0.02	**-0.16**	**0.22**
Reasonable-Compassionate	**-0.15**	-0.12	-0.03	-0.11	**0.31**
Questioning-Accommodating	0.10	0.02	-0.09	-0.03	0.07
Critical-Accepting	-0.02	**-0.14**	-0.02	**-0.17**	**0.18**
Tough-Tender	**-0.15**	0.01	**-0.15**	-0.06	0.12
J-P Facet Scales					
Systematic-Casual	**-0.27**	**0.16**	-0.01	0.05	-0.02
Planful-Open-ended	**-0.26**	**0.20**	-0.10	0.11	-0.03
Early Starting-Pressure Prompted	**-0.20**	0.10	0.05	0.00	0.06
Scheduled-Spontaneous	**-0.23**	**0.16**	-0.04	0.09	-0.05
Methodical-Emergent	**-0.16**	**0.15**	0.09	0.07	0.01

Notes: NUM = Numerical, OUT = Outdoor, PER = Persuasive, SCI = Scientific, SOC = Social Service; *N* = 216; **Bold** indicates a correlation coefficient significant at *p* < .05.
Source: 2008 MBTI®/The Birkman Method® study.

The Birkman Method® and MBTI® Summary

A number of salient points can be distilled from the tables above concerning The Birkman Method® and the MBTI®.

- *The Birkman Method® Orientation Usual scales (Social and Process) and MBTI® attitude scales (EI and JP) correlate highly*
- *The Birkman Method® Orientation Usual scales modestly correlate to the corresponding MBTI® SN and TF functions*
- *The Birkman Method® contains two non-personality scales, Personal Autonomy and Perspective Alignment, which·have no MBTI® equivalent*
- *The Birkman Method® contains 10 Interests scales with no MBTI® equivalent*

The Birkman Method® uses perceptions of "most people" to identify the perceptual orientations concerning others. The MBTI® has no equivalent measure.

The Birkman Method® and NEO Personality Inventory-Revised – International Personality Item Pool (NEO-R-IPIP) Comparison

The NEO-PI-R is a FFM personality measure developed by Costa and McCrae (1992). Birkman used the International Personality Item Pool version of the NEO-PI-R for convergent validity comparison with The Birkman Method®. The NEO-PI-R measures the Neuroticism, Extraversion, Openness to Experience, Agreeableness, and Conscientiousness dimensions of the FFM. Table 9.20 shows The Birkman Method® scale correlations with the NEO-R-IPIP. As shown, the Emotive Orientation Usual scale aligns positively with Neuroticism. The Social Orientation Usual scale has a strong correlation with Extraversion. The Process Orientation Usual scale is highly correlated with Conscientiousness, as expected. The Control Orientation Usual scale has a modest negative correlation with Agreeableness. The Change Orientation Usual scale has almost no correlation with Openness. This lack of correlation possibly can be accounted for by two explanations: 1) Openness to Experience is considered the weakest factor of the FFM (Eysenck, 1992), and 2) Openness to Experience is a broad construct of which the two scales may be accounting for variance from different construct space (Aluja, García, & García, 2003; Zuckerman, 1994). Significant correlations are bolded in Table 9.20.

The Birkman Method® and the Hogan Personality Inventory – International Personality Item Pool (HPI-IPIP) Comparison

In Table 9.21 and Table 9.22, The Birkman Method® scales are correlated with the HPI-IPIP (Hogan & Hogan, 2007). In Table 9.21, Emotive Orientation Usual is negatively correlated with the HPI-IPIP Adjustment scale, as expected. The Social Orientation Usual scale is positively correlated with Ambition, Sociability, and Likeability of the HPI-IPIP.

TABLE 9.20   CORRELATION OF THE BIRKMAN METHOD® SCALES AND NEO-R-IPIP

BIRKMAN SCALE	NEO-R-IPIP SCALE				
	NEO	EXT	OPEN	AGR	CON
Orientation Usual Scales					
Emotive	**.23**	**-.31**	-.01	-.12	**-.34**
Social	**-.23**	**.60**	**.27**	**.24**	.10
Process	**-.26**	.12	-.08	.18	**.63**
Control	.07	-.04	.04	-.17	-.13
Change	**.25**	.08	-.04	-.11	-.08
Orientation Needs Scales					
Emotive	.12	-.17	-.07	-.05	**-.27**
Social	-.09	.02	.00	.05	**.33**
Process	-.07	**.19**	.11	.12	.16
Control	-.04	-.15	-.14	-.08	-.02
Change	.12	**-.21**	-.03	-.06	-.11
Preference Usual Scales					
Activity	-.16	**.26**	.08	-.01	**.34**
Empathy	**.25**	**-.23**	.08	**-.19**	**-.29**
Thought	.15	**-.39**	-.10	-.11	-.18
Communication	**.28**	**-.45**	**-.22**	**-.23**	-.13
Interaction	-.11	**.58**	**.25**	**.19**	.04
Incentive	.12	-.11	-.03	-.14	**-.27**
Authority	.00	.04	.09	-.14	.05
Preference Needs Scales					
Activity	**-.20**	**.23**	.12	.02	**.25**
Empathy	.04	-.04	.00	-.04	**-.21**
Thought	.08	**-.31**	-.10	-.07	**-.28**
Communication	.15	-.03	.01	-.02	**-.20**
Interaction	-.02	.01	.00	.07	**.35**
Incentive	-.02	**-.21**	-.13	-.06	-.16
Authority	-.06	-.04	-.10	-.08	.14
Other Scales					
Personal Autonomy: Usual	**.23**	**-.30**	-.16	-.16	**-.31**
Personal Autonomy: Needs	.06	-.13	-.00	-.05	**-.29**
Perspective Alignment	.17	**-.22**	.02	-.13	-.05

Notes: NEO = Neuroticism, EXT = Extraversion, OPEN = Openness to Experience, AGR = Agreeableness, CON = Conscientiousness; $N = 106$; **Bold** indicates a correlation coefficient significant at $p < .05$.
Source: Birkman February 2007 Survey.

TABLE 9.21   CORRELATION OF THE BIRKMAN METHOD® SCALES AND THE HPI-IPIP SCALES

BIRKMAN SCALE	HPI-IPIP SCALE			
	ADJ	AMB	SOC	LIK
Orientation Usual Scales				
Emotive	**-.23**	-.01	-.03	-.16
Social	.08	**.34**	**.25**	**.28**
Process	.10	-.11	-.02	.04
Control	**-.25**	.04	.14	-.17
Change	-.17	.09	.03	.00
Orientation Needs Scales				
Emotive	-.14	-.06	.12	.01
Social	.01	.03	.06	.12
Process	-.10	.11	.14	.05
Control	.00	.11	**.21**	.01
Change	-.03	.03	.10	.02
Preference Usual Scales				
Activity	.05	-.04	-.01	.05
Empathy	**-.31**	-.01	-.04	**-.20**
Thought	-.09	-.12	-.02	-.05
Communication	-.09	**-.31**	-.15	**-.22**
Interaction	.04	**.28**	.27	**.26**
Incentive	**-.20**	.06	.15	**-.22**
Authority	**-.21**	.02	.08	-.07
Preference Needs Scales				
Activity	.12	.08	-.09	.04
Empathy	-.09	-.01	.13	.07
Thought	-.18	-.10	.06	-.05
Communication	-.06	-.01	.07	-.01
Interaction	-.03	.03	.14	.18
Incentive	-.01	.03	.15	-.13
Authority	.01	.14	**.20**	.14
Other Scales				
Personal Autonomy: Usual	**-.24**	-.10	-.15	-.19
Personal Autonomy: Needs	-.09	-.02	.11	-.03
Perspective Alignment	-.15	-.07	-.12	-.16

Notes: ADJ = Adjustment, AMB = Ambition, SOC = Sociability, LIK = Likeability; *N* = 103; **Bold** indicates a correlation coefficient significant at *p* < .05.
Source: Birkman April 2007 Survey.

TABLE 9.22 CORRELATION OF THE BIRKMAN METHOD® SCALES AND THE HPI-IPIP SCALES (CONTINUED)

	HPI-IPIP SCALE		
BIRKMAN SCALE	PRU	INT	LEA
Orientation Usual Scales			
Emotive	-.14	.00	.09
Social	.07	.17	-.03
Process	**.32**	-.08	-.15
Control	**-.27**	.07	-.12
Change	-.09	.05	-.12
Orientation Needs Scales			
Emotive	-.06	-.06	-.15
Social	.04	.11	.13
Process	.00	.13	.16
Control	-.14	.08	-.15
Change	-.08	.00	-.02
Preference Usual Scales			
Activity	.08	.02	.09
Empathy	-.17	.00	.18
Thought	.00	.06	.07
Communication	-.01	-.17	-.02
Interaction	.12	.13	-.07
Incentive	**-.31**	.00	-.06
Authority	-.14	.10	-.13
Preference Needs Scales			
Activity	.01	.08	**.26**
Empathy	-.08	-.03	-.01
Thought	-.04	-.09	-.19
Communication	-.04	-.10	-.13
Interaction	.03	.08	.09
Incentive	-.19	-.03	-.17
Authority	-.06	.16	-.08
Other Scales			
Personal Autonomy: Usual	-.18	-.09	-.01
Personal Autonomy: Needs	-.12	-.05	-.15
Perspective Alignment	-.13	.04	**.23**

Notes: PRU = Prudence, INT = Intellectance, LEA = Learning Approach; N = 103; **Bold** indicates a correlation coefficient significant at $p < .05$.
Source: Birkman April 2007 Survey.

The Birkman Method® and 16 Personality Factor Questionnaire - International Personality Item Pool (16PF-IPIP) Comparison

In Table 9.23 through Table 9.26, The Birkman Method® scales were correlated with the 16PF-IPIP (Conn & Rieke, 1994). In Table 9.23, Emotive Orientation Usual is negatively correlated with the 16PF Emotional Stability scale. The Social Orientation Usual scale is positively correlated with the Warmth scale of the 16PF. These relationships are expected since they are measuring similar constructs. The Activity, Empathy, and Thought Preference Usual subscales scales align as expected with Emotional Stability of the 16PF. The Authority Preference Usual subscale is positively correlated with the Assertiveness/Dominance scale of the 16PF. Other significant correlations are bolded in Table 9.23.

In Table 9.24, Social Orientation Usual and Interaction Usual align significantly with the 16PF Friendliness/Social Boldness and Gregariousness/Liveliness scales. Process Orientation Usual aligns with the 16PF Dutifulness/Rule-Consciousness scale. Communication Usual aligns with the 16PF Friendliness/Social Boldness scale. These relationships are expected due to the constructs they both are purporting to measure. Refer to bolded correlations in Table 9.24 for additional significant relationships.

In Table 9.25, the Emotive Orientation Usual is positively correlated with Distrust, Imagination/Abstractedness, and Anxiety/Apprehension of the 16PF. This is because Emotive describes someone who tends to be anxious and appears overly emotional when stressed. Social Orientation Usual and Interaction Usual are negatively related to Reserved/Privateness of the 16PF because they are measuring opposites of the same behavior, and the correlations are significant. Additional significant correlations are found in Table 9.25.

In table 9.26, it is shown that Emotive Orientation Usual is positively related to Emotionality/Tension of the 16PF. Process Orientation is positively related with Orderliness/Perfectionism because they are measuring similar constructs. Refer to the bolded correlations in Table 9.26 for additional significant correlations with The Birkman Method® and the 16PF-IPIP.

TABLE 9.23 CORRELATION OF THE BIRKMAN METHOD® SCALES AND THE 16PF-IPIP SCALES				
	16PF-IPIP SCALE			
BIRKMAN SCALE	WARM	INTE	STAB	ASSE
Orientation Usual Scales				
Emotive	.05	.03	**-.30**	-.06
Social	**.25**	.09	**.24**	**.32**
Process	**-.24**	-.10	.09	.05
Control	-.11	-.07	-.09	.20
Change	-.07	-.12	**-.31**	-.04
Orientation Needs Scales				
Emotive	.11	.05	-.15	.04
Social	-.04	-.05	.13	.15
Process	-.11	-.19	.01	-.04
Control	.03	-.10	-.13	.11
Change	.09	-.20	-.11	.06
Preference Usual Scales				
Activity	-.08	.01	**.29**	.08
Empathy	.04	.05	**-.22**	.02
Thought	-.04	.01	**-.23**	-.18
Communication	-.16	-.17	**-.27**	**-.32**
Interaction	**.27**	-.03	.13	**.22**
Incentive	-.01	-.16	-.15	.05
Authority	-.15	.02	-.01	**.25**
Preference Needs Scales				
Activity	.01	-.02	**.22**	.15
Empathy	.17	.05	-.07	.14
Thought	.06	.06	-.12	.04
Communication	.11	.06	-.18	-.10
Interaction	.04	-.02	.04	.15
Incentive	.03	-.14	-.18	-.05
Authority	.03	-.03	-.04	**.21**
Other Scales				
Personal Autonomy: Usual	-.01	-.03	-.23	-.03
Personal Autonomy: Needs	.03	-.02	-.18	.04
Perspective Alignment	-.16	-.08	-.12	-.12

Notes: WARM = Warmth, INTE = Intellectance/Reasoning, STAB = Emotional Stability, ASSE = Assertiveness/Dominance; *N* = 92;
Bold indicates a correlation coefficient significant at *p* < .05.
Source: Birkman June 2007 Survey.

TABLE 9.24 CORRELATION OF THE BIRKMAN METHOD® SCALES AND THE 16PF-IPIP SCALES (CONTINUED)

BIRKMAN SCALE	16PF-IPIP SCALE			
	GREG	DUTI	FRIE	SENS
Orientation Usual Scales				
Emotive	.11	-.11	-.09	.13
Social	**.23**	-.11	**.50**	.14
Process	-.10	**.27**	-.12	-.06
Control	.13	.01	.01	-.04
Change	.16	-.13	.03	.02
Orientation Needs Scales				
Emotive	.09	-.13	-.06	.15
Social	.11	.19	.08	-.06
Process	.10	**.26**	.06	-.09
Control	.13	-.11	.04	.00
Change	.10	.00	.07	.14
Preference Usual Scales				
Activity	-.01	.11	.16	-.17
Empathy	.16	-.12	-.01	.11
Thought	.05	.02	-.07	-.05
Communication	.00	.12	**-.30**	-.08
Interaction	**.40**	-.07	**.55**	.16
Incentive	.01	-.06	.01	.09
Authority	.18	.05	.01	-.12
Preference Needs Scales				
Activity	.05	-.05	**.21**	-.13
Empathy	.14	**-.22**	.04	.15
Thought	.09	-.08	-.07	.06
Communication	.10	-.12	-.02	.14
Interaction	**.27**	.18	.11	.04
Incentive	.08	- .18	-.01	.02
Authority	.14	-.02	.06	-.02
Other Scales				
Personal Autonomy: Usual	.04	-.05	-.15	.07
Personal Autonomy: Needs	-.08	-.19	-.07	.03
Perspective Alignment	.00	.17	-.15	-.11

Notes: GREG = Gregariousness/Liveliness, DUTI = Dutifulness/Rule-Consciousness, FRIE = Friendliness/ Social Boldness, SENS = Sensitivity
$N = 92$; **Bold** indicates a correlation coefficient significant at $p < .05$.
Source: Birkman June 2007 Survey.

TABLE 9.25   CORRELATION OF THE BIRKMAN METHOD® SCALES AND THE 16PF-IPIP SCALES (CONTINUED)

BIRKMAN SCALE	16PF-IPIP SCALE			
	DIST	IMAG	RESE	ANXI
Orientation Usual Scales				
Emotive	**.21**	**.35**	.06	**.29**
Social	**-.26**	-.05	**-.42**	**-.35**
Process	-.03	**-.37**	.16	.03
Control	.07	.17	-.16	**.21**
Change	.09	.10	-.02	**.28**
Orientation Needs Scales				
Emotive	.06	**.31**	-.13	.17
Social	-.18	-.19	-.08	-.09
Process	-.01	-.19	.07	.02
Control	.17	**.28**	-.17	.15
Change	.15	.13	-.09	.18
Preference Usual Scales				
Activity	**-.26**	**-.25**	-.15	-.19
Empathy	.13	**.35**	-.02	**.30**
Thought	.15	.20	.03	.18
Communication	**.34**	.09	.19	**.44**
Interaction	-.10	.01	**-.52**	-.14
Incentive	.17	.18	-.15	**.33**
Authority	-.02	.10	-.13	.06
Preference Needs Scales				
Activity	-.17	-.14	-.08	**-.24**
Empathy	.00	**.32**	**-.23**	.11
Thought	.03	**.27**	-.10	.10
Communication	**.22**	**.27**	-.01	**.25**
Interaction	-.07	-.04	-.14	.09
Incentive	**.31**	**.33**	-.11	.18
Authority	-.01	.15	-.17	.08
Other Scales				
Personal Autonomy: Usual	.24	.23	.05	.36
Personal Autonomy: Needs	.25	.26	-.09	.14
Perspective Alignment	.08	-.03	**.21**	.16

Notes: DIST = Distrust, IMAG = Imagination/Abstractedness, RESE = Reserve/Privateness, ANXI = Anxiety/ Apprehension; N = 92; **Bold** indicates a correlation coefficient significant at $p < .05$.
Source: Birkman June 2007 Survey.

TABLE 9.26 CORRELATION OF THE BIRKMAN METHOD® SCALES AND THE 16PF-IPIP SCALES (CONTINUED)

BIRKMAN SCALE	16PF-IPIP SCALE			
	COMP	INTR	ORDE	EMOT
Orientation Usual Scales				
Emotive	.10	.09	**-.28**	**.25**
Social	.16	-.17	.08	-.37
Process	-.19	.03	**.38**	.07
Control	.01	-.10	-.02	**.34**
Change	-.18	-.19	-.10	**.37**
Orientation Needs Scales				
Emotive	.17	.20	-.18	-.03
Social	-.10	**-.32**	.07	.09
Process	**-.20**	**-.22**	.08	.16
Control	.12	.00	-.11	.13
Change	.02	-.04	.06	.11
Preference Usual Scales				
Activity	-.09	-.18	**.22**	**-.23**
Empathy	.11	.04	**-.28**	**.22**
Thought	.01	-.06	-.16	.11
Communication	**-.21**	-.03	-.10	**.50**
Interaction	.06	**-.32**	.04	-.12
Incentive	.02	.08	.08	**.38**
Authority	.00	-.20	-.08	**.21**
Preference Needs Scales				
Activity	-.04	**-.26**	.07	-.10
Empathy	**.21**	.09	**-.23**	-.07
Thought	.14	**.24**	-.07	-.10
Communication	.12	**.21**	-.17	.10
Interaction	-.06	**-.30**	-.05	**.23**
Incentive	.15	.14	-.14	.15
Authority	.05	-.13	-.05	.08
Other Scales				
Personal Autonomy: Usual	-.04	-.01	-.11	.40
Personal Autonomy: Needs	.10	.25	-.02	.06
Perspective Alignment	-.17	-.20	-.09	**.38**

Notes: COMP = Complexity/Openness to Change, INTR = Introversion/Self-Reliance, ORDE = Orderliness/ Perfectionism, EMOT = Emotionality/Tension; N = 92; **Bold** indicates a correlation coefficient significant at $p < .05$.
Source: Birkman June 2007 Survey.

The Birkman Method® and Abridged Big Five-Dimensional Circumplex (AB5C-IPIP) Comparison

In Table 9.27 and Table 9.28, The Birkman Method® scales were correlated with the AB5C-IPIP (Hofstee, de Raad, & Goldberg, 1992). As shown in Table 9.27, Emotive Orientation Usual is negatively related to Assertiveness of the AB5C-IPIP. Social Orientation Usual is positively correlated with Assertiveness of the AB5C-IPIP. Control Orientation Usual is negatively associated with Empathy of the AB5C-IPIP.

In Table 9.28, it is shown that Social Orientation Usual is positively related to Gregariousness of the AB5C-IPIP. Control Orientation Usual, Incentive Usual, and Authority Usual are negatively related to Sympathy and Tenderness of the AB5C-IPIP because they are inversely related. Interaction Preference Usual is positively related to Gregariousness of the AB5C-IPIP, being a subscale of Social Orientation. Additional significant correlations are found in Table 9.28.

The Birkman Method® and the Jackson Personality Inventory (JPI-R-IPIP) Comparison

In Table 9.29, The Birkman Method® scales were correlated with JPI-R-IPIP (Jackson, 1994).

DIVERGENT CONSTRUCT VALIDITY

Besides establishing what The Birkman Method® measures, it is important to determine what The Birkman Method® does not measure. The associations of The Birkman Method® scales with a verbal aptitude measure, a general aptitude measure, and a clerical speed and accuracy measure are shown in Table 9.30. The average correlation absolute values are 0.06, 0.06, and 0.05, for the ability measures respectively. These statistics demonstrate that The Birkman Method® does not measure variance associated with these constructs. The highest correlation absolute values are 0.18, 0.15, and 0.17, respectively, which is additional empirical evidence that The Birkman Method® does not measure "abilities".

The Birkman Method® and the Job Descriptive Index (JDI) Comparison

Job satisfaction was measured with 25 items (5 items per facet) from an abbreviated version of the Job Descriptive Index (JDI; Smith, Kendall, & Hulin, 1969; revised by Roznowski, 1989; Stanton, et al., 2002). For each dimension, respondents indicated the extent to which they believed various aspects of their employment over the past four months could be described using terms such as "gives sense of accomplishment" (work satisfaction), "well paid" (pay satisfaction), "good chance for promotion" (promotion satisfaction), "praises good work" (supervision satisfaction), and "helpful" (coworker satisfaction). In Table 9.31, The Birkman Method® scales were correlated with the JDI. Note that although there were few significant correlations, Birkman scales do not consistently align with the JDI scales. This is due to the difference in measures. The Birkman Method® measures personality and social perceptions, whereas the JDI measures job satisfaction.

TABLE 9.27   CORRELATION OF THE BIRKMAN METHOD® SCALES AND THE AB5C-IPIP

BIRKMAN SCALE	AB5C SCALE		
	ASSE	EMPA	FRIE
Orientation Usual Scales			
Emotive	**-.43**	-.19	-.08
Social	**.44**	.03	.21
Process	.21	-.10	.07
Control	-.24	**-.40**	-.20
Change	-.01	-.07	.17
Orientation Needs Scales			
Emotive	**-.38**	-.02	-.09
Social	.13	.02	.11
Process	.17	**-.26**	.09
Control	**-.32**	-.03	-.15
Change	-.07	.06	-.12
Preference Usual Scales			
Activity	**.31**	.05	.13
Empathy	**-.41**	-.21	.00
Thought	**-.35**	-.20	-.15
Communication	**-.42**	.05	-.05
Interaction	**.36**	.11	**.33**
Incentive	-.21	**-.41**	-.15
Authority	-.20	**-.27**	-.18
Preference Needs Scales			
Activity	.23	-.01	-.02
Empathy	**-.35**	-.04	-.07
Thought	**-.38**	.01	-.24
Communication	-.09	.01	-.02
Interaction	.13	.04	.15
Incentive	**-.28**	-.04	-.16
Authority	**-.28**	-.01	-.10
Other Scales			
Personal Autonomy: Usual	**-.31**	**-.29**	-.09
Personal Autonomy: Needs	-.20	.00	-.16
Perspective Alignment	-.11	-.18	-.04

Notes: ASSE = Assertiveness, EMPA = Empathy, FRIE = Friendliness; *N* = 64; **Bold** indicates a correlation coefficient significant at *p* < .05.
Source: Birkman December 2007 survey.

TABLE 9.28 CORRELATION OF THE BIRKMAN METHOD® SCALES AND THE AB5C-IPIP (CONTINUED)

BIRKMAN SCALE	AB5C SCALE		
	GREG	SYMP	TEND
Orientation Usual Scales			
Emotive	-.11	-.01	-.05
Social	**.39**	.06	.11
Process	.03	-.09	-.13
Control	-.09	**-.36**	**-.30**
Change	.10	.00	.11
Orientation Needs Scales			
Emotive	-.11	-.04	.02
Social	.03	.11	.12
Process	.12	-.03	-.04
Control	-.14	-.04	-.15
Change	-.19	-.06	-.07
Preference Usual Scales			
Activity	.13	-.04	-.10
Empathy	-.04	-.01	-.07
Thought	-.18	-.09	-.22
Communication	-.19	.07	.05
Interaction	**.51**	.18	.24
Incentive	-.13	**-.36**	**-.28**
Authority	-.03	**-.26**	-.23
Preference Needs Scales			
Activity	.04	-.06	-.16
Empathy	-.08	-.09	-.06
Thought	-.22	-.03	.01
Communication	.02	-.08	-.05
Interaction	.06	.11	.14
Incentive	-.12	-.08	-.12
Authority	-.12	.01	-.14
Other Scales			
Personal Autonomy: Usual	-.16	-.18	-.18
Personal Autonomy: Needs	-.12	-.12	-.13
Perspective Alignment	-.10	-.03	-.03

Notes: GREG = Gregariousness, SYMP = Sympathy, TEND = Tenderness; $N = 64$; **Bold** indicates a correlation coefficient significant at $p < .05$.
Source: Birkman December 2007 survey.

TABLE 9.29 CORRELATION OF THE BIRKMAN METHOD® SCALES AND JPI-R-IPIP

BIRKMAN SCALE	JPI SCALE		
	NONC	NONT	RT
Orientation Usual Scales			
Emotive	-.09	.19	-.14
Social	.15	-.19	.16
Process	-.04	-.09	-.13
Control	-.04	.03	-.18
Change	-.12	.05	-.02
Orientation Needs Scales			
Emotive	-.11	-.04	-.04
Social	-.01	.10	.14
Process	-.02	.03	-.03
Control	.01	-.05	.04
Change	.08	-.13	.06
Preference Usual Scales			
Activity	.04	-.10	.06
Empathy	-.13	.19	-.15
Thought	.01	.19	-.14
Communication	**-.27**	.17	-.22
Interaction	.00	-.16	.08
Incentive	-.05	.09	-.12
Authority	-.02	-.03	-.17
Preference Needs Scales			
Activity	.15	.04	-.01
Empathy	-.07	.00	-.02
Thought	-.07	-.11	-.13
Communication	-.14	-.03	-.13
Interaction	-.11	.13	.11
Incentive	-.08	.01	-.02
Authority	.09	-.10	.09
Other Scales			
Personal Autonomy: Usual	-.12	.05	-.07
Personal Autonomy: Needs	.03	-.11	-.02
Perspective Alignment	-.06	.24	-.08

Notes: NONC = Non-Conformity, NONT = Non-Traditionalism, RT = Risk-Taking; *N* = 64; **Bold** indicates a correlation coefficient significant at *p* < .05.
Source: Birkman December 2007 survey.

TABLE 9.30   CORRELATION OF THE BIRKMAN METHOD® SCALES AND ABILITY SCALES

BIRKMAN SCALE	ABILITY SCALE		
	VA	GA	Clerical S/A
Orientation Usual Scales			
Emotive	**-.11**	**-.11**	.08
Social	**.06**	**.13**	-.04
Process	**.07**	.02	.04
Control	**-.05**	**.04**	.02
Change	-.02	.00	.07
Orientation Needs Scales			
Emotive	**-.04**	-.01	.02
Social	-.02	.01	-.04
Process	**-.06**	**-.05**	.02
Control	**-.05**	**-.06**	.07
Change	**-.06**	**-.05**	.17
Preference Usual Scales			
Activity	**.10**	**.10**	-.14
Empathy	**-.08**	**-.08**	.00
Thought	**-.12**	**-.11**	.12
Communication	**-.06**	**-.11**	.11
Interaction	**.05**	**.11**	.07
Incentive	**-.07**	.01	.00
Authority	-.02	**.06**	.03
Preference Needs Scales			
Activity	.01	.00	-.05
Empathy	**-.05**	-.01	.01
Thought	**-.05**	**-.04**	-.03
Communication	**.04**	-.01	.09
Interaction	.00	.01	.02
Incentive	**-.06**	**-.06**	.07
Authority	**-.04**	**-.04**	.07
Other Scales			
Personal Autonomy: Usual	**-.16**	**-.15**	-.08
Personal Autonomy: Needs	**-.12**	**-.07**	-.02
Perspective Alignment	**-.07**	**-.06**	-.01

Notes: Verbal Aptitude (VA) = Birkman Word Matching Survey, *N* = 2,613; General Aptitude (GA) = Wonderlic Personnel Test: Form V, *N* = 2,767; Clerical S/A = Clerical Speed and Accuracy - DAT: Differential Aptitude Tests for Personnel and Career Assessment, *N* = 51; **Bold** indicates a correlation coefficient significant at *p* < .05.
Source: Random Birkman online examinees from 01/01/2007 to 02/01/2008.

TABLE 9.31 · CORRELATION OF THE BIRKMAN METHOD® SCALES AND JDI SCALES

BIRKMAN SCALE	JDI SCALE				
	CW	PAY	PRO	SUP	WORK
Orientation Usual Scales					
Emotive	-.22	.06	-.19	-.15	**-.32**
Social	.02	.03	.04	-.14	.09
Process	-.11	-.13	-.09	-.11	-.10
Control	-.06	.13	-.01	-.21	-.23
Change	.11	-.09	.08	.02	.13
Orientation Needs Scales					
Emotive	.12	.25	-.17	.17	-.09
Social	-.02	-.21	-.13	**-.26**	-.10
Process	-.12	-.04	-.05	-.23	-.06
Control	.12	.20	.02	.17	-.10
Change	.23	.12	.11	.19	.11
Preference Usual Scales					
Activity	.12	-.08	.19	.09	**.28**
Empathy	-.24	.05	-.16	-.16	**-.29**
Thought	-.19	.03	-.14	-.17	**-.27**
Communication	-.02	.01	-.01	.11	-.06
Interaction	.02	.05	.06	-.14	.10
Incentive	-.07	.12	-.11	-.24	**-.31**
Authority	-.02	.10	.08	-.12	-.10
Preference Needs Scales					
Activity	-.17	**-.27**	.10	-.09	.01
Empathy	.08	.21	-.16	.16	-.13
Thought	.08	.18	-.16	.22	-.06
Communication	.13	.25	.19	**.37**	.21
Interaction	.09	-.11	-.04	-.09	.02
Incentive	.06	.19	-.06	.13	-.15
Authority	.14	.15	.09	.17	-.02
Other Scales					
Personal Autonomy: Usual	-.07	.05	-.10	-.05	-.09
Personal Autonomy: Needs	.02	.14	-.04	.12	-.08
Perspective Alignment	-.22	-.19	-.07	**-.34**	-.19

Notes: CW = Coworkers, PRO = Promotion, SUP = Supervision; $N = 62$; **Bold** indicates a correlation coefficient significant at $p < .05$.
Source: Birkman September 2007 survey.

The Birkman Method® and Emotional Intelligence - International Personality Item Pool (EI-IPIP) Comparison

Emotional intelligence (EI) is the ability to be aware of and regulate emotions of the self or others. In Table 9.32 and Table 9.33, The Birkman Method® scales were correlated with the EI-IPIP (Barchard, 2001). There are virtually no significant relationships between The Birkman Method® scales and EI-IPIP constructs. EI is thought to be distinct from personality in that it refers to an internal cognitive state of being able to recognize emotions. Birkman scales involving emotions are part of one's perceptions and personality, not ability.

The Birkman Method® and Personal Attribute Survey - International Personality Item Pool (PAS-IPIP) Comparison

In Table 9.34, The Birkman Method® scales were correlated with the PAS-IPIP (Buss, 1980; Paulhus, 1991; Snyder, 1974).

The Birkman Method® and Positive and Negative Affect Schedule – Expanded Form (PANAS-X) Comparison

The Positive and Negative Affect Schedule – Expanded Form (PANAS-X; Watson & Clark, 1994; Watson, Clark, & Tellegen, 1988) is a measure that assesses state (e.g., how one feels "right now"). Examples include "excited," "enthusiastic," "nervous," "irritated," etc. In Table 9.35 through Table 9.37, The Birkman Method® scales are correlated with the PANAS-X.

In Table 9.35, The Birkman Method® Emotive Orientation Usual scale correlates highly with Negative Affect and Fear, and negatively with Positive Affect. Since Emotive Orientation in essence measures neuroticism, these relationships with the PANAS-X scales are expected. The same can be said for The Birkman Method® Preference subscales Activity, Empathy, and Thought Usual and the previously mentioned PANAS-X scales. Significant correlations between The Birkman Method® and the PANAS-X are bolded and found in Table 9.35 through Table 9.37. Although affect and personality are different constructs, terms used in the PANAS-X items are words commonly found in descriptors of personality traits; and some high correlations would be expected.

The Birkman Method® and Six Factor Personality Questionnaire (6FPQ-IPIP): Independence Facet, Multidimensional Personality Questionnaire (MPQ-IPIP): Risk-Avoidance Facet, and HEXACO Personality Inventory (HEXACO-IPIP): Unconventionality Subfacet of Openness Facet Comparison

In Table 9.38, The Birkman Method® scales were correlated with 6FPQ-IPIP Independence facet (Jackson, Paunonen, & Tremblay, 2000), MPQ-IPIP Risk-Avoidance facet (Tellegen, 2000), and HEXACO-IPIP Unconventionality subfacet of Openness facet (Lee & Ashton, 2004) scales.

TABLE 9.32   CORRELATION OF THE BIRKMAN METHOD® SCALES AND EI-IPIP SCALES

BIRKMAN SCALE	EI-IPIP SCALES			
	AE	EBDM	EC	NE
Orientation Usual Scales				
Emotive	.06	.12	-.02	.09
Social	.07	.06	-.08	.02
Process	-.02	-.18	.05	-.13
Control	-.02	-.05	-.17	.11
Change	-.02	.16	-.15	.04
Orientation Needs Scales				
Emotive	.00	.11	-.03	-.11
Social	-.08	-.10	.10	.12
Process	**-.24**	-.04	.07	-.10
Control	-.10	-.03	-.15	-.05
Change	.09	.13	.04	-.16
Preference Usual Scales				
Activity	-.10	-.07	-.09	-.12
Empathy	.02	.16	-.10	.06
Thought	.05	-.02	.05	.06
Communication	.04	-.06	.15	.04
Interaction	.17	.04	.02	.08
Incentive	.02	.00	-.06	.10
Authority	-.05	-.09	**-.23**	.10
Preference Needs Scales				
Activity	.04	.01	-.07	**.20**
Empathy	.03	.16	-.08	-.06
Thought	-.01	.08	-.02	-.02
Communication	.05	.07	.01	-.17
Interaction	-.07	-.09	.16	.05
Incentive	-.04	-.03	.02	-.07
Authority	-.13	-.02	**-.25**	-.01
Other Scales				
Personal Autonomy: Usual	-.01	.12	-.04	.06
Personal Autonomy: Needs	.07	.15	-.07	-.12
Perspective Alignment	-.06	-.02	.08	.17

Notes: AE = Attention to Emotions, EBDM = Emotional-Based Decision-Making, EC = Empathic Concerns, NE = Negative Expressivity; $N = 74$; **Bold** indicates a correlation coefficient significant at $p < .05$.
Source: Birkman April 2007 survey.

VALIDITY

TABLE 9.33   CORRELATION OF THE BIRKMAN METHOD® SCALES AND EI-IPIP SCALES (CONTINUED)

	EI-IPIP SCALES		
BIRKMAN SCALE	PE	RD	RJ
Orientation Usual Scales			
Emotive	.00	-.11	-.13
Social	.16	.04	.12
Process	-.10	-.08	-.04
Control	-.08	-.17	-.18
Change	.07	.03	.18
Orientation Needs Scales			
Emotive	.09	-.13	-.10
Social	-.03	.04	.10
Process	**-.29**	-.11	-.14
Control	-.01	-.15	.08
Change	-.02	-.13	.01
Preference Usual Scales			
Activity	-.08	.01	.07
Empathy	-.01	-.13	-.13
Thought	-.12	-.16	-.17
Communication	-.22	.01	-.18
Interaction	.06	.07	.04
Incentive	.00	-.11	-.14
Authority	-.14	-.20	-.18
Preference Needs Scales			
Activity	-.09	.04	.12
Empathy	.03	-.18	-.08
Thought	.16	-.02	-.05
Communication	.05	-.08	-.04
Interaction	.00	.00	.12
Incentive	.01	-.12	-.01
Authority	-.03	-.13	.14
Other Scales			
Personal Autonomy: Usual	.08	-.18	-.02
Personal Autonomy: Needs	.05	-.11	.02
Perspective Alignment	-.17	.01	-.12

Notes: PE = Positive Expressivity, RD = Responsive Distress, RJ = Responsive Joy; $N = 74$; **Bold** indicates a correlation coefficient significant at $p < .05$.
Source: Birkman April 2007 survey.

184

TABLE 9.34 CORRELATION OF THE BIRKMAN METHOD® SCALES AND PAS-IPIP SCALES

BIRKMAN SCALE	PAS-IPIP SCALE			
	IM	PRIVATE SC	PUBLIC SC	SM
Orientation Usual Scales				
Emotive	**-.21**	.19	.19	.07
Social	.07	-.11	**-.30**	**.26**
Process	**.24**	.01	-.10	**-.21**
Control	**-.33**	.02	-.04	.08
Change	-.13	.09	**.21**	.15
Orientation Needs Scales				
Emotive	-.16	**.29**	.07	-.07
Social	.02	-.10	-.12	.04
Process	.03	-.03	-.13	.04
Control	-.05	.05	.11	.00
Change	.14	-.02	.03	.00
Preference Usual Scales				
Activity	.16	**-.27**	-.18	.05
Empathy	**-.25**	.12	.12	.14
Thought	-.04	.08	**.27**	.03
Communication	-.11	.14	**.38**	-.12
Interaction	.00	-.05	-.14	**.33**
Incentive	**-.31**	.00	.04	.04
Authority	**-.22**	.03	-.11	.09
Preference Needs Scales				
Activity	.12	**-.36**	-.03	.07
Empathy	-.15	.20	.06	-.02
Thought	-.13	.15	.09	-.14
Communication	-.02	.12	.16	.00
Interaction	.01	-.07	-.06	.08
Incentive	-.09	.06	.10	.00
Authority	.00	.03	.08	.00
Other Scales				
Personal Autonomy: Usual	**-.21**	-.02	.10	-.06
Personal Autonomy: Needs	-.04	.15	.07	-.11
Perspective Alignment	-.13	-.06	.07	.04

Notes: IM = Impression Management, SC = Self-Consciousness, SM = Self Monitoring; *N* = 87; **Bold** indicates a correlation coefficient significant at *p* < .05.
Source: Birkman July 2007 survey.

TABLE 9.35   CORRELATION OF THE BIRKMAN METHOD® SCALES AND THE PANAS-X SCALES

BIRKMAN SCALE	PANAS-X SCALE				
	NEAF	POAF	FEAR	HOST	GUILT
Orientation Usual Scales					
Emotive	**.38**	**-.26**	**.31**	.19	.21
Social	**-.28**	**.24**	-.20	-.21	**-.26**
Process	-.11	.13	.02	-.18	-.15
Control	.03	-.19	.05	.13	-.01
Change	.09	-.01	.07	.01	.11
Orientation Needs Scales					
Emotive	**.22**	-.07	**.22**	.18	.19
Social	-.15	-.02	-.17	-.09	-.08
Process	.05	.01	.02	.08	.03
Control	.12	-.07	.13	.05	.06
Change	.16	-.05	.23	.04	.09
Preference Usual Scales					
Activity	**-.22**	**.22**	-.12	-.08	-.10
Empathy	**.44**	**-.23**	**.38**	**.25**	**.24**
Thought	**.23**	**-.22**	**.23**	.10	.19
Communication	**.31**	-.14	**.26**	.16	**.22**
Interaction	-.17	**.27**	-.07	-.21	**-.23**
Incentive	.10	-.13	.05	.15	.03
Authority	-.04	-.17	.03	.07	-.03
Preference Needs Scales					
Activity	-.11	-.01	-.04	-.10	-.03
Empathy	**.23**	-.09	**.24**	.17	.20
Thought	.14	-.07	.21	.14	**.23**
Communication	.19	.06	**.23**	.07	.02
Interaction	-.08	.02	-.08	-.09	-.11
Incentive	.13	-.07	.14	.05	.08
Authority	.07	-.05	.09	.03	.01
Other Scales					
Personal Autonomy: Usual	.14	-.21	.08	.05	.12
Personal Autonomy: Needs	.16	.00	.16	.14	.17
Perspective Alignment	.12	-.21	.02	.12	.10

Notes: NEAF = Negative Affect, POAF = Positive Affect, HOST = Hostility; $N = 83$; **Bold** indicates a correlation coefficient significant at $p < .05$.
Source: Birkman August 2007 survey.

TABLE 9.36   CORRELATION OF THE BIRKMAN METHOD® SCALES AND THE PANAS-X SCALES (CONTINUED)

BIRKMAN SCALE	PANAS-X SCALE				
	SADN	JOVI	SEAS	ATTE	SHYN
Orientation Usual Scales					
Emotive	**.37**	-.16	-.20	**-.32**	**.24**
Social	**-.27**	.17	.15	.15	**-.35**
Process	-.12	.06	-.01	.21	-.02
Control	.08	-.11	.03	**-.22**	-.08
Change	.07	.01	.08	-.08	-.06
Orientation Needs Scales					
Emotive	**.31**	-.08	-.03	-.08	.20
Social	**-.26**	-.06	-.01	.11	-.07
Process	-.13	.10	-.13	.04	.08
Control	**.28**	-.07	.06	.01	.11
Change	**.31**	.02	-.03	-.08	.07
Preference Usual Scales					
Activity	**-.28**	.20	**.23**	**.26**	-.13
Empathy	**.38**	-.12	-.14	**-.30**	**.23**
Thought	**.24**	-.07	-.19	**-.25**	**.29**
Communication	**.22**	-.07	-.14	-.11	**.26**
Interaction	**-.24**	**.23**	.12	.15	**-.34**
Incentive	.16	-.05	.08	-.17	.00
Authority	.00	-.13	-.01	-.19	-.12
Preference Needs Scales					
Activity	-.15	.05	.09	.07	-.06
Empathy	**.31**	-.07	.02	-.07	.19
Thought	**.27**	-.08	-.02	-.05	**.25**
Communication	**.22**	.08	-.03	-.10	.06
Interaction	**-.22**	-.02	-.04	.09	-.06
Incentive	**.28**	-.06	.07	-.01	.13
Authority	.20	-.06	.02	.03	.05
Other Scales					
Personal Autonomy: Usual	.15	-.03	-.10	**-.25**	.08
Personal Autonomy: Needs	**.31**	.05	.10	-.05	.21
Perspective Alignment	-.03	-.11	-.15	-.19	.09

Notes: SADN = Sadness, JOVI = Joviality, SEAS = Self Assurance, ATTE = Attentiveness, SHYN = Shyness; *N* = 83; **Bold** indicates a correlation coefficient significant at *p* < .05.
Source: Birkman August 2007 survey.

9 VALIDITY

BIRKMAN SCALE	PANAS-X SCALE		
	FATI	SERE	SURP
Orientation Usual Scales			
Emotive	**.32**	-.09	.02
Social	**-.23**	.04	.07
Process	-.02	-.13	.04
Control	.08	-.01	-.04
Change	.09	-.11	.00
Orientation Needs Scales			
Emotive	**.38**	.01	.09
Social	-.17	-.12	-.18
Process	-.07	-.21	-.03
Control	.18	.11	.06
Change	.18	-.03	.08
Preference Usual Scales			
Activity	**-.31**	.10	.04
Empathy	**.29**	-.09	.04
Thought	.20	.00	.07
Communication	.13	-.10	-.04
Interaction	**-.26**	-.04	.08
Incentive	.08	.00	.08
Authority	.05	-.01	-.12
Preference Needs Scales			
Activity	**-.27**	.01	-.14
Empathy	**.35**	.03	.04
Thought	**.27**	-.04	.05
Communication	.16	.03	.17
Interaction	-.13	-.18	-.14
Incentive	.17	.15	.08
Authority	.13	.04	.03
Other Scales			
Personal Autonomy: Usual	.08	.02	-.13
Personal Autonomy: Needs	**.23**	.12	.18
Perspective Alignment	-.04	-.14	-.15

TABLE 9.37 CORRELATION OF THE BIRKMAN METHOD® SCALES AND THE PANAS-X SCALES (CONTINUED)

Notes: FATI = Fatigue, SERE = Serenity, SURP = Surprise; N = 83; **Bold** indicates a correlation coefficient significant at $p < .05$.
Source: Birkman August 2007 survey.

188

TABLE 9.38 CORRELATION OF THE BIRKMAN METHOD® SCALES AND 6FPQ-IPIP: INDEPENDENCE FACET, MPQ-IPIP: RISK-AVOIDANCE FACET, AND HEXACO-IPIP: UNCONVENTIONALITY SUBFACET OF OPENNESS FACET SCALES

	6FPQ, MPQ, & O SCALE		
BIRKMAN SCALE	FA INDE	RA	UNCO
Orientation Usual Scales			
Emotive	-.10	.12	.06
Social	.08	-.09	.03
Process	.02	.00	-.15
Control	.00	.04	-.06
Change	-.01	-.04	-.01
Orientation Needs Scales			
Emotive	-.01	.07	.22
Social	-.01	-.08	-.18
Process	-.08	-.05	-.19
Control	.08	-.02	.17
Change	.09	-.04	.16
Preference Usual Scales			
Activity	.17	-.10	-.10
Empathy	-.07	.10	.04
Thought	.06	.12	-.02
Communication	-.20	.15	-.12
Interaction	-.04	-.02	-.06
Incentive	-.08	.00	-.10
Authority	.06	.07	-.01
Preference Needs Scales			
Activity	.14	-.02	-.17
Empathy	.07	.05	.21
Thought	-.04	.14	.14
Communication	-.15	.12	.15
Interaction	-.12	-.03	-.16
Incentive	-.04	-.04	.16
Authority	.18	.00	.13
Other Scales			
Personal Autonomy: Usual	-.05	-.02	.08
Personal Autonomy: Needs	.12	.03	.24
Perspective Alignment	-.11	.03	-.21

Notes: INDE = Independence, RA = Risk-Avoidance, UNCO = Unconventional; *N* = 64; **Bold** indicates a correlation coefficient significant at *p* < .05.
Source: Birkman December 2007 survey.

ADJECTIVE CHECKLIST VALIDITY

For additional construct meaning for The Birkman Method® Usual scales, the Multiple Affect Adjective Check List-Revised (John, 1990) was correlated with each scale. The highest adjective correlates for each Birkman Method® Usual scale are shown in Table 9.39 and Table 9.40.

TABLE 9.39 CORRELATION OF THE BIRKMAN METHOD® ORIENTATION USUAL SCALES AND ADJECTIVE CHECKLIST

EMOTIVE		SOCIAL		PROCESS		CONTROL		CHANGE	
Temperamental	.21	Subdued	-.47	Daring	-.23	Gentle	-.28	Disciplined	-.21
Irritable	.23	Solitary	-.38	Careful	.21	Warm-Hearted	-.26	Edgy	.25
Moody	.25	Timid	-.37	Obedient	.22	Helpful	-.21	Dramatic	.30
Worried	.26	Distant	-.26	Efficient	.31	Bossy	.23		
Hesitant	.28	Sociable	.41	Neat	.31	Hard-Hearted	.23		
Fickle	.29	Talkative	.41	Organized	.31	Combative	.25		
		Vivacious	.41	Disciplined	.35	Commanding	.27		
		Outgoing	.42	Precise	.35				
		Gregarious	.50	Orderly	.41				
		Lively	.51						

Notes: N = 86.
Source: Birkman March 2007 survey.

TABLE 9.40 CORRELATION OF THE BIRKMAN METHOD® PREFERENCE USUAL SCALES AND ADJECTIVE CHECKLIST

ACTIVITY		THOUGHT		INTERACTION		EMPATHY		COMMUNICATION	
Subdued	-.32	Suspicious	.26	Subdued	-.50	Touchy	.21	Daring	-.42
Hesitant	.25	Nervous	.27	Solitary	-.37	Temperamental	.22	Tough	-.37
Hard-Working	.27	Hesitant	.29	Distant	-.26	Moody	.22	Powerful	-.35
Lively	.30	Fickle	.32	Vivacious	.37	Oversensitive	.23	Forceful	-.32
		Timid	.40	Lively	.38	Suspicious	.29		
				Sociable	.41				
INCENTIVE				Outgoing	.42			AUTHORITY	
Commanding	.21			Talkative	.45			Gentle	-.22
Self-Admiring	.25			Gregarious	.53			Bossy	.23
Self-Centered	.29							Combative	.30

Notes: N = 86.
Source: Birkman March 2007 survey.

CRITERION-RELATED VALIDITY

Numerous studies (e.g., Furnham & Fudge, 2008; Judge, Bono, Ilies, & Gerhardt, 2002; Judge, Heller, & Mount, 2002) have shown the FFM to be related and predictive of many job-related criteria (e.g., job performance, job satisfaction, turnover, retention, leadership, organizational fit, safety, sales, customer service, teamwork). The Birkman Method® has been shown to measure the FFM, environmental needs, and interests. Studies (e.g., Arvey & Dewhirst, 1979) also have shown that occupational interests are predictive of work-related criteria (e.g., job satisfaction, tenure). The following paragraph discusses one of the criterion studies used to directly establish criterion-related validity with The Birkman Method®. Additional criterion-related validity studies can be provided as requested.

Work Satisfaction

One facet of job satisfaction is work satisfaction. Work satisfaction is defined as a worker's feelings toward the tasks that make up the job (Smith, Kendall, & Hulin, 1969). Via Pearson product correlations and stepwise multiple regression, data were analyzed to examine the predictability of work satisfaction by The Birkman Method® scales. Results are shown in Tables 9.41 and 9.42.

TABLE 9.41 CORRELATION OF THE BIRKMAN METHOD® SCALES AND WORK SATISFACTION

	WORK SATISFACTION
Orientation Usual Scales	
Emotive	**-.29**
Social	**.21**
Process	.15
Control	-.13
Change	-.07
Orientation Needs Scales	
Emotive	**-.22**
Social	.13
Process	.16
Control	-.18
Change	-.08
Preference Usual Scales	
Activity	**.25**
Empathy	**-.27**
Thought	**-.22**
Communication	**-.22**
Interaction	.14
Incentive	-.15
Authority	-.09
Preference Needs Scales	
Activity	.19
Empathy	**-.20**
Thought	-.15
Communication	-.10
Interaction	.12
Incentive	-.18
Authority	-.13
Other Scales	
Personal Autonomy: Usual	**-.26**
Personal Autonomy: Needs	-.19
Perspective Alignment	-.03

Notes: N = 17,375; **Bold** indicates a correlation coefficient equal to or greater than .20.

TABLE 9.42   STEPWISE REGRESSION RESULTS

BIRKMAN SCALE	ADJUSTED R SQUARED	R SQUARED CHANGE
Emotive Orientation Usual	.09	.085
Incentive Preference Need	.09	.007
Social Orientation Usual	.10	.005
Incentive Preference Usual	.10	.003
Process Orientation Need	.10	.002

Notes: $N = 17{,}375$.

CHAPTER 9 SUMMARY

In Chapter 9, face, construct (convergent & divergent) validity, and criterion-related evidence were presented as support of the validity of The Birkman Method®. In addition, The Birkman Method® scales' association with other constructs was examined to gain a better understanding of how The Birkman Method® aligns with other psychological and sociological themes.

SECTION III SUMMARY

This section answers: "What are the specific psychometric properties of The Birkman Method®?"

In order to answer that question, this section explained the detailed psychometric properties of The Birkman Method®. Chapter 7 described the construction of the factors and subfactors, as well as the CTT and IRT properties of the instrument. Chapters 8 and 9 covered reliability and validity, respectively, including comparisons of The Birkman Method® to other assessments. Together, these chapters demonstrate that The Birkman Method® has rigorous psychometric properties for use in the non-clinical context.

SECTION IV

ADMINISTRATION & INTERPRETATION

CHAPTER 10
Administering & Scoring

CHAPTER **10**
OVERVIEW

In This Section

- Certification Training
- Appropriate Populations
- Instructions and Scoring
- Confidentiality
- Accommodations

Today's organizations operate in a rapidly changing environment. Consequently, one of the most important assets for an organization is the ability to manage change. The Birkman Method® is administered and delivered from a proprietary web-based platform, BirkmanDirect®, to provide ongoing organizational development and analysis. As the organization compiles Birkman data, this information can be used repeatedly as people move through organizations.

BIRKMAN CERTIFICATION TRAINING

The Birkman Method® is administered by qualified Birkman consultants trained in application and interpretation of the instrument. BI trains and certifies professionals for The Birkman Method®. Certification provides full understanding and interpretation for the full suite of Birkman reports. Over 2,000 consulting and organizational professionals across the world have been certified. For those organizations with immediate needs, BI can connect them with the appropriate Birkman expert to fulfill their program or developmental needs. Completion of the certification program is required for all consultants who wish to use The Birkman Method® directly. These courses are designed so that consultants become experts in the definition and interpretation of all Birkman scales and their multi-faceted applications to the real world. Certified consultants are required to complete 20 hours of professional development every three years to ensure that they remain current with the latest knowledge and trends regarding The Birkman Method®.

Consultants that are certified in The Birkman Method® come from a variety of backgrounds with most meeting at least one or more of the following criteria:

- *Several years of management consulting experience either internally within an organization or an externally as an independent practitioner*
- *Senior level organizational development or human resource position within an organization*
- *Ph.D., L.S.W., or C.S.W. in private practice*
- *A bachelor's or master's degree from an accredited college or university*

"In 1966, we were the first to apply computer scoring with computer generated narratives based on integrated scoring combinations. We were not well received in the psychological community because of it. Now, almost everyone is doing it. I guess it is hard on the innovators within any domain."

-Roger W. Birkman

APPROPRIATE POPULATIONS

Personality traits are known to be relatively stable and are usually solidified by adulthood. Therefore, caution should be taken in interpreting results for individuals under the age of 18. The Birkman Method® is recommended for individuals that have established themselves in the workforce and have gained life experiences beyond school. Typically, it is meant for individuals in the workforce 18 years of age and above. More reliable results from both Component scales and Interests scales are obtained using this age group. The instrument is also intended for use in educational settings (e.g., colleges and universities). The Birkman Method® does not measure dysfunctional personality and is recommended only for normally functioning adults in the general population, preferably in the workforce. The Birkman Method® is written in simple, everyday language, and for readability, at the third grade reading level. Various age comparisons studies were conducted for the 2000 revision of the instrument (Refer to Appendix B).

MODES OF ADMINISTRATION

The Birkman Method® is administered online as part of the BirkmanDirect® online system. This system allows for secure and confidential administration of all Birkman questionnaires and reports. BirkmanDirect® offers online access and management of questionnaires and reports; dynamic generation of over 40 reports available in 13 different languages; analytical capabilities for organizational and cultural assessment; and database sorting and searching for strategically managing an organization's human capital. BirkmanDirect® is a web-based platform for 24 hour worldwide access. Dynamically generated reports are available seconds after completion of the questionnaire.

BI recommends respondents take The Birkman Method® online through BirkmanDirect®. However, in certain situations, computer testing may not be an option. In such cases, Birkman provides test booklets in a paper-and-pencil version of The Birkman Method®. It is the responsibility of the Birkman certified consultant to maintain the security of test booklets to prevent compromising the integrity of the instrument. Completed booklets are returned to Birkman for scoring, and results in the form of requested reports are sent to the Birkman consultant.

TEST INSTRUCTIONS AND SCORING

It is important that the examinee follow instructions carefully for accurate results of test scores. The questionnaire should be taken in a quiet place to allow the respondent to complete it free of interruptions. Typically, a computer with Internet access is required, and participants must have a valid email address in order to access the questionnaire. The Birkman certified consultant authorizes the questionnaire and sends a link in an email to the participant. Upon clicking the link, participants are redirected to take the assessment using a User ID and password.

After logging on to the system, certain demographic information is required to continue through the assessment. Although mandatory, this information is kept strictly confidential and is used for Birkman to gather information to ensure the assessment complies with EEOC regulations and does not contain bias on the basis of gender, ethnicity, or age. After this information is entered, a participant continues on to take the assessment.

The questionnaire contains three parts and takes about 30-45 minutes to complete. Participants are informed that it is not a test that they can pass or fail, that there are no right or wrong answers, and that all information provided is kept confidential. The first section contains statements about "MOST PEOPLE," and participants are asked to indicate if they feel the statement is true or mostly true. Following this set of items, they are asked to read statements about themselves (i.e., "YOUR-SELF") and if they feel the statement is true or mostly true. The last section is the Interests section which asks participants to choose a first and second occupation that interests them the most out of a group of four. All items must be answered to complete the assessment.

The Birkman Method® is scored immediately upon completion of the BirkmanDirect® online system. The scoring mechanism is proprietary information to Birkman International, Inc., and The Birkman Method® can only be scored by BirkmanDirect® or authorized Birkman International, Inc. personnel. Results are available to Birkman consultants upon a participant's completion of the questionnaire.

PROTECTING CONFIDENTIALITY

All data from respondents of The Birkman Method® are kept strictly confidential on a secure server. Under no circumstances does Birkman disclose responses by any individual unless written approval is provided by the individual. Occasionally, Birkman conducts reliability and validity studies to refine and update the instrument. These results are published as white papers for public distribution; however, the results are presented as an aggregate, and individuals' results are not disclosed.

ACCOMMODATIONS FOR INDIVIDUALS WITH DISABILITIES

Birkman International can provide certified consultants and test administrators guidelines and recommendations for administering The Birkman Method® to individuals with disabilities. In most cases, recommendations are provided on a case by case basis. Ultimately, it is the responsibility of the Birkman consultant to be familiar with the Americans with Disabilities Act of 1990 when using The Birkman Method® for individuals with disabilities.

CHAPTER 10 SUMMARY

The Birkman Method® is administered by trained Birkman certified consultants familiar with the application and interpretation of the instrument. It does not measure dysfunctional personality. For the most reliable results, The Birkman Method® is meant for normally functioning individuals, preferably in the workforce, 18 years of age and above. It can also be used in educational settings. BirkmanDirect® is the web-based platform where The Birkman Method® is administered. Scores are computed by Birkman International and all data are kept strictly confidential. The administration and scoring of The Birkman Method® is similar to and consistent with other instruments and best practices for assessments with similar applications.

CHAPTER 11
Application & Interpretation

This chapter defines each of the 11 Component scales that make up the Component scores of The Birkman Method®. It also describes a representative selection of the many Birkman reports, applications, and interpretations.

The first nine Components are organized according to the FFM of personality. Since The Birkman Method® is a non-clinical assessment, any references to the FFM have been converted to less clinical language according to Table 11.1 below.

TABLE 11.1	FFM AND THE BIRKMAN METHOD® CONSTRUCT COMPARISON
FFM CONSTRUCTS	**BIRKMAN ORIENTATIONS**
Neuroticism	Emotive Orientation
Extraversion	Social Orientation
Conscientiousness	Process Orientation
Agreeableness	Control Orientation
Openness	Change Orientation

The last two Components deal with social conventionality and perspective and are beyond the scope of the FFM. Additionally, Preferences are Components that are subfactors of the Orientations. The breakdown of The Birkman Method® Orientations and Preferences are shown in Table 11.2.

EMOTIVE ORIENTATION

Emotive refers to responding emotionally to life events. Individuals who score low tend to be calm, stable, or steady during periods of change or instability. Individuals who score high tend to experience intense, positive or negative emotions in these same conditions.

"Over the years we have seen incredible growth in the number of applications that The Birkman Method® and internet delivery can address. Right now, I'm most excited about our research into making many of our products and services interactive. When we get that rolled out, there is no telling how it will change the domain."

-Roger W. Birkman

Empathy (Feelings or emotional expressiveness) Preference

The Empathy scales describe a construct that addresses the degree to which an individual is comfortable with emotional expression and involvement of feelings. This construct involves emotional volatility, mood changes, and feelings for others.

- *Low scores reflect unemotional behavior, a preference for practical tasks and unemotional relationships, and a tendency to appear to be unfeeling or to avoid emotional issues when stressed by encounters with emotional behavior or issues.*
- *High scores reflect emotionally expressive, emotionally creative behaviors; a preference for open expression of emotions; and open involvement with emotional issues and a tendency to appear overly emotional when stressed by perceived lack of attention to emotions or excessive demands for pragmatism and urgency of action.*

Empathy is closely associated with, and a subfactor within, Neuroticism.

Thought (Decision-Making) Preference

The Thought scales describe a construct concerning the degree to which an individual approaches forming conclusions and making decisions, concerns for making the right decision the first time, and concerns over consequences of decisions. The Thought construct addresses approach to deciding; and an action versus thought orientation.

- *Low scores reflect quicker decision making, ease of changing decisions, preference for action over cautious consideration of many options, and a tendency to appear rash or impulsive when stressed by perceived lack of action by others or complicated risk factors and options.*
- *High scores reflect cautious decision making, consideration of many options, a preference for time to think things through, preference for abundance of information to evaluate, and a tendency to appear indecisive and anxious when stressed by perceived pressure to decide (or act) or inadequate information.*

Thought is closely associated with, and a subfactor within, Neuroticism.

Activity (Physical and mental energy) Preference

The Activity scales describe a construct that addresses preferred pace of action and aspects of style of planning and decision making. This construct includes the degree to which an individual prefers action, quick thinking, and physical expression of energy.

- *Low scores reflect thoughtful, paced approaches to tasks, a preference for intellectual or emotional involvement instead of action, and a tendency to become indecisive, lose energy, and have trouble moving forward when stressed by tasks or relationships that aren't perceived to allow time for thought, careful planning, or emotional involvement.*
- *High scores reflect energetic, decisive and results-driven behavior, a preference for activities requiring quick action and practical results, and a tendency to be impulsive and impatient when stressed by perceived need to wait or indecisiveness.*

Activity is closely associated with, and a subfactor within, Neuroticism.

SOCIAL ORIENTATION

Social refers to initiating interpersonal relationships. Individuals who score low tend to select introverted behaviors and also tend to be independent, subdued, or individualistic. Individuals who score high tend to select extraverted behaviors and also tend to be lively, sociable, and outgoing.

Esteem/Communication Preference
The Esteem scales describe a sensitivity-based construct that includes shyness, saying no, praising and being praised, sensitivity about correcting others or being corrected by others, getting one's feelings hurt, and concerns about embarrassing or being embarrassed. This self-consciousness-related construct addresses how a person may deal with (or prefers others deal with) approval related topics and how they relate to individuals.

- *Low scores reflect candid, direct behavior, a preference for candid and direct relationships, and blunt behavior when under stress or in reaction to perceived overly-sensitive behavior by others.*
- *High scores reflect diplomatic, sensitive behavior, a preference for personal, supportive relationships, and a tendency to become overly-sensitive when others are perceived to be too direct.*

Esteem is closely associated with, and a subfactor within, Extraversion.

Acceptance/Interaction (Sociableness/Gregariousness) Preference
The Acceptance scales describe a sociability-based construct that addresses the manner of relating to people in groups. It includes the degree to which an individual wants to be talkative, enjoy people in groups, enjoy social laughter (sometimes at one's own expense), comfort in talking to strangers, enjoying parties and group activities, and approachability.

- *Low scores reflect quiet, independent and one-on-one behavior, a preference for individual assignments, freedom from social demands, and a tendency to withdraw when stressed by perceived demand for sociability.*
- *High scores reflect outgoing, gregarious behavior, a preference for group activities, and a tendency to be too easily swayed by groups when under stress of loneliness or feeling left out.*

Acceptance is closely associated with, and a subfactor within, Extraversion.

PROCESS ORIENTATION

Process refers to creating and maintaining visible structures in order to achieve goals. Individuals who score low tend to be comfortable with minimal formal organization and maximum spontaneity. Individuals who score high tend to be careful, organized, and orderly.

Structure (Insistence)

The Structure scales describe an orderliness-based construct that includes the degree to which an individual wants to give or receive clear direction, follow instructions carefully, finish tasks, deal with detailed tasks, work for accuracy, and use systematic approaches.

- *Low scores reflect flexible, adaptable, "start-up" behavior, a preference for new, less planned and open tasks, and a tendency to become disorganized, disjointed in giving instructions, and "last minute" in behavior, especially when stressed by perceptions of too much control by others or overly detailed and controlling procedures.*
- *High scores reflect orderly, instruction-conscious, detail-oriented behavior, a preference for planned and controlled tasks, a desire for schedules and controls, and a tendency to become overly constrained by existing plans, procedures, or ways of doing things, especially when stressed by rapid change of approach, lack of predictability, or feelings that tasks are out of control.*

Structure is significantly aligned with Conscientiousness.

CONTROL ORIENTATION

Control refers to preferring a direct or indirect style of influence. Individuals who score low tend to be described as agreeable, helpful, and interested in the needs of others. Individuals who score high tend to be described as commanding, opinionated, and interested in self needs.

Authority (Verbal dominance) Preference

The Authority scales address approaches to directing and influencing or persuading others in verbal exchanges. This construct describes a dominance-based construct that includes the degree to which an individual wants to persuade, speak up, express opinions openly and forcefully, and/or argue.

- *Low scores reflect agreeable, easy going, low-key behavior, a preference for low key and non-aggressive interactions about ideas, and a tendency to appear to give in or disengage when stressed by perceived aggression or argumentativeness from others.*
- *High scores reflect persuasive, competitive, forceful behavior, a preference for strong give and take about issues, and a tendency to become argumentative and domineering, especially when stressed by perceived lack of engagement (or listening) from others or a feeling that others are trying to "win the argument."*

Authority is closely associated with, and a subfactor within, Agreeableness when inversely coded.

Advantage/Incentive (Approach to tangible incentives) Preference

The Advantage scales describe another dominance-based construct that includes the degree to which an individual prefers to drive for personal rewards or to share in team rewards. This construct addresses the approach to idealism, and team vs. individual approaches to winning competitions and incentives. It also encompasses cautiousness about giving trust, involvement with money (as incentive), placing money over friendship, and seeking personal advantage.

- *Low scores reflect team-minded, idealistic behavior, a preference for relationships where trust is high, and a tendency to appear naïve and excessively self-sacrificing under stress of perceiving that others are not being trustworthy, or perceptions that self interest (especially monetary self interest) will control a relationship or interaction.*
- *High scores reflect competitive, opportunity-minded and money-conscious behavior, a preference for careful establishment of trust in relationships, a concern for personal advantage, desire for personalized incentive, and a tendency to become overly pessimistic, distrusting, and "win-at-all-costs" oriented when stressed by perceptions that others may take advantage or win rewards coveted by the individual.*

Advantage is closely associated with, and a subfactor within, Agreeableness.

CHANGE ORIENTATION

Change refers to openness to new personal experiences. Individuals who score low tend to prefer repetitive effort, minimal personal disruptions, and predictable responsibilities. Individuals who score high tend to seek new experiences and explore novel approaches, even within stable environments.

Change (Restlessness)
The Change scales describe a construct that addresses dealing with shifting of current focus or attention at a personal level. Change does not mean resistance to or comfort with structural or organizational change. This construct involves focused or wandering attention, the ease or trouble in sitting still, the frequency of needing to change focus, and working fast enough to optimize the inflow of new stimuli.

- *Low scores reflect patient attention to the task at hand, resistance to distraction, a preference for tasks that allow protection from interruption, and a tendency to appear to be resistant to demands for shifts of attention or requirements for unplanned shifts in goals.*
- *High scores reflect quickly shifting attention, attending to intrusions or interruptions easily, a preference for many quick, attention-shifting tasks, and a tendency to appear to be excessively restless and unfocused when stressed by perceived boring tasks or demand to stay focused on one goal for long periods of time.*

Change is aligned with Openness.

SOCIAL ENVIRONMENT ANCHORED SCALES

Freedom/Personal Autonomy (Individuality)
The Freedom scales describe a construct concerning the degree to which an individual provides

conventional or unconventional answering patterns across the instrument. The scales involve content from several of the other constructs with emphasis on agreeing or disagreeing with "conventional responses" to the content of these constructs. The construct addresses independence of thought and personal independence.

- *Low scores reflect group oriented or conventional thought and action, a preference for tasks and involvement based on precedence and agreement, and a tendency to appear overly constrained by precedent or group pressure when stressed by perceived lack of control or idiosyncratic approaches by others.*
- *High scores reflect independence of thought and action, taking initiative, a preference for tasks that allow freedom from control, and a tendency to appear rebellious and self-protective when stressed by perceived control by others or restrictive policies and procedures.*

Challenge/Perspective Alignment

The Challenge scale is the 11th construct of the section and is different in construction from the preceding ten. Scale construction results in a single score that is then utilized to represent Usual, Needs, and Stress aspects of an individual. It involves the way in which a person approaches and understands the issues of socially correct behavior and especially social image. The scale addresses issues on managing social image and social expectation and impacts how one goes about imposing demands on self (and others). High scores reflect public risk-taking, setting high demands on self (and others), a preference for believable approval balanced with evenhanded critique, and a tendency to over commit, self blame, and over demand when stressed in any manner, especially on commitment or obligation issues. Low scores reflect public charm, setting achievable demands for self (and others), a preference for public approval with socially supportive critique, and a tendency to appear risk-averse and others-blaming when stressed in any manner, especially on public image issues.

It is important to keep in mind what the Components are actually describing:

- *Self-Consciousness: NEED for ESTEEM*
- *Sociableness: NEED for ACCEPTANCE*
- *Insistence: NEED for STRUCTURE*
- *Verbal Dominance: NEED for AUTHORITY*
- *Materialism: NEED for ADVANTAGE*
- *Energy: NEED for ACTIVITY*
- *Emotional Expressiveness: NEED for EMPATHY*
- *Restlessness: NEED for CHANGE*
- *Individuality: NEED for FREEDOM*
- *Indecision: NEED for THOUGHT*
- *Perspective: NEED for CHALLENGE*

BIRKMAN SCALES AND SUBSCALES (FIVE FACTOR MODEL)	"LOW" SCALE NAMES	"HIGH" SCALE NAMES	ORIGINAL COMPONENT TITLE	ASSOCIATION WITH NEW LABEL	ASSOCIATION WITH ORIENTATION
Emotive Orientation (Neuroticism)	Consistent	Variable			
Empathy Preference	Indifferent	Sensitive	Empathy	Positive	Positive
Activity Preference	Managed	Energetic	Activity	Positive	Negative
Thought Preference	Decisive	Thorough	Thought	Positive	Positive
Social Orientation (Extraversion)	Introverted	Extraverted			
Communication Preference	Direct	Indirect	Esteem	Positive	Negative
Interaction Preference	Independent	Gregarious	Acceptance	Positive	Positive
Process Orientation (Conscientiousness)	Adaptable	Systematic	Structure	Positive	Positive
Control Orientation (Agreeableness)	Distributed	Localized			
Authority Preference	Distributed	Localized	Authority	Positive	Positive
Incentive Preference	Distributed	Localized	Advantage	Positive	Positive
Change Orientation (Openness)	Focused	Open	Change	Positive	Positive
Personal Autonomy	Conventional	Non-Conventional	Freedom	Positive	Positive
Perspective Alignment	Maintain	Enhance	Challenge	Positive	Positive

TABLE 11.2   THE BIRKMAN METHOD® SCALES AND SUBSCALES

INTERPRETING A REPORT

This section addresses the process of report interpretation using the scales associated with the Areas of Interest, the 11 Component scores, and the Life Style Grid®. Utilizing a sample report, the interpretive process will be demonstrated to illustrate the process of report analysis and how the information is combined to create a richer understanding of the respondent.

Interpreting a Birkman report is a combination of data analysis, logical thinking, and experience to offer prescriptive insights tied to the objective of the report administration. The review of the report can be performed at multiple levels ranging from the quick identification and description of independent scales to the much more complex method of combining factor and subfactor information to formulate a deeper, richer picture of competency level attributes.

In the event of interpreting a report, it is important to remember that the issue or situation will guide the analysis of the data. Using the data to try and anticipate issues will be met with limited success and time utilized in preparation may be ineffective due to focusing on areas that may not have much impact for the respondent. Let the situation determine the course of interpretation and not the other way around.

Standard interpretation of a report should follow a basic process to insure thorough review. Steps of the process include:

- *Understanding the Issue*
- *General Overview of the Report*
- *Areas of Interest*
- *Analyzing the Factors and Subfactors*
- *Life Style Grid® Summary*
- *Identification of Top Strengths*
- *Identification of Top Opportunities*
- *Prescriptives Based on Interpretation Objectives*

Understanding the Issue

Prior to the interpretation of the report, an effort must be made to understand the context and details of the situation that the data will support and provide insight. Knowledge of the situation or issue can be gained through a variety of methods including client observation, interviews, multi-rater assessment results, or performance metrics.

A report interpretation begins with a report generated for an individual. Figure 11.1 represents the Birkman report scales for a male project engineer working for a large oil and gas company. Prior to analysis of the report, effort should be taken to understand the background of the report respondent. The respondent is a 40 year-old male that has been employed with the organization for five years. Previous positions have been similar to current one with a 20-year history in the same industry.

The organization has recognized the skill set of the respondent and sees him as a person that can make a great contribution to the organization. He is currently participating in the company's leadership development program and is working with a coach to build the requisite competencies identified by the organization to advance in his career.

Based on observation and multi-rater feedback from colleagues and direct reports, it has been identified that the subject is a responsive and energetic person that is tenacious regarding meeting goals on time. Performance metrics support his goal-oriented approach and show how he has gain efficiencies in the project cost and process. The largest opportunity comes from his relational style. Feedback has indicated that his response to individuals is abrupt and commanding. It is widely seen that he treats direct reports as additional tools to achieve objectives and is unable to connect with them at a level that encourages collaboration and input.

He has a long tenure in the field that has given him experience, and it is felt that this experience is used to shut others out in the collaboration process. His direct reports show a lack of motivation to perform and only do so out of need to retain employment and meet their own individual goals.

FIGURE 11.1   SUMMARY ONE REPORT FOR SAMPLE EMPLOYEE

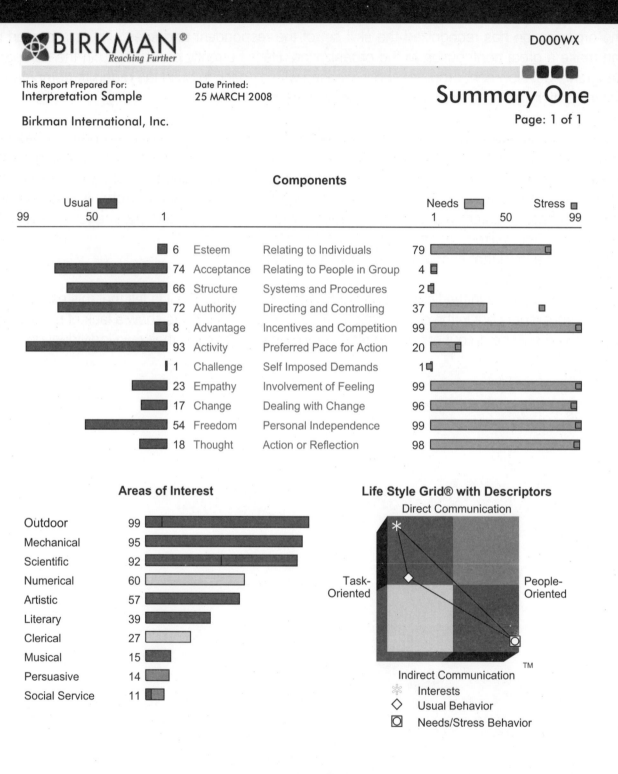

In prior engagements, the subject has been made aware of similar feedback and has expressed that the organization's main priority is to deliver the required product to the customer on time and within budget. He does not feel that subjectivity has a place in the work setting and is frustrated when it appears as though his direct reports need constant affirmation.

The subject has a better relationship with his peers as supported by the multi-rater feedback. There are indications of the same type of communication issues; but since many are not in his direct reporting chain, impact is minimized.

The issue of focus for report analysis will be the communication style of the subject and how the subject responds to the demands of the work objectives as well as those from his work team. Upon review, focus will be placed on how he prioritizes his efforts, the types of activities that he engages in most often, his behavior in getting results from his reports, and the expectations of support he has from the environment and others around him.

General Overview of the Report

In the initial review of the report, focus should be placed on any themes that become apparent and may be relevant to the feedback process. It is used to assess the general archetype of behavior to which the subject most closely aligns. From that archetype major themes can be identified and general issues understood.

The first step of review is looking at the scores for Areas of Interest. Focus should be placed on the order and degree of variance in all ten scales. Also, looking for patterns between similar types of scales should be part of the focus. These are identified by the color associated with each scale. For three of the interest scales, there will be multiple colors applied. The ratio of colors for each of these areas will remain consistent with only the respondent's percentage score changing from subject to subject. The scales containing multiple colors are Social Service, Scientific, and Outdoor.

Based on the subject's scores, it can be seen that Red interest areas rate the highest while more persuasive and relational activities and Green rank the lowest. The variance shows us that there is a clear demarcation of top interests to those that fall in the midrange and of those that are of little attraction. The distribution of scores is not smooth indicating definite preference in a targeted area. Based on the individual's unique scales, it can be determined that the subject is oriented strongly toward activities involving hands-on work with tangible results. From this pattern, it can also be determined that the subject will approach problems and view goals with this filter influencing actions. Problems and tasks will be approached with a sense that execution and urgency are important and results the only thing that matter.

Shifting focus to the factor and subfactor scales, the first aspect of analysis includes reviewing the extremities of scores and the differences between Usual behavior and Expectations (Needs). The report for the respondent shows many scores that are predominantly moving towards either the high or low end of the scoring spectrum. These values suggest intensity in the behaviors manifested and the support expected from the environment. This has implications for the subject since many will find the behaviors relatively extreme compared to others, and the environment will be naturally tempered making it difficult for expectations to be met.

The gap between Usual behavior and Needs is used to understand how the individual will act in an environment against the behaviors expected from others. With the gap being substantial in the case of the respondent, it can be inferred that the individual will portray behaviors that are quite opposite those that he expects from others. Observed social behavior patterns suggest that most individuals will react to an individual based on the behavior that is exhibited. If this action transpires for those interacting with the subject, it will be counter to the actual support expected making the probability of stress behaviors almost certain.

The subject has also answered the questionnaire in a manner that applies positive, social desirable behaviors towards self while answering the opposite for most people. This relationship of scores will influence the subject's perspective alignment. The result will influence how feedback is given and how developmental suggestions should be approached. With a perspective of maintaining image, as evidenced in the Challenge score, feedback will have to focus on building trust and the recognition of success and achievement. Developmental feedback will have to approach in a manner as to not threaten the image of the respondent.

Lastly, a brief analysis is done on the Life Style Grid® to gain a general perspective of interest, relational style and expectations of the respondent. The Life Style Grid® is used a summary, or companion piece, to the Interest scales and factor scales to understand how the individual's attribute align with the most discretionary, generalized behavioral archetypes. From the subject's scores, it can be determined that attraction will be strongest towards activities associated with tasks and direct interaction with others and a style that suggests a similar approach to those tasks. The behavior will reflect an approach that emphasizes action and urgency while keeping feelings minimized. Communication is direct and focused on issues appearing assertive yet friendly in nature. The expectations suggest a desire from others to be supportive providing affirmation, respect, and independent control over schedules and activities that directly affect the subject.

Areas of Interest

Once the general overview is performed, attention should be directed at the individual scales. Analysis begins by reviewing information provided by the ten Areas of Interest scales (Figure 11.2). The Areas of Interest provide information related to the types of activities in which the subject will engage and gain the most energy. The patterns associated with the Interest scales also provide insight on how the individual will filter and process information from the world around them and give insight on content and context of communication.

The first step of analysis focuses on looking at each of the ten scales independently. Each area is represented by a percentile scale from 1-99, indicating degree of interest as compared to a representative sample group. Each scale is also associated with a general color representing the general description or archetype that best represents the activities associated with the scale. All scales have a singular color except for three: Social Service, Outdoor, and Scientific. These scales each have two colors representing the multiple attributes that influence each. The ratio of colors will remain constant within these scales with only the length of bar changing for each respondent.

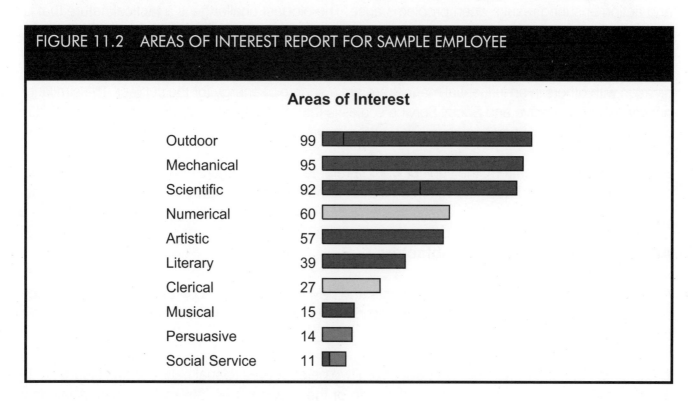

FIGURE 11.2 AREAS OF INTEREST REPORT FOR SAMPLE EMPLOYEE

Areas of Interest

Outdoor	99
Mechanical	95
Scientific	92
Numerical	60
Artistic	57
Literary	39
Clerical	27
Musical	15
Persuasive	14
Social Service	11

The respondent shows a strong attraction to the Outdoor, Mechanical, and Scientific areas. Each of these scores is represented by a value above 90 indicating a strong attraction. The attraction is so significant that it becomes a motivating influence for the respondent, and it will be important that the individual participate in these activities either socially or vocationally. From these data, it can be ascertained that it will be important that the subject will prefer an environment or role that affords for constant movement or connection to the outdoors. Hobbies likely include outdoor activities such as sports, and the best occupational role will include one that allows for movement between job sites or frequent travel. The high Outdoor Interest also suggests a propensity for physical work, in contrast to sitting behind a desk.

The high Outdoor score is also supported by a high Mechanical score, suggesting that there is a preference for hands-on activities that allow for tangible results. Activities may include working with machinery directly or a role that is directly related to machines and tangible work processes. The high Scientific score shows a preference for engaging in roles where a natural curiosity can be explored to understand why things work in a particular way.

Based on the pattern of the scores that are the strongest, it can be determined that there is similarity between scales associated with a common theme – a strong inclination towards roles and tasks that are defined and include an element of personal involvement and hands-on activities. This pattern also can be used to determine that the primary filter the individual will use to process information from the world around him will be strongly influenced by the task versus relationship involved. Solutions to problems will be in the form of direct execution with minimal focus placed on the participants that are involved in carrying out the task. The strength of this pattern is execution and action ensuring results when problems arise. The biggest challenge is a tactical nature that is often confused with strategic vision.

As focus is shifted to the lowest scales, it can be determined that activities involving direct communication with others in an influential manner are not a source of energy for the subject. The similarity between the Persuasive and Social Service scales is that of personal relationships and using influence and the power of persuasion to bring others towards agreement.

Based on the overall pattern, the subject would prefer to address others and promote ideas based on technical merits and quantitative features than rely strictly on his power to persuade others with his relational skills alone.

Analyzing the Factors and Subfactors

As attention is shifted away from the Interests, the next step is to focus on the basic relational approach of the individual and assess how expectation may align or diverge from the overtly manifested behaviors.

The Birkman Method® measures behavior from two perspectives (Usual behavior and Needs) with a third perspective derived from the relationship of the previous two (Stress behavior). Analyzing the factor patterns provide a broad assessment of the overall approach of the individual and the relationship he has to the world around him (Figure 11.3).

Emotive Orientation for the individual's Usual behavior shows a pattern of consistent emotional response. Using the subfactors of Empathy, Activity, and Thought, it can be determined that the individual will appear consistent in emotional response without letting feelings influence actions. Focus is placed on execution and decision making with the ability to stay calm during periods of change and instability. The overall pattern suggests one of stability that is not affected easily as the dynamics around him are constantly shifting.

As focus is directed towards the Needs, the opposite pattern is revealed. Although the individual will appear less affected by emotional interjections, he will be receptive to them. The pattern shows a high degree of sensitivity to the emotional signals that are present, and he may even expect others to operate with a high level of emotional expression. This suggests that the subject has the expectation that the world is more variable in its emotional response. Based on the pattern presented

FIGURE 11.3 COMPONENTS SCALES FOR SAMPLE EMPLOYEE

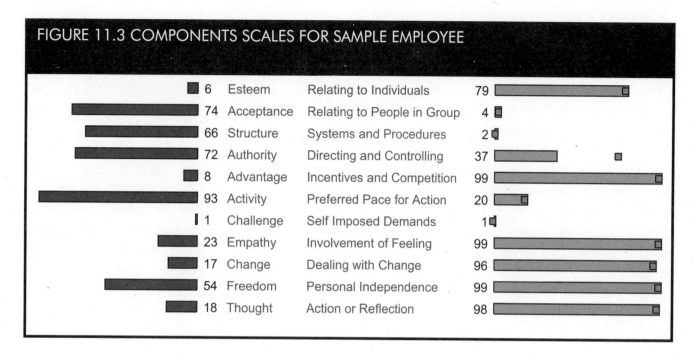

6	Esteem	Relating to Individuals	79	
74	Acceptance	Relating to People in Group	4	
66	Structure	Systems and Procedures	2	
72	Authority	Directing and Controlling	37	
8	Advantage	Incentives and Competition	99	
93	Activity	Preferred Pace for Action	20	
1	Challenge	Self Imposed Demands	1	
23	Empathy	Involvement of Feeling	99	
17	Change	Dealing with Change	96	
54	Freedom	Personal Independence	99	
18	Thought	Action or Reflection	98	

in the subfactors, it can be seen that preference is going to be directed to a work environment and relationships that provide support and freedom to set one's own pace. It will be important that the work environment acknowledges the subject as an individual while allowing for trust so that he can operate in a manner that is conducive for him.

The difference between the behavior overtly shown to the world and that of expectation may be a significant source of stress for the individual. This sample pattern difference will be seen as the report analysis continues. This will set the primary objectives in determining prescriptive insights, as this is an attribute that is heavily impacting the relationships with others around the subject.

The next factor reviewed is Social Orientation. As evidenced by the Usual behavior using the subfactors of Communication Preference (Esteem) and Interaction Preference (Acceptance), the subject shows strength in the ability to engage with others easily and communicate messages succinctly. Others may even describe him as gregarious. This appears as an extraverted behavior, and others may assume that teamwork and constant interaction are the preferred manner of operation.

This assumption breaks down as attention is shifted over to the Needs where it can be seen that the strongest motivator for the individual is work of an independent nature with respect and sensitivity shown for him in conversations. He will derive energy from his time alone and may feel that large groups of people are socially unsafe, preferring the company of a very few close colleagues or friends. This aspect will affect management style, as he may not proactively seek out opportunities to communicate, instead relying on people to come to him.

The Process Orientation factor involves creating and maintaining visible structures in order to achieve goals. Based on the score, the scale of Conscientiousness (Structure), we find a Usual behavior that resides close to the middle of the behavior spectrum. With this mid-range score, it is likely that this attribute will operate differently depending on the situation in which the subject is engaged. The mid-range score indicated a balance, or adaptability, to combine an insistence to process while not overburdening with an excessive amount of detail. Communication and delegation will be clear but not drawn out to include minutiae. Since the score is not extreme, the behavior may not appear as intense to others around him.

The relationship between the Usual behavior and Needs continues to follow the same pattern with the score dropping extremely to the low end of the spectrum. The scores suggest that the subject prefers not to have to follow meticulous instruction and not be overwhelmed with many points of data and detail. The subject will be most receptive to an environment that allows for flexibility without appearing to confining of the workflow. This gives strength of being flexible in the face of constant change and organizational dynamics that may be unpredictable. The challenge may lie in the fact that since the subject does not prefer to receive much of the detail, he may be less inclined to actively share details and information with others even though he may have the information. It will be up to the direct report and others to seek the information directly from him versus waiting for him to share.

Control Orientation focuses on the preference of the style of influence one uses or expects from others. It is a measure of one's Agreeableness and if an individual appears receptive to collaboration and sharing, fostering a sense of fairness and equity or he is more assertive, commanding, and motivated by personal gain.

Based on the subject's responses for the Authority Preference subfactor (Authority), the approach will be seen as assertive with the ability to stand behind one's positions. Emphasis will be placed on taking contrarian views to solicit debate as a means of collecting more information about the matter at hand. The subject will also display a respect for boundaries that are formally set through position or role and may appear territorial over the domain in which he is responsible.

As focus is shifted to the Needs, it becomes evident that even though the subject is assertive himself, the preference is for other to be more agreeable and not challenge him directly. The subject will respond best when others ask his opinions and engage him in dialogue. The subject prefers autonomy in how he is managed and too much overt control or direction is likely going to be a source of frustration. This pattern on the Authority Preference is observed often in managerial and leadership positions as it represents a strong assertive style that does not like to be challenged, preferring that others be much more democratic. This opposite relationship between the Usual behavior and the Needs will result in a domineering localized reaction when stressed, further breaking down the ability to communicate effectively and stripping power and autonomy from others.

The Incentive Preference (Advantage) is also a form of dominance focused on reward and competition. This scale addresses one's approach to tangible incentives and identifies the individual's motive with respect to incentives and rewards. Based on the subject's score, it is identified that the subject operated with a distributed mode of reward. Actions will appear cooperative and emphasis will be placed on the team accomplishing its goals as a unit. Fairness is promoted, with everyone feeling as though they will have an equal chance at potential reward.

When shifting to the Needs, the same shift that occurs with other scores continues to be present. The subject will operate in a manner conducive to maximizing team effort even though there is an appreciation for individual reward. This expectation is common in society as evidenced in the social norm patterns where individuals know that it is socially desirable to work with the team even though they prefer rewards based on individual merits. For a leader, this attribute is likely displayed in the reward structures that are created for the team. They will take the form of individual bonuses, promotion opportunities, and individualized acknowledgements at social functions. When under stress, the behavior appears self-promotional and distrusting of others. Based on the expectation of the subject, it will be important to ascertain the level of mistrust that may be present with respect to others that have a direct working relationship with him.

The Control Orientation domain shows a dichotomous flip of subfactor attributes indicating an overt localized perspective of control and authority while distributing incentive structures. A sample comment will be, "Do as I instruct and everyone will be fairly rewarded." Based on the change in the direction of scores for Needs, internally the subject views the world as "if others would not challenge me, I could achieve success."

The fourth factor is Change Orientation that aligns closely with Openness and provides an indication if the subject is more focused in approach or more receptive to new experiences. This factor addresses focus and attention. It does not indicate the ability of a person to adapt to structural or organizational Change.

The subject shows strength in the ability to focus direct on tasks that are a priority and work them towards completion to the extent that it is possible. He will have the ability to withstand constant distractions to achieve work objective or goals placed before him, but this style may appear as resistance to entertaining new information that may present itself during the course of the work project. Once the plan is set, diligence prevails until the work is complete, shutting off the ability to be influenced by outside input, otherwise perceived as distractions.

The shift in scores witnessed in the move from Usual behavior to Needs suggests that the subject prefers an environment that is highly charged, offering plenty of opportunities to pick up new tasks. Counter to his own behaviors, he expects people to be responsive to him and address his concerns in the moment. It is an expectation that others thrive in a restless environment and remain nimble when it comes to new views and opinions.

The last two scales analyzed are unique to The Birkman Method® and stand independent of the five major factors that align directly with the Five Factor Model. The first of these is the Personal Autonomy (Freedom) reflecting the degree of conventionality one expresses.

Upon analysis of the subject's scores on this scale, the behavior that will be seen by others will appear as balanced between understand the historical perspective on how tasks have been accomplished and pushing the boundaries from time to time to challenge current thinking. This attribute will be beneficial when it comes to withstanding pressure from the group to conform but may also make the subject appear more detached from the rest of the group.

The shift of focus from Usual behavior to Needs shows the same pattern as seen previously with the scores proceeding to go very high suggesting that the subject expects that many in the world around him do not conform to traditional standards. He expects others to take their own initiative and think and operate independently. Based on his scores between Usual and Needs, it can be seen that he views himself relatively grounded compared to the world around him. Others though, based on norms seen in the population, will consider him to be quite novel and non-conforming in his own approach. This conflict has the potential to impact many of the relationships around him, as he does not see the degree of his own non-conformity instead believing himself to be very consistent and traditional.

This pattern indicates a desire to forge his own path and do things as he sees they should be done. When forced to conform, he may become frustrated and become more rebellious creating a situation where the next action appears spontaneous and cannot be predicted. Another result of stress would be resistance to others input and suggestions, instead believing that his solution is the only solution.

The last factor to address is Perspective Alignment (Challenge). Perspective Alignment is different from the other score in that it is a single score that looks at the relationship between all of the Usual behaviors and Needs. The score that is seen for the subject directly represents the large shifts seen between the perspectives on each of the subfactor scales. It provides valuable information regarding the subject's own view of self.

The low score for the subject suggests that self-image is concentrated on the maintenance of self-image. The subject will appear confident and charismatic attracting others to follow him based on the operating style. He is inclined to set realistic goals for the teams and ensure that the team does not fail for it will be a reflection of his own leadership. The most difficult aspect for the individual will be the inability to hear strong feedback or development suggestions that appear to criticize current abilities and actions. In the engagement with the subject, trust must be built to allow for receptivity to the coaching suggestions. It will be vital to not appear attacking, as it will solicit a defensive reaction and potential non-acceptance of the analysis. It is best to approach this type of individual from a position of appreciative inquiry allowing time for them to identify the development goals with guidance. This same potential defensiveness may present itself to the rest of the work team whenever a work project or task is criticized or questioned as it reflect upon the individual's own self-image of success. This will result in minimizing situations that directly threaten the individual's place or role.

Life Style Grid® Summary

The Life Style Grid® provides a general picture of an individual's interests, approach, and expectations. As part of the analysis process, it is utilized to confirm aspects seen throughout the rest of the scales. The areas of Interests and Relational Components capture the unique elements that comprise each individual while the Life Style Grid® places them in the context of standard behavioral archetypes to understand general differences from others.

There are four symbols represented on the Life Style Grid®. The first is the asterisk representing Interests and the types of activities the individual prefers. The next is the diamond, summarizing the elements of the overt Usual behaviors and the predominant operating style of the respondent. The final two symbols are represented together, the circle and the square, representing the Needs and Stress respectively. These symbols will always be together due to the stress behavior being an outward reaction an underlying expectation that is not being met.

The Life Style Grid® is comprised of four quadrants, each representing a standard behavioral archetype. They are not inclusive as one might assume. As symbols fall closer to the border of another color or towards the center of the grid, the individual will show a blending of characteristics that may come from one or more of the quadrants. If the symbols are oriented towards the far, outside corners of the quadrants, the interests and behaviors shown will be more intense and characteristic of the individual quadrant.

The subject's symbol placement confirms many of the attributes recognized in the earlier analysis of the individual scales (Figure 11.4).

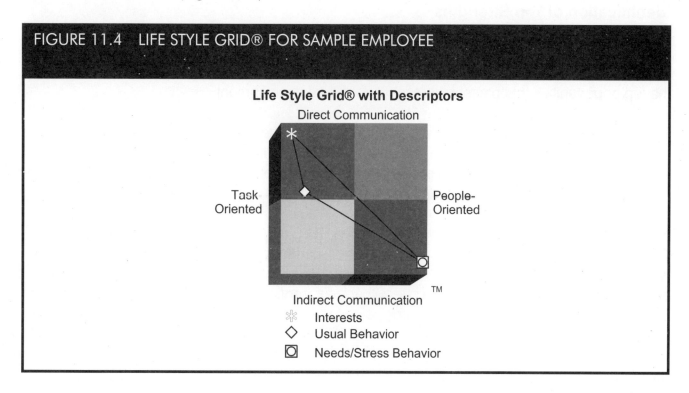

FIGURE 11.4   LIFE STYLE GRID® FOR SAMPLE EMPLOYEE

Life Style Grid® with Descriptors

Direct Communication

Task Oriented

People-Oriented

Indirect Communication

* Interests
◇ Usual Behavior
◻ Needs/Stress Behavior

The asterisk is position strongly in the upper left corner of the Red quadrant confirms the strong orientation toward tasks and activities that produce tangible results and are hands-on. This focus may also indicate that communication content and context is kept strictly on methods and actions versus the expression of thoughts and concerns for people.

The diamond is placed near the border of the Red and Yellow quadrants suggesting a blending of behaviors that are categorized by their stable nature and orientation towards objective matters. Behaviors seen will include the exertion of energy, communicating candidly, fostering casual relationship around the work process and operating with a degree of consistency in approach.

The large difference comes from the distance that is seen from the overt behaviors of the Usual style to the expectations represented by Needs/Stress behaviors shown as the circle/square. The circle/square is found in the bottom right side of the Blue quadrant, indicating a preference for autonomy, diplomatic relationships, reflection and independence. As previously identified, this difference from the overt behaviors holds the potential of conflict when relating to the subject and presents a situation where it will be difficult for the subject to get his Needs met.

As the symbols and their placement are analyzed further, it is seen that the two areas that motivate the individual to operate from a position of strength are in opposite quadrants. This suggests that if the subject were to work on activities that appeal to him, the potential to receive the support he expects will be minimized. Conversely, if he works in a position where his Needs have the opportunity to be met, he will be working in areas that do not align with interests, thereby causing fatigue and potential burnout.

Identification of Top Strengths

The process of analysis should not stop at the interpretation of the scales but continue to tie common themes and attributes together to identify the top strengths the subject can capitalize on and the top opportunities that present themselves for future development.

The information provided in the subject's report indicates that he values execution and does not consider projects complete until tangible results are seen. This sense of action and urgency will be seen from others as he seeks to create additional operational efficiencies. The manner of communication is direct and matter-of-fact, not shying away from issues or topics even though it may be hard for others to hear.

The subject also understands that in the work setting, emphasis should be placed on solutions withstanding the influence of feelings and emotion. This style appears stable and consistent in an environment undergoing change, and he will appear confident making it easy for people to get behind him as long as they share the same value for execution and results.

The most important strength that the subject has is the difference between the Usual style and Needs for each of the subfactors. This strength will be contingent on a strong self-awareness and a desire to use it to achieve results from other people. The differences seen suggest that the subject is aware or the broader spectrum of behaviors and attributes of others since he, himself responds to a different level of support than the one he provides. Self-awareness and the ability to use it can be a powerful tool to modify behaviors to better meet the expectations of those he is leading. The obstacle that stands in the way is the subject's perspective alignment, which allows him to maintain an image of success, and he may not understand readily the tools he has to expand his range to achieve better results and build relationships.

Identification of Top Opportunities

The shift of scores between the Usual style and the Needs can be one of the most important strengths for the individual, although it will likely be the source of greatest conflict.

Without self-awareness and the desire to try and modify behaviors, the subject will continue to operate in a manner that is not conducive to meeting the needs of others (extreme overt behaviors) and will find it difficult to get his own extreme Needs met. The potential is that others will see a person that has a hard time being in a setting with people similar to self. The message he delivers is clear and assertive while stressing results; but when the same demands are asked of him, the result is stress. This difference can lead to assumptions from others about the true motives of the subject as they contemplate about what he really is like or what he really believes. When this is compounded with the high Incentive Preference Needs, the subject will also be questioning the intent and motives of others actions.

The Control Preference also provides another opportunity for development. Direct reports may respond to the assertive style, but the style is not conducive to listening. It creates the appearance of running over others in conversation and shutting people down. When this is combined with the Emotive Preference of consistency and stability, the behavior appears detached and uncaring.

The strong stable style of the subject combined with the Interest and filter of execution and tasks leaves a blind spot in understanding how communication and relationship building can further influence the results of the team. The role of individuals as part of the process and goal should not be treated as though It is a part of a mechanized process, which the subject may be more inclined to see them as.

Prescriptives Based on Interpretation Objectives

The final step in the analysis and interpretation of a report is to identify the areas that the subject can focus on to continue strengthening certain behaviors while modifying others that have been making it difficult to see results.

As seen in the initial case, the subject was seen as a top performer by the management team, always meeting goals on time and creating operational efficiencies saving the organization money. The challenge lies in how his work team related to him and how he directly motivated them.

From the list of top strengths and opportunities, the first goal would be to establish trust with the subject. This is done through the acknowledgment of past success while showing where the strengths are derived from. Based on Interests and Usual behavior, there is natural alignment to the work that is performed and the culture of the organization.

Once the trust has been established and affirmation given to success achieved, the next step is to explore the scores at greater length to understand how it impacts the subject. Based on the Perspective Alignment, the suggested course of action would be to address the Needs as attributes that the individual sees in others and question why he feels that way. Attention should remain on an external target to minimize any feelings of threat or display of defensiveness. Once an understanding is established on the response patterns and expectation he has of others, dialogue cannot progress to the impact it has for the subject. Care must be taken not to become to pejorative as it may create a sense of attack on self-image. After trust has been established and acceptance is given to the information contained in the report, it is time to identify top developmental opportunities. Start small as to not overwhelm and make the goals realistic. The assertiveness aspect would make a good first step to try something new. The subject could be asked to minimize the control in message by adding a simple question on the end of a statement such as, "and what are your thoughts on that?" Simple modifications can create results that confirm why behavior modification can expand the range in which one relates to others. In the case of the subject with a low Challenge score, it will be imperative that he feels as though he is controlling the pace and timing of the modifications. Accountability is maintained by continued engagement acting as a support network for the subject, which also will help validate his own expectations.

The largest challenge facing the subject is the natural understanding of the role of relationships and planning as part of the business cycle and workflow. This general perception will be difficult to change and will not come easily or quickly. The approach should be from the behavior side with actions taking the form of more personal questions asked of team members, placing more trust in team members to perform, and listening. It will be a conscious effort on the part of the subject; but upon seeing increased motivation and performance on the part of the team, it will also lend itself to his own goals and sense of individual reward and recognition.

COMPARATIVE ANALYSIS

In addition to reports designated for the individual, The Birkman Method® contains an array of formats incorporating data from multiple individuals. The use of comparative analysis allows one to understand how individual dynamics influence the function of groups and teams.

The process of interpretation and analysis for a pair or individuals or a group of individuals begins with the same methodology used for the individual. As more members are added to the dynamic, consideration must be given to the interplay of overt behaviors and expectations.

After initial review of each individual report for two individuals, review the Usual scores of one of the individuals and match to the Needs of the other individual. The individuals will be inclined to work more productively together when the scores are in alignment. Most pairing will show random alignment with intervention efforts focus on areas that contain the largest difference.

Differences in Needs also play a role in the interaction between individuals. When two people are motivated by different support structures, the activities and behavior of each will be in response to getting those expectations met. The more divergence observed between the expectations, the greater the potential conflict.

The Birkman Method® provides several report formats that illustrate primary differences between pairs (Comparative Report) and teams (Group Reports).

REPORTS

The Birkman Method® has over 40 report sets at the present time. They are classified into one of three categories. Individual reports describe various behaviors and motivations focus on the individual as compared to the general population. Paired reports compare specific behaviors and motivations of one individual with another. Group reports either portray one individual to a specific group or portray all the individuals within the whole group.

Generally, the reports focus on one of the following applications:

- *Career development and selection*
- *Leadership development*
- *Team building*
- *Coaching*

While most reports require certificated consultants, some do not. For example, the following individual and paired report examples require fully credentialed consultants. The third example, the Team Building Report, requires minimal consultant preparation. It was developed as a "high impact per cost" team development assessment. While not shown, a facilitator guideline provides step-by-step instructions on how to maximize the effectiveness of this report.

FIGURE 11.5 STRENGTHS AND NEEDS REPORT EXAMPLE

	D000CH

Strengths and Needs

This Report Prepared For:
DOUGLAS JONES

Date Printed:
25 MARCH 2008

Page: 3 of 13

Birkman International, Inc.

PERSONAL STRENGTHS AND NEEDS

ESTEEM: *ONE-ON-ONE RELATIONSHIPS*

You project a certain ease and confidence as a result of your ability to be direct and to-the-point. People tend to notice how relaxed and comfortable you are around others.

Strengths:

>   frank and direct
>   unevasive
>   matter-of-fact

NEED: In contrast to your usual style of behavior, you have an underlying need to feel the genuine respect and appreciation of those who are close to you. You must have ample opportunity to explain and justify your point of view.

CAUSES OF STRESS: Because your needs are not obvious from your usual behavior, it   is easy for others to mistakenly assume that you need to be treated in a frank and   direct manner. This may result in your having your feelings hurt on occasion.

Possible stress reactions:

>   embarrassment
>   shyness
>   over-sensitivity

SAN/1

Birkman Direct® by Birkman International, Inc.
Copyright © 1985 - 2002, Roger W. Birkman, Ph.D. Houston, Texas. All rights reserved.
Only Birkman-certified consultants or persons working under the direct supervision of such consultants, are authorized to give you information on this page.

FIGURE 11.6   STRENGTHS AND NEEDS REPORT EXAMPLE (CONTINUED)

BIRKMAN®
Reaching Further

D000CH

This Report Prepared For:
DOUGLAS JONES

Date Printed:
25 MARCH 2008

Strengths and Needs

Birkman International, Inc.

Page: 4 of 13

PERSONAL STRENGTHS AND NEEDS

ACCEPTANCE: *SOCIAL RELATIONSHIPS*

Your natural friendliness toward others keeps you interested and involved in the activities of groups. As a rule, you are accepting of people and are at ease in most social situations. Genuine social awareness is one of your real strengths.

Strengths:

      sociable
      communicative
      at ease in groups

NEED: However, it is necessary for you to have a reasonable amount of time to spend by yourself or in the company of one or two other people. A balance of group and private activities is best, as this allows you to maintain your sense of well-being.

CAUSES OF STRESS: Too much time spent on solitary activities can result in feelings of loneliness; but you may also find yourself anxious to relieve the pressure of continuous social or group activities.

Possible stress reactions:

      withdrawal
      over-eagerness to please the group

SAN/1

Birkman Direct® by Birkman International, Inc.
Copyright © 1985 - 2002, Roger W. Birkman, Ph.D. Houston, Texas. All rights reserved.
Only Birkman-certified consultants or persons working under the direct supervision of such consultants,
are authorized to give you information on this page.

FIGURE 11.7   COMPARATIVE REPORT EXAMPLE - ISSUES TO WATCH

Issues to Watch
D000CH DOUGLAS JONES
D000CG CATHERINE JONES
25 March 2008

The Issues to Watch report describes significant similarities and *differences* between two people, and how those may impact their working together and with others

Self Awareness and Relating to Individuals

Issues around Self Awareness and Relating to Individuals often affect the areas of Managing performance problems and performance reviews, Awareness of feeling and special needs of others, Using candor as an interpersonal tool, Dealing with sensitive or tough business issues

1. Working with one another and with others

1a. **CATHERINE JONES** and **DOUGLAS JONES** have similar strengths and assets. They:

- tend to be direct and frank with one another and with other people
- keep one-to-one discussions brief and to the point
- are usually untroubled by self-conscious feelings

1b. *CATHERINE JONES* and *DOUGLAS JONES* have different expectations.

CATHERINE JONES prefers the direct and straightforward approach from others, and responds best to candid and open dialog. By contrast, *DOUGLAS JONES* responds better to a more sensitive and individualized approach where any criticism is tempered with respect.

1c. *CATHERINE JONES* and *DOUGLAS JONES* behave differently when their expectations are not met.
CATHERINE JONES may become too terse and direct, and upset others without realizing it. By contrast, *DOUGLAS JONES* may become over-sensitive, particularly to real or imagined criticism.

2. Key Recommendations

2a. When working with **CATHERINE JONES**, **DOUGLAS JONES** should remember:
- to keep one-on-one discussions brief, forthright, and to the point
- to get to the point rapidly, with a minimum of preliminary courtesies
- that a direct approach is preferable to beating about the bush

2b. When working with **DOUGLAS JONES**, **CATHERINE JONES** should remember:
- to temper directness with a certain sensitivity, particularly if criticism is involved
- to be sure that exchanges are courteous and diplomatic
- that time spent giving individualized attention will prove more effective than being candid or over-abrupt

Esteem
C: 6/31/31 D: 9/79/79
Copyright © 2004-2007 by Birkman International, Inc., Houston, Texas USA. All rights reserved.

FIGURE 11.8   COMPARATIVE REPORT EXAMPLE - ISSUES TO WATCH (CONTINUED)

Issues to Watch
D000CH DOUGLAS JONES
D000CG CATHERINE JONES
25 March 2008

The Issues to Watch report describes significant similarities and   *differences* between two people, and how those may impact their working together and with others

Gregariousness and Relating to People in Groups

Issues around Gregariousness and Relating to People in Groups often affect the areas of Social enthusiasm, participation in meetings, Open lines of communication, Comfort in interacting with groups, Spontaneous expression

1. Working with one another and with others

1a. **CATHERINE JONES** and **DOUGLAS JONES** have similar strengths and assets. They:

- are friendly and meet people easily
- tend to be at ease in group settings
- can use social situations for productive purposes

1b. There are no consistent similarities or differences in the social expectations of   **CATHERINE JONES** and **DOUGLAS JONES**

1c. There are no consistent similarities or differences in the less-than-productive behaviors that **CATHERINE JONES** and **DOUGLAS JONES** exhibit when their expectations are not realized

2. Key Recommendations

2a. When working with **CATHERINE JONES, DOUGLAS JONES** should remember:

- to approach **CATHERINE JONES,** where possible, in a team, social, or group context
- that **CATHERINE JONES** is strongly motivated by group involvement
- that addressing issues in a more social context is likely to be more productive than talking one-on-one

2b. When working with **DOUGLAS JONES, CATHERINE JONES** should remember:

- to offer **DOUGLAS JONES** a certain amount of group activity, while giving opportunities for working alone or with one or two other people
- to avoid isolating **DOUGLAS JONES** socially, or forcing participation in ongoing group-based work
- that **DOUGLAS JONES** does not expect, or want, excessive exposure to group involvement or protracted amounts of time alone

Copyright © 2004-2007 by Birkman International, Inc., Houston, Texas USA. All rights reserved.

Acceptance
C: 99/92/92   D: 92/51/51

FIGURE 11.9   COMPARATIVE REPORT EXAMPLE - ISSUES TO WATCH (CONTINUED)

Issues to Watch
D000CH DOUGLAS JONES
D000CG CATHERINE JONES
25 March 2008

The Issues to Watch report describes significant similarities and *differences* between two people, and how those may impact their working together and with others

Conscientiousness, Planning and Organizing

Issues around Conscientiousness, Planning and Organizing often affect the areas of Managing meetings effectively, Clarity of delegation, Project management/Time management, Sustaining the system and procedures

1. Working with one another and with others

1a. There are no consistent similarities or differences in **CATHERINE JONES** and **DOUGLAS JONES's** strengths and assets

1b. **CATHERINE JONES** and **DOUGLAS JONES** have similar expectations. They:

- respond most readily to a flexible environment
- are motivated by surroundings that do not over-emphasize procedures and policies
- prefer broad schedules and a minimum of routine

1c. **CATHERINE JONES** and **DOUGLAS JONES** behave similarly when their expectations are not met. They:
- may fail to follow through on necessary routine matters
- can underestimate the importance of precedent and procedure

2. Key Recommendations

2. When working with **CATHERINE JONES** and **DOUGLAS JONES**, other people should remember:
- to provide broad, rather than strict, guidelines where possible
- to keep formal procedures to a minimum and permit informal access to people and data
- that offering broad suggestions is preferable to trying to control them with rules

Structure
C: 42/29/29 D: 99/7/7

Copyright © 2004-2007 by Birkman International, Inc., Houston, Texas USA. All rights reserved.

FIGURE 1-1.10 COMPARATIVE REPORT EXAMPLE - ISSUES TO WATCH (CONTINUED)

Issues to Watch
D000CH DOUGLAS JONES
D000CG CATHERINE JONES
25 March 2008

The Issues to Watch report describes significant similarities and *differences* between two people, and how those may impact their working together and with others

Directing and Controlling

Issues around Directing and Controlling often affect the areas of Cooperation, Conflict management, Use of authority, Listening skills, Openness to others. ideas, Emphasis in delegation

1. Working with one another and with others

1a. There are no consistent similarities or differences in **CATHERINE JONES** and **DOUGLAS JONES's** strengths and assets

1b. **CATHERINE JONES** and **DOUGLAS JONES** have similar expectations. They:

- need to know exactly who is the dominant authority figure
- respond well to direct orders from those whose authority they respect
- prefer authoritative but fair superiors

1c. **CATHERINE JONES** and **DOUGLAS JONES** behave similarly when their expectations are not met. They:
- may become domineering and aggressive
- can "take over" in the absence of formally delegated authority

2. Key Recommendations

2. When working with **CATHERINE JONES** and **DOUGLAS JONES**, other people should remember:

- that it is important for them both to know exactly who is "in charge"
- to be fairly assertive when giving orders
- that a strongly directive approach is to be preferred to trying to be pleasant and agreeable

Copyright © 2004-2007 by Birkman International, Inc., Houston, Texas USA. All rights reserved.

Authority
C: 98/91/91 D: 51/96/96

FIGURE 11.11 GROUP REPORT EXAMPLE – TEAMBUILDING REPORT

TEAMBUILDING REPORT

Drew Lefty A45197 in <u>Team Central 79154A</u>

BIRKMAN TEAMS

Introduction

Teams are one of today's most powerful resources in organizations. The collaborative effects of a team facilitate optimal solutions to many of the challenges commonly faced in companies by harnessing multiple levels of experience, skill and expertise.

The Birkman Teambuilding Report offers diagnostic information for the team as well as the individual team contributor on four primary competencies required for team success. This powerful data can be utilized to initiate dialogue addressing important team issues and guide activities to strengthen team dynamics.

Effective teams demonstrate successful behaviors in four core competency areas:

- **Collaborating with Others**
- **Dealing with Change**
- **Organization and Accountability**
- **Productivity and Decision Making**

The Birkman Teambuilding Report focuses on each of these primary areas and offers insights on the team as a functional group and how you, as an individual contributor, influence and impact the team dynamic.

Each competency area illustrates how the team operates, how it is supported, and discussion points. The first section provides information on the overall team operating style – how it contributes and achieves results for the organization. The next section examines how the team is best supported, by the organization as well as other team members. In the final section, insights and discussion points are given to allow for team members to guide development efforts to increase the overall effectives of the team in achieving its objectives.

Reading the Graphs

The graphs on each page provide a visual representation of team member data for the attributes associated with each competency.

Style Example: Handedness (for the team: Lefties for Leadership)

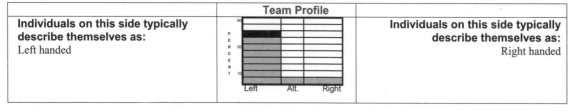

Individuals on this side typically describe themselves as: Left handed	Team Profile	Individuals on this side typically describe themselves as: Right handed

Columns indicate behavioral or social preferences for the <u>Left</u> side preferences, <u>Right</u> side preferences, or a preference for <u>Al</u>ternating between the left and right preferences.

Green Blocks indicate the percentage of team members distributed across the preferences.

Solid Black Box indicates your preference as compared to the other team members.

FIGURE 11.12 GROUP REPORT EXAMPLE – TEAMBUILDING REPORT (CONTINUED)

TEAMBUILDING REPORT OVERVIEW
Drew Lefty A45197 in <u>Team Central 79154A</u>

The following page summarizes the Team Building Report information for this team.

Collaboration with Others
This team has a conventional style of collaboration. On average, members speak plainly and initiate sufficient meetings or team member interactions. However, these same members are best supported when they get a fairly even distribution of respectful and expedient conversations, as well as significant amount of time to work alone without interruptions.
You probably prefer working alone much of the time and speaking directly to the point at hand when you are with others. While your contributions are well received by the majority, your direct style of speaking combined with your private orientation leave a number of your team members "less than motivated."

Dealing with Change
The style of this team is objective and purposeful. It is unlikely to introduce unwarranted changes. However, many of the members need personal time to examine all the possibilities and while others need to avoid "over-processing" the data. This team is best supported when members get some choice in whether to follow focused processes, or the ability to engage in many different activities during each day.
You probably prefer to change your focus from "one thing to another" throughout the day. This keeps you aware of many events that some other members miss. This tendency makes you open to change, at times, more open than some other members appreciate.

Organization & Accountability
For the most part, this team systematically works through its plans and trusts members to make choices that will benefit the team. Some members are best supported by this predictable style. A number of the members also need a significant amount of non-routine activities if they are to be best supported. Most members also want significant amounts of personal autonomy.
Your style is balanced, but edges toward being self assertive and competitive. At times, your style of influence will be needed to push the team to where it needs to go; however, it might also create reactions that make it less than productive.

Productivity & Decision Making
This team likes to move straight toward results in a pleasant, agreeable style. It is best supported when both objective and subjective aspects of the issue are woven into the discussions. This team also prefers a balance of teamwork opportunities, and times for personal initiative and leadership.
Your style contributes significant, direct influence upon the team. If you make room for both tactful conversations and non-competitive team decisions, it will help this team to stay productive.

Summary
This team has many of the attributes and issues common to most teams. To make this team even more productive, review the detailed sections most important to the team. This information and the exercises you will go through, should provide useful insights and suggestions that will help you in your efforts to become even more productive.

Note: Teams comprised of six or fewer members tend to work together in more "one-on-one" exchanges, while larger teams tend to work together based on the interactions of the whole membership. Consider this as you interpret your detailed information.

FIGURE 11.13 GROUP REPORT EXAMPLE – TEAMBUILDING REPORT (CONTINUED)

TEAMBUILDING REPORT
Drew Lefty A45197 in Team Central 79154A

COLLABORATING WITH OTHERS
Team Operating Style

Collaboration involves communication, gregariousness and working together. When done well, it enables a team to develop its own way of working together effectively. Collaboration includes communication, cooperation, trust, cohesion, participation, openness and fairness. Hindrances to collaboration include: over use of position or rank, withholding information, reluctance to speak up or speaking up to the degree that others cannot participate. Low levels of collaboration negatively impact team productivity and decision-making.

Personal Communication Style

Individuals on this side typically describe themselves as:	Team Profile	Individuals on this side typically describe themselves as:
Outgoing, lively Not easily embarrassed Frank, direct and matter-of-fact Not troubled by self-conscious thoughts		Diplomatic, appreciative Able to get along with others Attuned to subjective nuances Sensitive and respectful of others

Like most teams, this team's strength is communicating objective "facts and data" information. Relatively few team members have the natural skills to effectively deal with subjective topics or people issues. Your communication style is even more consistently direct and straightforward than the rest of your team. Internally, you align with the majority of the team and most of the time. However, that does not mean that either you, or the team, will coordinate well with outsiders, especially if these relationships require diplomatic skills.

Gregariousness Preference

Individuals on this side typically describe themselves as someone who:	Team Profile	Individuals on this side typically describe themselves as someone who:
Conserves social energy Thinks and speaks independently Is comfortable to be alone and work alone Prefers one-to-one interactions with others		As pleasant and outgoing Enjoys people, group activities Sociable and a good communicator Someone who expends social energy

This team is primarily comprised of team members that enjoy gathering together, engaging in spirited conversations and solving group problems through group participation. Ideas (or topics) are discussed, dropped, picked up again, modified and re-used without ceremony or effort. You also enjoy engaging in group activities, working in teams and meeting people. It is common for you to gather team members around you so that you can "think out loud." Your level of extraversion means you consistently seek to engage others in your activities.

FIGURE 11.14 GROUP REPORT EXAMPLE – TEAMBUILDING REPORT (CONTINUED)

TEAMBUILDING REPORT
Drew Lefty A45197 in <u>Team Central 79154A</u>

COLLABORATING WITH OTHERS
How the Team is <u>Best Supported</u>

This page describes less observable considerations that support the team's underlying motivational structure. The underlying principle is the Platinum Rule: "Treat others the way they want to be treated." In short, these graphs describe what team members want to experience in the team – which is often different than the way they act.

Personal Communication – Desired Style

Individuals on this side typically prefer:	Team Profile	Individuals on this side typically prefer:
• Others to be direct and to the point • Others to deal with you factually and on the basis of reason. • Not to deal with subtlety, shyness or evasiveness in others		• Receiving genuine respect and appreciation from others • Formality, tact and diplomacy from others • Not to be treated in a frank and forthright way

The team's desired style of collaboration and communication is processing:
- straightforward, yet thoughtful correction
- objective praise combined with personal appreciation
- "facts and data" information combined with subjective insights
- direct statements with enough context to get multiple perspectives

You are most effective when:
- you have the respect of your team members and leaders
- you have the reassurance of having many friends
- you have a large number of acquaintances
- you have criticism balanced with praise

Gregariousness – Desired Style

Individuals on this side typically prefer:	Team Profile	Individuals on this side typically prefer:
• To periodically, spend some time with your close friends and associates • Adequate time to be by yourself • Not to be pressured to attend to many team meetings or social situations		• An environment that emphasizes group involvement and a focus on casual relationships • A broad circle of friends and acquaintances • Approval and acceptance

This team's desired collaboration style is to:
- solve problems through group participation
- gather together and engage in spirited conversations
- discuss ideas (or topics), drop them for a while, pick them up again, modify them and re-use them without ceremony or effort

You desire an environment that provides you with:
- respect, including easy access into conversations so you don't have to speak in a loud voice to enter into those conversations
- gives you adequate time alone to perform your personal work
- plenty of work that requires minimal interpersonal contact
- invitations to contribute your independent analysis

FIGURE 11.15 GROUP REPORT EXAMPLE – TEAMBUILDING REPORT (CONTINUED)

TEAMBUILDING REPORT
Drew Lefty A45197 in Team Central 79154A

COLLABORATING WITH OTHERS
Insights and Discussion Points

IF THIS TEAM IS NOT FUNCTIONING UP TO ITS POTENTIAL YOU MIGHT EXPERIENCE THE FOLLOWING:
- Team members find a new team focus during every meeting. In one meeting, everyone is talking in short staccato sentences and in a "take it of leave it" manner. In the next meeting, of the same members, everyone is deferring to everyone else and trying to be "nice."
- Inconsistency of topic and tone makes it hard to know whether you should speak up, or work the issues outside the meeting.
- Team members actively seek meeting together and talking about various non-team topics.
- Meetings are scheduled so frequently that individual work cannot be accomplished between the meetings.
- Meetings may be called without considering an agenda.

HOW YOU CAN SUPPORT THE TEAM:
- Don't start "side conversations."
- Find out what kind of meeting protocols are most effective for this team and make sure meetings are structured accordingly.
- Support those who try to introduce new ideas to the team, and also try to integrate them so they don't pull the team off the agenda.
- Call for "one meeting" if others begin disturbing the agenda driven conversation.
- Put a time limit on conversations and/or determine the cost of a 1 minute conversation for the whole team and keep account of when the team spends $100 of team time on a $10 decision.
- Develop an expectation that once the agenda items are complete, there will be time to open up the meeting to other topics or general conversation.

IF NOT RECEIVING SUPPORT FROM TEAM:
- Record your successes as a reminder of your personal strengths and achievements
- Find roles that let you work with others who have insights into interpersonal issues
- Seek out team members with whom you can express your concerns and considerations
- Ask for an agenda to be sent out before meetings and adherence to the agenda during the meetings
- Request that a team meeting is not scheduled unless it's purpose is firmly established.
- Request sufficient time betweens meetings to accomplish significant personal work.

HOW THE TEAM CAN SUPPORT YOU:
- Make a team commitment to show respect and support each team member
- Provide team members some time to ask questions and receive high quality answers
- Make sure that accomplishments of team members are celebrated with the rest of the team
- Provide team members some opportunities to work in smaller groups
- Stop side conversations when someone "has the floor."
- Avoid interruptions

FORMAT SELECTION

The Birkman Method® system contains over 40 report formats that may be selected individually or in combination to fit the specific application for which the instrument is being used.

Individual Formats

Formats for the individual are the most numerous within the system with each reflecting the respondent's unique data in many variations. Some formats are narrative in construction whereas others rely on graphical representation of scores.

Samples of individual formats include:

- *Areas of Interest*
- *Guide Pages*
- *Managerial & Organizational Style Report*
- *Strengths and Needs*
- *Summary One*

- *Coaching Page*
- *Interpersonal Needs*
- *Needs Graph*
- *Strengths and Needs Graph*

- *Components at a Glance*
- *Color Grid Reports*
- *Needs at a Glance*
- *Stress Pages*

Comparative Formats

Several formats are included that compare two individuals and focus on the similarities and differences between each to understand how each with work with one another on a relational level. Formats are both narrative and graphical in nature.

Samples of comparative formats include:

- *Differences to Watch*
- *Issues to Watch*
- *Comparative Graph*

Group Formats

Several formats are available that allow for multiple individuals to be included in the same data set. Some formats are formatted as a spreadsheet to allow for quick group analysis whereas other are formatted specifically for working with groups and teambuilding efforts allowing for easy viewing of team data with manageable information for easy understanding.

Samples of group formats include:

- *Comprint*
- *Group Graph*
- *Group Grid*

Areas of Interests

The graphical report illustrates the ten general areas of interests with scores representing a percentile score indicating the degree of interest compared to normative samples. It indicates the primary areas that the respondent has indicated an attraction towards.

- *One page*
- *Suggested uses include coaching, teambuilding, career development, managerial training and development, diversity management, hiring/selection, and outplacement*

FIGURE 11.16 SAMPLE AREAS OF INTEREST REPORT

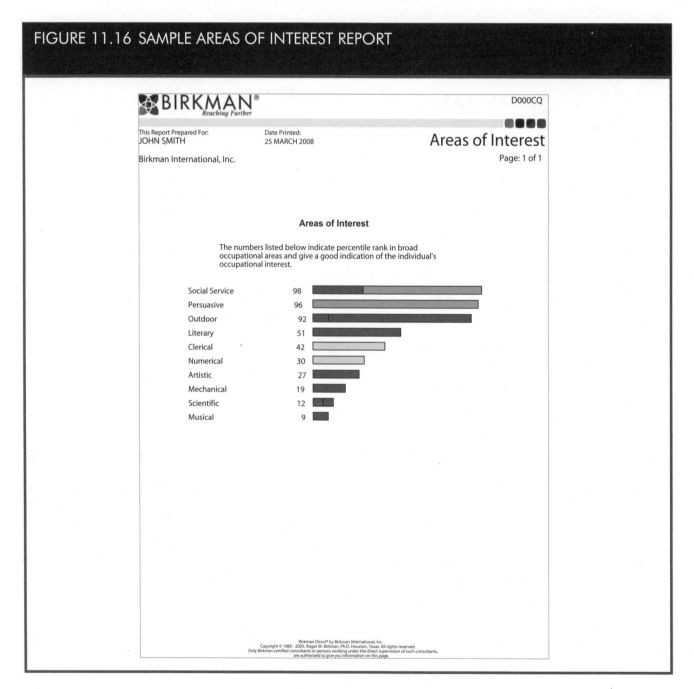

Coaching Page

The summary page is in narrative format describing operating style in four situational areas while highlighting Needs and expectations based on each of the subfactor scales.

- *Provides brief summary of Needs for quick reference*
- *Suggested uses include coaching, teambuilding, conflict resolution, management training and development, career management, and stress management*

FIGURE 11.17 SAMPLE COACHING REPORT

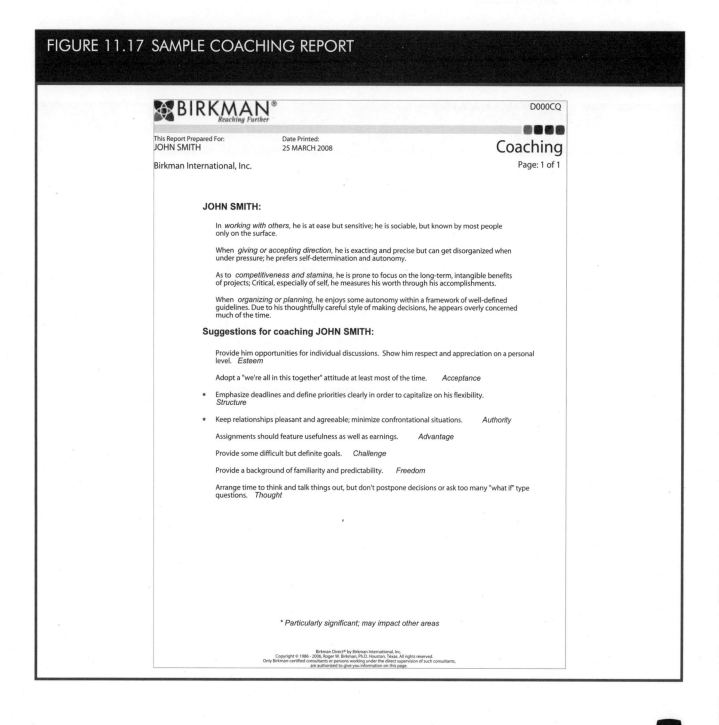

BIRKMAN®
Reaching Further

D000CQ

This Report Prepared For:
JOHN SMITH

Date Printed:
25 MARCH 2008

Coaching

Birkman International, Inc.

Page: 1 of 1

JOHN SMITH:

In *working with others*, he is at ease but sensitive; he is sociable, but known by most people only on the surface.

When *giving or accepting direction*, he is exacting and precise but can get disorganized when under pressure; he prefers self-determination and autonomy.

As to *competitiveness and stamina*, he is prone to focus on the long-term, intangible benefits of projects; Critical, especially of self, he measures his worth through his accomplishments.

When *organizing or planning*, he enjoys some autonomy within a framework of well-defined guidelines. Due to his thoughtfully careful style of making decisions, he appears overly concerned much of the time.

Suggestions for coaching JOHN SMITH:

Provide him opportunities for individual discussions. Show him respect and appreciation on a personal level. *Esteem*

Adopt a "we're all in this together" attitude at least most of the time.   *Acceptance*

* Emphasize deadlines and define priorities clearly in order to capitalize on his flexibility. *Structure*

* Keep relationships pleasant and agreeable; minimize confrontational situations.   *Authority*

Assignments should feature usefulness as well as earnings.   *Advantage*

Provide some difficult but definite goals.   *Challenge*

Provide a background of familiarity and predictability.   *Freedom*

Arrange time to think and talk things out, but don't postpone decisions or ask too many "what if" type questions. *Thought*

* Particularly significant; may impact other areas

Birkman Direct® by Birkman International, Inc.
Copyright © 1986 - 2006, Roger W. Birkman, Ph.D. Houston, Texas. All rights reserved.
Only Birkman-certified consultants or persons working under the direct supervision of such consultants, are authorized to give you information on this page.

Color Grid Reports

The Color Grid Reports are a narrative and visual representation of the respondent's goals, usual style, motivation, and stress behavior using four symbols within a four-color grid. It is made up of ten pages.

- *Suggested uses include coaching, teambuilding, management training and development, and organizational development applications*
- *Variations include:*

- Life Style Grid® Report - Leadership Style Grid℠ Report - Negotiating Style Grid℠ Report
- Sales Style Grid℠ Report - Business Development Style Grid℠ Report
- Business Development Style Grid℠ for Attorneys Report - Customer Service Style Grid℠ Report

FIGURE 11.18 SAMPLE LIFE STYLE GRID®

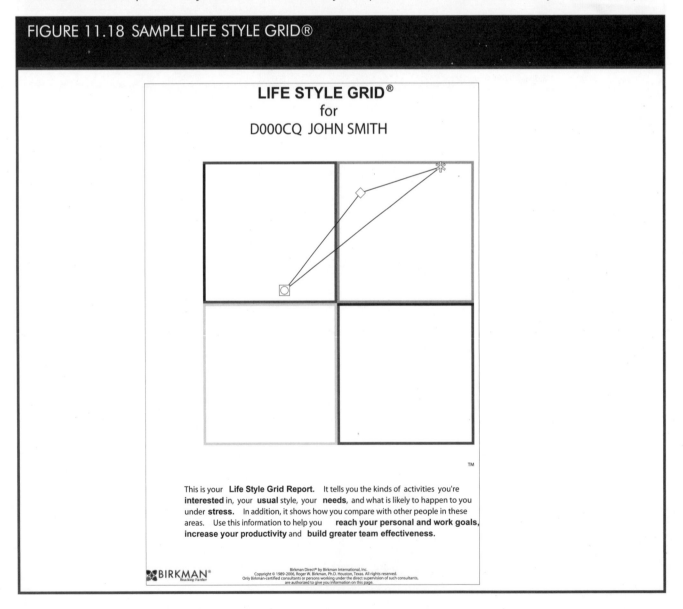

LIFE STYLE GRID®
for
D000CQ JOHN SMITH

™

This is your **Life Style Grid Report.**   It tells you the kinds of activities you're **interested** in, your **usual** style, your **needs**, and what is likely to happen to you under **stress.**   In addition, it shows how you compare with other people in these areas.   Use this information to help you   **reach your personal and work goals**, **increase your productivity** and **build greater team effectiveness.**

Birkman Direct® by Birkman International, Inc.
Copyright © 1989-2006, Roger W. Birkman, Ph.D. Houston, Texas. All rights reserved.
Only Birkman-certified consultants or persons working under the direct supervision of such consultants,
are authorized to give you information on this page.

BIRKMAN®

Guide Pages

The Guide Pages are in narrative format providing detailed descriptive information centered on each of the primary factors. Descriptions are based on the combination of subfactors related to each factor unique to the respondent.

- *Five pages*
- *Usual behavior, Needs, and Stress behavior shown for each of the five primary factors*
- *Suggested uses include coaching, management training and development, leadership development, and organizational development*

FIGURE 11.19 SAMPLE GUIDE PAGES

BIRKMAN®
Reaching Further

D000CQ

This Report Prepared For:
JOHN SMITH

Date Printed:
25 MARCH 2008

Guide Pages

Birkman International, Inc.

Page: 1 of 5

GUIDE PAGE TO

EMOTIONAL STABILITY

USUAL BEHAVIOR

You see action as the key to solving most problems. You are naturally inclined to take action personally and to encourage others to do the same -- a consequence of your high level of physical energy. You approve of a style which emphasizes practical, hands-on involvement over a more thoughtful approach which may involve unnecessary delay.

You tend to be objective and practical in outlook. You prefer to reduce issues to their logical foundations and to exclude more subjective considerations which may cloud matters. This practical and more detached approach permits you to get to the core of the issue and avoid distractions of a more emotional nature.

Your decision-making style is an effective balance between the extremes of impetuousness and unnecessary delay. You have a degree of tolerance for ambiguity that can permit you to work with matters that are not clear-cut. At the same time, you are able to reduce the issue to its basics without undue trouble.

Generally, therefore, your focus is on action and concrete results. However, you like to take a little time over decisions, particularly those that are important or more complex.

UNDERLYING NEEDS

You prefer an environment that offers a balance with respect to the issues described above, where you can avoid having to deal with extremes.

STRESS BEHAVIOR

Under pressure, you can respond poorly to extreme demands on your energies. An over-demanding schedule can cause you to delay unnecessary action, while an absence of demands on your time may prompt you to get involved in matters that are not your direct concern.

You also may find it hard to find a balance from an emotional point of view. Too much talk about feelings on the part of others makes you uncomfortable with and sometimes dismissive of emotional matters. But if you believe that subjective matters are being completely ignored, you can begin to experience negative feelings yourself.

In these more stressful circumstances, you can begin to give over-much attention to decisions. Your decision-making begins to slow, as you start to look too closely at minor issues that may not really be important. Under great pressure, you may refuse to commit yourself to any decision at all.

Your main tendency, then, is to slow your decision-making to the point that you defer unnecessarily or even abandon completely any attempt at a decision.

Birkman Direct® by Birkman International, Inc.
Copyright © 1966 - 2002, Roger W. Birkman, Ph.D. Houston, Texas. All rights reserved.
Only Birkman-certified consultants or persons working under the direct supervision of such consultants,
are authorized to give you information on this page.

Managerial & Organizational Style Report

The Managerial & Organizational Style Report is a narrative of the respondent's preferred management styles in significant areas. Its focus is placed on unique attributes where the respondent's scores deviate from the norm indicating behaviors that may be unexpected yet operate as strengths.

- *Up to six pages, depending on individual's style*
- *Suggested uses include leadership development, management training and development, coaching, outplacement, diversity management, and organizational development*

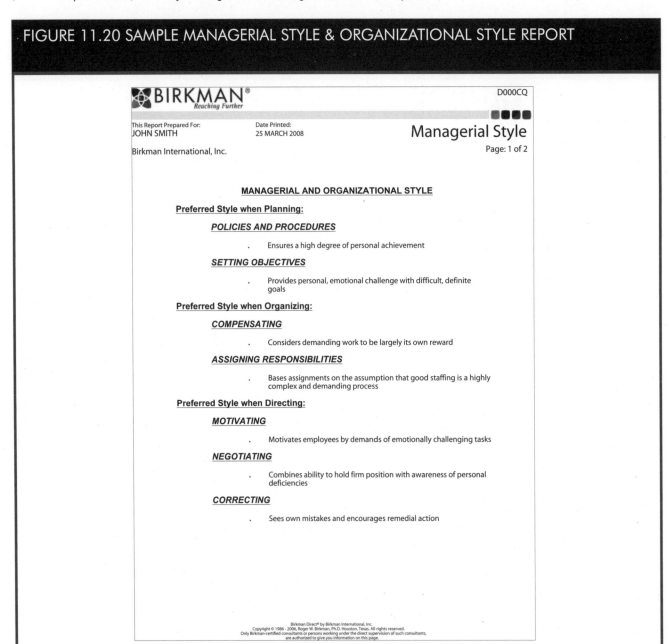

FIGURE 11.20 SAMPLE MANAGERIAL STYLE & ORGANIZATIONAL STYLE REPORT

Needs-At-A-Glance

The Needs-At-A-Glance displays a narrative based on component scores that summarize Usual behavior and Needs.

- *One to two pages in length*
- *Option available to have numerical scores displayed or leave them absent*
- *Suggested uses include hiring/selection, career development, outplacement, teambuilding, and diversity management*

FIGURE 11:21 SAMPLE NEEDS AT A GLANCE

BIRKMAN®
Reaching Further

D000CQ

This Report Prepared For:
JOHN SMITH

Date Printed:
25 MARCH 2008

Birkman International, Inc.

Needs at a Glance

Page: 1 of 1

Relating to People Individually
Prefers to combine a certain directness with an awareness of others' feelings; but has a need to feel the genuine respect and appreciation of people in return.

Relating to People in Groups
Enjoys working in a group and is socially at ease with people; and needs to feel the acceptance and support of the group.

Systems and Procedures
Prefers freedom of action and a minimum of routine; but needs organizational support and guidance and the benefit of recognized systems and procedures.

Direction and Control
Likes to be self-assertive and actively enjoys supervising and directing others; but needs in turn to be offered suggestions and persuasion rather than categorical orders.

Teamwork and Individual Competitiveness
Prefers to be trustful and to value an approach based on intangibles rather than competition; and needs trusting, team-based assignments which minimize competitive rivalry.

Preferred Pace for Action
Likes to be very active and displays a high energy level; but needs an environment that offers opportunity for reflection as well as stimulating action.

Demands of Work
Responds well to difficult and demanding tasks and goals; and needs the stimulus of personally challenging life and work situations.

Involvement of Feeling
Prefers to be objective in outlook, detached in feelings and practical in approach; but needs to feel an element of sensitivity in the work environment rather than total objectivity.

Dealing With Change
Likes to introduce a good deal of variety and novelty into personal routine; but needs an environment that combines opportunities for change with the encouragement of a fixed routine.

Personal Independence
Prefers to combine a degree of restraint and conformity with the exercising of a certain individuality; but needs in general the support of a familiar and predictable environment.

Action or Reflection
Likes to take some time before committing to a decision; and needs to be offered some opportunity for reflection.

Birkman Direct® by Birkman International, Inc.
Copyright © 1986 - 2002, Roger W. Birkman, Ph.D. Houston, Texas. All rights reserved.
Only Birkman-certified consultants or persons working under the direct supervision of such consultants, are authorized to give you information on this page.

Needs Graph

The Needs Graph is a graphical display of the respondent's scores for each of the factor subfactors. Three bars are separately displayed for Usual behavior, Needs (Expectations), and Stress behavior with the respondent's score encircled on each bar.

- *Shows behavioral description at each end of the spectrum for Usual, Needs, and Stress to allow for understanding of the entire range of behaviors for each subfactor*
- *Suggested uses include coaching, management training and development, diversity management, and teambuilding*

FIGURE 11.22 SAMPLE NEEDS GRAPH

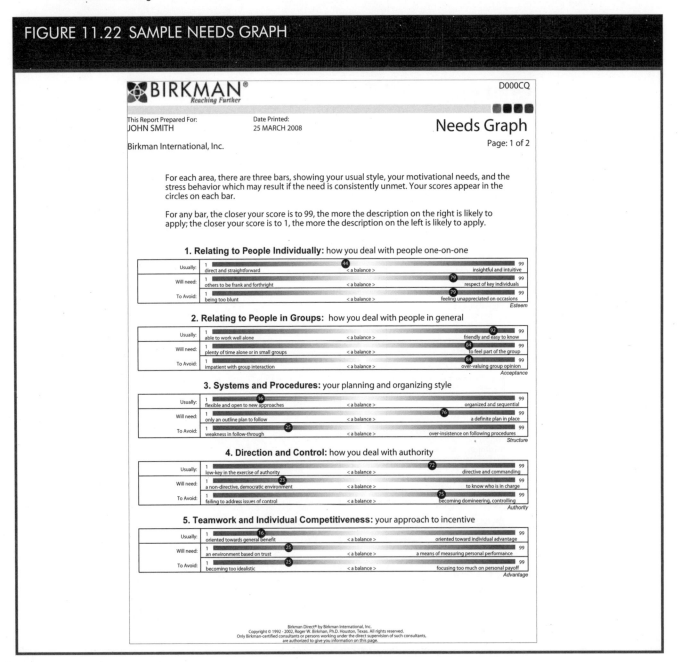

Strengths and Needs

The Strengths and Needs are written summaries of general interests and subfactors presented without scores.

- *Twelve pages*
- *Suggested uses include coaching, teambuilding, stress management, management training and development, and outplacement*

FIGURE 11.23 SAMPLE STRENGTHS AND NEEDS

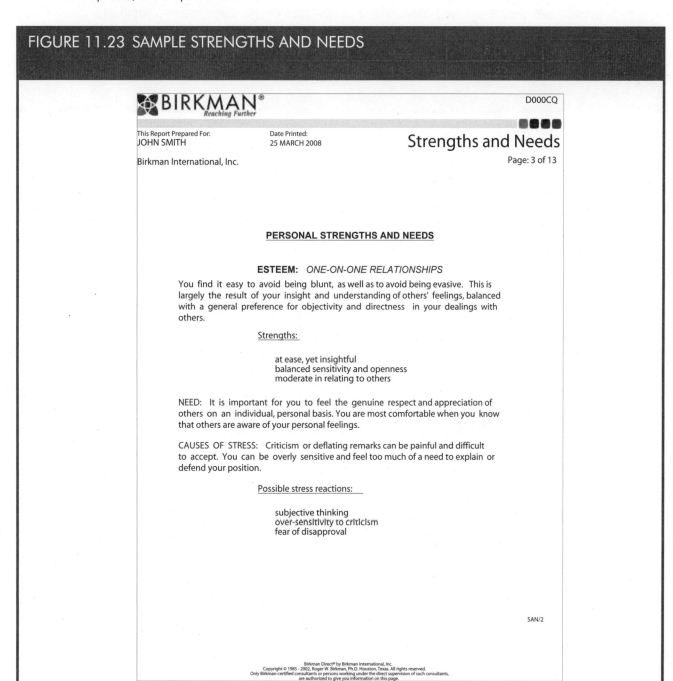

Strengths and Needs Graph

The Strengths and Needs Graph is a written summary of general interests and subfactors combined with graphical representations of each scale.

- *Twelve pages*
- *Shows behavioral description at each end of the spectrum for Usual, Needs, and Stress to allow for understanding of the entire range of behaviors for each subfactor*
- *Suggested uses include coaching, teambuilding, stress management, management training and development, and outplacement*

FIGURE 11.24 SAMPLE STRENGTHS AND NEEDS GRAPH

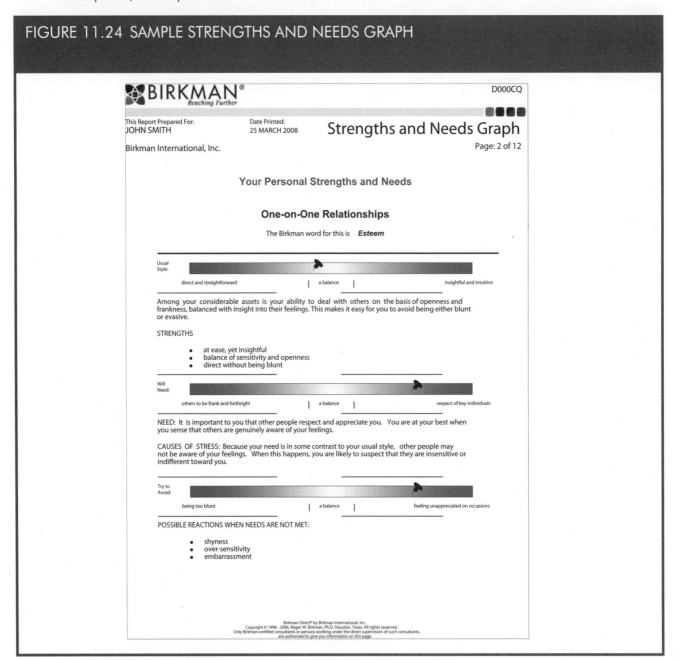

Stress Pages

The Stress Pages are written summaries pertaining to four situational areas where stress is most prominent. They are formatted based on a stress management technique involving managing stress behaviors when manifested and then meeting needs to negate future stress reactions in similar situations.

- *Eight pages*
- *Suggested uses include stress management, teambuilding, management training and development, conflict resolution, career development, diversity management, leadership development, and coaching*

FIGURE 11.25 SAMPLE STRESS PAGES

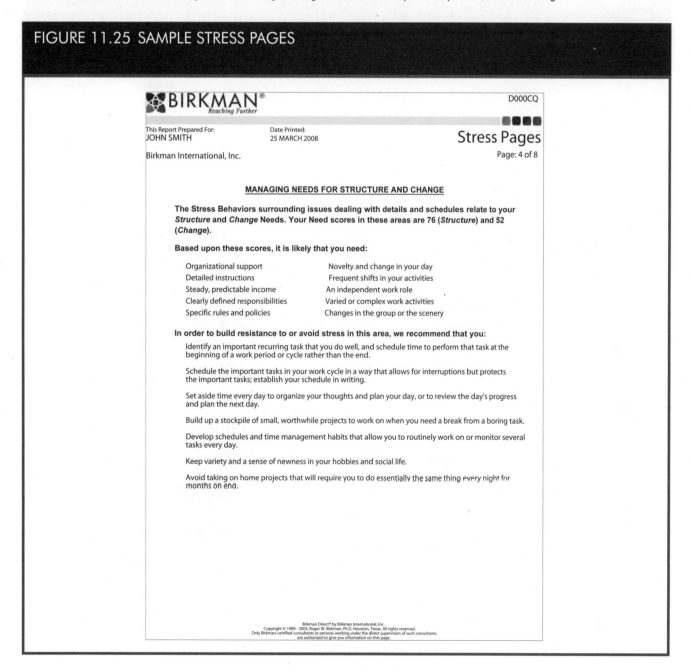

BIRKMAN®
Reaching Further

D000CQ

This Report Prepared For:
JOHN SMITH

Date Printed:
25 MARCH 2008

Stress Pages

Birkman International, Inc.

Page: 4 of 8

MANAGING NEEDS FOR STRUCTURE AND CHANGE

The Stress Behaviors surrounding issues dealing with details and schedules relate to your *Structure* and *Change* Needs. Your Need scores in these areas are 76 (*Structure*) and 52 (*Change*).

Based upon these scores, it is likely that you need:

Organizational support	Novelty and change in your day
Detailed instructions	Frequent shifts in your activities
Steady, predictable income	An independent work role
Clearly defined responsibilities	Varied or complex work activities
Specific rules and policies	Changes in the group or the scenery

In order to build resistance to or avoid stress in this area, we recommend that you:

Identify an important recurring task that you do well, and schedule time to perform that task at the beginning of a work period or cycle rather than the end.

Schedule the important tasks in your work cycle in a way that allows for interruptions but protects the important tasks; establish your schedule in writing.

Set aside time every day to organize your thoughts and plan your day, or to review the day's progress and plan the next day.

Build up a stockpile of small, worthwhile projects to work on when you need a break from a boring task.

Develop schedules and time management habits that allow you to routinely work on or monitor several tasks every day.

Keep variety and a sense of newness in your hobbies and social life.

Avoid taking on home projects that will require you to do essentially the same thing every night for months on end.

Birkman Direct® by Birkman International, Inc.
Copyright © 1989 - 2003, Roger W. Birkman, Ph.D. Houston, Texas. All rights reserved.
Only Birkman-certified consultants or persons working under the direct supervision of such consultants,
are authorized to give you information on this page.

Summary One

Summary One displays factor subfactors, Areas of Interests, and Life Style Grid® graphically. It is a summary of multiple formats for quick reference.

- *One page*
- *Suggested uses include coaching, hiring/selection, teambuilding, management training and development, and career development*

FIGURE 11.26 SAMPLE SUMMARY ONE

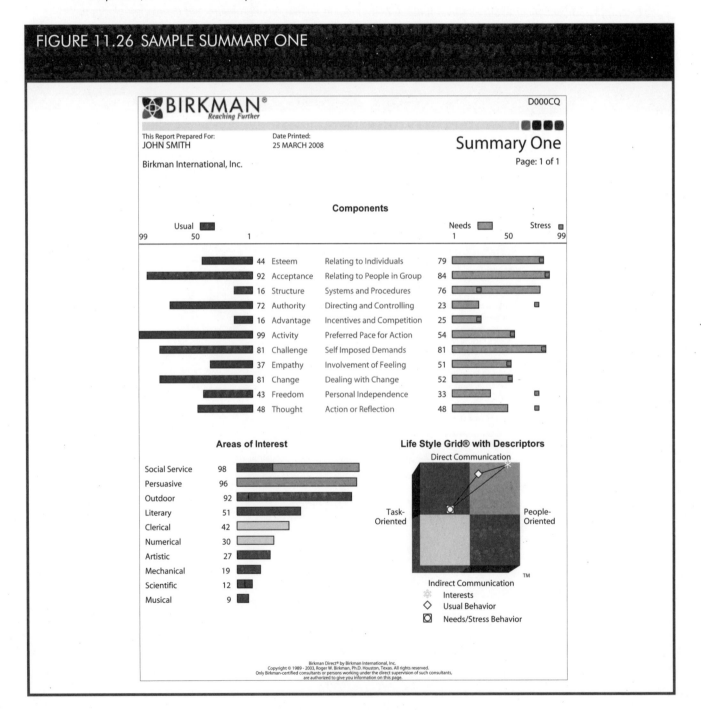

Differences to Watch

The Differences to Watch is a narrative consisting of individualized statements regarding how two people are likely to relate to one another. It only highlights significant differences in Needs between individuals.

- *Two versions: Primary/Secondary (for non-peer relationships) and Peer/Peer*
- *Suggested uses include relationship management, teambuilding, conflict resolution, stress management, and diversity management*

FIGURE 11.27 SAMPLE DIFFERENCES TO WATCH

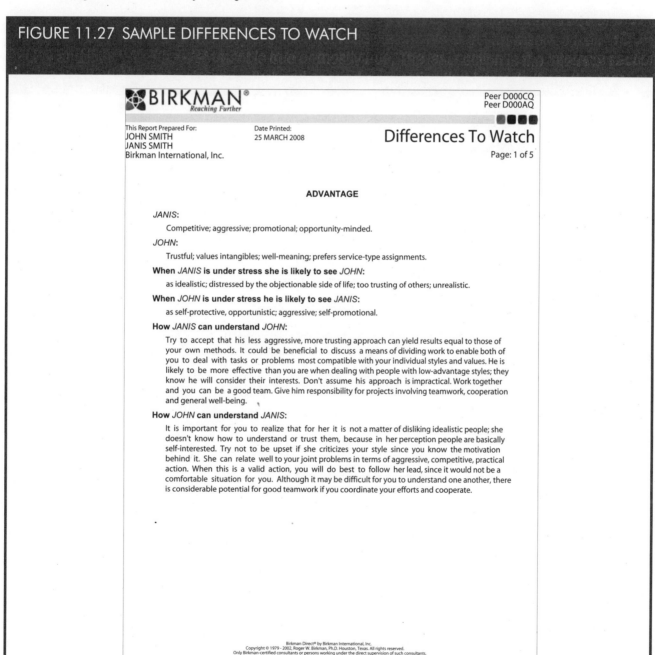

Issues to Watch

The Issues to Watch is a narrative consisting of individualized statements regarding how two people are likely to relate to one another. The report highlights significant differences, as well as similarities, in Usual styles, Needs, and Stress behaviors between individuals.

- *Contains prescriptive insights offering suggestions that each individual can use to relate better with the compared individual*
- *Suggested uses include relationship management, teambuilding, conflict resolution, stress management, and diversity management*

FIGURE 11.28 SAMPLE ISSUES TO WATCH

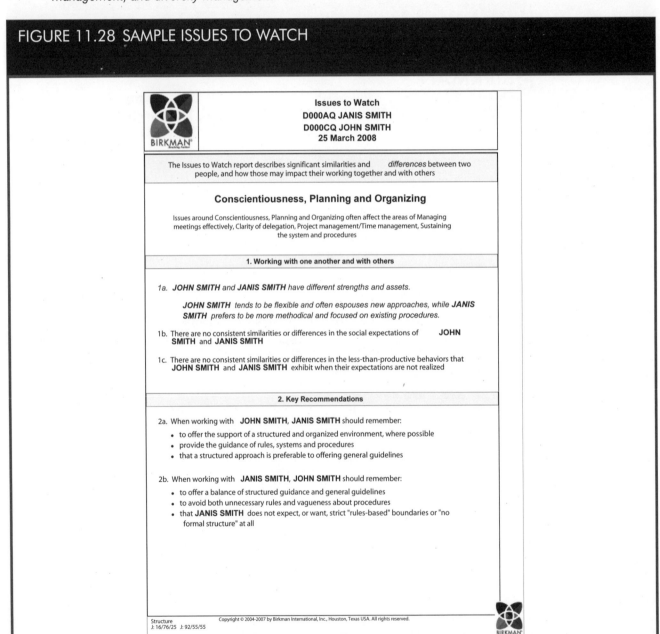

Issues to Watch
D000AQ JANIS SMITH
D000CQ JOHN SMITH
25 March 2008

The Issues to Watch report describes significant similarities and *differences* between two people, and how those may impact their working together and with others

Conscientiousness, Planning and Organizing

Issues around Conscientiousness, Planning and Organizing often affect the areas of Managing meetings effectively, Clarity of delegation, Project management/Time management, Sustaining the system and procedures

1. Working with one another and with others

1a. **JOHN SMITH** and **JANIS SMITH** have different strengths and assets.

  JOHN SMITH tends to be flexible and often espouses new approaches, while **JANIS SMITH** prefers to be more methodical and focused on existing procedures.

1b. There are no consistent similarities or differences in the social expectations of **JOHN SMITH** and **JANIS SMITH**

1c. There are no consistent similarities or differences in the less-than-productive behaviors that **JOHN SMITH** and **JANIS SMITH** exhibit when their expectations are not realized

2. Key Recommendations

2a. When working with **JOHN SMITH**, **JANIS SMITH** should remember:
- to offer the support of a structured and organized environment, where possible
- provide the guidance of rules, systems and procedures
- that a structured approach is preferable to offering general guidelines

2b. When working with **JANIS SMITH**, **JOHN SMITH** should remember:
- to offer a balance of structured guidance and general guidelines
- to avoid both unnecessary rules and vagueness about procedures
- that **JANIS SMITH** does not expect, or want, strict "rules-based" boundaries or "no formal structure" at all

Structure
J: 16/76/25   J: 92/55/55

Copyright © 2004-2007 by Birkman International, Inc., Houston, Texas USA. All rights reserved.

Comparative Graph

The Comparative Graph graphically compares the respondent's Usual behaviors, Needs, and Stress with another individual with arrows flagging significant differences.

- *Two pages*
- *Suggested uses include relationship management, conflict resolution, teambuilding, and hiring/ selection*

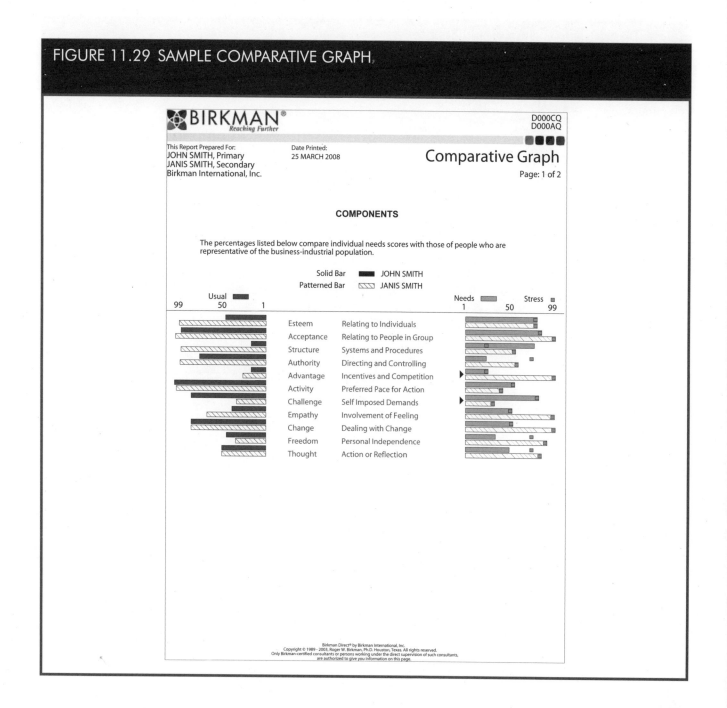

FIGURE 11.29 SAMPLE COMPARATIVE GRAPH

Comprint

The Comprint numerically displays each respondent's Interests, Usual behaviors, Needs, and Stress in a group. It is formatted in spreadsheet style containing group averages represented graphically and numerically.

- *For the advanced Birkman user or consultant*
- *Suggested uses include hiring/selection, teambuilding, management training and development, diversity management, and organizational development*

FIGURE 11.30 SAMPLE COMPRINT

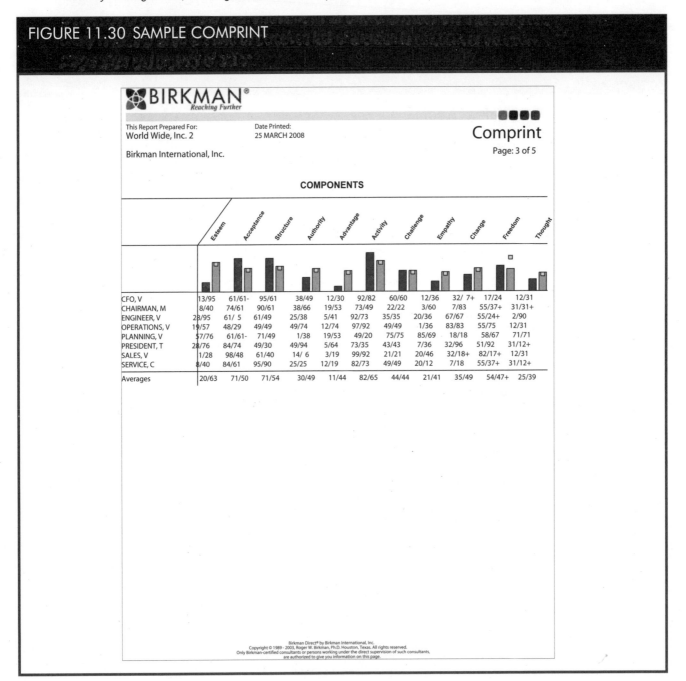

BIRKMAN®
Reaching Further

This Report Prepared For:
World Wide, Inc. 2

Date Printed:
25 MARCH 2008

Comprint

Birkman International, Inc.

Page: 3 of 5

COMPONENTS

	Esteem	Acceptance	Structure	Authority	Advantage	Activity	Challenge	Empathy	Change	Freedom	Thought
CFO, V	13/95	61/61-	95/61	38/49	12/30	92/82	60/60	12/36	32/ 7+	17/24	12/31
CHAIRMAN, M	8/40	74/61	90/61	38/66	19/53	73/49	22/22	3/60	7/83	55/37+	31/31+
ENGINEER, V	28/95	61/ 5	61/49	25/38	5/41	92/73	35/35	20/36	67/67	55/24+	2/90
OPERATIONS, V	19/57	48/29	49/49	49/74	12/74	97/92	49/49	1/36	83/83	55/75	12/31
PLANNING, V	57/76	61/61-	71/49	1/38	19/53	49/20	75/75	85/69	18/18	58/67	71/71
PRESIDENT, T	28/76	84/74	49/30	49/94	5/64	73/35	43/43	7/36	32/96	51/92	31/12+
SALES, V	1/28	98/48	61/40	14/ 6	3/19	99/92	21/21	20/46	32/18+	82/17+	12/31
SERVICE, C	8/40	84/61	95/90	25/25	12/19	82/73	49/49	20/12	7/18	55/37+	31/12+
Averages	20/63	71/50	71/54	30/49	11/44	82/65	44/44	21/41	35/49	54/47+	25/39

Birkman Direct® by Birkman International, Inc.
Copyright © 1989 - 2003, Roger W. Birkman, Ph.D. Houston, Texas. All rights reserved.
Only Birkman-certified consultants or persons working under the direct supervision of such consultants,
are authorized to give you information on this page.

Group Graph

The Group Graph utilizes horizontal bar graphs, and compares each respondent's subfactors with those of others in the group.

- *Fourteen pages for groups up to 14 individuals. Additional pages are added for groups larger than 14*
- *Suggested uses include hiring/selection, teambuilding, management training and development, stress management, diversity management, organizational development, and coaching*

FIGURE 11.31 SAMPLE GROUP GRAPH

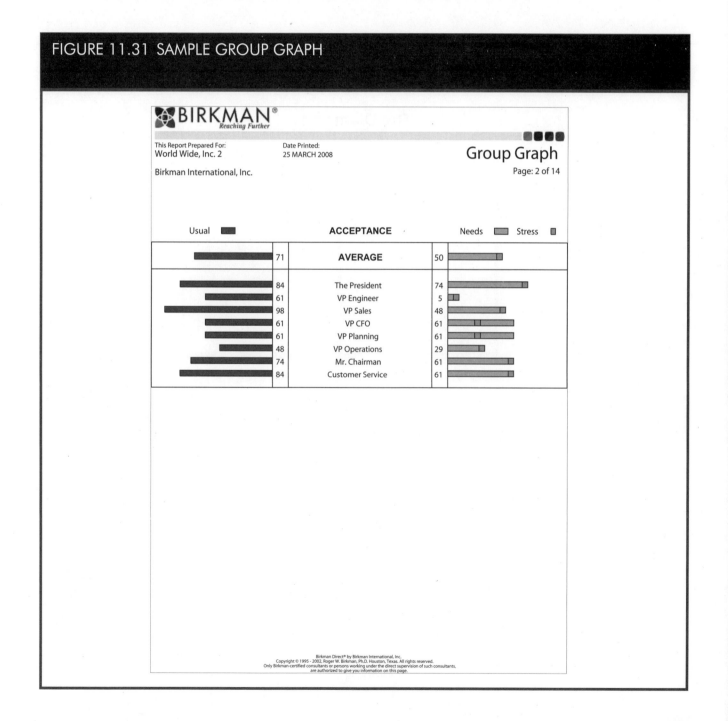

Group Grid

The Group Grid is a Life Style Grid® summary of a group on a four-color grid highlighting Interests, Usual behavior, Needs, and Stress with each on a separate page.

- *Provides a quick and effective overview of the group's distribution*
- *Suggested uses include diversity management, teambuilding, management training and development, conflict resolution, stress management, coaching, and organizational development*

FIGURE 11.32 SAMPLE GROUP GRID

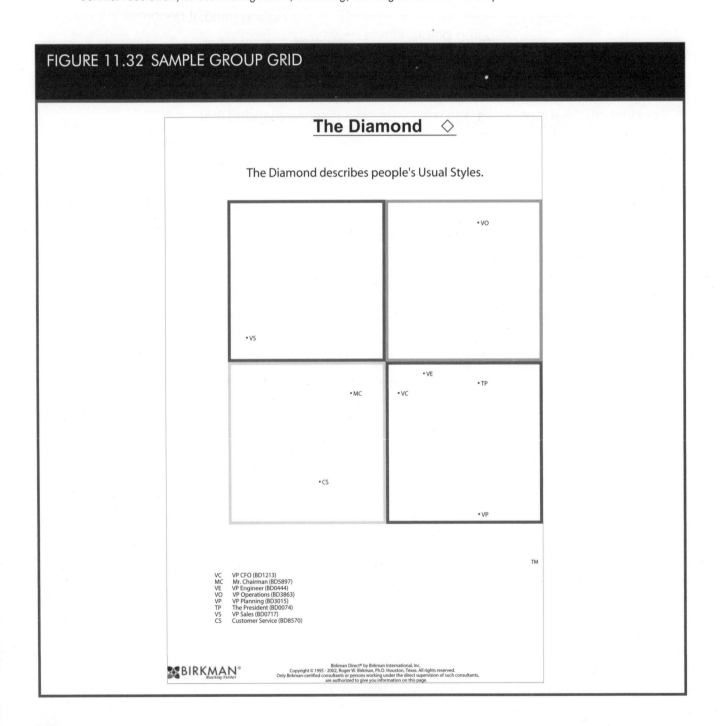

The Diamond ◇

The Diamond describes people's Usual Styles.

• VS	• VO
• MC	• VE • TP • VC
• CS	• VP

VC   VP CFO (BD1213)
MC   Mr. Chairman (BD5897)
VE   VP Engineer (BD0444)
VO   VP Operations (BD3863)
VP   VP Planning (BD3015)
TP   The President (BD0074)
VS   VP Sales (BD0717)
CS   Customer Service (BD8570)

Birkman Direct® by Birkman International, Inc.
Copyright © 1995 - 2002, Roger W. Birkman, Ph.D. Houston, Texas. All rights reserved.
Only Birkman-certified consultants or persons working under the direct supervision of such consultants, are authorized to give you information on this page.

BIRKMAN®
Reaching Further

DELIVERING FEEDBACK

Providing feedback to a participant on their own Birkman Method® report is the cornerstone for any relational work that a consultant provides. Using information found within each of the Birkman scales, a respondent's level of self-awareness rises exponentially, while also realizing the impact of that behavior within various contexts.

Feedback is a relational mechanism to help the respondent understand himself more thoroughly and is a personal engagement leading to great impact. With this in mind, it becomes important for the consultant to be well prepared before sitting down with an individual to discuss results.

The Feedback Process

To conduct effective feedbacks with respondents, it is recommended that the following process be utilized. It will ensure that the consultant is thoroughly prepared and knows what pieces of information will have the greatest impact on the solution they are trying to provide. The feedback process can be broken down into five steps:

- *Identification of Purpose*
- *Selecting Appropriate Birkman Formats*
- *Birkman Report Analysis*
- *The Feedback Session*
- *Action Steps*

Identification of Purpose

The basis of any successful feedback is to make sure there is a clear purpose for the session with set objectives, even if the feedback is for personal discovery.

Identifying the purpose of the feedback helps the consultant:

- *Clarify what is to be accomplished*
- *Frame the context for the respondent*
- *Act as a guide through the feedback*
- *Select the appropriate formats and scales to use*

In structuring the session, a consultant must have a clear understanding of the goal of the feedback and of the expectations of the respondent. It may also be beneficial to uncover any concerns the respondent may have as a result of organizational history with The Birkman Method®.

Some specific feedback applications:

For Individuals

Coaching
Leadership Development
Conflict Resolution
Selection/Hiring
Career Management
…and more

For Teams

Team Development
Team Identity
Addressing Team Issues
Defining Culture
…and more

Selecting Appropriate Birkman Formats

Consultants often have difficulty in determining the most succinct, beneficial combination of formats to use during the feedback. The easiest way to decide is to make sure the formats that are chosen align with the purpose of the feedback. This purpose should guide the feedback process.

Another point to keep in mind is to be selective! You do not have to give the respondent every available format to have impact. If the purpose is coaching, the components are going to have the most value - don't try to overload with other scales unless they are warranted later.

The Birkman Method® reporting system consists of a variety of formats, some of them containing numerical scales and others that do not. It is with these numerical formats that the consultant will find themselves engaged in discussions of explanation as well as interpretation. Be sure to balance narrative formats alongside those with numbers to aid in the understanding of the data. If the report is distributed prior to feedback, be careful that the respondent does not make assumptions before they have had the opportunity to hear their scores thoroughly explained to them. One point to keep in mind is that the behavioral descriptions for each of the scales do not change with each different format, only the context in which they are presented.

A consultant must first decide on the type of information needed for the feedback. The Interest scales and behavioral scales are presented in numerous ways to convey importance depending upon the purpose and objective of the feedback.

Samples of available formats include:

- *Areas of Interests*
- *Coaching Page*
- *Components at a Glance*
- *Components Graph*
- *Guide Pages*
- *Interpersonal Needs*
- *Life Style Grid®*
- *Managerial and Organizational Style*
- *Needs Graph*
- *Needs at a Glance*
- *Strengths and Needs*
- *Strengths and Needs Graph*
- *Stress Pages*
- *Summary One*

For a detailed description of these formats, please refer to the "Format Selection" section.

Below you will find a listing of some recommended format combinations used in popular applications:

Leadership Development

Coaching Page
Life Style Grid® Summary
Managerial and Organizational Style
Strengths and Needs
Stress Pages
Summary One

Teambuilding

Coaching Page
Life Style Grid®
Strengths and Needs
Stress Pages
Summary One

Career Management

Coaching Page
Life Style Grid®

Managerial and Organizational Style
Needs Graph
Strengths and Needs
Stress Pages
Summary One

Birkman Report Analysis

To maximize your time when reviewing a report, you do not need to worry about every scale. Focus on the factors or subfactors with the most importance to the purpose of the feedback. It is also important to pay attention to those scales where values fall outside of normative patterns.

Areas of Interests

- *Focus should be placed on scores with extreme values such as 90 and above and 10 and below. Scores in these ranges carry great influence in the activities the respondent will be attracted towards and the activities that are rejected. Scores with high intensity will act as a strong motivator for the individual.*
- *Look for patterns in the color distribution of the Interest scales. Patterns will give an indication of overall preference and provide insight regarding how an individual will filter information from the world around them.*
- *Dedicate less time on scales falling between the values of 40 and 60 since they do not operate as strong attractors or strong detractors.*

Components

- *Review the patterns of the sub-scales under each factor. If the subfactors are different than what is seen in the common patterns, attention should be given to those scales.*
- *Look at scales with either very high or very low values (especially Needs). These very high or low scores indicate that behavior will appear very frequently, intensely or possibly pronounced. If this intensity is seen in the Needs, it is likely that the individual will have a difficult time finding an environment that can support them to the extent that is necessary.*
- *Focus on scales that have large gaps between the Usual behavior and the Needs. Large differences are an indication that others are not able to understand the expectations of the individuals and the potential for Stress behavior increases.*

In giving feedback, it is important to understand the respondent's Needs and the behavior and support expected from others. The Needs will provide the information necessary to give feedback with the most impact. Also, it is important for the practitioner to be aware of their own Birkman scores and style. The style that is comfortable for the consultant may not be for the respondent.

The Feedback Session

After preparation has taken place, it is time to review the information with the respondent. The introduction to the session should begin with clarifying the purpose of why the feedback is being given and what outcome is targeted. It may be necessary to provide background information on The Birkman Method® and how the instrument functions to create comfort on the part of the respondent. This will help lend credibility to the tool and reduce fears regarding the type of information that will be discussed.

Establishing a safe environment is important to establish trust and create willingness on the part of the respondent to engage in the process. Explaining the review's purpose and process early in the feedback helps acclimate those individuals who were asked to complete a questionnaire without explanation of why it is being administered and how results will be used and shared.

In any conversation, the best way to engage and allow for the respondent to open up is through the invitation to speak about oneself. Ask the respondent questions to understand their background and what they see as strengths and potential opportunities. In this conversation, listen for specific example that can be used later when describing the scales.

The delivery should be conversational in nature. By creating back and forth dialogue the respondent will be able to self-validate the information and become more receptive to the information being given. Word choice is important in this stage of the delivery so that the differences between behaviors exhibited versus those that are expected are kept clear and distinct.

If the respondent is hesitant to share and does not engage readily it is best to prompt conversation with questions. Ask for confirmation of behaviors that fit descriptions from the scales reviewed. Use opportunities to tie stories or situations that have been previously discussed to provide real examples of how a scale describes observed behaviors or points to an expectation.

Handling disagreement is a vital competency of anyone providing feedback on a behavioral assessment. Some individuals may not agree on the description or intensity of a scale, but it is rare to encounter an individual that does not agree on a wholesale level. If an individual appears to be hesitant to accept any information derived from the assessment, it is best to put the tool aside and investigate the process in which the instrument was administered. In some situations it may be due to lack of communication on purpose and how the instrument will be used, creating fear and insecurity on the part of the respondent. Assess if the administration was a voluntary or involuntary process and question the respondent about their expectations and clarify what the instrument measures and how it will be used. Many times, once fear has been removed, individuals are more open to discuss the data. In all cases, the goal is to establish that the report is comprised of statements made by others who answered like the individual receiving feedback. If the report is not representative, then they should explore what is true for the individual.

If disagreement is encountered on a particular scale, it is best to first listen to the concern of the respondent. Why do they feel the score does not describe them? Is it how it is defined or is it a matter of intensity? If an individual has a score towards the middle of the scoring spectrum, they may not resonate with the strong, distinct descriptions that sound more intense. Next, explore why they feel the score does not fit and look for other scores that may account for perceived behavior. In many instances it is a matter of the scale's definition being generalized or confused with an attribute that is best covered under a different scale.

If the disagreement still persists, ask the respondent to confirm with others that they know. Individuals may be unaware of how others perceive their own behavior and they may not resonate with the behavior even though others can provide confirmation. By receiving outside validation, the respondent is more inclined to accept the description. If the respondent still feels the score does not fit, do not justify or defend the description as accurate for them. Acknowledge that the scale may not fit and ask what part of the scoring spectrum they feel bests represents them. It is not uncommon when this happens; it is usually a matter of intensity that the disagreement arises from and not the opposite behavioral description for the scale.

Action Steps

The feedback does not end after the scores are explained to the respondent. Birkman information gives the respondent a large amount of insight into the person they are and the strengths they have, but knowledge of those characteristics is not sufficient in isolation. It is important that the respondent know what to do with the information after it has been delivered. Action steps allow the respondent to use the new information in ways to increase their own performance and productivity.

Some important tips when creating action steps include:

- *Align with purpose*
- *Reinforce assets*
- *Target data to immediately focus on next steps and offer prescriptive insights*
- *Though it may be tempting, do not overburden with too much data – create manageable action steps*

CHAPTER 11 SUMMARY

This chapter specifically defined each Birkman Method® scale describing both low and high attributes. Each was written with positive language and intent. Many report examples were provided, both to inform, as well as to assess the "look and feel" of The Birkman Method® reports. Consistently, Birkman consultants report that The Birkman Method® definitions, reports, and feedback illustrations work together to provide high quality, positive, and impactful client reviews.

SECTION IV SUMMARY

This section answers: "Does The Birkman Method® address real issues in practical ways?"

In order to answer that question, Chapter 10 explained that the administration of the instrument followed conventional protocols, safeguards, and accommodations. This chapter also described conventional interpretation protocols. Chapter 11 described the Five Factor Model of personality and how it is reflected in The Birkman Method®. This chapter also provided numerous report examples – for an individual, for paired individuals, teams, and groups. It also provided examples of specific report pages in order to demonstrate readability, utility, and practicality in the reports.

SECTION V

TRANSLATIONS

CHAPTER 12
Translation Process and Cross-Cultural/ Language Comparisons

BI continues to stretch its outreach beyond the U.S. borders to nations around the world using The Birkman Method® in numerous languages and cultures.

TRANSLATION PROCESS

Working towards adhering to the Standards for Educational and Psychological Testing (AERA, APA, NCME; 1999), the Standard Guide for Quality Assurance in Translation (ASTM, 2006), and the Code of Fair Testing Practices in Education (JCTP, 2004), all translations of The Birkman Method® instrument undergo multiple steps before being used operationally on a large scale. The primary steps are as follows:

1. *The Birkman Method® instrument is translated by translator A from English to the language of interest.*
2. *Translator B back-translates The Birkman Method® instrument into English.*
3. *Multiple content experts independently compare the initial and back-translated English version of The Birkman Method® instrument.*
4. *Discrepancies found between the two English versions are discussed with Translator B and resolved.*
5. *The finalized translation is piloted with a sample size greater than 50. The data are analyzed at the item level and scale level using CTT. Any discrepancies found are resolved.*

At this point, the new translation of The Birkman Method® instrument is made operational on a large scale. After being made operational, the following additional steps are taken to insure translation quality assurance (Davies & Wadlington, 2006; Little, Wadlington, & Turner, 2007).

6. *Once the sample size reaches 500, 1,000, and 3,000, CTT analyses are repeated.*
7. *Once the sample size reaches 3,000, IRT analyses are conducted. These analyses include the examination of differential item functioning (DIF) and differential test functioning (DTF).*

"Now we are translating The Birkman Method® into more than a dozen languages. One of the most wonderful aspects of leading this effort is realizing that individuals from around the world can become more effective using the Method. It's exciting."

-Roger W. Birkman

8. *Once the sample size reaches 3,000, a simultaneous factor analysis across several populations (SIFASP) is conducted to examine differences from a factor analytic standpoint (Wadlington, Drasgow, & Fritzgerald, 2002).*

Cross-Cultural/Language Comparisons

Data have been collected and analyzed for multiple languages and cultures. In Table 12.1 through Table 12.5, The Birkman Method® scales' psychometric properties are compared across languages and cultures. These five tables illustrate the similarities and differences regarding the central tendency and dispersion of The Birkman Method® scales.

TABLE 12.1	CTT STATISTICS FOR DIFFERENT LANGUAGES AND GEOGRAPHICAL AREAS					
	CHINESE		DUTCH		FRENCH (CANADIAN)	
BIRKMAN SCALE	M	SD	M	SD	M	SD
Orientation Usual Scales						
Emotive	7.23	5.32	5.20	4.53	6.28	4.59
Social	14.49	5.19	17.19	4.69	13.13	4.62
Process	9.50	2.76	8.73	2.61	10.40	2.53
Control	7.87	3.24	6.39	2.66	7.17	2.90
Change	2.12	1.72	3.23	1.74	3.26	1.73
Orientation Needs Scales						
Emotive	10.41	5.57	7.71	4.47	9.92	5.18
Social	9.53	5.27	11.37	4.33	9.19	3.59
Process	7.06	3.26	6.58	2.58	7.13	2.98
Control	11.06	3.62	8.65	3.18	10.08	3.40
Change	3.45	1.99	3.45	1.62	3.73	1.54
Preference Usual Scales						
Activity	3.51	1.90	4.47	1.65	4.07	1.63
Empathy	3.21	3.24	3.07	2.76	3.41	2.79
Thought	1.54	1.05	0.60	0.84	0.94	0.94
Communication	6.06	2.90	4.09	2.89	6.40	2.92
Interaction	8.54	3.05	9.28	2.55	7.53	2.53
Incentive	2.88	1.82	1.68	1.44	2.12	1.49
Authority	4.99	2.03	4.71	1.77	5.05	1.98
Preference Needs Scales						
Activity	2.67	1.88	3.83	1.56	2.77	1.76
Empathy	5.13	3.37	4.30	2.69	5.11	3.10
Thought	1.94	1.03	1.23	1.01	1.58	1.07
Communication	7.86	2.84	7.26	2.58	8.46	2.17
Interaction	5.39	3.05	6.64	2.51	5.65	2.36
Incentive	5.36	2.44	3.78	2.00	4.45	1.92
Authority	5.70	1.72	4.87	1.77	5.63	2.00
Other Scales						
Personal Autonomy: Usual	5.90	4.51	4.43	3.43	4.84	3.62
Personal Autonomy: Needs	9.67	5.49	6.93	3.94	8.10	4.80
Perspective Alignment	-13.76	12.99	-12.73	10.67	-13.77	11.05

Notes: These samples are not stratified and may come from a narrow cross-section of the population of interest. Cautious interpretation is strongly recommended; N = 145, 5,893, and 2,180, respectively.

TABLE 12.2	CTT STATISTICS FOR DIFFERENT LANGUAGES AND GEOGRAPHICAL AREAS (CONTINUED)					
	FRENCH (EUROPEAN)		GERMAN		JAPANESE	
BIRKMAN SCALE	M	SD	M	SD	M	SD
Orientation Usual Scales						
Emotive	5.81	4.19	5.68	4.68	7.33	4.97
Social	13.85	4.32	15.90	4.76	13.89	5.10
Process	9.98	2.43	9.02	2.71	8.52	2.67
Control	7.80	2.61	6.09	2.95	6.07	3.22
Change	3.63	1.50	2.67	1.77	2.69	1.58
Orientation Needs Scales						
Emotive	10.17	4.79	9.50	5.20	9.89	4.75
Social	9.74	3.45	9.87	4.38	9.98	3.63
Process	6.22	2.89	6.35	2.92	6.58	2.71
Control	10.76	3.10	8.97	3.52	6.90	3.62
Change	3.78	1.28	3.79	1.74	2.62	1.49
Preference Usual Scales						
Activity	4.25	1.53	4.12	1.73	3.19	1.87
Empathy	3.21	2.58	3.17	2.83	3.43	2.99
Thought	0.85	0.88	0.63	0.84	1.08	0.96
Communication	5.87	2.78	5.10	3.01	5.82	3.03
Interaction	7.71	2.46	9.00	2.52	7.71	3.02
Incentive	2.15	1.60	1.91	1.53	1.69	1.69
Authority	5.65	1.75	4.18	2.01	4.38	2.08
Preference Needs Scales						
Activity	2.98	1.67	3.07	1.70	2.37	1.57
Empathy	5.46	2.97	5.41	3.15	4.59	2.92
Thought	1.69	1.03	1.16	1.01	1.67	1.00
Communication	8.21	1.92	8.26	2.50	7.37	2.68
Interaction	5.94	2.30	6.13	2.62	5.36	2.28
Incentive	4.48	1.84	4.19	2.14	2.85	2.01
Authority	6.29	1.79	4.79	1.93	4.06	2.08
Other Scales						
Personal Autonomy: Usual	4.44	3.23	3.92	3.65	5.80	4.08
Personal Autonomy: Needs	7.72	4.34	7.10	4.95	7.27	4.01
Perspective Alignment	-15.19	9.59	-15.41	11.90	-9.25	10.30

Notes: These samples are not stratified and may come from a narrow cross-section of the population of interest.
Cautious interpretation is strongly recommended; $N = 126$, 929, and 608, respectively.

BIRKMAN SCALE	KOREAN		NORWEGIAN		PORTUGUESE	
	M	SD	M	SD	M	SD
Orientation Usual Scales						
Emotive	10.74	5.96	6.38	4.50	6.74	4.52
Social	12.94	5.10	16.80	4.88	15.68	4.29
Process	10.45	2.45	8.64	2.44	9.94	2.70
Control	7.38	3.34	6.08	3.31	6.17	3.03
Change	2.48	1.74	3.29	1.78	3.80	1.76
Orientation Needs Scales						
Emotive	13.18	5.35	8.20	4.56	10.16	5.44
Social	11.24	4.52	11.51	4.60	11.76	4.66
Process	8.21	3.19	7.10	2.47	5.76	3.36
Control	10.31	3.73	7.59	3.71	9.81	3.92
Change	3.05	1.81	3.23	1.66	4.20	1.67
Preference Usual Scales						
Activity	2.13	1.89	3.73	1.82	4.15	1.71
Empathy	5.33	3.82	3.33	2.47	3.99	2.61
Thought	1.54	1.05	0.78	0.97	0.90	0.96
Communication	7.16	2.93	4.48	3.13	5.52	2.76
Interaction	8.10	3.01	9.27	2.63	9.19	2.57
Incentive	2.89	1.88	2.09	1.76	1.67	1.57
Authority	4.48	2.16	3.99	1.96	4.50	2.03
Preference Needs Scales						
Activity	1.51	1.50	3.64	1.53	2.96	1.76
Empathy	6.92	3.58	4.69	2.74	5.26	3.35
Thought	1.77	0.98	1.15	1.03	1.86	1.03
Communication	7.81	2.54	7.98	2.73	7.07	2.63
Interaction	7.05	2.84	7.49	2.59	6.83	2.79
Incentive	4.79	2.23	3.46	2.10	3.97	2.31
Authority	5.51	2.06	4.13	2.10	5.84	2.11
Other Scales						
Personal Autonomy: Usual	8.76	4.83	4.08	3.50	4.88	3.71
Personal Autonomy: Needs	10.93	4.80	6.45	4.07	9.01	5.23
Perspective Alignment	-9.32	11.73	-10.17	9.78	-15.15	12.91

TABLE 12.3   CTT STATISTICS FOR DIFFERENT LANGUAGES AND GEOGRAPHICAL AREAS (CONTINUED)

Notes: These samples are not stratified and may come from a narrow cross-section of the population of interest. Cautious interpretation is strongly recommended; $N = 1,512, 143$, and 324, respectively.

TABLE 12.4	CTT STATISTICS FOR DIFFERENT LANGUAGES AND GEOGRAPHICAL AREAS (CONTINUED)					
	SPANISH (ALL)		SPANISH (MEXICO)		SPANISH (SPAIN)	
BIRKMAN SCALE	M	SD	M	SD	M	SD
Orientation Usual Scales						
Emotive	4.22	4.37	4.08	4.40	5.00	4.51
Social	16.90	4.07	17.07	3.96	16.02	4.30
Process	10.99	2.37	10.98	2.39	9.89	2.34
Control	5.98	2.87	6.29	2.84	6.64	2.71
Change	3.31	1.70	3.39	1.67	3.40	1.84
Orientation Needs Scales						
Emotive	8.35	5.73	7.68	5.51	8.65	5.16
Social	13.18	4.36	13.56	4.45	11.97	4.20
Process	7.09	3.31	7.01	3.36	6.31	2.97
Control	8.50	4.19	8.22	3.93	8.85	3.78
Change	3.63	1.56	3.46	1.54	3.64	1.51
Preference Usual Scales						
Activity	4.77	1.53	4.82	1.53	4.46	1.53
Empathy	2.28	2.58	2.25	2.61	2.53	2.64
Thought	0.71	0.90	0.65	0.88	0.93	0.98
Communication	3.90	2.63	3.58	2.44	4.49	2.77
Interaction	8.79	2.31	8.65	2.34	8.51	2.30
Incentive	1.55	1.50	1.61	1.44	2.05	1.71
Authority	4.43	1.96	4.68	1.96	4.58	1.86
Preference Needs Scales						
Activity	3.58	1.89	3.84	1.85	3.15	1.81
Empathy	4.58	3.50	4.25	3.29	4.37	3.12
Thought	1.35	1.02	1.27	1.04	1.43	0.94
Communication	6.38	2.87	6.02	2.94	6.92	2.72
Interaction	7.56	2.37	7.58	2.34	6.88	2.37
Incentive	3.55	2.51	3.46	2.47	3.81	2.36
Authority	4.95	2.16	4.77	2.05	5.03	2.03
Other Scales						
Personal Autonomy: Usual	3.02	3.46	2.98	3.50	3.32	3.40
Personal Autonomy: Needs	6.47	5.43	5.93	5.09	6.31	5.05
Perspective Alignment	-14.27	12.50	-13.02	12.13	-13.50	12.03

Notes: These samples are not stratified and may come from a narrow cross-section of the population of interest.
Cautious interpretation is strongly recommended; N = 1,418, 582, and 118, respectively.

TABLE 12.5	CTT STATISTICS FOR DIFFERENT LANGUAGES AND GEOGRAPHICAL AREAS (CONTINUED)	
	SWEDISH	
BIRKMAN SCALE	M	SD
Orientation Usual Scales		
Emotive	6.54	4.31
Social	17.14	4.51
Process	8.75	2.48
Control	5.58	2.54
Change	2.99	1.77
Orientation Needs Scales		
Emotive	8.67	4.20
Social	11.82	4.18
Process	7.51	2.72
Control	6.61	2.98
Change	2.96	1.54
Preference Usual Scales		
Activity	3.57	1.68
Empathy	3.38	2.60
Thought	0.73	0.87
Communication	4.61	2.87
Interaction	9.76	2.43
Incentive	1.64	1.41
Authority	3.95	1.67
Preference Needs Scales		
Activity	2.94	1.59
Empathy	4.48	2.51
Thought	1.13	0.97
Communication	7.60	2.55
Interaction	7.42	2.50
Incentive	2.69	1.89
Authority	3.91	1.65
Other Scales		
Personal Autonomy: Usual	3.37	3.31
Personal Autonomy: Needs	4.68	3.63
Perspective Alignment	-9.71	9.24

Notes: These samples are not stratified and may come from a narrow cross-section of the population of interest. Cautious interpretation is strongly recommended; $N = 932$.

REFERENCES

Adler, A. (1917). *The neurotic constitution: Outlines of a comparative individualistic psychology and psycho-therapy*. New York, NY: Moffat, Yard, and Company.

Allport, G. W., & Odbert, H. S. (1936). Trait names: A psycho-lexical study. *Psychological Monographs, 47*, No. 211.

Aluja, A., García, O., & García, L. F. (2003). Relationships between extraversion, openness to experience, and sensation seeking. *Personality and Individual Differences, 35*, 671–680.

American Educational Research Association, American Psychological Association, National Council on Measurement in Education (1999). *Standards for educational and psychological testing*. Washington, DC: American Educational Research Association.

ASTM Standard F2575-06 (2006). "Standard Guide for Quality Assurance in Translation," ASTM International, West Conshohocken, PA, www.astm.org.

Ames, A. (1951). Visual perception and the rotating trapezoidal window. *Psychological Monographs, 65*(7), iii.

Angleitner, A., Ostendorf, F., & John, O. P. (1990). Towards a taxonomy of personality descriptors in German: A psycho-lexical study. *European Journal of Personality, 4*, 89-118.

Arvey, R. D., & Dewhirst, H. D. (1979). Relationships between diversity of interests, age, job satisfaction, and job performance. *Journal of Occupational Psychology, 52*, 17-23.

Asch, S. E. (1940). Studies in the principles of judgments and attitudes: II. Determination of judgments by group and by ego standards. *Journal of Social Psychology, 12*, 433-465.

Ashton, M. C., & Lee, K. (2002). Six independent factors of personality variation: A response to Saucier. *European Journal of Personality, 16*, 63-75.

Baker, F. B. (2001). *The basics of item response theory*. College Park, MD: ERIC Clearinghouse on Assessment and Evaluation.

13 REFERENCES

Barchard, K. A. (2001). *Emotional and social intelligence: Examining its place in the nomological network.* Unpublished doctoral dissertation, University of British Columbia, Vancouver, BC, Canada.

Barrick, M. R., & Mount, M. K. (1991). The Big Five personality dimensions and job performance: A meta-analysis. *Personnel Psychology, 44*, 1-26.

Barry, B., & Stewart, G. L. (1997). Composition, process, and performance in self-managed groups: The role of personality. *Journal of Applied Psychology, 82*, 62-78.

Barrick, M. R., Stewart, G. L., Neubert, M. J., & Mount, M. K. (1998). Relating member ability and personality to work-team processes and team effectiveness. *Journal of Applied Psychology, 83*, 377-391.

Baumann, N., & Kuhl, J. (2005). How to resist temptation: The effects of external control versus autonomy support on self-regulatory dynamics. *Journal of Personality, 73*, 443-470.

Baumeister, R. F., Heatherton, T. F., & Tice, D. M. (1994). *Losing control: How and why people fail at self-regulation.* San Diego, CA: Academic Press.

Baumeister, R. F., & Vohs, K. D. (2004). *Handbook of self-regulation: Research, theory, and applications.* New York, NY: Guilford Press.

Berger, E. M. (1952). The relation between expressed acceptance of self and expressed acceptance of others. *The Journal of Abnormal and Social Psychology, 47*(4), 778-782.

Biernat, M., Manis, M., & Kobrynowicz, D. (1997). Simultaneous assimilation and contrast effects in judgements of self and others. *Journal of Personality and Social Psychology, 73*, 254-269.

Birkman, R. W. (1961). *Development of a personality test using social and self-perception inventories.* Unpublished doctoral dissertation, University of Texas, Austin, TX.

Birkman, R. W. (1997). *True Colors.* Nashville, TN: Thomas Nelson, Inc.

Birkman, R. W., & Sadler, T. G. (2001). *Birkman Reliability & Validity Manual.* Houston, TX: Birkman International, Inc.

Birnbaum, A. (1968). Some latent trait models and their use in inferring an examinee's ability. In F. M. Lord & M. R. Novick (Eds.), *Statistical theories of mental test scores.* Reading, MA: Addison-Wesley.

Blake, R. R., & Mouton, J. S. (1964). *The managerial grid.* Houston, TX: Gulf Publishing Company.

Blake, R. R., & Ramsey, G. V. (1951). *Perception: An approach to personality.* New York, NY: Ronald Press Company.

Bono, J. E., & Judge, T. A. (2004). Personality and transformational and transactional leadership: A meta-analysis. *Journal of Applied Psychology, 89*, 901-910.

Briggs-Myers, I., McCaulley, M. H., Quenk, N. L., & Hammer, A. L. (2003). *MBTI® manual: A guide to the development and use of the Myers-Briggs Type Indicator.* Mountain View, CA: CPP, Inc.

Browne, M. W., & Cudeck, R. (1993). Alternative ways of assessing model fit. In K. A. Bollen & J. S. Long (Eds.), *Testing structural equation models* (pp. 136-162). Newbury Park, CA: Sage Publications.

Bruner, J. S., & Goodman, C. C. (1947). Value and need as organizing factors in perception. *The Journal of Abnormal and Social Psychology, 42*, 33-44.

Bruner, J. S., & Postman, L. (1947). Emotional selectivity in perception and reaction. *Journal of Personality, 16*, 69-77.

Bruner, J. S., & Postman, L. (1948). Symbolic value as an organizing factor in perception. *The Journal of Social Psychology, 27*, 203-208.

Buss, A. H. (1980). *Self-consciousness and social anxiety.* San Francisco, CA: W. H. Freeman.

Cattell, R. B. (1943). The description of personality: Basic traits resolved into clusters. *Journal of Abnormal and Social Psychology, 38*, 476-506.

Cattell, R. B. (1946). *Description and measurement of personality.* New York, NY: World Book Company.

Cattell, R. B. (1966). *Handbook of multivariate experimental psychology.* Chicago, IL: Rand McNally.

Chowdhry, K., & Newcomb, T. M. (1952). The relative abilities of leaders and non-leaders to estimate opinions of their own groups. *The Journal of Abnormal and Social Psychology, 47*(1), 51-57.

Chuah, S. C., Lee, W. C., & Wadlington, P. L. (2001, April). *The UIUC IRT web tutorial.* Paper presented at the 16th Annual Conference of the Society for Industrial and Organizational Psychology, San Diego, CA.

Conn, S. R., & Rieke, M. L. (1994). *The 16PF fifth edition technical manual.* Champaign, IL: Institute for Personality and Ability Testing.

Costa, P. T., & McCrae, R. R. (1985). *The NEO Personality Inventory.* Odessa, FL: Psychological Assessment Resources.

Costa, P. T., & McCrae, R. R. (1988). Personality in adulthood: A six-year longitudinal study of self-reports and spouse ratings on the NEO Personality Inventory. *Journal of Personality and Social Psychology, 54*, 853-863.

Costa, P. T., & McCrae, R. R. (1992). *Revised NEO Personality Inventory (NEO-PI-R) and NEO Five-Factor Inventory (NEO-FFI) professional manual*. Odessa, FL: Psychological Assessment Resources.

Davies, S. A., Norris, D., Turner, J. V., & Wadlington, P. L. (2005, April). *Cheating, guessing, faking, and self-presentation in assessment responses*. Paper presented at the 20th Annual Conference of the Society for Industrial and Organizational Psychology, Los Angeles, CA.

Davies, S. A., & Wadlington, P. L. (2006, May). *Factor & parameter invariance of a Five Factor personality test across proctored/unproctored computerized administration*. In S. T. Hunt (Chair), "Empirical investigations of unproctored personality measures used for employee selection." Paper in the symposium presented at the 21st Annual Conference of the Society for Industrial and Organizational Psychology, Dallas, TX.

Davies, S. A., & Wadlington, P. L. (2007, April). *The impact of testing conditions on online assessment.* In J. A. Weiner (Chair), "Interactions in test administration settings: The effects of applicant personality." Paper in the symposium presented at the 22nd Annual Conference of the Society for Industrial and Organizational Psychology, New York, NY.

Digman, J. M. (1990). Personality structure: Emergence of the five-factor model. *Annual Review of Psychology, 41*, 417-440.

Embretson, S. E., & Reise, S. P. (2000). *Item response theory for psychologists*. Mahwah, NJ: Lawrence Erlbaum Associates.

Epstein, S., & Feist, G. J. (1988). Relation between self- and other-acceptance and its moderation by identification. *Journal of Personality and Social Psychology, 54*(2), 309-315.

Equal Employment Opportunity Commission (1978). Uniform guidelines on employee selection procedures. *Federal Register, 43*, 38, 290-38, 315.

Eysenck, H. J. (1992). Four ways five factors are not basic. *Personality and Individual Differences, 13*, 667–673.

Fiske, D. W. (1949). Consistency of the factorial structure of personality ratings from different sources. *Journal of Abnormal and Social Psychology, 44*(3), 329-344.

Fried, Y., & Ferris, G. R. (1987). The validity of the job characteristics model: A review and meta-analysis. *Personnel Psychology, 40*, 287-322.

Fromm, E. (1939). Selfishness and self-love. *Psychiatry: Journal for the Study of Interpersonal Processes, 2*, 507-523.

Furnham, A., & Fudge, C. (2008). The Five Factor model of personality and sales performance. *Journal of Individual Differences*, *29*(1), 11-16.

Gage, N. L., & Suci, G. (1951). Social perception and teacher-pupil relationships. *Journal of Educational Psychology*, *42*(3), 144-152.

Goffin, R. D., Rothstein, M. G., & Johnston, N. G. (1996). Personality testing and the assessment center: Incremental validity for managerial selection. *Journal of Applied Psychology*, *81*, 746-756.

Goldberg, L. R. (1981). Language and individual differences: The search for universals in personality lexicons. In L. Wheeler (Ed.), *Review of personality and social psychology* (Vol. 2, pp. 141-165). Beverly Hills, CA: Sage.

Goldberg, L. R. (1990). An alternate "Description of personality": The Big-Five factor structure. *Journal of Personality and Social Psychology*, *59*, 1216-1229.

Goldberg, L. R. (1992). The development of markers for the Big-Five factor structure. *Psychological Assessment*, *4*, 26-42.

Goldberg, L. R. (1999). A broad-bandwidth, public domain, personality inventory measuring the lower-level facets of several five-factor models. In I. Mervielde, I. Deary, F. De Fruyt, & F. Ostendorf (Eds.), *Personality psychology in Europe*, (Vol. 7, pp. 7-28). Tilburg, Netherlands: Tilburg University Press.

Goldberg, L. R., Johnson, J. A., Eber, H. W., Hogan, R., Ashton, M. C., Cloninger, C. R., & Gough, H. C. (2006). The International Personality Item Pool and the future of public-domain personality measures. *Journal of Research in Personality*, *40*, 84-96.

Goodman, H. (1953). Self-insight, empathy, and perceptual distortion: a study of the relationships between measures of self-insight, empathy, and perceptual distortion as obtained from ratings made by individuals on themselves and others in their group. *Dissertation Abstracts*, *13*, 120.

Guion, R. M., & Gottier, R. F. (1965). Validity of personality measures in personnel selection. *Personnel Psychology*, *18*(2), 135-164.

Hambleton, R. K., & Swaminathan, H. (1985). *Item response theory: Principles and applications*. Norwell, MA: Kluwer Academic Publishers.

Hanfmann, E., Stein, M. I., & Bruner, J. S. (1947). Personality factors in the temporal development of perceptual organization: A methodological note. *American Psychologist*, *2*, 284-285.

Healy, W., Bronner, A. F., & Bowers, A. M. (1930). *The structure and meaning of psychoanalysis*. New York, NY: Knopf.

Heller, M. (2005). Court ruling that employer's integrity test violated ADA could open door to litigation. *Workforce Management, 84*(9), 74-77.

Hendriks, A. A., Perugini, M., Angleitner, A., Ostendorf, F., Johnson, J. A., De Fruyt, F., Hrebickova, M., Kreitler, S., Murakami, T., Bratko, D., Conner, M., Nagy, J., Rodriguez-Fornells, A., & Ruisel, I. (2003). The Five-Factor Personality Inventory: Cross-cultural generalizability across 13 countries. *European Journal of Personality, 17*, 347-373.

Higgins, E. T. (1997). Beyond pleasure and pain. *American Psychologist, 52*, 1280-1300.

Hillson, J. S., & Worchel, P. (1957). Self concept and defensive behavior in the maladjusted. *Journal of Consulting Psychology, 21*(1), 83-88.

Hogan, R., & Hogan, J. (2007). *Hogan Personality Inventory Manual: Third Edition*. Tulsa, OK: Hogan Assessment Systems.

Hofstee, W. K., de Raad, B., & Goldberg, L. R. (1992). Integration of the Big Five and circumplex approaches to trait structure. *Journal of Personality and Social Psychology, 63*, 146-163.

Holland, J. L. (1976). Vocational preferences. In M. D. Dunnette (Ed.), *Handbook of industrial and organizational psychology*. Chicago, IL: Rand McNally.

Holtzman, W. H. (1958). *Holtzman Inkblot Technique*. San Antonio, TX: Psychological Corporation.

Hulin, C. L., Drasgow, F., & Parsons, C. K. (1983). *Item response theory: Application to psychological measurement*. Homewood, IL: Dow Jones-Irwin.

International Personality Item Pool: A Scientific Collaboratory for the Development of Advanced Measures of Personality Traits and Other Individual Differences (http://ipip.ori.org/). Internet Web Site.

Jackson, D. N. (1994). *Jackson Personality Inventory-Revised manual*. Port Huron, MI: Sigma Assessment Systems.

Jackson, D. N., Paunonen, S. V., & Tremblay, P. F. (2000). *Six Factor Personality Questionnaire Manual*. Port Huron, MI: Sigma Assessment Systems.

John, O. P. (1990). Dimensionality of the multiple affect Adjective Check List-Revised: A comparison of factor analytic procedures. *Journal of Psychopathology and Behavioral Assessment, 12*(1), 81-91.

Joint Committee on Testing Practices (2004). *Code of fair testing practices in education*. National Council on Measurement in Education.

Judge, T. A., & Bono, J. E. (2000). Five-Factor Model of personality and transformational leadership. *Journal of Applied Psychology, 85,* 751-765.

Judge, T. A., Bono, J. E., Ilies, R., & Gerhardt, M. W. (2002). Personality and leadership: A qualitative and quantitative review. *Journal of Applied Psychology, 87,* 765-780.

Judge, T. A., Heller, D., & Mount, M. K. (2002). Personality and job satisfaction: A meta-analysis. *Journal of Applied Psychology, 87,* 530-541.

Justice, B., & Birkman, R. W. (1972). An effort to distinguish the violent from the nonviolent. *Southern Medical Journal, 65,* 703-706.

Karniol, R. (2003). Egocentrism versus protocentrism: The status of self in social prediction. *Psychological Review, 110,* 564-580.

Kelly, E. L., & Fiske, D. W. (1951). *The prediction of performance in clinical psychology.* Ann Arbor, MI: University of Michigan Press.

Kickul, J., & Neuman, G. (2000). Emergent leadership behaviors: the function of personality and cognitive ability in determining teamwork performance and KSAs. *Journal of Business and Psychology, 15,* 27-51.

Kuder, F. (1946). *Revised Manual for the Kuder Preference Record.* Chicago, IL: Science Research Associates.

Lee, K., & Ashton, M. C. (2004). Psychometric properties of the HEXACO Personality Inventory. *Multivariate Behavioral Research, 39,* 329-358.

Lehner, G. F. (1949). Some relationships between scores for self and projected "average" scores on a personality test. *American Psychologist, 4,* 390.

Little, I. S., Wadlington, P. L., & Turner, J. V. (2007, April). *The cross-cultural measurement equivalence of personality using CFA and IRT.* In S. Bedwell (Chair), "Santa Claus, the Tooth Fairy, and perfect measurement equivalence." Paper in the symposium presented at the 22nd Annual Conference of the Society for Industrial and Organizational Psychology, New York, NY.

Lord, F. (1980). *Applications of item response theory to practical testing problems.* Hillsdale, NJ: Lawrence Erlbaum Associates.

Marple, C. H. (1933). The comparative susceptibility of three age levels to the suggestion of group versus expert opinion. *Journal of Social Psychology, 4,* 176-186.

McCrae, R. R., & Costa, P. T. (1987). Validation of the Five-Factor Model of personality across instruments and observers. *Journal of Personality and Social Psychology, 52,* 81-90.

McCrae, R. R., & Costa, P. T. (1997). Personality trait structure as a human universal. *American Psychologist*, *52*, 509-516.

McDougall, W. (1926). *Outline of abnormal psychology*. New York, NY: Scribner.

McIntyre, C. J. (1952). Acceptance by others and its relation to acceptance of self and others. *The Journal of Abnormal and Social Psychology*, *47*(3), 624-625.

Mead, G. H. (1934). *Mind, self, and society from the standpoint of a social behaviorist*. Chicago, IL: University of Chicago Press.

Mefferd, R. (1992). *Cross-cultural validity of The Birkman Method®: Comparison of Native American and Native Oriental graduate students in schools and business*. Houston, TX: Birkman & Associates, Inc.

Moore, H. T. (1921). The comparative influence of majority and expert opinion. *American Journal of Psychology*, *32*, 16-20.

Morgeson, F. P., Reider, M. H., & Campion, M. A. (2005). Selecting individuals in team settings: The importance of social skills, personality characteristics, and teamwork knowledge. *Personnel Psychology*, *58*, 583-611.

Muraven, M., & Baumeister, R. F. (2000). Self-regulation and depletion of limited resources: Does self-control resemble a muscle? *Psychological Bulletin*, *126*, 247-259.

Murray, H. A., & Morgan, C. D. (1945). A clinical study of sentiments (I & II). *Genetic Psychology Monographs*, *32*, 152-311.

Newcomb, T. M. (1943). *Personality and social change: Attitude formation in a student community*. Fort Worth, TX: Dryden Press.

Norman, W. T. (1963). Toward an adequate taxonomy of personality attributes: Replicated factor structure in peer nomination personality ratings. *Journal of Abnormal and Social Psychology*, *66*, 574-583.

Norman, R. D., & Ainsworth, P. (1954). The relationships among projection, empathy, reality and adjustment, operationally defined. *Journal of Consulting Psychology*, *18*(1), 53-58.

Omwake, K. T. (1954). The relation between acceptance of self and acceptance of others shown by three personality inventories. *Journal of Consulting Psychology*, *18*(6), 443-446.

Paulhus, D. L. (1991). Measurement and control of response bias. In J. P. Robinson, P. R. Shaver, & L. S. Wrightsman (Eds.), *Measures of personality and social psychological attitudes* (Vol. 1, pp. 17-59). New York, NY: Academic Press.

Paunonen, S. V., Jackson, D. N., Trzebinski, J., & Forsterling, F. (1992). Personality structure across cultures: A multimethod evaluation. *Journal of Personality and Social Psychology, 62,* 447-456.

Phillips, E. L. (1951). Attitudes toward self and others: A brief questionnaire report. *Journal of Consulting Psychology, 15*(1), 79-81.

Piotrowski, C., & Armstrong, T. (2006). Current recruitment and selection practices: A national survey of Fortune 1000 firms. *North American Journal of Psychology, 8*(3), 489-496.

Postman, L., Bruner, J. S., & McGinnies, E. (1948). Personal values as selective factors in perception. *The Journal of Abnormal and Social Psychology, 43,* 142-154.

Quenk, N. L. (1993). *Beside ourselves: Our hidden personality in everyday life.* Palo Alto, CA: CPP.

Quenk, N. L., Hammer, A. L., & Majors, M. S. (2001). *MBTI® Step II: Exploring the next level of type with the Myers-Briggs Type Indictor® Form Q.* Mountain View, CA: CPP, Inc.

Rogers, C. R. (1949). A coordinated research in psychotherapy: A nonobjective introduction. *Journal of Consulting Psychology, 13*(3), 149-153.

Rothstein, M. G., & Goffin, R. D. (2006). The use of personality measures in personnel selection: What does current research support? *Human Resource Management Review, 16,* 155-180.

Roznowski, M. (1989). An examination of the measurement properties of the Job Descriptive Index with experimental items. *Journal of Applied Psychology, 74,* 805-814.

Sala, F. (2003). Executive blind spots: Discrepancies between self- and other-ratings. *Consulting Psychology Journal: Practice and Research, 55,* 222-229.

Salgado, J. F. (1998). Big Five personality dimensions and job performance in army and civil occupations: A European perspective. *Human Performance, 11,* 271-288.

Salgado, J. F. (2003). Predicting job performance using FFM and non-FFM personality measures. *Journal of Occupational and Organizational Psychology, 76,* 323-346.

Sande, G. N., Goethals, G. R., & Radloff, C. E. (1988). Perceiving one's own traits and others': The multifaceted self. *Journal of Personality and Social Psychology, 54,* 13-20.

Schutz, W. (1994). *The human element: Productivity, self-esteem, and the bottom line.* San Francisco, CA: Jossey-Bass.

Segall, D. O., Moreno, K. E., Bloxom, B. M., & Hetter, R. D. (1997). Psychometric procedures for administering CAT-ASVAB. In W. A. Sands, B. K. Waters, & J. R. McBride (Eds.), *Computerized adaptive testing* (pp. 131-140). Washington, DC: American Psychological Association.

Sears, R. R. (1937). Experimental studies of projection: II. Ideas of reference. *Journal of Social Psychology*, *8*, 389-400.

Sheerer, E. T. (1949). An analysis of the relationship between acceptance of and respect for self and acceptance of and respect for others in ten counseling cases. *Journal of Consulting Psychology*, *13*(3), 169-175.

Sherif, M. (1935). A study of some social factors in perception. *Archives of Psychology (Columbia University)*, *No. 187*, pp. 60.

Sherif, M. (1936). *The psychology of social norms*. New York, NY: Harper and Bros.

SHL (1984a, 1993a). OPQ *Concept Model Manual and User's Guide*. Thames Ditton, UK: SHL Group.

Smith, P. C., Kendall, L., & Hulin, C. L. (1969). *The measurement of satisfaction in work and retirement: A strategy for the study of attitudes*. Chicago, IL: Rand McNally.

Snyder, M. (1974). Self-monitoring of expressive behavior. *Journal of Personality and Social Psychology*, *30*, 526-537.

Stanton, J. M., Sinar, E. F., Balzer, W. K., Julian, A. L., Thoresen, P., Aziz, S., Fisher, G. G., & Smith, P. C. (2002). Development of a compact measure of job satisfaction: The abridged Job Descriptive Index. *Educational and Psychological Measurement*, *62*, 173-191.

Stock, D. (1949). An investigation into the interrelations between the self concept and feelings directed toward other persons and groups. *Journal of Consulting Psychology*, *13*(3), 176-180.

Strong, E. K. (1927). *Vocational Interest Blank*. Stanford, CA: Stanford University Press.

Suinn, R. M. (1961). The relationship between self-acceptance and acceptance of others: A learning theory analysis. *The Journal of Abnormal and Social Psychology*, *63*(1), 37-42.

Sullivan, H. S. (1940). *Conceptions of modern psychiatry: The first William Alanson White Memorial Lectures*. New York: W. W. Norton & Company.

Sweet, L. (1929). *Personal attitudes test for younger boys*. New York, NY: The Association Press.

Tellegen, A. (2000). *Manual for the Multidimensional Personality Questionnaire*. Minneapolis, MN: University of Minnesota Press.

Tett, R. P., Jackson, D. N., & Rothstein, M. (1991). Personality measures as predictors of job performance: A meta-analytic review. *Personnel Psychology, 44,* 703-742.

Tobolski, F. P., & Kerr, W. A. (1952). Predictive value of the Empathy Test in automobile salesmanship. *Journal of Applied Psychology, 36*(5), 310-311.

Travers, R. M. W. (1941). A study in judging the opinions of groups. *Archives of Psychology (Columbia University), No. 266,* pp. 73.

Trull, T. J., & Geary, D. C. (1997). Comparison of the Big-Five Factor structure across samples of Chinese and American adults. *Journal of Personality Assessment, 69,* 324-341.

Tupes, E. C. (1957). *Personality traits related to effectiveness of junior and senior Air Force officers.* USAF Personnel Training Research Center Research Report, No. 57-125.

Tupes, E. C., & Christal, R. E. (1961). *Recurrent personality factors based on trait ratings* (ASD-TR-61-97). Lackland Air Force Base, TX: Aeronautical Systems Division, Personnel Laboratory.

Van Zelst, R. H. (1952). Empathy test scores of union leaders. *Journal of Applied Psychology, 36*(5), 293-295.

Vohs, K. D., & Heatherton, T. F. (2000). Self-regulatory failure: A resource-depletion approach. *Psychological Science, 11,* 249-254.

Wallen, R. (1943). Individuals' estimates of group opinion. *Journal of Social Psychology, 17,* 269-274.

Wadlington, P. L., & Davies, S. C. (2006, May). *Necessity, advantages, and requirements of dynamic testing in personnel selection.* In P. L. Wadlington (Chair), "Dynamic testing: An essential ingredient in personnel selection." Paper in the symposium presented at the 21st Annual Conference of the Society for Industrial and Organizational Psychology, Dallas, TX.

Wadlington, P. L., Davies, S. C., & Phillips, G. (2006, May). *Distributional projection: Solution to a small sample size.* In P. L. Wadlington (Chair), "Developing and Using Norms: Why, how, and what's new." Paper in the symposium presented at the 21st Annual Conference of the Society for Industrial and Organizational Psychology, Dallas, TX.

Wadlington, P. L., Drasgow, F., Fitzgerald, L. (2002, April). *The generalizability of sexual harassment models across heterogeneous organizations.* Paper presented in the symposium, "Sexual harassment in organizations: Multilevel perspectives for theory and research", presented at the 17th Annual Conference of the Society of Industrial and Organizational Psychology, Toronto, Ontario.

13 REFERENCES

Wadlington, P. L., Little, I. S., & Turner, J. V. (2007, April). *Methodology for the development and validation of new forms of personality assessments in an unproctored environment.* In F. Drasgow (Chair), "Advancing research on unproctored internet testing." Paper in the symposium presented at the 22nd Annual Conference of the Society for Industrial and Organizational Psychology, New York, NY.

Watson, D., & Clark, L. A. (1994). *The PANAS-X: Manual for the Positive and Negative Affect Schedule – Expanded Form.* University of Iowa.

Watson, D., Clark, L. A., & Tellegen, A. (1988). Development and validation of brief measures of positive and negative affect: The PANAS scales. *Journal of Personality and Social Psychology, 54,* 1063-1070.

Wiggins, J. S., & Pincus, A. L. (1992). Personality: Structure and assessment. *Annual Review of Psychology, 43,* 473-504.

Yang, K. S., & Bond, M. H. (1990). Exploring implicit personality theories with indigenous or imported constructs: The Chinese case. *Journal of Personality and Social Psychology, 58,* 1087-1095.

Zickar, M. J. (2001). Conquering the next frontier: Modeling personality data with item response theory. In B. W. Roberts & R. Hogan (Eds.), *Personality psychology in the workplace.* Washington, DC: American Psychological Association.

Zuckerman, M. (1994). *Behavioral expressions and biosocial bases of sensation seeking.* New York, NY: Cambridge University Press.

APPENDICES

APPENDICES

APPENDIX A

DESCRIPTIVE STATISTICS FOR 2007 NORMATIVE DATA SET

TABLE A.1   ETHNICITY

BIRKMAN SCALE	BLACK		ASIAN/PI		WHITE	
	M	SD	M	SD	M	SD
Orientation Usual Scales						
Emotive	4.17	4.01	5.42	4.97	5.49	4.89
Social	18.42	4.58	14.67	4.86	16.88	5.24
Process	10.52	2.88	9.96	2.87	9.47	2.95
Control	5.18	3.09	5.87	3.70	5.30	3.01
Change	2.38	1.75	3.12	1.82	3.42	1.94
Orientation Needs Scales						
Emotive	7.95	5.67	8.58	4.93	8.45	5.39
Social	12.64	5.01	11.68	4.23	11.40	4.81
Process	7.65	3.61	6.57	3.44	6.07	3.39
Control	9.14	4.36	9.22	4.23	8.43	3.86
Change	3.58	1.81	3.56	1.54	3.61	1.69
Preference Usual Scales						
Activity	4.23	1.81	4.03	1.87	3.88	1.98
Empathy	1.87	2.20	2.57	2.71	2.60	2.75
Thought	0.53	0.83	0.88	1.02	0.77	0.93
Communication	3.71	2.87	6.02	3.23	4.85	3.12
Interaction	10.13	2.48	8.70	2.66	9.73	2.91
Incentive	1.82	1.54	1.92	2.03	1.68	1.47
Authority	3.36	2.05	3.95	2.21	3.62	2.08
Preference Needs Scales						
Activity	3.29	1.91	2.88	1.77	2.99	1.92
Empathy	3.82	3.38	3.86	3.01	4.06	3.12
Thought	1.42	1.13	1.60	1.04	1.39	1.07
Communication	7.24	2.87	7.97	2.67	8.04	2.58
Interaction	7.88	2.87	7.65	2.74	7.43	2.99
Incentive	4.08	2.39	3.96	2.34	3.72	2.16
Authority	5.06	2.39	5.26	2.28	4.71	2.15
Other Scales						
Personal Autonomy: Usual	2.80	2.99	4.03	3.90	3.77	3.73
Personal Autonomy: Needs	5.81	5.10	6.18	4.73	5.72	4.91
Perspective Alignment	-16.39	13.33	-12.89	11.98	-14.97	12.74

Notes: PI = Pacific Islander; *N* = 414, 216, and 3,180, respectively.

TABLE A.2   ETHNICITY (CONTINUED)

BIRKMAN SCALE	HISPANIC		NA/AN	
	M	SD	M	SD
Orientation Usual Scales				
Emotive	4.40	4.39	4.58	4.99
Social	17.77	4.79	18.61	4.50
Process	10.38	2.60	10.24	2.41
Control	4.67	3.07	5.30	3.03
Change	3.12	1.91	3.44	1.80
Orientation Needs Scales				
Emotive	7.76	5.60	7.71	5.85
Social	12.97	4.85	12.64	5.13
Process	7.57	3.35	6.97	3.46
Control	8.13	4.42	8.29	3.99
Change	3.70	1.78	4.21	1.77
Preference Usual Scales				
Activity	4.33	1.74	4.38	1.89
Empathy	2.03	2.48	2.27	2.87
Thought	0.69	0.91	0.68	1.01
Communication	4.29	2.98	3.83	2.82
Interaction	10.06	2.54	10.44	2.53
Incentive	1.41	1.46	1.67	1.70
Authority	3.26	2.05	3.64	2.04
Preference Needs Scales				
Activity	3.40	1.88	3.39	2.01
Empathy	3.74	3.31	3.77	3.30
Thought	1.43	1.09	1.33	1.15
Communication	7.20	2.82	7.42	3.15
Interaction	8.17	2.89	8.06	2.79
Incentive	3.37	2.43	3.56	2.16
Authority	4.76	2.39	4.73	2.29
Other Scales				
Personal Autonomy: Usual	2.96	3.27	3.53	3.79
Personal Autonomy: Needs	5.58	5.19	5.70	5.43
Perspective Alignment	-14.43	13.22	-15.36	13.77

Notes: NA = Native American, AN = Alaskan Native; *N* = 344 and 66, respectively.

TABLE A.3   GENDER

BIRKMAN SCALE	FEMALE		MALE	
	M	SD	M	SD
Orientation Usual Scales				
Emotive	6.03	4.86	4.58	4.63
Social	16.49	5.11	17.59	5.14
Process	9.42	2.94	9.90	2.91
Control	4.55	2.81	5.90	3.15
Change	3.33	1.96	3.24	1.92
Orientation Needs Scales				
Emotive	8.43	5.19	8.29	5.60
Social	11.96	4.70	11.43	4.98
Process	6.44	3.32	6.34	3.59
Control	8.16	3.99	8.82	3.94
Change	3.70	1.69	3.54	1.71
Preference Usual Scales				
Activity	3.58	1.98	4.30	1.85
Empathy	2.70	2.71	2.28	2.67
Thought	0.92	0.97	0.60	0.86
Communication	5.38	3.10	4.09	2.97
Interaction	9.87	2.75	9.68	2.92
Incentive	1.50	1.37	1.85	1.61
Authority	3.05	1.97	4.05	2.08
Preference Needs Scales				
Activity	2.91	1.87	3.18	1.95
Empathy	3.94	3.02	4.06	3.26
Thought	1.40	1.06	1.41	1.10
Communication	7.80	2.63	7.92	2.69
Interaction	7.76	2.90	7.35	3.01
Incentive	3.67	2.21	3.79	2.23
Authority	4.49	2.21	5.03	2.15
Other Scales				
Personal Autonomy: Usual	3.82	3.66	3.45	3.66
Personal Autonomy: Needs	5.51	4.74	5.96	5.12
Perspective Alignment	-13.51	12.32	-16.34	13.06

Notes: N = 2,038 for females, N = 2,262 for males.

TABLE A.4   AGE

BIRKMAN SCALE	<40		≥40	
	M	SD	M	SD
Orientation Usual Scales				
Emotive	5.66	4.91	5.11	4.75
Social	17.41	5.12	16.81	5.19
Process	9.89	2.99	9.51	2.90
Control	5.67	3.22	5.07	2.96
Change	3.44	1.93	3.22	1.94
Orientation Needs Scales				
Emotive	9.07	5.52	8.00	5.32
Social	12.12	4.93	11.37	4.78
Process	6.41	3.58	6.33	3.38
Control	8.95	4.10	8.29	3.88
Change	3.84	1.73	3.50	1.68
Preference Usual Scales				
Activity	3.81	1.98	4.02	1.94
Empathy	2.62	2.75	2.43	2.68
Thought	0.85	0.96	0.70	0.91
Communication	4.65	3.13	4.77	3.10
Interaction	10.06	2.76	9.58	2.88
Incentive	1.83	1.61	1.61	1.45
Authority	3.84	2.14	3.46	2.05
Preference Needs Scales				
Activity	2.80	1.96	3.18	1.88
Empathy	4.33	3.24	3.84	3.09
Thought	1.54	1.07	1.33	1.08
Communication	7.71	2.75	7.99	2.60
Interaction	7.82	2.95	7.36	2.97
Incentive	3.91	2.29	3.65	2.17
Authority	5.04	2.21	4.64	2.17
Other Scales				
Personal Autonomy: Usual	3.87	3.80	3.54	3.60
Personal Autonomy: Needs	6.32	5.08	5.47	4.86
Perspective Alignment	-15.46	12.78	-14.72	12.85

Notes: $N = 1{,}576$ for < 40, $N = 2{,}606$ for ≥ 40.

APPENDIX B

AGE GROUP COMPARISONS

TABLE B.1 COMPARISON OF SCALE MEANS FOR PERSONS OF DIFFERENT AGE GROUPS GATHERED BETWEEN 1995 AND 2000

SCALE NAME / AGE	13-16	17-19	20-24	25-30	31-40	41-50	51-60	61-70
SAMPLE SIZE	378	656	3,324	8,838	19,510	16,793	6,443	532
Esteem Usual	37.68	32.60	26.75	25.06	23.95	23.48	22.29	21.50
Esteem Needs	57.43	54.84	51.41	52.07	55.77	57.69	58.48	58.68
Acceptance Usual	76.07	76.41	80.90	79.91	77.02	74.51	74.37	74.21
Acceptance Needs	53.26	55.80	60.16	57.52	53.67	52.88	53.03	53.74
Structure Usual	52.87	64.29	75.70	71.97	67.46	66.26	66.69	68.25
Structure Needs	35.18	43.98	52.54	51.24	50.80	52.50	54.03	53.72
Authority Usual	71.72	64.86	53.77	52.91	52.71	51.54	51.84	47.64
Authority Needs	82.12	77.35	65.97	59.22	54.18	52.04	50.64	49.68
Advantage Usual	45.98	35.79	23.91	21.74	19.90	18.84	19.02	19.09
Advantage Needs	81.52	75.80	63.00	58.98	54.04	51.42	50.79	51.67
Activity Usual	59.06	64.33	77.04	77.81	79.13	79.55	81.29	79.03
Activity Needs	38.35	42.32	51.51	51.91	52.88	54.72	56.79	55.13
Challenge Usual	53.18	50.73	48.07	49.31	50.11	51.44	51.55	51.63
Challenge Needs	53.18	50.73	48.07	49.31	50.11	51.44	51.55	51.63
Empathy Usual	69.67	62.53	47.60	43.47	39.64	38.70	36.63	36.37
Empathy Needs	83.88	79.54	66.53	60.47	55.21	53.64	52.68	52.25
Change Usual	74.33	67.30	61.50	59.47	57.57	54.09	53.16	50.17
Change Needs	83.93	78.35	68.37	62.88	56.84	53.32	53.37	55.34
Freedom Usual	59.13	49.12	34.64	35.93	36.48	36.53	35.79	36.27
Freedom Needs	82.65	75.55	62.23	59.53	55.23	51.67	49.44	51.70
Thought Usual	71.11	61.48	44.26	41.20	37.88	36.32	33.25	35.69
Thought Needs	84.40	78.26	66.12	61.17	56.96	53.88	52.82	55.34
Persuasive Interest	62.85	59.62	55.52	52.98	53.36	53.25	55.60	58.21
Social Service Interest	42.97	46.39	51.80	50.51	48.80	47.23	45.97	47.88
Scientific Interest	54.23	53.43	52.45	53.81	52.70	51.28	48.85	45.19
Mechanical Interest	48.56	48.96	46.65	48.69	52.90	54.95	56.62	53.55
Outdoor Interest	42.92	42.96	41.12	46.03	51.86	53.96	55.46	48.92
Numerical Interest	50.21	50.55	56.64	54.50	52.45	50.49	51.37	53.88
Clerical Interest	64.77	63.31	60.40	52.79	48.19	46.11	47.06	51.78
Artistic Interest	51.51	49.15	46.26	48.97	48.38	48.21	44.90	43.31
Literary Interest	52.34	48.81	48.72	53.09	53.99	56.50	54.27	56.95
Musical Interest	51.37	50.41	51.07	53.76	54.45	55.73	51.26	51.43

APPENDIX C

FREQUENCY DISTRIBUTIONS FOR THE 2007 NORMATIVE DATA SET

TABLE C.1   CUMULATIVE FREQUENCY DISTRIBUTION FOR ORIENTATIONS USUAL SCALES

RAW	PERCENTILE				
	EMOTIVE	SOCIAL	PROCESS	CONTROL	CHANGE
0	14	0	0	3	7
1	26	0	0	10	21
2	37	0	1	20	38
3	46	1	3	32	56
4	54	1	5	44	71
5	62	2	9	57	84
6	67	3	16	69	94
7	73	5	23	78	100
8	78	8	34	85	
9	82	10	45	90	
10	85	13	57	94	
11	87	17	69	96	
12	90	21	81	98	
13	92	25	92	99	
14	94	30	98	100	
15	95	35	100	100	
16	97	40		100	
17	98	47		100	
18	99	54		100	
19	99	61		100	
20	100	68			
21	100	76			
22	100	86			
23		93			
24		98			
25		100			

Notes: N = 4,300.

TABLE C.2   CUMULATIVE FREQUENCY DISTRIBUTION FOR ORIENTATIONS NEEDS SCALES

RAW	EMOTIVE	SOCIAL	PROCESS	CONTROL	CHANGE
			PERCENTILE		
0	4	0	2	1	2
1	10	0	6	3	10
2	15	2	13	6	28
3	22	3	23	11	49
4	28	6	34	18	70
5	35	9	45	25	84
6	42	14	55	33	95
7	48	21	64	42	100
8	55	27	72	51	
9	61	35	79	60	
10	67	43	85	68	
11	72	52	90	76	
12	77	59	95	83	
13	81	66	98	88	
14	85	72	100	93	
15	88	78	100	96	
16	90	83		98	
17	93	87		99	
18	95	90		100	
19	97	93		100	
20	98	95			
21	100	97			
22	100	98			
23		99			
24		100			
25		100			

Notes: N = 4,300.

TABLE C.3 CUMULATIVE FREQUENCY DISTRIBUTION FOR PREFERENCES USUAL SCALES

RAW	PERCENTILE						
	ACT	EMP	THO	COM	INT	INC	AUT
0	8	26	52	5	0	23	5
1	16	48	79	17	0	54	17
2	24	63	94	30	1	76	34
3	34	74	100	42	3	88	52
4	52	81		53	6	94	69
5	70	86		62	9	98	82
6	100	90		70	15	99	90
7		93		78	22	100	96
8		95		86	31	100	98
9		97		91	40	100	100
10		98		96	50		100
11		99		99	65		
12		100		100	81		
13		100			100		

Notes: N = 4,300; ACT = Activity, EMP = Empathy, THO = Thought, COM = Communication, INT = Interaction, INC = Incentive, AUT = Authority.

TABLE C.4 CUMULATIVE FREQUENCY DISTRIBUTION FOR PREFERENCES NEEDS SCALES

RAW	PERCENTILE						
	ACT	EMP	THO	COM	INT	INC	AUT
0	13	13	26	1	0	8	2
1	26	25	54	2	2	19	7
2	40	38	80	5	5	33	16
3	55	51	100	8	10	46	29
4	73	62		13	17	62	46
5	89	72		18	26	76	63
6	100	80		26	37	88	78
7		85		37	49	96	88
8		89		53	60	99	95
9		93		70	71	100	98
10		96		85	81		100
11		97		96	90		
12		99		100	97		
13		100			100		

Notes: N = 4,300; ACT = Activity, EMP = Empathy, THO = Thought, COM = Communication, INT = Interaction, INC = Incentive, AUT = Authority.

TABLE C.5   CUMULATIVE FREQUENCY DISTRIBUTION FOR PERSONAL AUTONOMY SCALES

RAW	PERSONAL AUTONOMY: USUAL	PERSONAL AUTONOMY: NEEDS
0	6	3
1	24	13
2	44	27
3	61	40
4	73	52
5	82	63
6	88	71
7	92	77
8	95	82
9	97	87
10	98	90
11	99	93
12	100	95
13	100	97
14	100	98
15	100	99
16	100	100
17	100	100
18	100	100

Notes: N = 4,300.

TABLE C.6	CUMULATIVE FREQUENCY DISTRIBUTION FOR EMOTIVE ORIENTATION USUAL SCALE ACROSS GENDER, ETHNICITY, AND AGE								
	GENDER		ETHNICITY					AGE	
RAW	F	M	A/PI	B	H	NA/AN	W	< 40	≥ 40
0	9.0	17.8	11.1	17.4	20.1	18.2	12.5	12.6	14.0
1	19.3	32.6	24.6	33.3	32.3	36.4	24.8	24.2	27.2
2	28.8	44.4	35.7	45.4	43.6	50.0	35.2	32.9	38.8
3	37.4	53.0	44.4	54.3	51.7	57.6	44.0	40.7	47.8
4	46.0	60.5	53.2	61.1	60.5	63.6	51.9	49.7	55.2
5	54.8	67.7	64.3	69.8	69.5	69.7	59.5	57.7	63.3
6	60.6	73.6	68.3	76.1	75.3	69.7	65.5	64.7	68.4
7	67.8	78.3	73.0	81.6	78.8	74.2	71.8	70.2	74.6
8	72.8	82.0	78.6	85.3	83.7	81.8	75.9	75.2	78.6
9	77.7	85.7	81.0	88.2	87.8	84.8	80.5	79.6	82.8
10	81.5	87.8	84.1	91.1	89.2	86.4	83.6	82.9	85.4
11	84.7	89.7	84.9	92.8	91.3	87.9	86.4	85.7	87.9
12	88.1	91.6	88.1	95.2	94.5	90.9	89.0	88.5	90.5
13	90.6	93.1	91.3	96.4	94.5	92.4	91.1	90.7	92.4
14	92.6	94.8	91.3	97.8	95.9	93.9	93.2	93.0	94.1
15	94.4	96.1	93.7	98.8	97.4	95.5	94.7	94.6	95.6
16	95.7	97.3	96.8	99.3	97.7	97.0	96.1	95.9	96.9
17	97.5	98.4	97.6	99.8	98.8	97.0	97.7	97.7	98.0
18	98.4	98.9	98.4	99.8	99.1	97.0	98.6	98.6	98.7
19	99.0	99.3	98.4	99.8	99.4	98.5	99.2	99.1	99.2
20	99.7	99.6	99.2	100.0	99.7	100.0	99.6	99.6	99.7
21	100.0	99.8	100.0	100.0	99.7	100.0	99.9	100.0	99.8
22	100.0	100.0	100.0	100.0	100.0	100.0	100.0	100.0	100.0

Notes: N = 4,300; F = female, M = male; A/PI = Asian/Pacific Islander, B = Black, H = Hispanic, NA/AN = Native American/Alaskan Native, W = White; <40 = less than 40 years, ≥40 = 40 or more years.

TABLE C.7   CUMULATIVE FREQUENCY DISTRIBUTION FOR SOCIAL ORIENTATION USUAL SCALE ACROSS GENDER, ETHNICITY, AND AGE

RAW	GENDER		ETHNICITY					AGE	
	F	M	A/PI	B	H	NA/AN	W	< 40	≥ 40
0	0.0	0.0	0.0	0.0	0.0	0.0	0.0	0.0	0.0
1	0.0	0.0	0.0	0.0	0.0	0.0	0.0	0.0	0.0
2	0.1	0.2	0.0	0.0	0.3	0.0	0.2	0.2	0.2
3	0.6	0.4	0.0	0.0	0.3	0.0	0.6	0.6	0.5
4	1.1	0.9	0.8	0.0	0.3	0.0	1.3	1.1	1.0
5	2.1	1.5	1.6	0.5	0.3	1.5	2.1	1.6	1.9
6	3.7	2.6	3.2	1.7	1.5	1.5	3.5	2.7	3.5
7	5.9	4.3	7.1	2.7	2.0	1.5	5.7	4.0	5.9
8	8.7	6.7	8.7	4.6	4.7	1.5	8.5	6.5	8.5
9	11.3	9.2	15.1	6.0	6.7	1.5	11.1	9.1	11.1
10	14.9	11.9	20.6	7.2	9.3	9.1	14.4	12.2	14.3
11	18.9	15.2	31.7	10.1	12.5	9.1	18.0	16.1	17.8
12	23.8	19.1	38.9	13.8	16.6	12.1	22.4	19.9	22.4
13	28.0	22.5	44.4	15.7	19.5	13.6	26.5	22.5	26.9
14	33.4	26.9	51.6	19.3	25.9	16.7	31.1	28.1	31.5
15	38.6	31.4	54.8	22.5	30.8	22.7	36.2	32.2	36.8
16	45.0	36.2	61.1	28.7	36.3	27.3	41.8	38.2	42.1
17	52.4	41.8	68.3	34.8	42.4	34.8	48.2	44.3	48.8
18	58.9	49.2	75.4	41.8	48.5	47.0	55.2	50.5	56.1
19	65.6	56.2	81.0	48.3	56.7	51.5	62.0	57.2	63.0
20	73.8	62.9	86.5	57.7	64.5	60.6	69.2	65.4	70.0
21	81.2	72.0	90.5	71.5	72.4	66.7	77.1	73.7	78.4
22	89.2	82.3	95.2	82.6	82.3	75.8	86.1	83.7	86.7
23	95.2	90.5	96.8	90.1	91.3	86.4	93.1	91.4	93.5
24	98.8	97.5	99.2	98.1	98.0	98.5	98.1	97.7	98.4
25	100.0	100.0	100.0	100.0	100.0	100.0	100.0	100.0	100.0

Notes: N = 4,300; F = female, M = male; A/PI = Asian/Pacific Islander, B = Black, H = Hispanic, NA/AN = Native American/Alaskan Native, W = White; <40 = less than 40 years, ≥40 = 40 or more years.

TABLE C.8	CUMULATIVE FREQUENCY DISTRIBUTION FOR PROCESS ORIENTATION USUAL SCALE ACROSS GENDER, ETHNICITY, AND AGE								
	GENDER		ETHNICITY					AGE	
RAW	F	M	A/PI	B	H	NA/AN	W	< 40	≥ 40
0	0.1	0.0	0.0	0.0	0.0	0.0	0.1	0.1	0.0
1	0.4	0.1	0.0	0.0	0.0	0.0	0.3	0.3	0.2
2	1.3	0.5	0.0	0.2	0.6	0.0	1.0	0.7	1.0
3	2.9	2.2	0.0	1.7	1.5	0.0	2.8	2.6	2.5
4	5.4	4.3	2.4	4.1	2.3	0.0	5.3	5.1	4.8
5	10.3	8.8	8.7	6.0	4.7	4.5	10.5	9.8	9.6
6	17.5	14.3	15.1	9.7	8.4	9.1	17.5	14.9	16.5
7	25.4	21.6	23.0	15.2	12.8	15.2	25.7	21.7	24.7
8	37.4	30.9	31.0	24.9	23.3	22.7	36.5	31.7	35.8
9	48.9	41.1	42.1	31.9	34.3	33.3	47.8	40.9	47.6
10	61.0	53.5	52.4	45.9	47.1	48.5	59.8	52.7	60.1
11	73.0	66.2	63.5	58.9	60.5	69.7	71.9	65.4	72.1
12	83.5	78.9	77.8	69.3	77.0	80.3	83.0	78.1	83.0
13	93.1	90.7	89.7	86.5	91.3	92.4	92.5	90.4	92.8
14	98.1	97.4	98.4	94.0	98.0	100.0	98.1	97.3	98.0
15	100.0	100.0	100.0	100.0	100.0	100.0	100.0	100.0	100.0

Notes: N = 4,300; F = female, M = male; A/PI = Asian/Pacific Islander, B = Black, H = Hispanic, NA/AN = Native American/Alaskan Native, W = White; <40 = less than 40 years, ≥40 = 40 or more years.

TABLE C.9   CUMULATIVE FREQUENCY DISTRIBUTION FOR CONTROL ORIENTATION USUAL SCALE ACROSS GENDER, ETHNICITY, AND AGE

	GENDER		ETHNICITY					AGE	
RAW	F	M	A/PI	B	H	NA/AN	W	< 40	≥ 40
0	4.2	1.8	4.0	3.9	5.2	1.5	2.5	2.1	3.4
1	14.0	5.9	10.3	10.9	13.7	4.5	9.3	8.4	10.1
2	26.4	13.5	18.3	22.2	26.7	13.6	18.7	17.3	20.7
3	39.4	24.9	27.8	34.8	41.0	27.3	30.6	28.4	33.3
4	53.0	36.1	38.9	44.4	52.9	48.5	43.2	39.5	46.2
5	66.0	49.2	51.6	57.7	63.7	63.6	56.6	51.6	59.7
6	77.9	60.8	64.3	68.1	75.0	71.2	68.6	62.7	71.7
7	85.4	71.6	70.6	75.8	83.7	81.8	78.2	73.2	80.4
8	91.1	79.8	78.6	83.6	90.4	87.9	85.1	81.7	86.6
9	94.1	85.8	83.3	89.6	93.3	90.9	89.8	87.1	90.9
10	96.8	91.2	90.5	95.4	95.3	92.4	93.9	91.6	95.0
11	98.3	94.8	92.1	97.6	96.2	95.5	96.7	94.8	97.4
12	99.1	96.8	92.9	98.8	97.7	95.5	98.2	96.8	98.5
13	99.8	98.5	95.2	99.3	99.1	97.0	99.3	98.7	99.3
14	99.9	99.4	97.6	99.8	99.7	98.5	99.7	99.3	99.8
15	99.9	99.8	98.4	100.0	99.7	100.0	99.9	99.7	99.9
16	99.9	99.9	98.4	100.0	99.7	100.0	100.0	99.8	100.0
17	100.0	100.0	100.0	100.0	99.7	100.0	100.0	99.9	100.0
18	100.0	100.0	100.0	100.0	100.0	100.0	100.0	100.0	100.0
19	100.0	100.0	100.0	100.0	100.0	100.0	100.0	100.0	100.0

Notes: N = 4,300; F = female, M = male; A/PI = Asian/Pacific Islander, B = Black, H = Hispanic, NA/AN = Native American/Alaskan Native, W = White; <40 = less than 40 years, ≥40 = 40 or more years.

TABLE C.10   CUMULATIVE FREQUENCY DISTRIBUTION FOR CHANGE ORIENTATION USUAL SCALE ACROSS GENDER, ETHNICITY, AND AGE

	GENDER		ETHNICITY					AGE	
RAW	F	M	A/PI	B	H	NA/AN	W	< 40	≥ 40
0	6.6	7.6	7.1	15.5	7.3	3.0	6.1	5.8	7.6
1	20.6	20.7	20.6	35.0	23.8	16.7	18.5	18.3	21.7
2	37.3	38.6	38.1	57.0	42.2	30.3	35.1	35.0	39.3
3	55.6	55.8	60.3	75.1	59.0	51.5	52.5	52.2	57.1
4	70.0	72.4	78.6	86.7	73.0	75.8	68.9	68.1	72.6
5	83.0	85.4	86.5	93.5	87.2	86.4	82.7	82.6	85.1
6	93.7	95.0	96.8	98.8	95.6	92.4	93.6	93.9	94.5
7	100.0	100.0	100.0	100.0	100.0	100.0	100.0	100.0	100.0

Notes: N = 4,300; F = female, M = male; A/PI = Asian/Pacific Islander, B = Black, H = Hispanic, NA/AN = Native American/Alaskan Native, W = White; <40 = less than 40 years, ≥40 = 40 or more years.

TABLE C.11   CUMULATIVE FREQUENCY DISTRIBUTION FOR EMOTIVE ORIENTATION NEEDS SCALE ACROSS GENDER, ETHNICITY, AND AGE

RAW	GENDER		ETHNICITY					AGE	
	F	M	A/PI	B	H	NA/AN	W	< 40	≥ 40
0	3.0	5.5	0.8	5.8	5.2	6.1	4.2	3.9	4.4
1	7.6	12.4	5.6	14.5	12.8	15.2	9.6	8.8	10.7
2	13.0	17.7	11.1	20.5	19.5	22.7	14.7	13.8	16.0
3	19.3	24.0	19.8	26.8	27.0	30.3	20.9	19.5	22.9
4	26.3	30.3	23.8	31.4	34.6	40.9	27.5	24.7	30.3
5	33.3	36.6	33.3	38.2	41.3	47.0	34.0	30.3	37.4
6	40.2	43.0	38.1	45.7	50.3	50.0	40.5	36.2	44.5
7	47.8	48.9	42.1	53.1	57.0	51.5	47.4	41.6	51.9
8	54.9	54.8	47.6	60.9	61.3	54.5	53.9	47.4	58.7
9	61.0	61.2	58.7	64.5	65.4	62.1	60.7	53.2	65.4
10	67.3	66.0	67.5	68.8	68.9	71.2	66.3	60.2	70.1
11	72.9	71.6	73.0	72.9	74.7	74.2	71.9	67.1	75.0
12	78.3	76.2	80.2	77.1	78.2	78.8	76.8	73.0	79.1
13	82.2	80.4	83.3	81.4	81.4	83.3	80.9	77.7	82.9
14	85.7	83.8	85.7	85.5	84.6	83.3	84.3	81.7	86.1
15	88.6	87.2	88.1	88.2	87.2	84.8	87.7	85.3	89.0
16	91.3	89.7	92.9	90.3	90.7	90.9	90.3	88.5	91.4
17	93.9	92.4	94.4	91.5	93.6	93.9	93.1	91.6	93.8
18	95.7	94.6	97.6	93.7	95.3	93.9	95.2	94.3	95.5
19	97.1	96.7	99.2	95.9	97.1	97.0	96.9	96.4	97.0
20	98.4	98.5	99.2	98.6	98.3	98.5	98.4	98.2	98.6
21	99.6	99.7	100.0	99.8	99.4	98.5	99.7	99.6	99.7
22	100.0	100.0	100.0	100.0	100.0	100.0	100.0	100.0	100.0

Notes: N = 4,300; F = female, M = male; A/PI = Asian/Pacific Islander, B = Black, H = Hispanic, NA/AN = Native American/Alaskan Native, W = White; <40 = less than 40 years, ≥40 = 40 or more years.

TABLE C.12   CUMULATIVE FREQUENCY DISTRIBUTION FOR SOCIAL ORIENTATION NEEDS SCALE ACROSS GENDER, ETHNICITY, AND AGE

RAW	GENDER		ETHNICITY					AGE	
	F	M	A/PI	B	H	NA/AN	W	< 40	≥ 40
0	0.2	0.0	0.0	0.2	0.0	0.0	0.2	0.1	0.2
1	0.5	0.4	0.0	0.5	0.0	0.0	0.5	0.4	0.5
2	1.3	2.2	0.0	1.2	0.3	1.5	2.1	1.1	2.3
3	2.4	4.4	1.6	1.7	2.0	1.5	4.0	2.7	3.9
4	4.2	7.7	3.2	4.1	3.8	1.5	6.8	5.0	6.7
5	7.3	11.3	5.6	6.8	6.4	9.1	10.3	8.2	10.2
6	11.5	16.3	9.5	10.1	8.7	12.1	15.4	12.1	15.5
7	17.7	23.1	16.7	16.4	13.7	15.2	22.1	18.1	22.3
8	24.3	29.9	23.0	22.0	19.5	22.7	29.0	24.6	29.2
9	31.7	38.3	35.7	29.5	25.9	27.3	37.1	32.6	37.1
10	41.0	45.7	44.4	37.0	32.3	36.4	45.6	40.7	45.5
11	49.6	53.9	49.2	44.4	39.2	45.5	54.3	48.7	54.2
12	56.9	61.1	57.9	51.0	46.5	56.1	61.5	55.5	61.7
13	64.2	67.8	66.7	58.0	56.1	60.6	68.2	62.9	68.4
14	71.3	72.9	76.2	65.7	63.4	65.2	73.8	68.9	74.4
15	77.1	78.7	79.4	71.0	69.8	71.2	79.7	75.2	80.0
16	82.1	83.7	88.1	76.8	73.3	78.8	84.8	81.0	84.5
17	87.2	86.9	90.5	80.7	80.5	81.8	88.6	85.2	88.4
18	90.7	90.2	92.9	84.3	87.8	83.3	91.7	88.5	91.7
19	93.1	93.0	96.8	89.4	90.1	86.4	94.0	91.2	94.4
20	94.9	95.2	97.6	92.5	92.4	90.9	95.7	93.7	96.0
21	97.1	97.2	98.4	96.6	94.8	95.5	97.5	96.2	97.8
22	98.3	98.1	99.2	97.6	97.7	95.5	98.4	97.4	98.8
23	99.3	99.1	99.2	98.8	99.1	98.5	99.3	98.9	99.4
24	99.8	99.8	100.0	99.8	100.0	100.0	99.7	99.6	99.9
25	100.0	100.0	100.0	100.0	100.0	100.0	100.0	100.0	100.0

Notes: N = 4,300; F = female, M = male; A/PI = Asian/Pacific Islander, B = Black, H = Hispanic, NA/AN = Native American/Alaskan Native, W = White; <40 = less than 40 years, ≥40 = 40 or more years.

TABLE C.13   CUMULATIVE FREQUENCY DISTRIBUTION FOR PROCESS ORIENTATION NEEDS SCALE ACROSS GENDER, ETHNICITY, AND AGE

RAW	GENDER		ETHNICITY					AGE	
	F	M	A/PI	B	H	NA/AN	W	< 40	≥ 40
0	1.1	2.0	0.8	0.5	0.6	0.0	1.8	2.0	1.3
1	4.9	7.2	4.8	2.4	3.2	6.1	7.0	6.4	6.0
2	11.4	15.2	9.5	8.0	7.0	9.1	15.2	14.1	13.2
3	21.5	25.3	21.4	14.3	12.2	13.6	26.2	23.7	23.6
4	32.0	35.9	31.7	23.9	20.1	25.8	37.3	34.3	34.2
5	43.3	46.6	42.1	32.6	28.2	39.4	48.7	45.6	45.1
6	53.5	55.6	54.8	40.3	39.0	47.0	58.2	55.6	54.5
7	64.3	64.4	62.7	49.3	51.5	62.1	67.5	65.1	64.4
8	73.1	71.6	73.0	57.0	61.0	68.2	75.5	72.3	72.8
9	80.2	78.1	78.6	66.2	68.3	75.8	81.9	78.6	79.8
10	86.4	84.1	84.1	74.9	76.5	80.3	87.6	83.5	86.5
11	91.4	89.2	88.9	83.1	86.0	87.9	91.8	88.9	91.3
12	95.5	94.2	95.2	89.4	92.4	92.4	95.8	93.2	96.0
13	98.3	97.6	96.8	94.4	97.4	95.5	98.6	97.0	98.6
14	99.6	99.5	98.4	99.0	99.4	100.0	99.7	99.2	99.7
15	100.0	100.0	100.0	100.0	100.0	100.0	100.0	100.0	100.0

Notes: N = 4,300; F = female, M = male; A/PI = Asian/Pacific Islander, B = Black, H = Hispanic, NA/AN = Native American/Alaskan Native, W = White; <40 = less than 40 years, ≥40 = 40 or more years.

TABLE C.14 CUMULATIVE FREQUENCY DISTRIBUTION FOR CONTROL ORIENTATION NEEDS SCALE ACROSS GENDER, ETHNICITY, AND AGE

	GENDER		ETHNICITY					AGE	
RAW	F	M	A/PI	B	H	NA/AN	W	< 40	≥ 40
0	1.1	0.6	0.0	1.0	2.3	0.0	0.7	0.6	1.0
1	3.1	2.2	0.8	1.9	4.9	3.0	2.6	2.0	2.9
2	7.3	5.3	4.0	6.0	12.2	4.5	6.0	5.9	6.2
3	13.3	9.4	8.7	11.6	19.2	7.6	10.7	10.7	11.4
4	20.6	15.5	17.5	17.1	24.7	19.7	17.3	16.6	18.5
5	27.5	22.2	21.4	22.2	30.8	27.3	24.5	22.4	25.7
6	37.0	29.3	27.8	29.0	39.0	34.8	33.0	30.2	33.9
7	45.2	38.4	35.7	37.4	44.8	48.5	42.0	37.3	43.7
8	54.4	47.1	42.1	45.4	52.6	53.0	51.4	45.1	53.2
9	63.5	56.7	56.3	54.8	61.0	65.2	60.5	54.4	62.8
10	71.3	65.8	63.5	62.6	68.0	72.7	69.2	63.9	70.8
11	78.6	74.3	70.6	70.0	76.2	78.8	77.4	72.0	78.8
12	84.9	81.4	77.0	75.4	82.8	86.4	84.4	79.7	84.9
13	89.7	86.9	83.3	81.6	86.3	90.9	89.4	85.0	90.0
14	93.9	92.0	88.1	87.0	92.2	92.4	93.9	90.6	94.1
15	96.1	95.2	91.3	90.8	95.1	95.5	96.5	94.1	96.4
16	97.9	97.5	94.4	94.9	97.1	95.5	98.3	96.8	98.2
17	99.0	98.8	96.0	97.8	98.8	97.0	99.2	98.5	99.1
18	99.7	99.6	99.2	99.3	99.4	98.5	99.7	99.5	99.7
19	100.0	100.0	100.0	100.0	100.0	100.0	100.0	100.0	100.0

Notes: N = 4,300; F = female, M = male; A/PI = Asian/Pacific Islander, B = Black, H = Hispanic, NA/AN = Native American/Alaskan Native, W = White; <40 = less than 40 years, ≥40 = 40 or more years.

TABLE C.15 CUMULATIVE FREQUENCY DISTRIBUTION FOR CHANGE ORIENTATION NEEDS SCALE ACROSS GENDER, ETHNICITY, AND AGE

	GENDER		ETHNICITY					AGE	
RAW	F	M	A/PI	B	H	NA/AN	W	< 40	≥ 40
0	1.7	3.0	1.6	3.9	1.5	3.0	2.4	1.7	2.7
1	8.8	11.8	8.7	12.6	13.7	7.6	10.0	8.6	11.4
2	26.7	29.0	26.2	29.7	29.4	15.2	27.5	24.0	29.8
3	47.6	50.7	48.4	49.5	43.0	34.8	49.9	44.2	51.9
4	68.1	70.8	73.8	69.3	66.3	54.5	69.9	64.3	72.1
5	82.8	85.3	88.1	83.1	82.0	72.7	84.7	80.0	86.4
6	94.3	95.5	97.6	93.5	94.2	90.9	95.1	93.2	95.8
7	100.0	100.0	100.0	100.0	100.0	100.0	100.0	100.0	100.0

Notes: N = 4,300; F = female, M = male; A/PI = Asian/Pacific Islander, B = Black, H = Hispanic, NA/AN = Native American/Alaskan Native, W = White; <40 = less than 40 years, ≥40 = 40 or more years.

TABLE C.16 CUMULATIVE FREQUENCY DISTRIBUTION FOR ACTIVITY PREFERENCE USUAL SCALE ACROSS GENDER, ETHNICITY, AND AGE

	GENDER		ETHNICITY					AGE	
RAW	F	M	A/PI	B	H	NA/AN	W	< 40	≥ 40
0	10.5	6.0	7.1	6.3	4.1	6.1	8.8	8.9	8.0
1	20.2	11.5	13.5	9.9	9.6	12.1	17.3	17.8	14.8
2	29.8	18.9	22.2	19.1	17.2	18.2	25.4	26.8	23.1
3	41.9	27.4	31.0	27.8	26.2	25.8	36.1	37.4	33.1
4	61.2	43.5	50.8	46.4	45.1	40.9	53.4	55.3	50.4
5	78.2	62.7	72.2	67.1	65.1	59.1	70.9	72.5	69.0
6	100.0	100.0	100.0	100.0	100.0	100.0	100.0	100.0	100.0

Notes: N = 4,300; F = female, M = male; A/PI = Asian/Pacific Islander, B = Black, H = Hispanic, NA/AN = Native American/Alaskan Native, W = White; <40 = less than 40 years, ≥40 = 40 or more years.

TABLE C.17 CUMULATIVE FREQUENCY DISTRIBUTION FOR EMPATHY PREFERENCE USUAL SCALE ACROSS GENDER, ETHNICITY, AND AGE

	GENDER		ETHNICITY					AGE	
RAW	F	M	A/PI	B	H	NA/AN	W	< 40	≥ 40
0	22.3	30.0	24.6	34.1	33.4	30.3	24.7	24.1	27.4
1	42.9	52.6	42.9	58.7	56.1	59.1	45.8	45.7	48.8
2	58.5	67.1	62.7	70.0	69.2	69.7	61.5	61.0	63.7
3	71.1	76.5	74.6	80.9	80.2	75.8	72.3	71.7	74.8
4	79.5	83.1	81.0	87.7	86.6	83.3	80.0	80.0	81.8
5	85.0	87.8	84.1	92.5	90.4	87.9	85.4	85.2	87.0
6	89.0	91.0	91.3	95.2	93.3	89.4	89.1	89.1	90.4
7	92.1	93.8	93.7	96.9	95.3	92.4	92.3	92.1	93.4
8	95.0	95.7	94.4	98.8	97.1	92.4	94.8	94.7	95.6
9	97.0	97.0	96.8	99.3	97.1	95.5	96.8	96.8	97.0
10	98.4	98.3	97.6	99.5	98.8	97.0	98.3	98.4	98.3
11	99.3	99.0	99.2	99.5	99.1	100.0	99.2	99.0	99.2
12	99.9	99.7	100.0	100.0	99.7	100.0	99.8	99.9	99.7
13	100.0	100.0	100.0	100.0	100.0	100.0	100.0	100.0	100.0

Notes: N = 4,300; F = female, M = male; A/PI = Asian/Pacific Islander, B = Black, H = Hispanic, NA/AN = Native American/Alaskan Native, W = White; <40 = less than 40 years, ≥40 = 40 or more years.

TABLE C.18   CUMULATIVE FREQUENCY DISTRIBUTION FOR THOUGHT PREFERENCE USUAL SCALE ACROSS GENDER, ETHNICITY, AND AGE

RAW	GENDER		ETHNICITY					AGE	
	F	M	A/PI	B	H	NA/AN	W	< 40	≥ 40
0	42.5	61.0	46.8	64.5	55.2	62.1	50.7	47.0	54.9
1	74.3	84.0	77.0	86.5	82.6	78.8	78.5	75.4	81.2
2	91.4	95.5	88.1	95.7	93.3	90.9	93.6	92.6	94.0
3	100.0	100.0	100.0	100.0	100.0	100.0	100.0	100.0	100.0

Notes: N = 4,300; F = female, M = male; A/PI = Asian/Pacific Islander, B = Black, H = Hispanic, NA/AN = Native American/Alaskan Native, W = White; <40 = less than 40 years, ≥40 = 40 or more years.

TABLE C.19   CUMULATIVE FREQUENCY DISTRIBUTION FOR COMMUNICATION PREFERENCE USUAL SCALE ACROSS GENDER, ETHNICITY, AND AGE

RAW	GENDER		ETHNICITY					AGE	
	F	M	A/PI	B	H	NA/AN	W	< 40	≥ 40
0	3.3	7.4	4.8	7.5	6.1	10.6	5.1	6.3	4.9
1	10.9	22.3	7.9	27.1	18.9	24.2	15.7	17.3	16.4
2	21.4	37.6	16.7	43.5	35.2	40.9	28.0	31.2	28.9
3	32.2	50.6	26.2	56.5	46.5	48.5	39.8	43.1	40.7
4	43.3	61.4	37.3	64.7	60.5	59.1	50.8	53.7	51.7
5	53.9	69.9	43.7	76.6	68.3	72.7	60.2	62.6	61.7
6	62.6	77.2	50.8	82.9	74.7	84.8	68.5	70.6	69.6
7	72.3	83.8	63.5	87.4	81.4	90.9	76.9	78.0	78.2
8	81.6	90.0	73.8	91.8	89.0	92.4	85.2	85.6	85.9
9	88.4	94.1	84.1	94.4	94.2	95.5	90.8	91.4	91.2
10	93.4	97.4	91.3	96.6	97.4	97.0	95.2	96.0	95.1
11	98.3	99.1	97.6	100.0	98.8	100.0	98.6	98.9	98.6
12	100.0	100.0	100.0	100.0	100.0	100.0	100.0	100.0	100.0

Notes: N = 4,300; F = female, M = male; A/PI = Asian/Pacific Islander, B = Black, H = Hispanic, NA/AN = Native American/Alaskan Native, W = White; <40 = less than 40 years, ≥40 = 40 or more years.

TABLE C.20   CUMULATIVE FREQUENCY DISTRIBUTION FOR INTERACTION PREFERENCE USUAL SCALE ACROSS GENDER, ETHNICITY, AND AGE

	GENDER		ETHNICITY					AGE	
RAW	F	M	A/PI	B	H	NA/AN	W	< 40	≥ 40
0	0.1	0.0	0.0	0.0	0.0	0.0	0.1	0.1	0.1
1	0.2	0.4	0.0	0.0	0.3	0.0	0.3	0.2	0.3
2	0.7	1.6	0.8	0.2	0.6	1.5	1.4	1.0	1.4
3	2.4	3.6	2.4	1.0	1.7	1.5	3.5	2.8	3.3
4	4.4	6.6	6.3	2.4	2.9	3.0	6.3	4.5	6.3
5	7.9	10.5	13.5	4.8	4.9	4.5	10.2	7.2	10.7
6	13.6	16.6	23.8	9.4	9.6	7.6	16.3	13.3	16.5
7	21.4	23.0	34.1	16.9	16.9	13.6	23.0	18.8	24.6
8	29.5	31.5	46.8	26.8	26.7	19.7	30.8	26.7	33.0
9	39.2	40.8	54.8	35.5	38.7	33.3	40.2	35.5	42.9
10	49.5	51.4	69.0	46.1	47.4	42.4	50.7	46.1	53.2
11	63.5	65.4	84.1	63.5	63.4	53.0	64.2	61.0	66.8
12	80.3	80.7	94.4	80.0	80.8	75.8	80.1	76.4	82.9
13	100.0	100.0	100.0	100.0	100.0	100.0	100.0	100.0	100.0

Notes: N = 4,300; F = female, M = male; A/PI = Asian/Pacific Islander, B = Black, H = Hispanic, NA/AN = Native American/Alaskan Native, W = White; <40 = less than 40 years, ≥40 = 40 or more years.

TABLE C.21   CUMULATIVE FREQUENCY DISTRIBUTION FOR INCENTIVE PREFERENCE USUAL SCALE ACROSS GENDER, ETHNICITY, AND AGE

	GENDER		ETHNICITY					AGE	
RAW	F	M	A/PI	B	H	NA/AN	W	< 40	≥ 40
0	24.5	20.9	32.5	21.3	31.4	22.7	21.3	20.7	23.2
1	59.5	49.8	53.2	48.6	61.9	62.1	54.3	50.8	56.1
2	80.5	71.8	67.5	71.0	82.0	78.8	76.4	72.5	77.5
3	91.4	84.6	78.6	87.4	90.7	84.8	88.3	85.2	89.1
4	96.1	92.7	89.7	93.7	95.6	93.9	94.5	92.4	95.2
5	98.6	96.9	92.9	97.3	98.3	93.9	97.9	96.6	98.3
6	99.7	98.8	95.2	99.0	99.1	97.0	99.4	98.9	99.4
7	99.9	99.6	98.4	99.8	99.7	100.0	99.8	99.6	99.8
8	100.0	100.0	100.0	100.0	100.0	100.0	100.0	100.0	100.0
9	100.0	100.0	100.0	100.0	100.0	100.0	100.0	100.0	100.0

Notes: N = 4,300; F = female, M = male; A/PI = Asian/Pacific Islander, B = Black, H = Hispanic, NA/AN = Native American/Alaskan Native, W = White; <40 = less than 40 years, ≥40 = 40 or more years.

16 APPENDIX C

TABLE C.22 CUMULATIVE FREQUENCY DISTRIBUTION FOR AUTHORITY PREFERENCE USUAL SCALE ACROSS GENDER, ETHNICITY, AND AGE

	GENDER		ETHNICITY					AGE	
RAW	F	M	A/PI	B	H	NA/AN	W	< 40	≥ 40
0	7.6	2.6	4.8	5.1	6.7	1.5	4.7	3.7	5.7
1	24.3	10.7	14.3	20.0	20.9	12.1	16.8	14.5	18.4
2	43.6	24.8	25.4	37.9	40.1	28.8	32.9	30.1	35.3
3	62.3	42.2	44.4	57.5	58.7	56.1	50.4	46.3	54.0
4	77.9	60.6	62.7	72.2	73.5	75.8	68.0	63.8	71.0
5	87.9	76.1	78.6	83.8	85.8	83.3	81.2	77.7	83.5
6	94.6	86.3	85.7	91.1	93.9	89.4	90.0	87.9	91.3
7	98.0	93.9	92.9	97.3	95.9	93.9	95.9	94.3	96.6
8	99.0	98.0	96.8	99.0	98.8	95.5	98.6	97.7	98.9
9	99.9	99.6	99.2	99.8	99.7	100.0	99.8	99.8	99.7
10	100.0	100.0	100.0	100.0	100.0	100.0	100.0	100.0	100.0

Notes: N = 4,300; F = female, M = male; A/PI = Asian/Pacific Islander, B = Black, H = Hispanic, NA/AN = Native American/Alaskan Native, W = White; <40 = less than 40 years, ≥40 = 40 or more years.

TABLE C.23 CUMULATIVE FREQUENCY DISTRIBUTION FOR ACTIVITY PREFERENCE NEEDS SCALE ACROSS GENDER, ETHNICITY, AND AGE

	GENDER		ETHNICITY					AGE	
RAW	F	M	A/PI	B	H	NA/AN	W	< 40	≥ 40
0	14.0	11.9	11.9	10.1	9.0	10.6	13.8	16.1	11.3
1	27.5	25.3	25.4	22.0	20.6	22.7	27.5	32.2	23.3
2	41.9	37.5	41.3	36.2	32.3	36.4	40.6	45.8	36.3
3	58.7	51.5	61.1	49.3	46.5	47.0	56.0	60.7	51.8
4	75.6	69.8	79.4	67.1	65.1	62.1	73.7	75.8	70.9
5	91.7	86.1	92.9	86.2	86.0	81.8	89.1	89.1	88.6
6	100.0	100.0	100.0	100.0	100.0	100.0	100.0	100.0	100.0

Notes: N = 4,300; F = female, M = male; A/PI = Asian/Pacific Islander, B = Black, H = Hispanic, NA/AN = Native American/Alaskan Native, W = White; <40 = less than 40 years, ≥40 = 40 or more years.

TABLE C.24 CUMULATIVE FREQUENCY DISTRIBUTION FOR EMPATHY PREFERENCE NEEDS SCALE ACROSS GENDER, ETHNICITY, AND AGE

| RAW | GENDER | | ETHNICITY | | | | | AGE | |
	F	M	A/PI	B	H	NA/AN	W	< 40	≥ 40
0	11.7	13.5	11.1	17.6	16.0	15.2	11.9	11.1	13.2
1	23.8	26.5	26.2	31.4	32.0	31.8	23.9	22.8	26.4
2	37.3	38.3	39.7	44.0	43.9	48.5	36.5	33.6	39.9
3	51.3	50.7	52.4	54.8	58.1	54.5	49.8	45.6	53.6
4	62.9	61.6	65.9	64.0	66.9	63.6	61.4	57.3	64.7
5	73.4	70.6	73.0	72.7	73.5	72.7	71.5	67.8	74.0
6	81.3	78.0	77.8	78.7	79.1	77.3	79.7	75.9	81.5
7	86.9	83.8	87.3	85.0	85.2	80.3	85.1	82.9	86.3
8	90.8	87.8	91.3	88.9	88.7	92.4	89.1	87.6	89.9
9	94.0	91.7	93.7	91.3	92.2	93.9	92.9	91.5	93.4
10	96.2	95.0	98.4	94.2	94.5	97.0	95.7	94.7	95.9
11	97.7	97.2	98.4	96.1	97.7	97.0	97.5	96.8	97.8
12	99.3	99.3	99.2	99.0	98.8	98.5	99.4	99.0	99.4
13	100.0	100.0	100.0	100.0	100.0	100.0	100.0	100.0	100.0

Notes: N = 4,300; F = female, M = male; A/PI = Asian/Pacific Islander, B = Black, H = Hispanic, NA/AN = Native American/Alaskan Native, W = White; <40 = less than 40 years, ≥40 = 40 or more years.

TABLE C.25 CUMULATIVE FREQUENCY DISTRIBUTION FOR THOUGHT PREFERENCE NEEDS SCALE ACROSS GENDER, ETHNICITY, AND AGE

| RAW | GENDER | | ETHNICITY | | | | | AGE | |
	F	M	A/PI	B	H	NA/AN	W	< 40	≥ 40
0	24.3	27.2	18.3	28.5	24.4	31.8	25.9	21.2	28.3
1	31.1	25.8	27.0	23.7	30.5	25.8	28.6	27.6	28.5
2	24.9	26.1	31.0	25.4	22.7	19.7	25.8	27.3	24.7
3	19.7	20.9	23.8	22.5	22.4	22.7	19.6	23.9	18.5

Notes: N = 4,300; F = female, M = male; A/PI = Asian/Pacific Islander, B = Black, H = Hispanic, NA/AN = Native American/Alaskan Native, W = White; <40 = less than 40 years, ≥40 = 40 or more years.

TABLE C.26   CUMULATIVE FREQUENCY DISTRIBUTION FOR COMMUNICATION PREFERENCE NEEDS SCALE ACROSS GENDER, ETHNICITY, AND AGE

RAW	GENDER		ETHNICITY					AGE	
	F	M	A/PI	B	H	NA/AN	W	< 40	≥ 40
0	0.7	0.8	0.8	0.5	1.2	3.0	0.7	1.1	0.5
1	2.4	2.3	1.6	3.6	4.7	4.5	1.8	3.2	1.7
2	4.7	5.1	4.0	8.7	7.3	6.1	3.9	6.1	4.1
3	8.0	8.4	7.9	14.5	11.0	10.6	6.9	9.0	7.6
4	12.9	12.6	13.5	18.8	17.7	21.2	11.1	14.3	11.7
5	18.5	18.3	19.0	25.4	27.6	28.8	16.2	20.7	17.0
6	27.1	25.7	27.0	35.5	36.9	37.9	23.7	28.6	24.5
7	38.9	35.7	35.7	45.9	47.1	45.5	34.7	39.2	35.4
8	53.7	51.4	43.7	61.6	63.7	59.1	50.2	54.0	51.0
9	70.9	68.5	69.0	75.4	75.9	69.7	68.0	70.9	68.3
10	86.0	83.6	84.9	88.4	89.0	80.3	83.7	85.7	83.9
11	96.2	95.4	96.0	97.3	98.0	90.9	95.3	96.2	95.4
12	100.0	100.0	100.0	100.0	100.0	100.0	100.0	100.0	100.0

Notes: N = 4,300; F = female, M = male; A/PI = Asian/Pacific Islander, B = Black, H = Hispanic, NA/AN = Native American/Alaskan Native, W = White; <40 = less than 40 years, ≥40 = 40 or more years.

TABLE C.27   CUMULATIVE FREQUENCY DISTRIBUTION FOR INTERACTION PREFERENCE NEEDS SCALE ACROSS GENDER, ETHNICITY, AND AGE

	GENDER		ETHNICITY					AGE	
RAW	F	M	A/PI	B	H	NA/AN	W	< 40	≥ 40
0	0.4	0.3	0.0	0.5	0.3	0.0	0.4	0.3	0.4
1	1.4	2.3	0.8	1.2	1.7	0.0	2.2	1.5	2.2
2	3.7	6.2	2.4	2.2	4.4	1.5	5.8	3.9	5.8
3	8.2	11.3	7.9	6.8	7.6	4.5	10.5	8.4	10.8
4	14.7	19.3	13.5	14.0	11.6	10.6	18.1	14.7	18.8
5	23.1	28.6	21.4	22.2	17.4	18.2	27.5	23.4	27.6
6	34.2	40.1	39.7	33.6	27.6	31.8	38.7	33.5	39.8
7	46.3	50.6	47.6	43.2	39.5	47.0	50.0	44.7	51.0
8	56.8	62.0	57.1	56.8	49.1	53.0	61.3	55.5	62.1
9	69.2	73.4	70.6	68.6	64.2	69.7	72.5	67.8	73.9
10	79.8	82.8	81.7	78.7	77.0	78.8	82.1	79.2	83.0
11	89.1	91.0	93.7	87.4	86.9	84.8	90.7	88.6	91.2
12	96.8	96.9	98.4	96.4	95.6	93.9	96.9	95.9	97.5
13	100.0	100.0	100.0	100.0	100.0	100.0	100.0	100.0	100.0

Notes: N = 4,300; F = female, M = male; A/PI = Asian/Pacific Islander, B = Black, H = Hispanic, NA/AN = Native American/Alaskan Native, W = White; <40 = less than 40 years, ≥40 = 40 or more years.

TABLE C.28   CUMULATIVE FREQUENCY DISTRIBUTION FOR INCENTIVE PREFERENCE NEEDS SCALE ACROSS GENDER, ETHNICITY, AND AGE

	GENDER		ETHNICITY					AGE	
RAW	F	M	A/PI	B	H	NA/AN	W	< 40	≥ 40
0	8.0	7.3	7.9	7.7	14.8	4.5	6.8	7.8	7.3
1	19.4	18.8	18.3	16.2	28.8	22.7	18.4	18.3	19.3
2	34.0	31.9	30.2	29.2	42.4	33.3	32.6	30.6	33.8
3	47.5	45.0	42.1	42.0	54.1	48.5	46.1	43.1	47.7
4	63.1	60.8	57.9	55.6	63.4	71.2	62.5	57.8	63.8
5	77.2	75.1	71.4	69.1	76.2	78.8	77.0	72.4	78.0
6	89.0	87.6	84.1	83.3	88.1	90.9	89.1	85.4	89.8
7	96.2	95.5	93.7	92.0	96.8	95.5	96.3	94.9	96.4
8	99.0	98.9	98.4	96.6	98.8	98.5	99.3	98.7	99.1
9	100.0	100.0	100.0	100.0	100.0	100.0	100.0	100.0	100.0

Notes: N = 4,300; F = female, M = male; A/PI = Asian/Pacific Islander, B = Black, H = Hispanic, NA/AN = Native American/Alaskan Native, W = White; <40 = less than 40 years, ≥40 = 40 or more years.

TABLE C.29   CUMULATIVE FREQUENCY DISTRIBUTION FOR AUTHORITY PREFERENCE NEEDS SCALE ACROSS GENDER, ETHNICITY, AND AGE

RAW	GENDER		ETHNICITY					AGE	
	F	M	A/PI	B	H	NA/AN	W	< 40	≥ 40
0	2.2	0.9	0.0	1.7	2.9	1.5	1.4	0.9	1.9
1	8.5	5.0	4.8	6.5	9.3	9.1	6.6	5.0	7.5
2	19.7	12.8	9.5	16.7	18.9	16.7	16.0	14.1	16.9
3	34.7	24.4	20.6	28.3	31.4	27.3	29.7	25.9	30.9
4	52.0	41.3	44.4	41.3	46.8	47.0	47.3	40.7	49.0
5	67.9	59.0	58.7	56.8	62.2	66.7	64.2	58.7	65.5
6	81.6	74.8	68.3	70.8	75.6	80.3	79.6	73.8	80.4
7	90.2	86.7	81.7	83.8	85.8	90.9	89.3	85.8	89.8
8	95.7	94.1	89.7	91.3	93.9	93.9	95.6	93.2	95.7
9	98.3	98.3	96.0	97.1	97.4	93.9	98.7	97.8	98.6
10	100.0	100.0	100.0	100.0	100.0	100.0	100.0	100.0	100.0

Notes: N = 4,300; F = female, M = male; A/PI = Asian/Pacific Islander, B = Black, H = Hispanic, NA/AN = Native American/Alaskan Native, W = White; <40 = less than 40 years, ≥40 = 40 or more years.

GLOSSARY

a parameter. An IRT item parameter characterizing the slope of the ICC for an item. Also known as the discrimination parameter.

a posteriori. A probability that is calculated with prior knowledge known.

Acceptance. The Acceptance scales describe a sociability-based construct that addresses the manner of relating to people in groups. It includes the degree to which an individual wants to be talkative, enjoy people in groups, enjoy of social laughter, comfort in talking to strangers, enjoying parties and group activities, and approachability. The Acceptance Preference is a subfactor of the Social Orientation. The Acceptance Preference is also titled Interaction. See Table 11.2.

Activity. The Activity scales describe a construct that addresses preferred pace of action and aspects of style of planning and decision making. This construct includes the degree to which an individual prefers action, quick thinking, and physical expression of energy. Activity is a subfactor of the Emotive Orientation. See Table 11.2.

Advantage. The Advantage scales describe a dominance-based construct that includes the degree to which an individual prefers to drive for personal rewards or to share in team rewards. This construct addresses the approach to idealism, and team vs. individual approaches to winning competitions and incentives. It also encompasses cautiousness about giving trust, involvement with money (as incentive), placing money over friendship, and seeking personal advantage. The Advantage Preference is a subfactor of the Control Orientation and is also known as Incentive. See Table 11.2.

Artistic. The Artistic Interest scale measures a preference for career and/or opportunities involving photography, architecture, design, and representational art endeavors.

Authority. The Authority scales address approaches to directing and influencing or persuading others in verbal exchanges. This construct describes a dominance-based construct that includes the degree to which an individual wants to persuade, speak up, express opinions openly and forcefully, and/or argue. The Authority Preference is a subfactor of the Control Orientation. See Table 11.2.

b parameter. An item parameter identifying an item's location on the θ continuum. Also known at the "difficulty" parameter.

Big Five. See Five Factor Model (FFM).

BirkmanDirect®. A proprietary, web-based platform for administering The Birkman Method® and generating reports.

c parameter. An item parameter indicating the lower asymptote. Also known as the "pseudo-guessing" parameter.

CFA. See Confirmatory Factor Analysis.

Challenge. Challenge involves the way in which a person approaches and understands the issues of socially correct behavior and especially social image. The scale addresses issues on managing social image and social expectation, and impacts how one goes about imposing demands on self (and others). Also known as Perspective Alignment.

Change. The Change Orientation refers to openness to new personal experiences. Individuals who score low tend to prefer repetitive effort, minimal personal disruptions, and predictable responsibilities. Individuals who score high tend to seek new experiences and explore novel approaches, even within stable environments. See Tables 11.1 and 11.2.

classical test theory (CTT). A theory of test measurement based on observed scores consisting of true scores and an error term.

Clerical. The Clerical Interest scale measures a preference for career and/or opportunities involving internal administrative support, secretarial, and public contact administrative or service activities.

coefficient alpha. A reliability statistic computed from average inter-item correlation conditional on the number of items for the scale. Also known as Cronbach's alpha.

Communication. The Communication scales describe a sensitivity-based construct that includes shyness, saying no, praising and being praised, sensitivity about correcting others or being corrected by others, getting one's feelings hurt, and concerns about embarrassing or being embarrassed. The Communication Preference is a subfactor of the Social Orientation. Communication is also known as Esteem. See Table 11.2.

Components. One of the fundamental scales used within The Birkman Method® system. Each Component, except Perspective Alignment, is further differentiated into Usual, Needs, and Stress scales.

conditional standard error (CSE). The amount of standardized error at a specific point on the θ continuum.

confirmatory factor analysis (CFA). A method for testing the factor structure using a priori hypotheses of the existing factor structure.

construct validity. The validity that characterizes what a scale measures and does not measure.

continuum. The continuous range of a construct's magnitude on which examinees fall.

Control. The Control Orientation correlates with the FFM Agreeableness scale. It is comprised of two subscales, Authority and Incentive. See Tables 11.1 and 11.2.

convergent construct validity. The validity that establishes what construct a scale does measure.

CTT. See classical test theory.

d. Statistic that measures effect sizes in significant variable mean differences. Used to determine to what degree significant differences are observable. Also known as Cohen's d.

divergent construct validity. The validity that establishes what construct a scale does not measure.

EAPS. See Expected A Posteriori Scoring.

EEOC. See Equal Employment Opportunity Commission (EEOC).

EFA. See Exploratory Factor Analysis.

Emotive. The Emotive Orientation correlates with the FFM Neuroticism scale. Emotive refers to responding emotionally to life events. Individuals who score low tend to be calm, stable or steady during periods of change or instability. Individuals who score high tend to experience intense, positive or negative emotions in these same conditions. It is comprised of three subscales, Activity, Empathy and Thought. See Tables 11.1 and 11.2.

Empathy. The Empathy scales describe a construct the degree to which an individual is comfortable with emotional expression and involvement of feelings. This construct involves emotional volatility, mood changes, and feelings for others. Empathy is a subfactor of the Emotive Orientation. See Table 11.2.

Equal Employment Opportunity Commission (EEOC). United States federal agency responsible for enforcing employment discrimination laws including Title VII of the Civil Rights Act of 1964 (Title VII), the Equal Pay Act of 1963 (EPA), the Age Discrimination in Employment Act of 1967 (ADEA), Title I and Title V of the Americans with Disabilities Act of 1990 (ADA), Section 501 and 505 of the of the Rehabilitation Act of 1973, and the Civil Rights Act of 1991. The agency prohibiting discrimination based on age, disability, ethnicity, gender, religion, and other demographics. Additionally, the agency provides oversight and coordination of federal equal employment opportunity regulations, practices, and policies.

Esteem. The Esteem scales describe a sensitivity-based construct that includes shyness, saying no, praising and being praised, sensitivity about correcting others or being corrected by others, getting one's feelings hurt, and concerns about embarrassing or being embarrassed. The Esteem Preference is a subfactor of the Social Orientation. The Esteem Preference Also known as Communication. See Table 11.2.

Expectations. See Needs.

Expected A Posteriori Scoring (EAPS). An IRT scoring methodology.

exploratory factor analysis (EFA). A method for finding possible a factor structure for constructs while capitalizing on chance.

face validity. A type of validity used to describe whether a measure appears to be valid at first look.

factor analysis. Statistic analysis used to determine how factors align.

FFM. See Five Factor Model (FFM).

Five Factor Model (FFM). A popular model of personality that has five constructs.

Freedom. The Freedom scales describe a construct concerning the degree to which an individual provides conventional or unconventional answering patterns across the instrument. The scales involve content from several of the other constructs with emphasis on agreeing or disagreeing with "conventional responses" to the content of these constructs. Freedom is also known as Personal Autonomy.

Incentive. The Incentive scales describe a dominance-based construct that includes the degree to which an individual prefers to drive for personal rewards or to share in team rewards. This construct addresses the approach to idealism, and team vs. individual approaches to winning competitions and incentives. It also encompasses cautiousness about giving trust; involvement with money (as incentive); placing money over friendship; and seeking personal advantage. The Incentive Preference is a subfactor of the Control Orientation and is also known as Advantage. See Table 11.2.

Interaction. The Interaction scales describe a sociability-based construct that addresses the manner of relating to people in groups. It includes the degree to which an individual wants to be talkative; enjoy people in groups; enjoy of social laughter (sometimes at one's own expense); comfort in talking to strangers; enjoying parties and group activities; and approachability. The Interaction Preference is a subfactor of the Social Orientation. The Interaction is also known as Acceptance. See Table 11.2.

Interests. Occupations and/or areas that attracts or motivates individuals.

IRT. See item response theory (IRT).

item pool. Database of items that can be drawn from to measure constructs.

item response theory (IRT). A theory of test measurement based on modeling the association between an individual's response and the construct being measured.

item-total correlation. Pearsonian correlation of an item with the total of scores on all other items.

Literary. The Literary Interest scale measures a preference for career and/or opportunities involving writing, editing, reporting, and general involvement with books and the literary arts.

Mechanical. The Mechanical Interest scale measures a preference for career and/or opportunities involving skilled and semi-skilled mechanical crafts, repair and trouble-shooting responsibilities, hands-on electronics work, and engineering.

most. The "most" perspective is comprised of the first 125 items in the questionnaire that ask the respondent to select the preferences of "most people."

Musical. The Musical Interest scale measures a preference for career and/or opportunities involving performing music, working with musical instruments, or general involvement with music and the musical arts.

Needs. Environmental conditions necessary for effectiveness. Needs are the expectations which need to be met in order for the individual to behave in a natural, confident and productive manner.

norms. A representative sample of the population of interest.

Numerical. The Numerical Interest scale measures a preference for career and/or opportunities involving bookkeeping and accounting, auditing, financial and statistical analysis, and mathematics.

Orientation. The five Birkman Orientations are the equivalent to the Five Factors in the Five Factor Model of personality. See Table 11.2.

Other perspective. The "other" perspective is comprised of the first 125 items in the questionnaire that ask the respondent to select the preferences of "most people."

Outdoor. The Outdoor Interest scale measures a preference for career and/or opportunities involving agricultural and building activities, adventure oriented activities (performed outside), and working with animals.

Personal Autonomy. The Personal Autonomy scales describe a construct concerning the degree to which an individual provides conventional or unconventional answering patterns across the instrument. The scales involve content from several of the other constructs with emphasis on agreeing or disagreeing with "conventional responses" to the content of these constructs. Personal Autonomy is also known as Freedom.

Perspective Alignment. Perspective Alignment involves the way in which a person approaches and understands the issues of socially correct behavior and especially social image. The scale addresses issues on managing social image and social expectation, and impacts how one goes about imposing demands on self (and others). Also known as Challenge.

Persuasive. The Persuasive Interest scale measures a preference for career and/or opportunities involving persuading, selling, communicating, and various influencing responsibilities such as management.

Preference. Term used to describe scales that measure subfactors.

Process. Process refers to creating and maintaining visible structures in order to achieve goals. These scales describe an orderliness-based construct that includes the degree to which an individual insists on to giving or receiving clear direction, following instructions carefully, finishing tasks, dealing with detailed tasks, working for accuracy, and using systematic approaches. Process is also known as Structure. The Process Orientation correlates with the FFM Conscientiousness scale. See Tables 11.1 and 11.2.

reliability. Reliability describes a scale's internal consistency and stability over time.

RMSEA. See root mean square error of approximation (RMSEA).

root mean square error of approximation (RMSEA). A fit statistic used to describe how well factor structure model fit the data of interest.

Scientific. The Scientific Interest scale measures preference for career and/or opportunities involving medicine (and allied professions), research, and applied sciences.

SE. See standard error (SE).

SEA. See social environment anchored (SEA).

Self perspective. The "self" perspective is comprised of the second 125 items in the questionnaire that ask the respondent to select their own preferences.

SEM. See standard error of measurement (SEM).

Social. The Social Orientation refers to initiating interpersonal relationships. Individuals who score low tend to select introverted behaviors and also tend to be independent, subdued or individualistic. Individuals who score high tend to select extraverted behaviors and also tend to be lively, sociable and outgoing. The Social Orientation correlates with the FFM Extraversion scale. See Table 11.2.

Social Environment Anchored (SEA). The Social Environment Anchored scales are comprised of the Personal Autonomy and Perspective Alignment scales. Personal Autonomy is a contrarian score that compares self and most scores of the respondent to the typical self and most scores of the population. The Perspective Alignment scale compares the self responses to the most people responses of the respondent. This identifies the degree to which the respondent sees himself or herself as similar to their society. Both of these scales are distinctly separate from personality and have impact on social expectations and behaviors.

Social Service. The Social Service Interest scale measures a preference for career and/or opportunities involving counseling, supporting, guiding, educating, and ministering to others as clergy.

standard error (SE). A standardized statistics which characterize how much variance is due to error as opposed to the construct of interest.

standard error of measurement (SEM). A reliability statistic that characterized the level of precision obtained.

Stress behaviors. Behaviors which are less than productive or undesirable.

Structure. Structure refers to creating and maintaining visible structures in order to achieve goals. These scales describe an orderliness-based construct that includes the degree to which an individual insists on to giving or receiving clear direction, following instructions carefully, finishing tasks, dealing with detailed tasks, working for accuracy, and using systematic approaches. Structure is also known as Process. Structure correlates with the FFM Conscientiousness scale. See Tables 11.1 and 11.2.

TCC. See test characteristic curve (TCC).

test characteristic curve (TCC). A curve/function that characterizes the probability of endorsement across the θ continuum.

test information function (TIF). A function that characterizes the amount of information across the θ continuum.

test standard error function (TSEF). A function that characterizes the amount of standard error across the θ continuum.

test-retest reliability. A type of reliability that describes the repeatability of scale results.

theta (θ). Theta is a point on the continuum of a construct.

Thought. The Thought scales describe a construct concerning the degree to which an individual approaches forming conclusions and making decisions, concerns for making the right decision the first time, and concerns over consequences of decisions. Thought is a subfactor of the Emotive Orientation. See Table 11.2.

three-parameter logistic model (3PL). The 3PL is an IRT model with three parameters used to characterize each item on a scale.

TIF. See test information function (TIF).

TSEF. See test standard error function (TSEF).

Usual behaviors. Behaviors which are productive and create few, if any, negative consequences, in and of themselves. Usual behaviors can be natural or learned behaviors.

validity. A term used to describe to what extent a scale measures what it is supposed to measure and that the resulting information is accurate.

CONTRIBUTORS

Roger W. Birkman, Ph.D., is the creator of The Birkman Method®, the founder of Birkman International, Inc., and the company's current chairman of the board. Since 1951, Dr. Birkman has dedicated himself to understanding of how human behaviors and motivations can be revealed through "self" and "other" perceptual assessments. His goal, to improve the effectiveness of individuals, teams, organizations, and cultures through his work. In particular, Dr. Birkman is interested in serving faith communities worldwide. His current project extends reporting capabilities of The Birkman Method® into interactive, online, and real-time report generation.

Paul Cruz, Ph.D., served for several years as a research assistant for Birkman International, Inc., performing extensive statistical analyses of the validity and reliability of the instrument. He is currently an organizational development specialist for NASA.

Scott Davies, Ph.D., is a manager of psychometric services at Pearson Educational Measurement.

Fabian Elizondo, M.S., is a psychometrician in the Research and Development department at Birkman International, Inc., and specializes in psychological measurement and test development. He works on various projects researching personality assessments and their applications in the workforce. These applications include developing personality profiles for companies, for the purposes of employee selection, development, and succession planning. In addition, he assists Spanish-speaking clients with the interpretation and translation of The Birkman Method®.

Lynn A. Greene, was a staff member of Birkman International, Inc. from 1978 to 1987. He was involved in research, material development, consulting, and training activities. Presently, Mr. Green works as a founding Member of Performance Enhancement Group, Ltd. Mr. Greene's expertise is in developing and facilitating a wide range of business development processes aimed at increasing individual, team, and organizational performance. He continues to work with BI as a co-facilitator of the Birkman Level II Certification training.

Frank Larkey, Ph.D., has over 20 years experience in the applied and academic psychology domains. He followed Tim Sadler as the next director of Research and Development at Birkman International, Inc. He performed a number of validity and reliability studies and provided leadership in translating The Birkman Method® into a dozen languages. Currently Larkey is the president of the Reed Larkey Research Group and continues to work with Birkman International, Inc. on joint projects.

18 CONTRIBUTORS

Larry G. Lee, Ph.D., is the Senior Director of Research and Development at Birkman International, Inc. since 2006. He is a subject matter expert in The Birkman Method® applications. In addition to his Birkman research and management responsibilities, he teaches and consults on Leadership Development and Executive Coaching. Prior to this role, Dr. Lee was the Leader of Instrument Assessment Practice and a senior executive coach at The Boeing Company corporate level. This dual position required him to evaluate and select assessments for the company based on reliability, validity, versatility, and applied effectiveness requirements.

The late **Roy B. Mefferd**, Jr., Ph.D., was a man of many talents. He held professorships at a number of universities, including a period when he was a professor of both psychiatry and Physiology at Baylor University. He was also the President and Director of Research for the Birkman-Mefferd Research Foundation. In that role, he published The Birkman Method® for Manpower Selection, Classification, Assessment, Motivation, Counseling, and Training: Its Reliabilities and Validities as of March 1972. He led the research and development efforts at Birkman International, Inc. starting in the mid 1960s until 1995, when he retired from Birkman International, Inc.

Timothy G. Sadler, Ph.D., worked for Roy Mefferd (beginning 1971) for over 20 years before taking over the directorship of Research and Development at Birkman International, Inc. from 1995 to 2002. During that time, he directed numerous research projects and applied projects including the developing of training programs, revising scales of The Birkman Method®, creating the 2000 Birkman scale norms, and working with consultants and clients across many business sectors. After his retirement, Sadler continued to contribute to Birkman through his research, teaching, and consulting.

Elizabeth A. Wadlington, Ph.D., is a professor of Teaching and Learning at Southeastern Louisiana University. She works with preschool through secondary teachers to help them effectively meet the needs of all students, including those with learning disabilities. She has published in Childhood Education, Reading Research and Instruction, the Reading Professor, Reading Improvement, Preventing School Failure, and various other respected journals. Recent works include ACEI Speaks: What Teachers Need to Know About Dyscalculia and Teachers with Dyslexia and Dyscalculia: Effects on Life.

Patrick L. Wadlington, Ph.D., is a senior psychometrician at Birkman International, Inc. and specializes in psychological measurement and test development. He works on various projects researching and developing quantitative methods for cognitive, social perception, and personality assessment development and validation. Dr. Wadlington specializes in integrating classical and item response test theory to produce web-based psychological instruments for personnel selection and development purposes.

Matthew Zamzow, M.A., is the Director of Training for Birkman International, Inc. He is responsible for the development and implementation of numerous programs targeted to support the interpretation, application and integration of The Birkman Method® in organizational development initiatives. Matt has worked with clients in the development of strategic competencies, developed programs to establish selection processes, and coached individuals to achieve success in career.

329